The Discovery
of Society

The Discovery of Society

Fifth Edition

Randall Collins

and

Michael Makowsky

McGraw-Hill, Inc.
New York St. Louis San Francisco Auckland Bogotá
Caracas Lisbon London Madrid Mexico City Milan
Montreal New Delhi San Juan Singapore
Sydney Tokyo Toronto

THE DISCOVERY OF SOCIETY

6 7 8 9 0   DOC   DOC   9 0 9 8 7 6 5 4

ISBN 0-07-011841-8

This book is printed on acid-free paper.
This book was set in Palatino by The Clarinda Company.
The editors were Phillip A. Butcher, Katherine Blake, and Bernadette Boylan.
The cover was designed by Carol Couch.
R. R. Donnelley & Sons Company was printer and binder.

Library of Congress Cataloging-in-Publication Data

Collins, Randall, (date).
     The discovery of society/Randall Collins, Michael Makowsky.—
   5th ed.
       p.   cm.
     Includes bibliographical references and index.
     ISBN 0-07-011841-8
     1. Sociology—History.   I. Makowski, Michael.   II. Title.
   HM19.C64   1993
   301'.09—dc20   92-9953

About the Authors

RANDALL COLLINS is Professor of Sociology at the University of California, Riverside. He received his A.B. at Harvard (1963), M.A. at Stanford (1964), and Ph.D. at the University of California, Berkeley (1969). He is the author of a number of books and articles, including *Conflict Sociology: Toward an Explanatory Science* (1975), *The Credential Society* (1979), *Three Sociological Traditions* (1985), *Weberian Sociological Theory* (1986), and *Theoretical Sociology* (1988). Some of his books and articles have been translated into Italian, Dutch, Spanish, Japanese, Korean, Chinese, Rumanian, German, and Arabic.

MICHAEL MAKOWSKY is organizational consultant to Musart Company. He attended New York University's Washington Square College, where he received his B.A. in 1962. He received his M.A. in Sociology from the University of California at Berkeley in 1967. He has taught at the University of California, Berkeley and Davis, Chabot College, College of San Mateo, Goddard College, the California Institute of Integral Studies, and the Cultural Integration Fellowship during the past thirty years. He is the author of *Minstrel of Love: A Biography of Satguru Sant Keshavadas* (1980), *Breath of the Eternal: The Way of Self-Knowledge: The Concept of Atman in Four Upanishads* (1990), and numerous articles in contemporary journals. He is currently president of his own company, Deal Glamour Media and Educational Productions. His fields of specialization include comparative religion, social psychology, race relations, sports, and show business.

Contents

The Discovery
of Society

INTRODUCTION

Society and Illusion

We all conceive of ourselves as experts on society. In fact, however, the social world is a mystery—a mystery deepened by our lack of awareness of it. Society is our immediate, everyday reality, yet we understand no more of it merely by virtue of living it than we understand of physiology by virtue of our inescapable presence as living bodies. The history of sociology has been a long and arduous effort to become aware of things hidden or taken for granted: things we did not know existed—other societies in distant places and times, whose ways of life make us wonder about the naturalness of our own; things we know of only distortedly—the experiences of social classes and cultures other than our own; the realities of remote sectors of our own social structure, from inside the police patrol car to behind the closed doors of the politician and the priest; things right around us unreflectingly accepted—the network of invisible rules and institutions that govern our behavior and populate our thought, seemingly as immutable as the physical landscape but in reality as flimsy as a children's pantomime. Most obscure of all, our own feelings, actions, thoughts, and self-images—the tacit bargains that we make and remake with friends, lovers, acquaintances, and strangers and the paths we steer amid emotions, habits, and beliefs. All these things are beneath the usual threshold of our awareness.

We think of ourselves as rational, choice-making masters of our actions if not of our destinies; in reality, we know little about the reasons for either. And if the social world is shrouded from us today, it becomes even more illusory the further back we go into our history. We need go only a few hundred years back in European history to an era when authority of kings and aristocracies was legitimized by divine right, when unexpected behavior from our fellows was attributed to witchcraft and seizures of the devil, and foreign lands were populated not merely by bloodthirsty Communists or the terrible Turk but by werewolves and Cyclopes. "History is a nightmare from which I am trying to awake!" James Joyce declared. Sociology has been part of that very slow awakening.

The social world as we know it and have known it is mostly illusion. Yet, if we were all completely deluded, there would be no point in trying to investigate and explain, and this writing as well as any other would be worthless. The existence of illusions is not incompatible with the existence of facts and of the principles of logic. But facts and logic are inextricably

1

mixed with concepts and theories, and in the study of society the concepts and theories involved are ones that we daily act upon as well as use to explain how things are and why.

Sociology is not an impossible science, but it is a very difficult one. It has progressed by disengaging the web of everyday belief, not all at once but little by little, as one taken-for-granted assumption after another has been questioned and replaced. As was once said of philosophy, sociology is like rebuilding a boat, plank by plank, while floating on it in the middle of the ocean. The history of sociology is a progression of worldviews, each an advance on some other in that it asks some previously unasked question, avoids some previous confusion, or incorporates some previously unobserved fact. Each worldview, including our own, has its illusions; waving the banner of science is no more absolute a guarantee of truth than any other. Nevertheless, there has been a series of major breakthroughs in understanding, including some quite recent ones, and we can be confident now that we are on the right path.

THE SOURCES OF ILLUSION

At the center of the web that clouds our vision is the realization that our knowledge is both subjective and objective. "Facts" are things that independent observers can agree upon; but we must look for facts in order to see them, and what we look for depends on our concepts and theories. What questions we can answer depends on what questions we ask. But the form of the question cannot be the only determinant of the answer, or else our knowledge would never go beyond the subjective point of view of the particular questioner. Any completely subjective viewpoint undermines its own validity, since there is no reason for anyone else to accept it. If there are no objective standards, then the person who claims that there are no such standards can never prove that claim to be true.

There is a realm of objectivity, then, based on shared observations and the exigencies of logical communications. We do not know, however, whether any particular theory or even any particular belief about the facts is true. The problem of separating illusions from reality has been an especially difficult one for sociology, since it begins in the midst of the social world of everyday ideas and ideologies. Until we begin to notice phenomena and ask questions about them, we cannot start to check our theories against the facts or even to check our assumed facts against careful observations. It took many centuries of controversy about ideological and practical issues before some people realized that their ordinary ideas might not be accurate and hence were in need of logical ordering and empirical testing. Even after there arose a community of individuals dedicated to this purpose, much of the raw material of human illusion remained mixed in with the more solid part of sociological knowledge. Progress has come not because sociologists were convinced that a particular theory was right, but because the scholarly community generated a cutting edge of objectivity out of its own controversies and research efforts that has moved it onward in the right direction.

We cannot usually notice something unless we have a name for it. This is true of the physical world—the botanist notices dozens of species of plants where the layman sees only a field—and it is especially important in understanding society. No one has ever seen a "society," although we have all seen the people who belong to one; no one has ever seen an organization, only its members, the buildings and equipment that belong to it, and its name or emblem written on signs and pieces of paper. We live in a social world of symbols: of symbolic entities such as "property"—land that would "belong" to no one but for a social convention, a set of rules as to how various people must behave toward it and what words they must use in talking about it—and of symbolic acts such as "marriage"—a recorded ceremony that enables middle-class Americans to recognize the otherwise indiscernible difference between a couple "illicitly" living together and a "respectable" family. These symbols are by no means obvious if one has never thought about them. The fish apparently does not notice the water until he is out of it. The idea of a *society*, as distinct from the *state*, did not develop until the commercial and industrial changes of the eighteenth century and the French Revolution woke people up to the recognition that there were two different forms of social institutions, each going its own way. One hundred years later, thinkers such as George Herbert Mead came to recognize the symbolic nature of society and thus provided us with concepts with which to analyze the operations of this world that we have so long taken for granted.

Much of sociology has developed by uncovering facts that had not previously been known, either because they were remote from ordinary experience or because they had been deliberately ignored. The earliest efforts at sociology were inspired by European explorations in the Orient, the Americas, Africa, and the South Seas. Familiar ways of life in Europe could no longer be accepted as the natural order of God but had to be explained in light of practices now found to exist in vastly different cultures. The first efforts in this direction were naive and consisted mainly of doctrines of progress, which accounted for the European culture simply as a social advance over other cultures. Such theorizing, nevertheless, began a tradition of thought concerned with explaining society. It was an early thinker on social evolution, Auguste Comte, who first gave sociology its name and thus helped to create that "invisible college" of thinkers who have ever since asked questions about society.

Many facts, to be sure, could have been discovered without the voyages of Captain Cook. But the voyage to the other side of town is harder to make than a trip around the world, and a voyage of discovery in one's own home is the hardest of all. Conventional biases against looking for or recognizing facts that touch on one's life have been greater impediments to sociological understanding than the lack of facts themselves. These same biases that have kept most of social reality obscure have prevented us from seeing that they *are* biases. Not the least important aspect of an illusion is the fact that one believes it to be the truth. The great sociologists have contributed to the sociology of knowledge as an intrinsic part of their work. They have broken through illusions by analyzing the ways in which the conditions of social life determine the contents of our consciousness. The history of sociology has been a progressive sophistication about our own thought, uncovering sources of bias that we did not know existed.

The uncovering began with Karl Marx, the first great thinker to see life from the standpoint of the common worker. Marx did not discover social classes, of course; ancient and medieval law as well as social thought spoke openly of the various ranks of society, which indeed everyone knew about from daily experience. Ideological denial of stratification is an innovation of modern America. What Marx discovered was that our own thought is a product of our social circumstances and that much of what we believe to be reality is but a reflection of our socially determined interests. Marx may have defined "interests" too narrowly in economic terms, but there is no doubt of the validity of this general principle. Marx was not the first to notice that governments tell lies or that newspapers, writers of books, and individuals in conversation put forward alleged facts and explanations that are actually selected and distorted according to the interests of their formulators. Much of the thought of the Enlightenment is epitomized by Voltaire's effort to unmask the absurdity of supernatural explanations for human events. Marx went beyond Voltaire when he pointed out how the socially conservative attitudes adopted by the Church were only to be expected from the leaders of a wealthy, landowning institution whose higher ranks were filled from the aristocracy and whose leaders, like Cardinals Mazarin and Richelieu, often served in the government of the kings.

Marx's dictum "Religion is the opiate of the masses" is a puzzle in its own terms, however: If ideas reflect material interests, how could the lower classes hold ideas that did not reflect their own interests? It took Max Weber's analysis of the relation between ideas and power and Emile Durkheim's recognition of the effects of ritual on solidarity to provide the keys to this paradox. But the opening wedge first driven by Marx has never been retracted, even though there is a constant danger that our ideas will be molded in keeping with the prevailing political orthodoxy.

We know now that ideas are upheld as conventions within particular social groups and that the ideas of the group tend to take the form that will most enhance its status and advance its interests. We know that people associate closely only with persons of similar outlook and that individuals modify their ideas to fit the groups they join. And we also know how it is possible for people to have some freedom from ideological bias by institutionalizing a *competition* of ideas, especially among those whose interests are based on their achievements within the collective enterprise of science or scholarship.

Marx's recognition of ideological bias in social ideas is not a counsel of despair. The bias cannot be wished away, but it can be gradually pushed back by continuous effort to examine our own and others' ideas for their adequacy in explaining the full range of facts about society. This is not to say that biases cannot be found in modern social science. They are deeply embedded, especially in the areas of politics, deviance, and stratification. But we can have some faith that the search for the most powerful explanatory theory will lead us away from ideological distortion, whether from the right, the left, or the center.

One result of Marx's unveiling of ideology has been a distinction (first emphasized by Max Weber) between depictions of reality and evaluations of it, between "facts" (here used broadly to refer both to empirical data and to theories summarizing and explaining the data) and "values." This seems obvious enough: It is one thing to find out what the state of affairs is in the world, another thing to decide whether we think it is good or bad, just or unjust, beautiful or ugly. This distinction is important because most of our thought about the social world is evaluative: We are more interested in finding wrongdoers to condemn and heroes to praise than in explaining what happens or even in ascertaining the facts. Just after World War II it was popular to point to the "big lie" techniques of propaganda as a sign of totalitarian regimes and to stereotypes and distortions as the warning signs of extremist political thought. A closer acquaintance with serious sociology would have shown that such distinctions are naive: that all governments try to manipulate their own legitimacy, that all politics deals in slogans and ideology, and that the popular worldview is made up of stereotypes. If we are to expose the authoritarian and the brutal, deeds are much better indicators than words.

The distinction between facts and values thus has a twofold usefulness: It warns us to note which statements are saying something about reality and which are only assuming something about that reality in order to arouse our feelings about the good or evil of it, and it points us to the hard discipline of separating out and testing a body of knowledge whose validity does not depend merely on our moral point of view.

In the history of sociology the struggle against value biases is far from won. Indeed, controversy currently rages over this very issue. There is a strong tendency, especially among younger sociologists whose personal sympathies are vehemently on the side of dominated racial minorities in America and oppressed peasants in the Third World, to declare that all sociology must be value-biased and hence that the only choice is the moral one: Which side are you on? In support of this position, it is pointed out that academic social scientists have claimed to be value-neutral and yet have created theories that extol the virtues of American democracy, minimize the plight of oppressed groups, and rationalize military support for brutal dictatorships in Chile, Central America, and elsewhere. But the lesson is not clearly drawn. Propaganda for the left is no more valuable *intel-*

lectually than propaganda for the right or the center, whatever one may think of its *moral* virtue.

The distinction between facts and values remains crucial, even in this context. If we do not make an effort to uphold the ideal of intellectual objectivity in assessing theories and facts, no valid knowledge is possible—even the sort of knowledge that practical and activist people claim to have about the problems of the world. If objectivity is not maintained, both serious theory and intelligently guided action will be impossible. A successful explanatory theory is universally acceptable as knowledge; but in the realm of value judgments, everyone's basic values are as good as everyone else's, and no logical argument can force people to change their minds. This means that *applied* sociology will be much more diverse than *pure* sociology; and it is for applied sociology that the arguments of radical sociologists hold true: It comes down to the moral question of in whose interests you choose to apply the arguments. The attack on some of the older sociologists, then, is a legitimate attack only on their applied work; their pure sociology, on the other hand, must be judged by the standards of scholarly objectivity, comprehensiveness, and consistency, and if mistakes are made here, they will be corrected by normal advances in research. If some of these people have misleadingly claimed value-neutrality in an effort to make others accept the conclusions of their applied work, carried out in the interests of cold-war politics, the blame cannot fall on the doctrine that distinguishes between facts and values but on the misuse these individuals have made of that doctrine. In the end the fact-value distinction remains absolutely crucial, and not only for the development of objective sociological theory. Whatever our values may be, only by taking a position of detachment are we able to see society realistically enough to act on it with any insight into our chances of success.

The fact-value distinction is important to keep in mind in the following chapters. We have attempted throughout to present the successive developments in sociological theory and to assess their objective validity. Since most of these developments are far from complete in terms of formalizing the logic of their arguments and testing their factual predictions, our judgments on them must reflect the balance of existing evidence and the most promising prospects for future elaboration. But all this is an attempt to move forward within the realm of objective sociological knowledge. We have also tried from time to time to discuss some applications of these theories to particular practical issues of today. It should be clear that these applications are made from a particular point of view and in that sense we cannot make a claim on others to agree with us unless they happen to share our particular sets of values. These values are heavily on the side of maximizing personal liberty and are slanted toward the point of view of those coerced by systems of power. There are, of course, many other points of view from which theory could be applied; we have given little attention to practical questions as seen from the viewpoints of military officers, politicians, businessmen, administrators, or dominant classes and status groups. For the theoretical side of sociological knowledge presented here, we would like to claim as much objectivity as the considerable progress of the sociological enterprise allows. For our practical applications, we claim no more than that an effort has been made to see the world accurately as it bears on our particular values.

The fate of Karl Marx's insights warns us of how arduous the path to sociological understanding is. The fact that one person, even a famous one, makes an advance is no guarantee that other social thinkers will maintain it. Marx's thought had little impact on the respectable thinkers of his day. It lived on mainly in the underground until a twentieth-century generation of German sociologists (Ferdinand Toennies, Max Weber, Robert Michels, Karl Mannheim) recaptured some of its key insights. Marx's contributions did not fare much better in the revolutionary underground. Instead of being treated as a theory to be developed and refined as new facts and new insights became available, Marxism became a dogma to be polemically defended against all revisions. Near the end of his life, Marx was moved to cry out against his own followers, "I am not a Marxist!" When the Russian Revolution enshrined Marxism as an official state ideology, Marx's thought virtually ceased to be a fruitful source of new insight except, ironically, for non-Marxists or for Marxist heretics. The lesson applies not only to Marx; the uncompromising political realism of Weber and Michels has also proved too much for most respectable thought to incorporate, and it remains semihidden in an academic underground.

Marx found one source of illusion about society in the realm of ideology; Sigmund Freud made an analogous discovery at the turn of the twentieth century when he discovered repression. Freud struck even closer to home. If ideology prevents us from understanding the larger processes that link us to countless others through the economy, politics, and social stratification, repression prevents us from seeing what is right before our eyes, including the motivations for our own actions. Again, the discovery was more in the way of seeing than in the sight itself. Freud was not the first one to notice that men lust for women who are not their wives (and vice versa) or that people can bitterly hate each other even while carrying on polite, and even intimate, relationships. Freud's insight was to see how widespread such desires and feelings are and to see that they can exist even in people who would be ashamed and guilty to realize that they felt anything of the sort. Freud unmasked the respectable society of the nineteenth century at its most vulnerable point—the place that was kept most hidden. Repression, like layers of clothing upon bodies, points to what is concealed by the very act of covering it.

Respectable social thought of the nineteenth century, epitomized by Herbert Spencer and the British utilitarians, saw people in modern society as rational and respectable, the upholders of contractual rules that regulated the individual for the common good. Freud looked into those conscious, rationalistic beliefs and those proper, middle-class ideals and found that they could be explained in terms of something else: passions of love and hate turned in upon the self in response to the social restraints that kept them from being outwardly expressed. Where preceding thinkers saw a rational human making decisions to follow the rules, Freud discovered what had long been excluded from such a worldview: that the human is still a physical animal, a creature of instincts and emotions, and that the civilized, rational part shaped by socialization does not displace the physical creature, but only reshapes it, sometimes in a mutilated form.

The fate of Freud's insights has been much like the fate of Marx's. In some cases, his ideas have gained considerable notoriety among people who have heard of him only secondhand and who think that they can dismiss him with the observation that "obviously there's more to life than sex." In this way, his insight into repression has been itself repressed, along with the recognition that *anything* in the world is the result of sex, hate, or any other emotions impelling our rational behavior. Freud has also suffered from dogmatic followers who have given the theory a bad name in scientific circles, especially through polemics against equally dogmatic behaviorists in psychology. Between these two extremes, Freud has done much to orient us toward investigating how childhood socialization makes us members of society. The central insights—the view of humans as emotional animals who live in groups, the existence of repression and identification—are yet largely unexplored, but they are not lost. Freud's discoveries are more appropriately investigated in group interaction than individual behavior. It is in the socially oriented analyses, conducted by such thinkers as the psychiatrist Fritz Perls and the sociologist Erving Goffman, that Freud's insights are beginning to find their explanation and their place in an integrated body of social theory.

We have touched on a number of sources of illusion in our views of social reality: taking our social arrangements for granted because we know of no others, ideological distortions based on the interests and perspectives of our social positions, inability to detach ourselves from an evaluative stance, repression of things that make us feel shameful or guilty. By the time these sources of bias came to light, sociology was on the eve of the twentieth century. We shall touch on only two kinds of illusions and thereby bring ourselves up to the present: the fallacy of psychological reductionism and the misconceptions that a too-literal identification with physical science can engender. The man who cut through the first of these most strikingly was Emile Durkheim.

People will commonly attempt to explain social events by the actions of individuals: to look for great individuals in history, agitators in riots, traitors in defeats. By the end of the nineteenth century the dominant evolutionist thinkers—speaking especially in defense of a laissez-faire economic policy—described society as the interplay of individual decisions, in which deliberate social policy could have little effect. Nevertheless, their basic mode of explanation was individualistic. People struggle for a livelihood and rise and fall according to their individual qualities; modern society it-self exists because of contracts between individuals.

Durkheim struck through in a new direction: The distinctive thing about social institutions is that they persist while individuals come and go; they have a force of their own such that individuals who violate social norms not only do not change the norms but are punished as deviants. Furthermore, society can never be logically explained in terms of the motives of individuals. As Durkheim put it, society is a reality *sui generis*. "Social facts," such as the rules that people enforce upon each other, the forms of the institutions within which people act, and even the ideas that they hold, cannot be explained by examining the workings of an individual and multiplying the result a millionfold. These facts must be explained by *social*—that is, supraindividual—causes. Living organisms are made up of chemical molecules; yet physiology must be explained on its own level, in terms of the functioning of the parts in relation to each other. By the same token, society is made up of individuals but is not explicable simply in terms of individual psychology. With his emphasis on social structure as the subject matter of sociology, Durkheim gave the field a distinctive focus of its own. He also showed that such supposedly individual phenomena as suicide, crime, moral outrage, and even our concepts of time, space, God, and the individual personality are socially determined. With Durkheim nineteenth-century individualistic rationalism commits suicide. We know now that we are all social creatures and there is no turning back to the naive optimism of the nineteenth century that could see in the rational education of the individual the solution to all social ills.

The final major development of sociology took place in the early twenti-eth century, for the most part in the United States. Instead of relying on his-torians, newspapers, and their own speculations, sociologists began to go and see for themselves: first with community studies, then with surveys, participant observation of organizations, and small group experiments. This research tradition has done much to counteract illusions based on ide-ology and on other biases. We have discovered, for example, that the con-servative claims that crime is due to hereditary degeneration or racial traits (theories once popular among biologically oriented sociologists of the evo-lutionist school) are false, as are liberal outcries that social mobility has been declining in the United States. The great merit of an active research tradition is that it is largely self-correcting; as long as we insist that theories must explain facts, their biases are likely to reveal themselves sooner or later.

But even this research tradition has its dangers and illusions. One of these is the problem of overspecialization and technicism. Sociology has be-come a large-scale cooperative enterprise; and, as in any large bureaucracy, the individual members tend to lose sight of the overall goals—producing and testing theories to explain all of social behavior and institutions—and become caught up in the immediate details of day-to-day research. One danger, then, has been the trivializing of research and a tendency to substitute purely technical standards, such as statistical refinements, for substantial contributions to our knowledge about society.

The physical sciences provided a model for the modern research enterprise; they have also provided a final, distinctively modern illusion about society. Many American social scientists, especially those who have not fully absorbed the great breakthroughs of Durkheim, Weber, Freud, and Mead, still find their ideas in a version of nineteenth-century tradition. Like the British utilitarians and their American followers, they continue to take the natural sciences as an uncriticized model for understanding society. Utilitarian rationalism has been modernized as behaviorism, the doctrine that asserts that human behavior is to be explained in terms of external stimuli—rewards and punishments—without any reference to scientifically inadmissible concepts such as "mind." In sociology, the old positivist doctrine shows up in the notion that the only valid material for a scientific theory is quantitative data, such as those collected in large-scale questionnaire surveys, carefully measured experimental behaviors, and census tabulations. Only "hard data," consisting of observed and preferably quantified behaviors or enumerations, are valid; "soft data," encompassing the experiences of participant observers, in-depth interviews, case studies, historical writings, and introspection, are excluded.

The merit of this distinction turns out to be an illusion. Human social behavior and social institutions are basically symbolic. Society exists and affects the observable behavior of individuals only through systems of invisible names, rules, and positions that individuals can identify with and orient toward. As might be expected, strictly behavioristic theories have not borne much fruit in psychology; rather, it has been in the area of cognitive development and functioning that progress has been made. In sociology the extreme positivists have been found mostly among researchers who have been caught up in short-run technical concerns and hence have contributed little to advancing theories that explain society. It has been by insisting on the principle that we be able to explain *all* the facts that social science corrects itself, even against illusions created by an excessive zeal to emulate the methods of the natural sciences. Symbolic reality is *the* empirical reality for sociologists; it is life as all individuals experience it. Numbers derived by totaling the answers of many individuals to a few short questions about what they believe or have done are quite a long way from the firsthand experience of those individual lives that we are ultimately trying to explain. In this sense Erving Goffman and his students, with their firsthand accounts of how people manipulate the social reality they present for each other to experience, are the latest of the important innovators in sociology.

We are coming to see that there is no necessary battle between "hard" and "soft" in the social sciences. Both quantitative but superficial data and direct phenomenological experience of a few situations have their values and weaknesses. When used to complement each other, they help us both to understand in depth and to check up on the generalizability of the understanding. Like a navigator plotting the position of a point from his or her own moving ship, we are learning to "triangulate" our accounts of social reality from several vantage points.

THE CONTRIBUTIONS OF SOCIOLOGY

It is often said that the social sciences lag behind the natural sciences and that the latter have created the problems of atomic war, overpopulation, and industrial change that the former must now solve. This view betrays a naive analogy between the natural sciences and the social sciences, ignoring how unamenable to control by deliberate action the structures of a society are, except—and even here there are serious organizational limitations—by a form of political control that would be likely to create more evils than it solves. If we judge the social sciences not by the popularistic criterion of practicality, but by their advance toward a comprehensive and powerful explanatory theory of social behavior and institutions, their advance is much greater than has been recognized. Such a theory may not yet be found assembled in the textbooks, but the major pieces have been in existence for some time, and we are slowly learning to put them together. From a time when social thought was little more than myth, ideology, and speculation, we have broken through illusion after illusion, and with each destruction of old belief we have discovered something new and solid.

The great breakthroughs that provide the basis for our modern knowledge took place around the turn of the twentieth century. Durkheim discovered the dynamics of social solidarity, providing us with a way to *explain* how society can operate as a moral order, instead of merely to justify or debunk it. Weber showed how ideas and ideals interact with material and power interests, how we can understand social order in the midst of conflict by seeing society not as a reified abstraction but as a stratified network of groups and organizations. In addition, Weber gave us the most penetrating vision of world history yet produced. Freud revealed the human as a social animal in whom civilized mind and physical body guide and torture each other. Mead showed both individual minds and social institutions to be the result of symbolic communication. Since then we have come to see how the unexplained or overlooked facets of one theory could be clarified by the insights of another. Weber synthesized leads from Marx and Friedrich Nietzsche; Goffman synthesized leads from Durkheim, Simmel, and Mead. Empirical research has fleshed out our general insights, especially on organizations and stratification, where we are beginning to see a core uniting much of sociological theory and research.

This development is not yet widely recognized. Of the great figures in sociology, only Freud and Marx are names widely known to the general public. Durkheim, Weber, and Mead are little known or understood outside the bounds of academic sociology. Even within sociology progress has been obscured, most notably by the conflict between hard and soft approaches and by other controversies over the application of sociology to political issues. Sociologists caught up in these peripheral disputes have thereby blinded themselves, in a way that Marx's analysis of ideology would have predicted, to their opponents' contributions to sociological theory and have even themselves often forgotten that a comprehensive explanatory theory is the major goal of the discipline. But in science as elsewhere nothing succeeds like success. As the demonstrated power of the central sociological tradition is increasingly brought into the light, it advances steadily.

The sociological tradition has shaped our views of the world throughout the last century without our knowing it. It has been the major source of political worldviews: Radicalism derives mostly from the views of Marx; liberalism in both its laissez-faire and its welfare-state versions from the British utilitarians and evolutionists; corporate statism in Europe from the tradition of Saint-Simon; fascism from, among other sources, the racist varieties of nineteenth-century evolutionism. What is striking about this list is that modern political ideologies all derive from nineteenth-century social thought. The far more profound thought of the great breakthrough—the Durkheim-Weber-Freud-Mead contributions—has as yet had little influence on our thinking about social and political issues. Popular thought lags fifty or seventy years behind the forefront of sociological knowledge. Even the university-oriented liberal proponents of the modern American welfare state have offered little more than a benevolent reformer's belief in the "bad environmental" causes of crime and social unrest and a faith in social work and public education as panaceas. Political ideologists have yet to appreciate the hard Weberian truths about the dynamics of status stratification and the scarcely controllable momentum of bureaucratic organizations and the Durkheimian and Freudian discoveries of the personal strains in a world of impersonal rules and emotionless organizations.

Modern sociology does not recommend itself to those in search of easy solutions, whether these be of the left, right, or center. Indeed, one of sociology's great contributions is to show that the center is just as subject to illusion as are the extremes. Perhaps we can now see why sociology does not offer easy practical applications in the way that advances in the physics of electricity gave rise to color television sets. If we wish our knowledge to advance, we cannot spell out what that knowledge must consist of in advance of the facts. The facts are not what most people would wish them to be, and social science cannot be called in to tell them what they want to hear.

The early social thinkers of the Enlightenment thought they had the key to the world: Humans are basically rational; the evils of despotism and war are due to ignorance and superstition. Let people only learn to see things in a rational way, and utopia would be ushered in. This dream has died hard. The generation of Durkheim destroyed its last remnants as far as serious thinkers were concerned, although it has hung on in naive public ideologies—a further illustration of how little our social behavior fits the Enlightenment dream. Politicians and social movements pursue their own ideologies and try to impose their ceremonies on reality; the applied sociologist advising them is usually in the position of an anthropologist telling the aborigines what is wrong with their fertility rites.

If sociology has a contribution to make, it is this: If we can be more realistic about our world, more wary of the dilemmas of social organizations, more aware both of the necessities of social coordination and of the dangers of social coercion, and more sophisticated about the illusions with which our institutions populate social reality, we can perhaps make our world more livable. It may be that if enough people realized the connections between political illusion and political coercion and the deadening effect of psychic chimeras on our everyday encounters, the quality of life would improve a great deal. A significant part of the new generation has already shown itself more realistic than those before it—more capable of cutting through social hypocrisies about sex and politics, through rituals of status deference and illusions about personal relationships. Whether a new culture of honesty and personal emancipation will enable us to control the coercive and alienating institutions of modern society is still in doubt, but greater illumination is one of our few weapons.

THE BOUNDARIES OF SOCIOLOGY

A final note should be made on the subject of disciplinary boundaries. We have attempted to present a brief history of sociology, but we have not insisted on any rigid classification of thinkers, and occasionally we move far beyond what a strictly Durkheimian view of the field would include. One of the reasons for the looseness of boundaries is that sociology did not become a distinct discipline until the twentieth century. Up to that time, it was often not distinguished from economics, and many of the important sociologists—Marx, Weber, Pareto, Parsons—spent some or all of their lives as economists. As economics came to concentrate more and more on the technical analysis of money, prices, wages, and employment, it gradually became a distinct intellectual enterprise as well as a separate university department, although even today institutional and developmental economists, such as James O'Connor, Arghiri Emmanuel, Samuel Bowles, and Herbert Gintis, discuss many of the same concepts and issues as sociologists. Robert Heilbroner's *The Worldly Philosophers* tells much of the side of the story we have omitted here.

Another discipline whose history is entwined with that of sociology is anthropology. The main difference between the two fields is primarily a historical one: Anthropologists became identified as the investigators of the newly discovered tribal societies of the colonial era, whereas sociologists were concerned with modern societies. The distinction has since broken down. As primitive tribes have been colonized or destroyed, anthropologists have come to study modern Western and non-Western societies, and sociologists to study traditional ones. Today there is little difference between what most anthropologists and sociologists do, although anthropology includes some fields—physical anthropology, archaeology, and linguistics—that are rather remote from the work of most sociologists. It is mainly for reasons of space that this volume does not deal with the great anthropologists, although Spencer, Durkheim, and Freud must be viewed as key figures in both histories. The interested reader is referred to Marvin Harris's book *The Rise of Anthropological Theory* for a sketch of the great discoverers in anthropology.

Political science had origins rather distinct from those of sociology. It originated largely in the study of constitutional law, and its main function has been to train public administrators and high-school government teachers. This background has meant that its orientation has been too philosophical and too ideologically biased to make any very notable contributions to a scientific theory of society. Since World War II the behavioral movement has developed in American political science, and political scientists now do work in areas such as political sociology, organizations, and social change, which overlap sociology.

Psychology has long been both distinct from and intertwined with sociology. Its distinct branch deals with nonsocial determinants of individual behavior in such areas as physiological psychology, perception, learning, and motivation. The overlapping branch is social psychology, the study of the individual in relation to others. It has been carried on in modern American universities both in sociology and in psychology departments and sometimes in a separate department of its own. We have set the boundaries of sociology rather far over in the field of social psychology out of the feeling that disciplinary boundaries often do more harm by compartmentalizing studies that should be carried on in a broad perspective: than they do good by allowing the concentration of attention. Freud, in particular, might be considered primarily a psychologist, but we give him rather full treatment here for two reasons. First, although Durkheim is surely right that social structures cannot be explained purely in terms of individuals, society is nevertheless created only by individuals, and our explanations of social order must be founded on knowledge of how individuals function, especially in relation to others. Second, Freud has exerted a great deal of influence on sociology and anthropology—indeed more than on psychology (although perhaps less than on the medical field of psychiatry). American academic psychology has been the bastion of behaviorist orthodoxy, and much of the best thought about cognitive functioning—by Mead and Schutz as well as by Freud—has had to find refuge in sociology. Psychology's loss has been sociology's gain, but one that may eventually be repaid, as the work of the symbolic interactionists, ethnomethodologists, and sociolinguists promises much progress in understanding the psychological functioning of individual human beings.

Finally, history has considerable overlap with sociology. It would be difficult to place earlier thinkers like Alexis de Tocqueville, Fustel de Coulanges, Weber, Henri Pirenne, Marc Bloch, Otto Hintze, Michael Rostovtzeff, and many modern historians such as Lawrence Stone or Fernand Braudel decisively in one intellectual camp or the other. Like sociology, history is an all-encompassing discipline: Everything that has ever happened in the social world is potential material for its narratives, just as it is potential material for sociological theory. The main difference is in orientation: Sociology's is toward a generalizing theory, history's toward the description and explanation of particular sequences of events. The distinction between *generalizing* theory and *particularistic* histories is not an absolute one, however. Historians often apply general principles as a means of ordering the myriad facts available to them, and one of the great tasks of sociology has always been to describe what a particular society (usually our own) is like and to explain the social changes that have led up to our world. In thinkers such as Marx and Weber, the two aims—creating generalizing explanations and capturing a particular historical drama—were carried side by side, to their mutual enrichment. As historians grow increasingly interested in probing beyond political and diplomatic events to social structures, we can expect the two disciplines to draw together even more closely.

Our history of sociology is thus mixed with those of most of the other social disciplines. We draw the boundaries here only to make our subject compact enough to handle. The various disciplines have learned much from each other in the past, and they have much to offer each other now and for the future if only we transcend narrow departmental labels. Having said this, perhaps our various colleagues will forgive us if we indulge in a little sociological pride: In the pages of this book, the reader will find the most illuminating tradition in modern social thought.

PART I

The Vicissitudes of Nineteenth-Century Rationalism

CHAPTER ONE

The Prophets of Paris: Saint-Simon and Comte

One sign that an era is over is that it begins to be romanticized. Medieval society had become remote enough from the educated French of the early nineteenth century for many of them to grow nostalgic about it. It had been a time of faith and order, they thought, when everyone from peasant to king knew his or her place, and social strife was unknown; when people were poor but happy, and the lords and priests watched paternally over their human flocks. The thinkers of the eighteenth century could hold no such illusions. They were too close to the realities of the Middle Ages and glad to have just escaped.

People certainly had been poor; but happy? The physical hardships of the Middle Ages were scarcely imaginable—peasants had nothing but bread to eat, and aristocrats were often little better off; dwellings were small, cold, crowded, unsanitary, and ridden with disease. Nor was there much order. Europe had been in continual warfare since the decline of the Roman Empire, and the threat of violence permeated everyday life. It was a world without police, in which individuals looked out for themselves. Towns locked their walls to keep out robbers, and masters could inflict harsh punishment on their servants, and fathers on their children. Torture was the common treatment for public suspects, and execution and mutilation were the punishments for trivial crimes. People knew their places only because they were kept in them; order existed only as violent oppression.

Nor was that period precisely the age of faith that the romanticists imagined it to be. Religious conflict was almost as chronic as political violence. The Protestant Reformation and the Catholic Counter Reformation were but the biggest and bloodiest battles over the world of the spirit. Heresies and persecutions abounded both before and after the time of Luther, Calvin, and Torquemada's Inquisition. The Church owned a third of the land in Europe and provided the financial and spiritual support for kings (and sometimes their soldiers, too), thereby giving virtually all conflicts a religious tone. It was an age of faith only in the sense that the Church was omnipresent, and the belief in heaven and hell was virtually unquestioned.

The universe was seen as highly ordered, as in Dante's description of the world starting with the heavenly spheres, where God dwelt with his angels, proceeding down through the social hierarchies of the earth to the nine underground levels of hell, where the damned were punished according to their sins. Virtually everyone believed dogmatically in this world order, but they disagreed with each other about just where everyone fitted into it—about who was to be Pope, which kings were to be sanctified, which theology should dominate, and whose morals should be absolute. Everyone was sure of his or her version of the truth and was ready to kill whoever stood in its way. In short, it was an era of waking nightmare, and when peace came and religion waned in the advanced kingdoms of England and France in the 1700s, thinking people heaved a sigh of relief. For them, it was an awakening, an "enlightenment."

Those who entertained the salons of Paris with their conversation were the first intellectuals since antiquity to find employment outside the Church. The *philosophes,* as such men as Voltaire, Diderot, Rousseau, Condorcet, and Turgot came to be known, had found a substitute for theology in science. Isaac Newton was the hero of the age, for his work on the laws of motion, published in 1687, showed how the universe ran of its own accord like a clock. Reason was the spirit of the times, and religion was its enemy. Humankind would at last be happy when the last king was strangled in the entrails of the last priest, declared the freethinker Jean Meslier, to which Voltaire gave assent—although under his breath, since he made a living by frequenting the courts of "enlightened despots" such as Frederick the Great. The *philosophes* rejected the theology of sin and declared that nature was reasonable and good. It was necessary only to discover the natural laws that governed the world and to put society in accordance with them. History ceased to be seen merely as the record of humankind's deeds between Adam and the Second Coming of Christ or a story of continual decline from the golden ages of Greece and Rome. Rather, people began to view history as the progress of scientific enlightenment, in which the eighteenth century stood out as an age of reason, an age of optimism.

The outbreak of the French Revolution in 1789 brought the opportunity people had been waiting for. Now they could be rid of the old order entirely and build a new one based on principles of reason and justice. The king was overthrown and beheaded, aristocrats dispossessed, and the feudal order abolished. But then the liberal supporters of the Revolution began to fall away. The republicans began to turn against themselves. The Assembly purged more and more of its members, and their heads rolled from the guillotine to the cheers of the Paris crowds. The Revolution became paranoid; enemies of freedom were everywhere at home, war was declared against it abroad. The Reign of Terror was instituted under Robespierre and his Committee of Public Safety. Finally, Robespierre himself went to the guillotine, and France began turning to the right. In 1799 the republican government was overthrown by a general named Napoleon Bonaparte, and the great experiment was almost over.

It took another decade and a half for the drama to play itself out. But behind the grand adventure of Napoleon's conquests and eventual defeat, it was becoming clear that an idea had failed. Reason could be a religion, too, and many people could be just as fanatical in defending the Enlightenment as any Grand Inquisitor. Paris in 1815, with a constitutional monarchy back on the throne, was superficially at order again, but intellectually it was in turmoil. Reformers, utopians, and cultists abounded with their explanations of what had gone wrong and what must be done to set it right. At this point entered Saint-Simon, and our story begins.

HENRI DE SAINT-SIMON (1760–1825)

Claude-Henri de Rouvroy, Comte de Saint-Simon, as his name tells us, was an aristocrat, born into one of the most eminent families in France. Like many of his contemporaries, he was brilliant, egotistical, and absolutely unprincipled. His opportunistic career sums up many of the contradictions of his age. He began with a wild and dissolute youth, during which he was even imprisoned by his family as the only means of controlling him (as was, incidentally, his sinister contemporary the Marquis de Sade). Saint-Simon then became an officer in the French army, went to America, and fought in the battle of Yorktown. But we must not think of him as a freedom-loving volunteer like Lafayette; Saint-Simon served purely under the orders of the absolute monarch, King Louis XVI, who for reasons of state supported the Americans in order to oppose the British. Saint-Simon's political motives did not prevent him from becoming an honorary member of the American patriotic Society of Cincinnatus. If Saint-Simon was cynical, it only reflected the general tone of his age.

Back in Europe, Saint-Simon chafed for some excitement. He cooked up schemes for building canals—one across Central America, another connecting Madrid to the sea—but could not successfully promote them. The French Revolution came along at just the right time. Saint-Simon took on the role of the great republican, making revolutionary speeches, presiding at the local assembly near his estate, proposing reforms, and befriending the peasants—while the chateaux of other aristocrats went up in flames. At the height of the republican fervor, Saint-Simon even renounced his title and took the name Bonhomme, equivalent to a Rockefeller today naming himself Jones.

Throughout the political turmoil, Saint-Simon was also busy with private affairs. The Revolution confiscated lands of the Church and of aristocrats who were beheaded or fled the country; Saint-Simon busily bought them up at a fraction of their cost. As the republic's paper currency steadily lost value, Saint-Simon speculated in money and paid for property in worthless *assignats*. To be sure, Robespierre had his eye on such speculators, and Saint-Simon was arrested under suspicion of being a foreign agent. But he had established his republican image well in the provinces, and he mustered enough impeccable supporters to have himself freed. The episode proved only a temporary setback, and while heads were rolling

from the guillotine, Saint-Simon amassed a fortune. He entertained lavish-
ly, kept a salon, and conversed grandly with a drawing room full of admirers and wits about his plans for reconstituting society.

But this was not to last. The French Republic was eclipsed in 1799 by
Napoleon's coup d'état, and not long after Saint-Simon found that he had
spent the last of his fortune. He began to harass his former business partners, his family, and whoever could give him money. He became regarded
as a nuisance. He turned again to ideas, wrote them up, and sent them in
petitions to Napoleon, to members of the Académie des Sciences, and to
anyone else who might put them into action. His favorite idea was that the
world could be saved if the scientists would form an international council
and take over the direction of society. Instead of war and strife, people
could then turn their attention to building canals and generally improving
conditions. Saint-Simon had taken a typical Enlightenment idea, the belief
in science, and given it a slightly more practical foundation.

Strangely, Napoleon and the other eminences were too busy for Saint-
Simon's schemes. His petitions were usually returned to him unopened.
Saint-Simon dropped further into destitution. He came to believe that the
scientists were in a conspiracy against him. His paranoia grew acute, and
for a while he was confined in the famous madhouse at Charenton (the setting for Peter Weiss's play *Marat/Sade*). He made an unsuccessful attempt at
suicide.

Eventually, his fortunes improved a bit. After the monarchy was restored in 1815, Saint-Simon began to make a living as a publicist. The confiscated properties of the aristocrats were now in the hands of a new class
of financiers and entrepreneurs, and with the downfall of Napoleon the
remaining émigrés returned and tried to reclaim them. The government
became the focus for a struggle between these two groups, and Saint-
Simon, who had a sharp eye for the winning side, began to put out papers
and pamphlets arguing the cause of the "industrialists," as he called
them. The word was soon to take on general currency. Saint-Simon's publications were always collapsing, but he made a living by making the rounds
of his supporters for contributions to each new venture. Out of this enterprise, Saint-Simon developed his theory of society and began to attract a
following.

Saint-Simon's main idea was that industrialism was a new era in history. Progress was not a matter of science alone, but affected all the conditions of life. This new society, growing out of a declining feudalism, would
provide the basis for solving all the old problems. Saint-Simon was one of
the first to discern the new order emerging, and he took on the role of
prophet concerning how it should operate.

One of Saint-Simon's famous statements sums up his philosophy:

Suppose that France suddenly lost fifty of her best physicists, chemists, physiol-
ogists, mathematicians, poets, painters, sculptors, musicians, writers; fifty of her
best mechanical engineers, civil and military engineers, artillery experts, archi-
tects, doctors, surgeons, apothecaries, seamen, clockmakers; fifty of her best

bankers, two hundred of her best businessmen, two hundred of her best farmers, fifty of her best ironmasters, arms manufacturers, tanners, dyers, miners, clothmakers, cotton manufacturers, silk-makers, linen-makers, manufacturers of hardware, of pottery and china, of crystal and glass, ship chandlers, carriers, printers, engravers, goldsmiths, and other metal-workers; her fifty best masons, carpenters, joiners, farriers, locksmiths, cutlers, smelters, and a hundred other persons of various unspecified occupations, eminent in the sciences, fine arts, and professions; making in all three thousand leading scientists, artists, and artisans of France.

These men are the Frenchmen who are the most essential producers, those who make the most important products, those who direct the enterprises most useful to the nation, those who contribute to its achievements in the sciences, fine arts and professions. They are in the most real sense the flower of French society; they are, above all Frenchmen, the most useful to their country, contribute most to its glory, increasing its civilization and prosperity. The nation would become a lifeless corpse as soon as it lost them. It would immediately fall into a position of inferiority compared with the nations which it now rivals, and would continue to be inferior until this loss had been replaced, until it had grown another head. It would require at least a generation for France to repair this misfortune; for men who are distinguished in work of positive ability are exceptions, and nature is not prodigal of exceptions, particularly in this species.

Let us pass on to another assumption. Suppose that France preserves all the men of genius that she possesses in the sciences, fine arts and professions, but has the misfortune to lose in the same day Monsieur the King's brother, Monseigneur le duc d'Angouleme, Monseigneur le duc de Berry, Monseigneur le duc d'Orleans, Monseigneur le duc de Bourbon, Madame la duchesse d'Angouleme, Madame la duchesse de Berry, Madame la duchesse d'Orleans, Madame la duchesse de Bourbon, and Mademoiselle de Conde. Suppose that France loses at the same time all the great officers of the royal household, all the ministers (with or without portfolio), all the councillors of state, all the chief magistrates, marshals, cardinals, archbishops, bishops, vicars-general, and canons, all the prefects and sub-prefects, all the civil servants, and judges, and, in addition, ten thousand of the richest proprietors who live in the style of nobles.

This mischance would certainly distress the French, because they are kindhearted, and could not see with indifference the sudden disappearance of such a large number of their compatriots. But this loss of thirty-thousand individuals, considered to be the most important in the state, would only grieve them for purely sentimental reasons and would result in no political evil for the State.[1]

By chance, a few days after this was published in 1819, an assassin took the life of the Duc de Berry. Saint-Simon was arrested as an instigator. But Saint-Simon had chosen his sides well, and he was acquitted.

The old era had been devoted to war and religion; aristocrats and priests had lived as parasites on the rest of society. The new era was to be devoted to the production of useful goods and services. Saint-Simon did not distinguish among bankers, manufacturers, engineers, laborers, poets, and scien-

[1]Henri de Saint-Simon, *Social Organization, The Science of Man, and Other Writings* (New York: Harper Torchbooks, 1964), pp. 72–73.

tists—all were producers, in contrast to the parasitic aristocracy. "All men must work" became Saint-Simon's slogan, whatever work one might be suited for. His disciples later put forward the formulation: "Each according to his capacity"—eventually to become famous as part of the motto of communism.

The Saint-Simonians were quite willing to call themselves "socialists," although they meant this in a rather vague sense. Modern ideologies had not yet crystallized, and the Saint-Simonians continued to believe in private property, although they did not assign it very much importance, and were more concerned with coordinating the activities of society through large and centrally directed enterprises. Great undertakings—like canals, railroads, and steamship lines—were the focus of their interest, and these things were "social" rather than individual in nature.

The modern era was to be one of peace. Force would no longer be necessary, since people would turn their powers against nature instead of against other men. The state would virtually cease to exist, at least in its old, coercive form; it would be replaced by a world council of scientists, financiers, and industrialists, who would plan and coordinate for the good of all.

Society would remain a hierarchy but would no longer be looked upon as stratified. People simply have different innate capacities: Some are more intellectually developed, and these would become scientists; others are more emotional and would become the poets and artists; those who are more motor-oriented would become the workers and organizers. The best of all three types would be given the top positions of leadership, and the others would array themselves below. All would be happy if they could fill their own true function, be it high or low. In sum, Saint-Simon believed in the rise of a perfect meritocracy.

What Saint-Simon developed has turned out to be the characteristic ideology of industrialism. It is found all over the world today, among the technocrats of the modern French state, in the British civil service, and in the great American bureaucracies from the universities to the RAND Corporation. It is a belief that progress is based on science and that new societies are created out of the old (in the developing nations of the world as well as in the more advanced countries of the East and West), without revolution or conflict, simply by putting the scientists and industrialists in charge. There is no real conflict of classes if everyone works and is able to rise according to his or her individual merit. The system is elitist, but no one would (or should) mind, since the experts at the top are working only for the common good. This ideology includes what may be called the belief in "the stateless state": that the government exists purely as a technical, neutral instrument for coordinating society, not as a means of oppression or the provider of special interests. As we shall see, even the Communists adopted this view of their own state, although they deny that it is true of the state in capitalist countries.

When Saint-Simon died in 1825, his young followers started off on an unexpected turn. Taking up one of Saint-Simon's last ideas, the creation of a "new Christianity" of social harmony, they began to preach love of humanity and formed a utopian community outside of Paris, where all would work for the common good. In a prim and proper fashion, they were the hippies of their day. The experiment collapsed after a year, when their leader Enfantin was brought to trial and sentenced to a year in jail for outraging public morals. After this romantic escapade, the Saint-Simonians settled down to become industrialists and financiers. Among them were the Pereire brothers, the financiers of Louis Napoleon's Second Empire and the organizers of the famous Credit Mobilier speculations. Another of these, Ferdinand de Lesseps, even brought one of Saint-Simon's earliest schemes to fruition: In 1869 he completed the Suez Canal.

AUGUSTE COMTE (1798–1857)

In 1817 Saint-Simon engaged as his private secretary a serious young man named Auguste Comte. Comte was well educated, having just graduated from Napoleon's new Ecole Polytechnique, where the best of modern science was taught. Saint-Simon saw his new assistant, trained in mathematics and all the sciences, as the disciple who could formulate his loose ideas into a complete system. They worked together for seven years, developing their views on history and on industrial society. From this enterprise was to emerge an entirely new social science.

They split up in 1824 after a series of quarrels. The final dispute came over the question of whose name was to appear on the title page of their most important work. Without a patron, Comte fell into dire straits. He demanded a position at the Ecole Polytechnique from which to teach his new science and was refused repeatedly. He eked out a living grading entrance examinations in mathematics, gave public lectures to whoever would listen, and wrote volume after volume about his system. Like his former employer, he barraged kings and officials all over Europe with petitions to support his work. He drew no response, for the garrets of Paris were crowded with starving writers of every variety, and his petitions were part of a deluge of such mail. Comte fulminated against those who rejected his ideas, which he felt could save the world. In classic style, he went through fits of raving mania and was confined for a while at Charenton asylum. He twice attempted suicide. Eventually, he began to gather a cult around him, and his system of Positivism gradually became known.

Comte's system derives from a basic principle, the law of the three stages of knowledge. Comte referred to this concept as "the great discovery of the year 1822" (when he had still been working for Saint-Simon); he had even written down the hour of the day at which he had begun each new page. It was over the publication of this work that the break with Saint-Simon had come.

The law of the three stages states that knowledge of any subject always begins in *theological* form (explanation by animism, spirits, or gods), passes to the *metaphysical* form (explanation by abstract philosophical speculation), and finally becomes *positive* (scientific explanation based on observation, experiment, and comparison). Accordingly, there is a historical sequence of the sciences, as the various areas of knowledge pass through these stages in order of difficulty. The simplest and most remote topics become scientific first, followed by increasingly complex and concrete matters. Thus the sciences develop in this order:

> mathematics
> astronomy
> physics
> chemistry
> biology
> sociology

Humans free themselves from theological and metaphysical notions first in those areas most remote from themselves—mathematics and astronomy; it is only after great advance that humans come to apply science to the realms of their own being—biology and sociology. This was, in fact, the first time that society was conceived of as an object for science, and Comte coined the term "sociology" for this new field.

There appears to be a missing link in this list of sciences—psychology. But this was no oversight on Comte's part. As far as he was concerned, the individual psyche or soul was merely a religious and philosophical superstition; a truly scientific psychology would treat humans as the activity of body and brain, and hence psychology was part of physiology, a division of biology. Comte's views on psychology at the time consisted of a belief in phrenology, the system that explained human temperaments as due to the enlargement of various areas of the brain. This survives today only as a memory of analyzing a person's character by feeling the lumps on his or her head. Comte's radical rejection of any subjectivistic psychology has its modern counterpart in behaviorism.

Comte's rejection of psychology has another important consequence. In his view, each science constitutes a separately organized level of existence. The social world, although composed of individuals, is not identical with those individuals, but is structured according to its own principles. Comte thus broke with the prevailing Enlightenment search for an answer to social problems in the elements of human nature. Society is not just the behavior of individuals, but something that accumulates across many generations. Just as language is created by individual people speaking, but nevertheless develops a vocabulary and a grammar that no one person ever does much to modify, society remains and unfolds by laws of its own, while individuals come and go. Comte thus hit on the concept of society as a cumulative *culture,* as we would now put it.

The task of the new science of sociology was to set forth the laws that governed this entity. Accordingly, sociology is divided into two parts: "social statics" and "social dynamics." Comte defined statics as the study of social order, and dynamics as the study of social change or progress.

Comte himself was well trained in the sciences of his day, and he held that sociology would develop by the scientific methods of observation, experimentation, comparison, and historical research. Unfortunately, he himself never did much of this kind of research, although he was fairly well versed in history. He was in too much of a hurry to finish his system, for he believed it contained the answer to the main problem of the day: how to put a society ravaged by revolution and strife back into order. With this in view, Comte invoked some methodological principles that provided short-cuts to his goal.

The first of these was the principle that isolated facts cannot be understood by themselves, but must be seen in their larger context: The whole must be grasped if one is to see the functions of the parts. This principle contains the fairly sophisticated idea, upheld by modern philosophy of science, that one must have an organizing paradigm or set of concepts before one can know what observations to make of the world. But Comte neglected the modern proviso that the concepts one begins with are only provisional, to be modified or rejected as the effort to fit in the facts goes on. Comte was confident that he had grasped the model of the whole at his first try.

According to this model, society is analogous to a biological organism. Society has its various parts (the family, the church, the state) just as a body has its various organs (the liver, the brain, the kidneys, and so on), each serving some function for the whole. Comte did not mean that society is literally an organism; it exists only as consciousness, not as physical individuals, and the various social institutions are parts of this set of ideas that are passed on from generation to generation. The roots of modern functionalism can be found in this analysis.

The various parts of society thus fitted together, and none could exist without the others. The harmonious society, then, was based on *consensus*, a feeling of belonging together as a moral unit. Here we can see how much more conservative Comte was than his mentor Saint-Simon. Saint-Simon was a thoroughgoing atheist and materialist, a believer in science and industry, whereas Comte felt that society could not be held together by reason alone, but demanded faith. Thus the family, the church, and the community are the core of society, for it is here that people's selfish tempers are controlled by the sentiments of love, duty, loyalty, and respect. Comte thus mixed Saint-Simon's revolutionary heritage with the ideas of the conservative opponents of the Revolution, who contrasted the chaos of the years of Robespierre with a romanticized view of feudal society. The most influential of these conservatives were the émigré aristocrats Joseph de Maistre and Louis de Bonald, whom we shall meet again when we come to Tocqueville. Social thought owes many of its advances to such mixtures.

This constituted Comte's social statics. Two other principles helped him formulate his system of social dynamics: the belief that social change everywhere goes through the same sequence and the belief that all the various elements of a society change together. According to the first of these, we do not need to investigate the history of all societies; we need only locate the most advanced society, and the stages of its history will show us the stages through which all others must pass. The evolution of one society can show the rest of the world the face of its future. Comte was thus able to place all known societies on a continuum of development, from the primitive tribes described by the explorers of America and the Orient, on through the empires of history, and culminating, needless to say, with nineteenth-century France.

The second of these principles tells us that progress occurs simultaneously in all spheres—intellectual, physical, moral, and political. This follows from the idea of society as an integrated whole or system. This provided another shortcut for Comte, for it meant that one kind of change could be taken as an index for all others. Comte chose to emphasize intellectual change, since this was the area he knew best. The result was this capsule summary of the stages of human history:

Intellectual	Material Form	Basic Social Unit	Basic Moral Sentiment
Theological	Military	Family	Attachment
Metaphysical	Legalistic	State	Veneration
Positive	Industrial	Humanity	Benevolence

Comte's basic ideas have had enormous influence on the development of sociology, both for good and for ill. Society is somewhat like an organism, but it is also unlike an organism in crucial ways. It is inherently full of conflict as well as harmony; and it is held together, when it is in fact held together, by coercion and economic self-interest as well as by moral sentiments. Comte's ideas about social change have been especially pernicious. They have a considerable appeal for the mentally lazy, who do not want to have to understand the intricate paths of history, which are arranged so inconveniently that they do not even progress toward the same goal. The elements of society do not all change together, and the outcomes are neither so inevitable nor so benevolent as Comte believed. For all humankind's hopes, France did not hold out the vision of the future for the rest of the world, nor does the United States for the Third World today. As we are beginning to understand, the so-called developing nations show few signs of creating our kind of politics, stratification, or even economy in the foreseeable future, and it has even become questionable whether they are "developing" at all. Today's world planners are guilty of the same haste for favorable conclusions as was Comte. There is no shortcut substitute for the scientific method of collecting, comparing, and analyzing the facts.

On the positive side, Spencer, Durkheim, and others were to make good use of many of Comte's leading insights: the recognition that society would have to be explained on its own level rather than by reduction to psychology, the division of labor among social institutions, and especially the role of moral sentiments in holding society together. Free of Comte's overwhelming ideological concerns, later sociologists have gone beyond merely advocating moral order to analyze it, to search for the conditions that create it at certain times and places, and, thus, to break through to an understanding of the emotions and rituals that harness people to each other below the level of their rational consciousness.

But this was to be in the future. Comte, indeed, ended by turning his new science into a cult. The cult took form after Comte, in 1844, had a melodramatic but strictly platonic love affair with a middle-aged woman. The object of his passion was a lady named Clothilde de Vaux, who had been deserted by her husband but still remained faithful to her marriage vow. The high point of the affair was an abortive liaison, complete with much handwringing and many protestations of duty and honor, which left Comte still physically denied but enraptured with worship of Clothilde's moral superiority. Not long after, she became deathly ill, and Comte forced his way into her bedroom and locked out her parents so that he might spend her dying moments with her alone.

Comte then began a series of ritual devotions, starting with daily obeisance to a lock of Clothilde's hair. He formed his followers into a Religion of Humanity, with Comte as its high priest. He began to refer to society as the "Great Being" and preached universal love and harmony through his system of industrial order. He envisioned mankind advancing to progressively higher levels of spirituality and even imagined a time in the future when love would dispense with gross material forms entirely, and women would be able to give birth without sexual intercourse. He formulated a new calendar, with days of devotion commemorating scientists, saints, poets, and philosophers alike. He planned a council of all such leaders, organized under the High Priest of Humanity, who would rule the world benevolently through the application of Positivism.

The cults of Comte and Saint-Simon, like the other utopian schemes of the nineteenth century, failed to save the world, of course, or even to have very much effect on it. Saint-Simonianism provided an ideology to justify the activity of some financiers and industrialists of the nineteenth century. Comte's Positivism attracted scattered adherents around the world, notably in the United States and Russia, and at the behest of some romantic Brazilian aristocrats it was made the official philosophy of Brazil. Indeed, Comte's motto *Ordem e Progresso* (Order and Progress) is still found on the Brazilian flag, an ironic commentary on the actual conditions of that beleaguered country.

The utopian prophets failed to change the world because they insufficiently understood it. They were too optimistic, too sentimental, and too eager for easy change to understand that history grinds out its conclusions through long and hard struggles. In the next chapter we meet the founder of the most successful social movement of modern times, a man willing to see the conflict at the core of things: Karl Marx.

CHAPTER TWO

Sociology in the Underground: Karl Marx

The social thinkers discussed so far have been respectable. They appeal to the established order. They talk of ideals and avoid looking too closely at unpleasant facts about the new industrial order. But the nineteenth century was not simply a glorious era of science, progress, justice, and brotherhood. Saint-Simon's harmonious hierarchy of industrial men or Comte's social organism made sense only if one closed one's eyes to what was going on in the mundane world. Black smoke was beginning to hang in the air over the industrial towns of England, France, and Germany, and on the streets behind the houses of the prospering businessmen were growing the tenements where workers crowded with their families in scenes of grime, poverty, and disease. The mines and factories were manned by a tubercular population of men, women, and children, working eleven-, thirteen-, or fourteen-hour days, six or seven days a week, without respite except through layoff or death. For Karl Marx the basis of reality was here, in the harsh facts of material and economic conditions, and the talk of philosophers, politicians, and priests was only a smoke screen designed to divert attention from it.

Marx was the great angry man of the nineteenth century. Indignant at what was happening to people and at the hypocrisy and blindness of those who covered it up, he set out to reveal what was going on, to explain both the inexorable workings of the economic substructure and the deceptions of the political and ideological superstructure. Marx was the first to come to grips with the realities of social conflict instead of wishing them away, and for this he doomed himself to a life in the underground. But this was the fate he wished. Free from the illusions of respectability, he thought he saw the system bringing its own destruction and the outlines of a newer, better world arising in its midst. Karl Marx, the man of conflict, was both a realist and a revolutionist.

It is not surprising that Marx is the most controversial of all modern thinkers, with the possible exception of Sigmund Freud. His writings have been the handbook of revolutionists and would-be revolutionists. With the success of his followers in Russia, China, and elsewhere, his ideas have been raised to the level of state dogma. In Moscow the Institute of Marxism-

Leninism faithfully recorded the events that took place every day of Marx's life. Marxism became a political orthodoxy. On the other side, virtually all opponents of communism have felt they must refute the Marxist system, usually by pointing out that revolution has occurred only in backward countries, where Marx did not expect it, and has not occurred in mature capitalistic nations, where Marx did expect it. The anti-Communist revolutions in Eastern Europe and Russia during 1989–1991 further discredited Marxism as a political and economic program.

Can we say, then, that Marxism is just a bizarre episode which the future will increasingly forget? Marx predicted that factory workers would be the gravediggers of the capitalist system; instead, the worldwide capitalism of the late twentieth century appears to be burying socialism. But let us make some distinctions among the various parts of Marx's ideas. His program of socialism did not work out as he expected. But Marx did not say much about socialism, only regarding this as a phase in the future which should be created when the time came. His work concentrated on capitalism and its internal conflicts. Ironically, the collapse of socialism makes the topic of capitalism even more central. This is the system we see almost everywhere, including in the old Soviet-bloc countries where capitalism is being introduced today. Socialism is certainly not a utopian end of history, but neither is capitalism. Capitalism is full of economic conflicts, and these inner workings of capitalism are even more on the center of the stage now that the conflict with socialism has virtually disappeared.

Marx's great contribution to sociology was in opening up the analysis of economic classes and economic conflict, and in proposing that they have a central place in the theory of how societies operate. Though Marxism was wrong about many things, the central insight remains an important one. Knowledge advances by using and revising ideas to account for the facts we turn up, building on strengths, shoring up weaknesses. In the long run we are best served by discovering as much as we can of the truth, not by rushing to act on half-truths or outright illusions. Marx's ideas can best be used if we are aware of both their weaknesses and their strengths, and that is what this chapter will try to display.

KARL MARX (1818–1883)

Marx was born in Trier, one of the small, legalistic states of the Rhineland, on the border between a progressive France and the more traditional parts of Germany. His father was a liberal, a Jew from a long line of rabbis, who had nominally converted to Christianity in order to maintain his career as a lawyer—that is, as a member of the local government bureaucracy, since lawyers were not independent professionals in Germany. Young Marx attended the University of Berlin, where he drank in taverns, acquired debts, fought the usual duel and got the usual scar on his face, and studied philosophy. In short, he prepared himself for an academic career.

But circumstances conspired to forbid him a respectable career as a brilliant professor. He became caught up in the intellectual movement known as the Young Hegelians. Georg Hegel (1770–1832) had been the dominant German philosopher of his day. He was a liberal, after the German fashion, which meant that he believed in the rule of laws rather than the arbitrary rule of humankind and hence supported the Prussian state. Hegel's philosophy was a culmination of the idealist tradition that began with Kant; it held that the essence of reality is Reason, but that the spirit of Reason manifests itself only gradually, revealing more and more facets of itself during the course of time. History, he held, is the growth of Reason to consciousness of itself, and the constitutional, legalistic state is the culmination of history. Hegel developed his philosophy while Napoleon seemed to be spreading the achievements of the French Revolution all over Europe. Later, in the reaction following Napoleon's final defeat in 1815, Hegel found it expedient to declare that history culminated in the bureaucratic Prussian state, and he became the official philosopher at Berlin.

Of course, there was no reason history should come to a halt in Prussia, especially when that state still lacked a true constitution, and after Hegel's death the revolutionary implications of his doctrine came to the fore again. One faction of Hegel's students, the left Hegelians, unleashed his historical relativism as an attack on the autocratic state and its ideological bulwark, the state church. Marx's teacher, Bruno Bauer, investigated the Bible as a historical document and declared the Gospels to be forgeries and Jesus a historical myth. For this Bauer was dismissed from his university post in 1842 as dangerous to the state. This ended Marx's chances for an academic career, since sponsorship was even more important in the universities of the time than it is now. It had been predicted that Marx would be the most eminent professor of his generation, but this path was now closed. Marx took his first step toward the underground.

He became the editor of a liberal newspaper in Cologne, a Westernized city on the Rhine River. Hard economic realities struck him immediately. He became embroiled in a controversy with the authorities over their decision to prohibit peasants from cutting firewood in the forest, although this was a traditional custom. The trees were protected by laws, Marx wrote acidly, while poor people froze. He began to view philosophy of all sorts as a distraction from the hard, material realities. Hegel's idealism stood history on its head, he later wrote; the task was to set it on its feet. The newspaper lasted five months before being suppressed by the government. The conservative papers accused him of being a Communist. Marx did not quite know what this meant, but he resolved to find out.

Now twenty-four years old, he went to Paris, the intellectual home of all radicals. He read the French historians, imbued with the Saint-Simonian idea of progress and the image of industrial society breaking out of the bonds of feudalism, and he encountered the advocates of utopian socialist communities. To his German Hegelianism and French radicalism he added the third leg of his system: the ideas of the British economists Adam Smith,

Thomas Malthus, and David Ricardo. These thinkers explained how the movements of people and goods in this new era were controlled by the invisible hand of the market.

Among Marx's radical acquaintances was Friedrich Engels, another idealistic young German, who had just returned from his father's textile factory in Manchester, bringing with him a harsh exposé entitled *The Condition of the Working Class in England in 1844.* Their ideas meshed, and they launched an intellectual partnership that was to last the rest of their lives. They were soon expelled from France for their radical writings. They went to Belgium and then to England. In 1847 they attended secret meetings in London of a new revolutionary coalition of labor unions (at that time illegal) called the Communist League. As its platform they wrote a manifesto, which ended with the following words:

> The communists disdain to conceal their views and aims. They openly declare that their ends can be attained only by the forcible overthrow of all existing social conditions. Let the ruling classes tremble at a communist revolution. The proletarians have nothing to lose but their chains. They have a world to win. WORKING-MEN OF ALL COUNTRIES, UNITE!

The *Communist Manifesto* was finished in January 1848. In February, during an economic crisis in Paris, a group of demonstrating unemployed workers were fired upon by soldiers, and the city erupted into riot. The French king abdicated, his government collapsed, and a wave of revolt was set off through the cities of Germany, Italy, Austria, and most of the rest of Europe. The nobility everywhere were frightened and on the defensive. In France the wealthy property owners took command of the Second Republic; a popular left-wing revolt in June was crushed by the army in six days of bloody fighting. Around Europe the right wing gradually regained confidence and began to reestablish its power. Marx, who edited the revolutionary newspaper in Cologne during the uprising there, was banished by the Prussian government.

Reaction had set in again. Marx went to London, his final place of refuge, and, watched by police spies, began again to write. With him came his wife, his childhood sweetheart and the daughter of a German aristocrat who had been the Marxs' neighbor in Trier. Life became a struggle to survive. For a while Marx made a living as a foreign correspondent for the New York *Tribune,* then under a liberal editor. At times the family nearly starved. They lived in the poorest working-class section of London. They pawned their possessions and borrowed money from Engels, who was then working in his father's business in Manchester. Several of Marx's children died of malnutrition and disease. Through it all he managed to work, sitting in the reading room of the British Museum from 10 A.M. to 7 P.M. every day for years. At last, in 1867, his researches were published as *Das Kapital,* a book that would help bring down half the world.

Marx's life work forms a comprehensive system, but for purposes of analysis it may be divided into three parts: his sociology, built around the analysis of class consciousness and class conflict; his economics, which develops the internal contradictions of capitalism; and his social and political philosophy, built around the notion of alienation and its solution in communism. These parts are not equally valid. Marx's sociology has turned out to be basically correct and has been very important for subsequent theories. His economics, on the other hand, is crucially flawed, although it points us to some important questions. His philosophy, in the final analysis, is based on value premises and ways of looking at the world that individuals can accept or reject as a source of inspiration as they see fit. In short, it is possible to get much from Marx without accepting his whole system.

MARX'S SOCIOLOGY

Classes and Class Consciousness

"The history of all hitherto existing society is the history of class struggles," Marx declares at the beginning of the *Communist Manifesto,* and classes are the core of his analysis. Marx did not invent the concept of class, of course. In his day one could scarcely avoid noticing them, and the danger was rather to take them for granted. What Marx did was to provide a theory of how classes are produced. He began from materialist premises. Since one could not survive without making a living, he reasoned, the source of one's living must be the most basic determinant of one's behavior. The economy of an era, with its different economic positions, was thus the source of its fundamental class divisions. In the society of ancient Greece and Rome the economy was organized around slavery; hence the basic classes were those whose living came from owning slaves (the patricians or citizens), the slaves themselves, and those who were neither slaves nor slaveholders (the plebeians or freemen). In the feudal society of the Middle Ages the basis of the economy was the manor; the main class was the nobility, who owned the land and the services of the peasants attached to it, and the serfs or peasants, who provided the agricultural labor. In modern or bourgeois society the economy is organized around industrial production and commercial exchange; and the main classes comprise the capitalists, who own the factories, the banks, and the goods to trade, and the proletarians, who own nothing but their own labor power.

Within these classes there could be further divisions. For example, in feudal society the nobility was divided into ranks from king down to knight and included the landowning clergy of the powerful medieval Church. There were also minor classes not based directly on the central economy, such as servants, guild masters, journeymen, apprentices, and free peasants. For Marx the property divisions were crucial because they marked the breaking lines in the social structure. When conflicts became intense, classes would have to group themselves along these divisions. Thus modern society includes financial capitalists (such as bankers and brokers) as well as industrialists and agricultural landowners; small capitalists as well as big ones; the petty bourgeoisie, consisting of handicraftspeople and shopkeepers who both own their own tools and shops and work in them; the working class or proletariat; and the poorest and most degraded class, full of criminals and people living from hand to mouth, the *lumpenproletariat*. Marx used all of these classes to analyze what happened in modern society, but he expected the conflicts to polarize more and more between the property owners as a whole and the propertyless workers, with the petty bourgeoisie and small capitalists being deprived of their property and dropping into the ranks of the proletariat.

This material organization of society produces what Marx calls "class consciousness." People do not have an objective view of the world; they see it from the restricted point of view of their own positions. Thus, bourgeois writers like John Locke saw private property as an inherent part of the order of nature; feudal lords saw the rights of hereditary nobility as given by God; and the ancient philosophers could not even imagine a world without slavery. This is not to say that people have *no* capacities for being objective or that they spend all their time thinking about their economic interests. They may occasionally be genuinely interested in the ideas of philosophy, religion, science, literature, history, or art, but where their ideas impinge on the social world, class consciousness goes into action.

Out of the array of available ideas, people select those to believe in that best fit their material interests. Thus, the medieval nobility supported the conservative Christian thinkers who preached the sanctity of worldly authority and diverted the peasants toward the spiritual world and away from the oppressions of the material one. This is the meaning of Marx's phrase, "religion is the opiate of the people." Occasionally, it could work the other way, as when the religious upheavals of the Lutheran Reformation provided some alternatives, and a peasant revolt broke out under the religious guise of the belief that the Second Coming of Christ was at hand. In modern society bourgeois interests found ideological support in beliefs about personal morality; extolling the virtues of hard work, individual success, self-control, frugality, and respect for law and property were ways of getting people to support the competitive system of free enterprise. In the same way, politicians make speeches about the eternal truths embodied in their laws, even though those laws frame a system of property that benefits the group those politicians belong to.

But there seems to be a contradiction here. If everyone selects ideas to fit his or her personal interests, how can religion be the "opiate of the people"? How can people have "false consciousness" and be taken in by the ideologies of their opponents? This was a serious question for Marx, since the workers did not always see the capitalists as their enemies, and until they did so, a revolution could not occur. Marx's writings imply two main answers. The first is simply that people's ideas can be controlled by coercion. He himself was familiar with government censorship, treason trials, and the denial of rights of speech to "subversive" thinkers by those who did not want their viewpoint contested. The second, somewhat subtler, answer is that consciousness depends on the material resources people have for formulating and communicating ideas. The dominant social classes have most of these resources: They get the most education, are most likely to be literate, and have the time and money to keep up on news and ideas. Furthermore, they can influence what ideas are produced by paying the salaries of teachers or priests, owning newspapers or controlling them by buying their advertisements (or, in the present era, giving research grants). The impoverished Saint-Simon, writing publicity for the French industrialists, provides an example of how the process works. The lower classes can criticize the upper classes under their breath but not in the center of public attention, and they lack the means to formulate ideas about things happening at a distance from them. The result, in Marx's words, is that "the ideas of the ruling class are in every epoch the ruling ideas."

As history moves, consciousness changes with it. The thinkers of the Enlightenment appeared because material conditions had changed in England and France, and the incipient bourgeois class was beginning to gather the resources to support thinkers of its own. Marx discerned another movement, culminating in the future. As capitalism brought workers into the cities and crowded them together in factories, it created material conditions that allowed the workers to communicate among themselves. Literacy and the press began to give the workers a chance to develop a worldview of their own. Beneath the public beliefs of bourgeois ideology an underground consciousness was growing. Here Marx found a role for himself not unlike that of Hegel: to raise the level of consciousness of the working class until it became fully aware of itself.

MARX'S THEORY OF POLITICS

All this culminates in Marx's theory of politics. Politics is the effort to control the state. The state fundamentally consists of the instruments of organized violence in society, and hence it is an enormous power for whoever can control it. The state is a crucial prop for the economy in that it establishes the system of property. Property, after all, is not so much the things that are owned as it is the right of owners to do what they please with them, and the denial of those rights to others. Land, for example, does not "belong to" anyone, even if it is used, until someone claims the exclusive right to use it and backs up the claim with either his or her own power or the power of the state. In this way, the state creates the rights of property in a system of slavery or serfdom or in a modern money economy. Marx was particularly interested in the fact that since the state creates private property, it can abolish it and substitute socialism. But that was for the future.

Ordinary politics is the struggle to control the state so that its powers can be used for one's personal advantage. The struggle may be between members of the same class (such as nobles fighting among themselves for power in the Middle Ages) or between different class sectors (in modern society, petty bourgeois interests versus industrialists, financiers versus landowners). Beneath the sonorous speeches of the politicians, the real business of politics concerns mundane economic issues—taxes, tariffs, monopolies, franchises, licenses—over which people struggle and bargain for nothing more noble than the opportunity for economic gain.

Occasionally, there are more important clashes. These occur in historical periods when new economic classes attempt to change the existing structure of property. Marx lived in the shadow of the French Revolution, when the entire feudal system of aristocratic privileges and monopolies was swept aside to create the basis for a market economy, transforming the noble into a holder of salable land and the peasant into a free laborer, and freeing the entrepreneur from old monopolies and restrictions. These basic, revolutionary conflicts draw together the members of the various classes. Nobles cease to fight among themselves, and the bourgeoisie unite in their common interest. An entire system is at stake.

Who wins in these struggles? There are two main determinants: the distribution of material resources that enable people to struggle successfully for power and the historical situation that favors a class whose time has come. While these are not entirely distinct, we can see that the first determinant is most important in ordinary politics, and the second is crucial in times of revolution.

During the feudal era, for example, ordinary politics was monopolized by the aristocracy, because they alone had the resources to engage in it. The peasants were tied down to the land; the merchants were a minor group, without military power. Men who owned enough property to afford a horse and armor could be knights; the great landowners could outfit whole armies. Thus the nobility constituted the only "political class," the only group with the time and resources to keep informed of what was going on, to make alliances with other nobles, and to take part in wars and court intrigues.

In the same way, in the industrial era the capitalists control communications, money, and time. They exert an influence over government far out of proportion to their numbers because they command the resources of business and finance. The network of business contacts gives them a class organization; their business and financial affairs keep them constantly aware of what the government is doing that may affect them; their wealth and organizational bases allow them to support politicians who will represent them in office. Not the least of this power is ideological. As we have seen, the class with the strongest resources can control the means of communication and hence hinder other classes' abilities to formulate their own interests. Within the capitalist class, as within the aristocratic class in its era of dominance, those who hold the largest resources will be able to advance their interests over those of their fellows. But when another class challenges, the class that holds the greatest resources as a whole will usually unite and thus prevail.

This brings us to the second determinant of power: the long-term historical changes in the economy that favor a particular class simply because that class's interests happen to coincide with the interests of the system as a whole. Marx was sure that the bourgeoisie would eventually prevail over the aristocracy in Germany, Russia, and the rest of the world, just as it had in France. Once capitalism developed to the stage where a society depended more on industrial production and trade than on subsistence agriculture for its livelihood, the capitalist economic system had to be supported by favorable state policies. To fail to give it this support would hurt everyone, especially the existing rulers, who would not want to go back to a preindustrial standard of living. But in Marx's time the old feudal laws and government hindered capitalism; kings could only ruin it with their old policies of sales of monopolies, indiscriminate taxation, and special rights for aristocrats. The means of production had outgrown the relations of production; the fetters had to be broken.

"Force is the midwife of every old society pregnant with a new one," declared Marx. The revolution came in France in 1789. The king went to the guillotine, eventually to be replaced by another in 1815—but now the old property system was gone, and a new one, suitable for the bourgeoisie, had taken its place. Instead of the old absolute monarchy, there were a constitution and a representative assembly in which the bourgeoisie could begin to shape laws to its economic needs.

The bourgeoisie won because its time had come. The economy had changed, giving them the resources to contend for power, the ideology to express their interests, and the favored position of being necessary for society's prosperity. A similar revolt in the Middle Ages could only have been a failure. Even if by some chance the capitalists had had the resources to win power, they would have been unable to change the laws upholding feudal society without creating a chaos of marauding warriors and defenseless peasants. They had to wait until history was prepared for them.

Marx's sight focused on another class maturing in the womb of history: the working class. Just as capitalism grew up within feudalism until their conflict kept both systems from operating and the old world had to be smashed to make way for the new, capitalism itself would begin to break up because of its internal contradictions. The periodic financial crises, with attendant bankruptcies and unemployment, were only symptoms of what was to come. As the industrial economy grew, it would come more and more into conflict with the free market and the system of private property that formed its structure. Eventually, a crisis would occur in which the interests of the *workers* alone would coincide with the *necessities* of keeping the system going. Only abolition of private property and the institution of socialism would restore economic order. The interests of the workers, then, would have at last become the interests of the whole system, and the capitalists would be displaced.

The process was really twofold. Not only would economic change make the workers the necessary dominant class, but it would also shift the balance of weapons with which to conquer power. The factories and industrial cities would bring the workers together in the strength of numbers, and technological change—the press, the telegraph, and so forth—would improve their capacities for communication and organization. Modern advances would thus bring them to full mobilization and full consciousness of their interests. When the moment struck, they would be prepared.

When properly understood, Marx's sociology appears to be basically correct. That is not to say that his predictions about the downfall of capitalism are right, as they obviously are not. But these are specific applications of the theory and not the theory itself. A considerable amount of modern research indicates that one's economic position (that is, occupation) is a major determinant of one's life style, interests, and beliefs; that economic change produces the lineup of classes in a particular historical era; and that the material resources for organization and communication, along with the functional necessities of governing to keep up the economy, tend to determine who will win political power. All of this, however, Marx plugs into a particular theory of *how the economy will develop.* His account of capitalism growing within European feudalism and bringing about the great waves of bourgeois revolutions seems basically accurate. But his theory about the inevitable tendencies of modern capitalism is wrong. It is because Marx's economics fails that the rest of the system does not turn out the way he expected it to. Marx did not, as is sometimes suggested, fail to take account of racial or religious strife that would keep the workers from unifying, or of social mobility that would make workers think of their individual chances of rising instead of their class interests in overthrowing the whole system. He merely expected such conflicts to be dwarfed by an economic crisis so great that people would have to unite along class lines simply to survive. The decline of racial animosity in the United States during the Depression of the 1930s suggests that Marx was right on this point. Similarly, he recognized the possibility of social mobility, but he believed that in a time of economic crisis the only social mobility would be *downward*. No, the problem is with Marx's prediction of an economic crisis that could be resolved *only* by socialism.

We turn, then, to a brief sketch of Marx's economics.

MARX'S ECONOMICS

Labor Theory of Value

Marx began with a premise common to Adam Smith, David Ricardo, and the other classical economists: that the value of anything is the amount of labor it takes to produce it. For example, if it takes one day's labor to produce a shirt and two days' labor to produce a pair of shoes, then two shirts are worth one pair of shoes. Given the fluctuations of supply and demand on the market, the market price should eventually come into equilibrium with the real value, and two shirts will sell for the price of a pair of shoes. The labor theory of value, then, describes the basic mechanism of production and exchange in the economy. It also has a special appeal to a socialist like Marx; for if *labor* is what produces value, justice would seem to require that workers receive the proceeds of their labor.

Profit as Exploitation

If the labor theory of value is correct, we are left with a paradox: Where does *profit* come from? The market moves toward equilibrium; everything gets exchanged for its true value; one day's labor is exchanged for one day's labor. How can individuals get more than they put in? Marx finds the answer in one commodity that sells for its true value yet can produce more than what it sells for. This commodity is human labor itself—the workers' exertions as they sell them on the labor market. According to Marx's chain of deductive reasoning, labor should tend to sell for its true value, which is equivalent to the amount of labor it takes to produce it—that is, if it takes an average of six hours' work by farmers, weavers, carpenters, and others to feed, clothe, and shelter a man for a day, he will be paid the equivalent of six hours' work. But if the employer pays him for six hours' work, he can nevertheless work him eight hours (or twelve hours or fourteen hours, as was more common in Marx's day). This is possible because the employers own the means of production—the factory and its tools—and hence they can demand this longer working day as a condition of giving the man a job. Profit, then, comes out of the extra hours of work, over and above what the worker is paid for. This extra work is called "surplus value," and profit can be said to be based on the exploitation of labor.

Law of the Falling Rate of Profit

The system can now be set in motion. As capitalists expand production, they compete with each other for labor. Thus, they bid up wages to attract workers. But rising wages cut into the margin of profit. This, in turn, motivates capitalists to install labor-saving machinery to cut their labor costs.

But here the capitalists start to cut their own throats. Machines do not produce profit, according to Marx's scheme; profit comes only from exploitation of labor. Any gains manufacturers may make with their new equipment will disappear just as soon as competitors catch up with them and install the same equipment. This drives the price of machinery up and the price of the produced goods down, so the upshot is merely that the capitalists have reduced the amount of labor they employ in comparison to machinery and other nonlabor costs. This means that profit has to fall, since exploitation of labor is the only source of profit, and less labor is being exploited. And in fact, the economists of Marx's day agreed that profits did tend to decline. (Modern economics has modified this principle: Profits fall *within* the business cycle, but not *across* cycles, where there can be long-term growth.)

Periodic Crises

This brings us to the characteristic drama of the capitalist economy. About every ten years throughout the nineteenth century there was a depression. As new machinery is installed, Marx explained, people are thrown out of work. This means there are fewer people drawing wages and hence fewer people who can afford to buy things. But the machinery has *increased* the rate of production. There are too many goods, too few buyers. Prices fall; profits go down. Manufacturers try to catch up by installing even more labor-saving machinery, but this only makes matters worse. Soon there are great warehouses of goods lying unused, while unemployment grows and people are destitute. Manufacturers go bankrupt, throwing even more people out of work.

Eventually, the crisis reaches a bottom. The stronger capitalists buy up the factories and machines of the bankrupts at a fraction of their value and begin to make a profit. The surplus is used up, workers can be hired for low wages, and employment begins to rise. Soon the cycle begins again: a boom of expansion and profit, then a bust of falling profit, mechanism, and unemployment. The system rises and falls with grim regularity, only each time there are fewer manufacturers, holding bigger and bigger shares of the market.

The Final Collapse of Capitalism

Capitalism, then, moves toward a gigantic industrial monopoly. The smaller capitalists are squeezed out; they lose their property and join the ranks of the proletariat. At the same time the system creates a great reserve army of the unemployed, which keeps the competition for jobs high and wages at a level just above starvation. The proletariat thus becomes larger and more disgruntled. Each successive crisis of the system is worse than the last, because the collapse of big firms throws more workers into destitution than the collapse of small ones. During this period, the economy becomes centralized through these gigantic monopolies, preparing the way for socialism. All that needs to be done is to overthrow the system of private property and let the workers run the system for the common good.

A last crisis occurs, and the workers rise up as a vast majority. The army, the politicians, and the defenders of the state can do nothing to stop them, for all are forced to see the inevitable solution. "The centralization of the means of production and socialization of labour at last reach a point where they become incompatible with their capitalist integument," Marx prophesied. "This integument bursts asunder. The knell of capitalist private property sounds. The expropriators are expropriated."

What went wrong? The capitalist system has not collapsed in the advanced industrial countries, whatever its strains; profits have not fallen in the long run; wages have not stayed near subsistence level. There have been cyclical crises, to be sure, and huge corporations with near monopolies dominate the business scene; but the crucial elements of Marx's picture are missing.

There are two main answers. The Marxist reply has been: imperialism. V. I. Lenin, whose theory was based on the ideas of the British economist John Hobson, pointed out that modern capitalism has become international. Thus the more advanced countries, like Britain, France, Germany, and the United States, have been able to avoid domestic economic ills by exploiting the rest of the world. If capitalist countries overproduce, they can dump their excess goods in the markets of India or South America. Extra capital to invest can go to the same places; even labor can be exploited internationally, by using low-cost native labor to produce raw materials cheaply. In short, by exploiting the rest of the world, the wealthy nations can keep their profits up and can even pay enough wages to content their workers.

But the crisis can only be put off, not evaded entirely. Once the entire world is brought into the capitalist orbit, the class conflict will become internationalized. War becomes an adjunct to revolution. Lenin saw World War I as a struggle of the great capitalist powers of Europe over colonial markets; the result could only be to speed up the inevitable chaos of the capitalist system. Thus, Russia underwent a socialist revolution in the economic devastation following its defeat by the Germans. World War II and the Japanese conquest were to have the same results in China. Cuba, Algeria, and Vietnam are only so many more steps along the road toward capitalism's final collapse.

There is another answer to the question of why Marx's predictions have not been realized, one that goes more to the core of the problem. That is: Marx's labor theory of value and the related labor exploitation theory of profit are wrong. Labor, we may reflect, is not the only thing out of which profits may be gotten by obtaining more production from it than it costs. Machinery and improved organization can provide this too, because they can increase the productivity of labor. The United States produced so much more per capita in 1970 than it did in 1870 because our technology is so much more powerful today. This means that it has been possible to produce much more than before; profits can remain high, yet workers can get more, too, by unionization and through government welfare programs. With this extra production the government can even intervene in economic crises, using the techniques of Keynesian economics (such as government employment, spending, and taxation) to keep widespread unemployment and underconsumption from happening.

None of this would be possible if Marx's inexorable economic machine really worked the way he said it did; but that machine is broken at the very center. Marx's thought forms a perfect system: The economy produces social classes, class consciousness, and class power to rule the state; the labor theory of value, the law of the falling rate of profit, and the inevitable progression of economic cycles turn the wheels of the system. But the labor theory of value is wrong; the mainspring falls out. Marx's sociological determinants go on, but free of their inexorable underpinnings. History lapses into indeterminacy.

Still, something may be salvaged from the wreck of Marx's economics. If economic crises are not necessarily inevitable, it is still true that they can occur or at least threaten to occur, and it is worth remembering Marx's prediction of their political effects. The capitalist societies of the West since the 1970s have become increasingly divided between the extremes of wealth and poverty. Marx's theory did not encompass the expansion of the middle classes between the two extremes; and we need to revise our theoretical understandings to take account of this. But the existence of the middle class does not eliminate economic conflict among classes; it only makes it more complicated. It appears what we have now is a conflict among four different classes: the wealthy property-owning capitalists at the top; the middle class; the working class; and a poverty class at the bottom subsisting on welfare and posing a specter of street crime. Class conflict now often takes place between the middle class and the poor, with the former in revolt against what they consider to be the burden of the welfare system and the threat of crime from below. But this too is class conflict, although more complex than Marx envisioned. We see tendencies, too, for the middle class to revolt against the upper class, reacting to the financial scandals and tax inequities that became so prominent in the 1980s. Class conflict obviously is not at an end. The Marxist theory bases its dynamics on an economic mechanism that does not quite work. It does not give us the answer, but points us to the crucial questions.

MARX'S SOCIAL AND POLITICAL PHILOSOPHY

Marx's philosophy is woven throughout the rest of his work. It centers around the ideas of alienation as the distinguishing feature of humankind's history and of communism as the end of history and the solution to alienation.

Alienation has become a common idea in the twentieth century; modern individuals have, it would seem, been infected by a malaise that was scarcely discernible one hundred years ago. We feel there is something about the world we have created that goes against our basic nature—that we are ruled by the impersonal forces of the market and the inhuman decisions of bureaucracies. We live in a world diagrammed by Kafka. Marx was one of the first to discern this malaise, although it remained for Weber and Freud to make empirical sense out of it. For Marx alienation was less an observable fact than a basic axiom, derived from Hegel and ultimately going back to a theological notion of sin. To understand what Marx meant, we must take a brief excursion back into Western philosophy.

The idealist tradition in philosophy can best be grasped if we begin with René Descartes (1596–1650). Descartes's famous phrase *"cogito ergo sum"* (I think therefore I am) was the one principle that he found *must* be true, even if one doubted everything else about the world. David Hume (1711–1776) extended the scope of skepticism by pointing out that we can never really *know* that something *causes* something else. If one event always follows another (at least has always done so up until now), we can only *suppose* that it is caused by the first event. We judge the probability that the same sequence will happen again. Causality, then, is something we impute to things out of our own minds, not something that   *absolutely* exists "out there." Immanuel Kant (1724–1804), the founder of the German idealist tradition, took this idea one step further. We cannot really know *anything* about the world, he argued, because we never *experience* anything except through our own subjective filters of understanding. Not only causality, but time, space, shapes, numbers, colors, and substance are all part of the framework of our own minds. The "things in themselves" can never be known; all one can know is the contents of one's own mind, imposed on the raw materials of unknowable reality.

This brings us to Hegel, Marx's mentor. Hegel drew the conclusion from Kant that humans *create* their world by the act of perceiving it. But this does not occur all at once; it takes all of history to fulfill. In effect, inert matter has no form until living creatures develop who can perceive it; the higher forms of beauty and truth do not appear until humans arrive to see the world through these spectacles. Moreover, an individual actively fashions the world, making tools, works of art, laws, states, and systems of ideas. Each of these progressively manifests more and more of the world of forms into the world of actuality. Eventually (we are nearing Hegel's own time), humans become aware that they are the agents of something greater than themselves—that the world is a spirit that unfolds more and more facets of itself until it is fully visible. This spirit is Reason, and it reaches its culmination in the constitutional state and in Hegel's philosophy, which is Reason at last conscious of itself.

Alienation enters into Hegel's system because it describes the relationship of humans to their creations up until the time they finally recognize reality for what it is—the unfolding spirit of Reason. That is, people create things but then fail to understand that they have created them. They mistake the world for something objective (at least, they did so up until the revelation of Kant). They worship objects as idols and lose sight of their own creativeness and of the spirit flowing through them. Thus, people are cut off, or alienated, from their essential selves.

Marx adopted this form of analysis from Hegel but took it off its spiritual foundation. For Marx people create the world through their labors but then become constrained by the very things they have created. They create religions out of the imaginings of their own brains and then fall down and worship their gods as if they really existed. They create the state and then cannot escape its rule. They create an economic system by the labors of their own hands and then find that they are compelled to sell themselves on the market they have created.

In a famous chapter in *Capital* entitled "The Fetishism of Commodities," Marx describes how money begins as a means of exchange to buy goods but soon becomes an end in itself. Goods become viewed in money value only, instead of in terms of their use to the consumer. A house is no longer a place to live but becomes a piece of real estate that one can afford to live in only if the market makes it feasible to keep it. The capitalist is a person who cannot enjoy owning goods but must turn them into as much profit as possible or else be wiped out by a competitor. In the capitalist system the workers are the most alienated of all, because they become cogs in a machine, selling their own labor as a commodity, and are stripped of any meaningful relation with the goods they produce for the capitalist to sell.

Alienation grows progressively worse throughout history. The final revolution that brings down capitalism, then, destroys not only a system of economic exploitation, but also a system of dehumanization. History ends with communism, for monopoly capitalism stretches human alienation to the final verge, at which it can at last be abolished. Communism was to be a society without alienation, where people no longer were to be controlled by the system they had created, but instead would control it for their own benefit. The division of labor itself would be destroyed. Humankind would at last reach absolute fulfillment.

Marx's notion of alienation is not really an empirical entity, but a whole way of looking at the world, of holding up a standard to evaluate it by. Modern sociologists have tried to measure just how alienated people are in various kinds of jobs, and the results are mixed. Certain kinds of labor, such as that on the assembly line, are considered by most workers to be rather dehumanizing. Most other kinds of work (and we must remember that most people, even in factories, do *not* work on assembly lines) elicit a fair amount of positive reaction; and some people, although a minority, even like working on the assembly line. Marx's response would no doubt be that people can be so oppressed by the system as to lose even their elementary human wants. In the final analysis Marx believed in untapped human potentialities and held up a high standard for society to emulate.

The idea of communism is easier to evaluate. Marx himself actively promoted the revolution he wrote about. He helped found the revolutionary trade-union movement, the International Workingman's Association ("the First International"), and Engels carried on the leadership after his death. In some places, notably in Germany, the unionists' Marxism became more and more rhetorical and irrelevant as their organization gained political recognition. But the revolutionary potential of Marxism would not be lost. Marx's most militant followers, inspired by his penetrating analysis of capitalism and by his assurances of the inevitability of their victory, created a state in Russia and elsewhere in his name. The Communist states emerged from the wreckage of states in World Wars I and II. In the second half of the twentieth century, the cold war and the nuclear arms race against the capitalist West strengthened control by the military and by an authoritarian Communist party over Soviet societies. The system became overwhelmingly unpopular with its own people; ironically, the political and economic crises which Marx envisioned for the end of capitalism came about instead in the socialist states. To explain why this system collapsed would take further advances in sociology; we will meet some of this analysis later in Chapter 15.

Marx would probably have rejected the Soviet system as a gross perversion of what he had in mind. He wanted a system to dignify the whole person, not to sacrifice everything to the military power of the state. But Marx never really devoted himself to the hard question of how his humanist utopia was to be brought about. It is easy to speak abstractly of people taking control of the system instead of being controlled by it, but it is harder to see just how this may be brought about. Indeed, much of subsequent sociology has carried on a debate with Marx's ghost, as Weber, Sorel, Michels, Mannheim, and others have questioned the possibility of controlling *power* in the same way that the *economy* might be reduced to management for the common good. Events have forced us to go beyond Marx. We have had to look for ways to escape from the Leviathan of the state as well as the Mammon of the marketplace.

THE MARXIAN LEGACY

Since Marx's death there has been a continuous strain of dogmatism among his followers. The movement he engendered made such strong organizational and emotional claims on its members that most of them seem to have had little inclination to think any new thoughts on their own. The movement has not been entirely stagnant, however; there have been those willing to build on some of Marx's themes and drop others. In the period just after Marx's death in 1883, for example, Friedrich Engels and other leading Marxists stressed the scientific, materialistic nature of Marxist thought. In the early twentieth century, writers like Lenin, Rosa Luxemburg, and Rudolf Hilferding brought about new developments on the economic side. These Marxists turned their attention to the role of imperialism, finance capitalism, and war in shaping society. Politically oriented Marxism, at the same time, began to claim that socialism could be achieved through parliamentary and political means. Its proponents included the German "revisionist" leader Eduard Bernstein, who preferred to speak of "evolution" instead of "revolution." The Italian theorist Antonio Gramsci, who spent many years in Mussolini's prisons, argued that the goal of Marxist politics was not merely to await the economic destruction of the capitalist class, but politically to overthrow the *hegemonic* (actually ruling) class by gaining control of the state.

In the 1920s intellectual Marxism began to shift away from materialism toward an idealistic philosophy. The first move in this direction was made by a young Hungarian intellectual, Georg Lukacs, who had previously been a follower of Hegel. Lukacs declared that the basic problem was not so much the surface issues of economic exploitation and political domination but the *reification* of the false ideologies upheld by capitalist domination. Lukacs thus cast Marx's doctrine of alienation (which is, of course, originally derived from Hegel) into a form that is both more philosophical and more sociological. It is people's attachment to the false ideals they use to shroud their own social striving and privileges that alienates them from a true, productive reality and from a truly honest self, according to Lukacs. And it is the working class that is least subject to reifications, because it is least attached to the dominant ideologies; its mission therefore is to liberate the more alienated, dominant society from its own false consciousness.

In the next few decades, the Frankfurt school in Germany brought Marxism into even closer harmony with Hegel. Herbert Marcuse argued that Hegel, with his dialectic of the development of Reason, was the great progressive philosopher, preparing the way for Marx. Max Horkheimer and Theodor Adorno went even further, declaring that Marxism was the sole embodiment of Reason in this era of fascist antireason brought about by the fatal irrationalities of advanced capitalism. In the 1960s leadership of the Frankfurt tradition was taken over by Jurgen Habermas. Habermas wrote of the ideological interests behind the scientific establishment by which modern government and business try to rationalize their decisions and of the legitimation crisis that has become for modern capitalism the equivalent of the traditional Marxian economic crisis. In France, meanwhile, Marxism has been integrated with existentialism by its leading proponent, Jean-Paul Sartre, and with structuralism by his opponent, Louis Althusser.

ENGELS' THEORY OF GENDER STRATIFICATION

Another part of the Marxian tradition which has become increasingly important in recent years is its analysis of male domination of the female. The main source was a book by Friedrich Engels, *The Origin of the Family, Private Property, and the State,* which appeared in 1884, just after Marx's death. Engels used Marx's notes and regarded this work as expressing the Marxian position.

Engels used the anthropology of his day, leading to criticisms of this work due to the fact that the older interpretations of anthropological data are not all accepted by scholars today. Engels drew, in particular, upon the American anthropologist Lewis Henry Morgan, who lived in upstate New York and was an expert on the Iroquois. This Indian tribe lived in its famous "long houses," which each contained several families living together. An especially striking feature of Iroquois society was the role of women: It was a fierce warrior society, but also a political democracy. Tribal leaders were elected, and were always men; but women had a full vote, and elder women were particularly powerful and were capable of deposing chiefs.

Moreover, Iroquois clans were basically organized around women. They followed the principle that Engels (and Morgan) called "mother right," and is now called *matrilineal descent*. Family lines were traced only through mothers and their children, and property was inherited only through females. Clans were exogamous, prohibiting marriage within their own ranks. Hence, a man married into a clan different from his own, but remained an outsider there. His children did not belong to his clan, nor did they inherit from him. Engels, like Morgan and some other anthropologists of the time, regarded this system as evidence of *matriarchy*, a universal stage in the early development of the family.

Another curious feature of Iroquois society was its kinship terminology. Iroquois children referred to their mother's sisters also as "Mother," and to their father's brothers as "Father." The children of these extra fathers and mothers, then, were not called cousins, but brothers and sisters. Engels, following Morgan, took this as evidence of a prior stage of group marriage which had once existed. At this time there was indiscriminate mating between all the wives of a set of brothers, or husbands of a set of sisters; hence, it was impossible to tell whose children were actually whose.

On this basis, Engels proposed the following sequence of stages in the development of the family. First, there was complete sexual promiscuity, a society of absolute freedom and equality. Next, incest between parents and their children was prohibited, but otherwise, sexual relationships were left wide open. Then, the incest prohibition was extended to siblings. Finally, this gave way to what Engels called "pairing marriage." This was exemplified by the Iroquois system of exogamous clans: The incest taboo had spread to everyone in the clan, and hence sexual partners had to be found outside, in another clan.

Engels regarded all of these, but particularly the earlier stages before pairing marriage, as a version of primitive communism. This had certain characteristics:

1. No private property existed. The clan as a group held all land, whether hunting grounds or farming plots. All clan members shared food, just as they cooperated in labor to produce it.
2. Similarly, communism reigned in the sexual realm. Although there were incest prohibitions of various sorts, women and men were not exclusive sexual partners of particular individuals, but were widely shared. (The degree of sexual freedom had become fairly limited by the time of the pairing marriage system of the Iroquois, but the terminology of the earlier stages survived.)
3. There was gender equality. Women had a respected position in society, and often shared political power. Engels regarded the economic basis of this equality as crucial: Women shared fully in the labor. They were the major producers of food in horticultural (primitive agricultural) societies, and even in hunting societies produced the most stable part of the diet by gathering wild plants. Women were not alienated from the products of their labor or from the central social process of production, and hence enjoyed a high status.

The rise of sexual domination of men over women was brought about by an economic change; chiefly, the growth of wealth, resulting from more advanced agricultural methods such as plowing and irrigation. As a result, Engels theorized, men wanted to pass on their property to their own children. Hence, they overthrew "mother right" (matrilinealism) and instituted "father right" (patrilineal descent). They also tended to reverse the older system of clan exogamy—since property stayed with the man's offspring—and endogamous clan rule was instituted to keep property within the clan. (Previously, under matrilinealism, the exogamous rule had had the same effect of keeping property within the clan.)

With patrilineal descent came the institution of monogamy. Since a man wanted to pass his property along to his children, he wanted to be sure which children were his. Hence, no more sexual promiscuity and no more group marriage were to be allowed. This new monogamy, however, was decidedly one-sided. As Engels noted, monogamy was primarily for the women. Men could allow themselves polygamy, when they could afford it, in the form of concubines, female slaves, or prostitutes.

The result of this change in the family system was the subjugation of women. "This revolution [was] one of the most decisive ever experienced by humanity," Engels declared. ". . . the overthrow of mother right was the *world historical defeat* of the feminine sex" (p. 120). With the shift from matriarchal to patriarchal society, women were excluded from the public economic sphere and consigned to household labor. Men had taken over heavy agriculture, leaving women only with menial domestic tasks. Males also gained complete control of politics, and excluded women largely from religion and public culture as well.

The new monogamous marriage was now concerned only with property. Love was excluded. Women were regarded simply as instruments by which men could propagate their property and their lineage. Engels seems to be saying that men did not care about propagating themselves through their offspring, but rather, that private property called for privately controlled heirs to whom one could pass it on. The family system thus became a kind of cult of perpetual private property. Engels regarded the rise of patriarchy as a revolutionary development in human history, not only in the position of women. It marked the first big turning point in the Marxian perspective—the rise of private property per se, and hence the rise of class society. Engels summed up: "The first class opposition that appears in history coincides with the development of the antagonism between man and woman in monogamous marriage, and the first class oppression coincides with that of the female sex by the male" (p. 129).

From that point on, Engels argued, love affairs could only occur outside of marriage. Among the ancient Greeks, he pointed out, the sphere of eros was confined to men's interests in courtesans, or in homosexual favorites. In medieval Europe, love was celebrated by the poetry of the troubadours in the form of a cult of adultery, forbidden love between knights and married women. Engels went on to mock the monogamous marriages of the bourgeoisie of his own day as inevitably producing their antithesis, prostitution and adultery. As long as the marriage was a property relationship first and foremost, love had to be found outside. Just as, historically, prostitution appeared at the same time as the beginnings of monogamous marriage, the combination, Engels declared, was indissoluble, and would exist as long as monogamy did.

Even in the modern capitalist societies where parents no longer choose their children's husbands and wives as part of a system of legal inheritance of property, the economic aspect of marriage predominates. The choice of marriage partners seems to be free, but it is only formally so. It is analogous to the freedom of the modern labor market, in which wage laborers are free to sell their labor to an employer or not; but the latter is merely freedom to starve if one owns no property. Hence, women have the freedom to marry or not, but in reality economic necessity forces them into subjugation to husbands who have the income to support them.

Is there any way out of this system? The Marxian analysis points the way to the solution. It is necessary to abolish private property, Marx said; this would make the motive for monogamy disappear, since there no longer would be private property to pass along to children. Women would enter the labor force on an equal basis with men, and would no longer be forced into marriage for reasons of financial support. Society would take over the support of children; concerns for legitimacy would disappear, and all restraints on "sex love," as Engels terms it, would disappear. Hence, at the end of capitalism, sexual freedom would reappear, along with the reinstitution of group marriage, as in primitive communism.

Actually, Engels was rather Victorian in his moral attitudes, and he went on to argue that when monogamy disappears, so will prostitution. There will no longer be any need for women to sell themselves, either long-term or short-term. Marriage, he argued, is selling oneself once and for all (long-term), instead of the economics of the prostitute who "lets out her body on piece work like a wage worker" (p. 134). But, without economic incentives, individuals could choose partners on the basis of sheer personal attraction. Engels rather romantically assumed such passions would be forever, and, hence, there would be lifelong love affairs in the Communist society of the future.

Engels' argument has various flaws, but it should be noted that his work did have an important practical effect. The socialist movement in Germany, following Marxian principles, was the first large-scale political movement to come out in favor of female equality, and the socialist party leader, August Bebel, wrote a popular book expounding Engels' thesis. As German socialists gained prominence in parliamentary politics, they gave a big impetus to the German feminist movement, the strongest one on the Continent, culminating in political enfranchisement of women after World War I. Another aspect of this great upheaval in sexual attitudes which occurred during the early twentieth century in Germany was a movement for erotic freedom, which was part of the milieu in which Freud first became popular. Max Weber's wife, Marianne Weber, was an important feminist leader, and was the first woman to be elected to public office in Germany.

On the theoretical side, there are numerous problems with Engels' theory. It was a pioneering formulation, and recent thought has gone considerably beyond it. There has been a great deal of criticism of its conception of the early anthropological stages of the family. It is doubtful that there ever was a stage of primitive promiscuity with no incest taboos. Also, there is no universal sequence from matrilineal to patrilineal societies. Many hunting-and-gathering societies (the oldest economic form) are patrilineal, and even more of them are bilineal (i.e., they trace descent on both sides, as we do today). Matrilineal societies seem never to have been a majority of societies at any time in history, although they are relatively frequent in horticultural societies, when women were most important in food production.

But if the picture of evolutionary stages must be abandoned, nevertheless, the more abstract principles in Engels' theory have opened up important lines of inquiry. Engels' was the first sociological theory of gender stratification, attempting to show the conditions that bring about different degrees of inequality or equality between the sexes. His general conception that monogamy is connected with a property system has proven fruitful, and so has his strategy of tracing sexual domination and subordination through economic relations.

Debates go on today among Marxists and feminists over the extent to which the position of women is part of the general struggle of workers under capitalism. The modern Marxian argument is that women in capitalism play a crucial but hidden role in the economic system by *reproducing the labor force.* This means, first of all, that women bear children who grow up to become workers; they also feed and clothe them, clean them, and bring them up. Women as mothers are thus an unpaid part of the capitalist system; without them, capitalism could not function. The same is true of women as wives; their household labor cares for their husbands' homes, feeds them, washes their clothes, and so forth. Women also put in the emotional labor of soothing the men's egos and, in general, absorbing the strains that men suffer working in the capitalist marketplace.

The conclusion drawn, then, is that women are exploited by the capitalist system, even when they are not directly employed by it. Women contribute to capitalist profits, which would be a good deal lower without unpaid female labor by housewives. From this point of view, the solution to sexual inequality is to overthrow capitalism, and thereby change the economic basis that fosters female exploitation.

It has been argued also, however, that women's struggle is separate from, if perhaps parallel to, the struggle of workers and other oppressed groups. Working-class men also benefit by dominating women in their homes. Sexist tradition keeps women who are employed outside the home in sex-segregated or other low-paying jobs, and thus keeps them from competing with men. Improving the position of workers per se, then, does not necessarily help women. The position of women in socialist societies, such as those existing in Russia and Eastern Europe, is not notably different from that in Western ones. They still do most of the domestic work, while outside the household they still tend to hold inferior jobs and few important political positions. It is also pointed out that women have made some improvements in their position in capitalist societies by organizing as a separate interest group for their own rights. Where women have been able to secure high-paying jobs, their status and power have improved, even within their own households. Along with a general expansion in women's labor force participation, the traditional monogamous family that Engels described so scathingly has given way to a much more fluid situation of premarital sexuality, divorces, and remarriages based on individual preference. And this, in fact, is what Engels predicted, only it did not take the abolition of private property to bring about increased job market participation for women.

The issue, though, continues to remain a vital one. While the feminist movement has had its greatest successes recently in the lives of upper-middle-class women, there remains a huge sector of women in manual and clerical jobs who constitute the most underpaid and exploited sector of the labor force. The Marxian theory may not be correct, but at least it points its finger at a crucial problem: The existence of a large category of female exploitation reminds us that there are still very large, potentially revolutionary forces that may explode some time in the future.

CHAPTER THREE

The Last Gentleman: Alexis de Tocqueville

Thought in the early nineteenth century was no more unitary than it is today. So far we have paid attention to the modernists: prophets of the industrial order like Saint-Simon and Comte and radicals like Marx who looked further ahead into the future. Not everyone believed in progress, however. The postrevolutionary situation had its conservatives, too, of whom the most famous were the Englishman Edmund Burke (1729–1797) and the French aristocrats Louis de Bonald (1754–1840) and Joseph de Maistre (1753–1821). The last two attacked modern society as the anarchy of mob rule and counterposed an ideology of order, obedience, ritual, religion, and hierarchy—all of which qualities were supposed to be found in the Middle Ages. Restoration France thus created the germs of the major modern ideologies: liberalism, communism, and fascism.

But the heritage of conservatism is more ambiguous than this, and new thought comes from strange mixtures. Comte combined the conservatism of Bonald and Maistre with the industrialism of Saint-Simon and produced sociology as the science of *order* in the new society. Conservatism also produced a man who represents the best of the old order—Alexis de Tocqueville. His conservative stance brought him not to vituperation against the new era, but to the detachment necessary for understanding it.

Modernists are essentially optimists. Tocqueville was a pessimist. He shared the classical Roman and Greek outlook: Life is a tragedy, with its eternal forces always in balance. His classical prose style aims to impose the only order possible upon the dilemmas of existence—the harmony of literature. Thus, equality improves most people's lives; but mediocrity is the price we must pay for it. Freedom is gained in some respects only by the loss of freedom in other respects. Tocqueville holds the classical idea of balance: An excess in any direction leads to a corresponding reaction. In an era of optimism Tocqueville's conservatism enabled him to tear off the veil blinding the eyes of his contemporaries. The others shared a belief in the withering away of the coercive powers of the state, whether this was to occur immediately, as Saint-Simon and the liberals believed, or in the revolutionary future, as Marx predicted. The idea of progress made the wars and tyrannies of twentieth-century governments inconceivable for these men; Tocqueville's more timeless viewpoint on the dangers of power, however, has kept him contemporary and relevant.

Tocqueville was virtually the last of the old school of gentleman-intellectuals. This sort of person was not a professor or a commercial writer, but a man of some wealth who owned a well-stocked library, wrote beautiful letters to his friends, and devoted his leisure to composing treatises and essays on philosophy, history, and everything else, to be circulated to his correspondents and sometimes published upon wider request. Some of these men dabbled in science—Darwin was to be perhaps the last of these—before the era of large university and government laboratories. It was a role existing only in aristocratic society and comprised only a very small section of the aristocracy. All in all, it was the best excuse that class had for its existence.

Tocqueville himself was on the margin of the French aristocracy— the *petite noblesse*. His father was a government official, a prefect (governor) in various parts of France. His parents were almost executed in the Revolution; they were saved only by the Thermidorian reaction—the anti-revolutionary shift of 1793—that sent Robespierre himself to the guillotine. Other relatives of Tocqueville did not escape.

Tocqueville studied law and took up a career as a lawyer—that is, as a salaried official of the royal court system. In 1830 riots in Paris led to the abdication of Charles X. When the dust had settled, the throne was still there but was occupied by Charles's cousin, Louis Philippe, of the rival house of Orléans. The Orléanists had been scheming for the throne for hundreds of years and at last achieved their aim by an alliance with the constitutionalists. (The alliance was to survive only eighteen years.) Tocqueville was forced to take an oath of loyalty to the new regime. But as a legitimist, he was opposed to this bastard monarchy, and his views caused much friction with his superiors.

The recurrence of revolution convinced Tocqueville that there was an inevitable trend toward equality and the destruction of aristocratic society, but that France was going about achieving it in the wrong way. He hit on a plan: a leave of absence and a commission to go to America to study penal reform, currently a topic of interest in France. His real reasons for wanting to go were to escape from an impossible situation for himself personally and to see what lessons could be learned for the future of France. He left in 1831 for nine months of travel in America. Out of the trip came his monumental work *Democracy in America.*

Tocqueville liked America, even though its surface was unappealing to an aristocrat. It was the land of "mob rule," where politics consisted of demagogic bombast and the maneuvers of politicians to stay in office and dispense patronage to their followers; where business dealings were incessant and all pervasive; where high culture and refined manners hardly existed; where the laws were in the hands of the people, and individuals shot each other down in the streets of the western territories. In other words, it was an America like that of today, only cruder, tougher, and above all, more puritanical. "I thought that the English constituted the most serious nation on the face of the earth, but I have since seen the Americans and changed my opinion," said Tocqueville. "An American, instead of going in a leisure hour to dance merrily at some place of public resort, as the fellows of his class continue to do throughout the greater part of Europe, shuts himself up at home to drink. He thus enjoys two pleasures: he can go on thinking of his business and can get drunk decently by his own fireside."[1]

Tocqueville liked this. He himself was rather serious, hardworking, devoutly religious, and prudish, and he admired the Americans for these same qualities. Beneath the surface he saw the Americans as like his beloved Romans—people who believed in laws and used them to rule themselves; who participated actively in public affairs; who showed patriotism, religiousness, and the discipline of moral self-control. Tocqueville romanticizes America a bit, especially in failing to see that the American democracy he describes was run by the middle class and not by the poor. Given these reservations, his analysis of America continues to be sound.

EQUALITY IN AMERICA

The basic premise of Tocqueville's system is the inevitable advance of equality, which Tocqueville took to be so characteristic of modernity as to be a sign of God's will. Equality (which Tocqueville uses interchangeably with the term "democracy") is contrasted with aristocracy, as the other great form of society. Equality means the free mobility of individuals; aristocracy means that positions are hereditary from birth. Equality means the extension of the political franchise from the few to the many. It means the end of legal differences in status, of noble ranks and titles with their attendant privileges, and of primogeniture within the family (by which the eldest son inherits all the wealth). In short, equality means an end of deference based on immutable differences between different ranks of society. Along with this, Tocqueville believed that people were becoming more equal in wealth, education, and culture.

In an effort to be balanced, Tocqueville tried to present both the good and the bad effects of the advance of equality, based on his observations of daily life in America. He pointed out that with the end of dominance by inheritable property and of primogeniture, equality had spread to the relations between fathers and sons and among brothers. The result was a decline in the old authority of the family. But the family did not fall apart, as the conservatives had predicted; the artificial bonds of property were replaced by stronger bonds of personal sentiment. As family members were no longer controlled by each other, they were able to like each other more. The same sort of freedom applied to unmarried women. Since they were no

---

[1]Alexis de Tocqueville, *Democracy in America*, Vol. 2 (New York: Alfred A. Knopf, 1945), p. 232. Copyright Alfred A. Knopf, Inc.

longer bartered by their parents for family connections, they were free to choose their own partners by falling in love. The result, Tocqueville shrewdly remarks, is that such marriages have much less infidelity than the aristocratic marriages of convenience, which make no claim on the feelings of the partners.

In the same vein Tocqueville remarks on the effects of equality on manners. The Americans are not great conversationalists who use talk as a display of rank, but rather talk plainly and openly without signs of deference. The British, he says, are caught in between the clear rankings of the French aristocracy and the equality of America, and the famous British standoffishness is the result. They still retain the aristocratic belief that people of rank should be given the proper deference, but equality has progressed enough so that it is hard to tell just what deference people are entitled to. The solution is to avoid speaking to people unless they are properly introduced.

Tocqueville found that equality also changed the relationship between employer and employee. Instead of a relationship between a proud master and submissive servants, it becomes a simple contract between individuals in which one bargains for a limited portion of the other's labor. One does not sell one's whole self, but only a part. The old loyalties to one's superior disappear, but they are replaced by new ideals, shared by all. In the field of politics, the prevailing sentiment is nationalism. In the field of personal virtues, the old military "honor" that had to be defended by fighting duels is replaced by the business virtues of hard work, reliability, and thrift. Modern society is thus not without honor; it is only that the honor appropriate to a time of armed self-defense is changed into the honor necessary in a time of commerce and industry.

Most impressive of all, Tocqueville thought, was the extension of personal sympathy in egalitarian society. He quotes a letter written by an aristocratic Frenchwoman of the seventeenth century, in which she blithely mingles descriptions of the fine weather with news about the tortures that were imposed on the local peasants who were revolting against a new tax. This lady was not an unkind person, Tocqueville explains; her letters show that she was full of kindness to her relatives and friends. It is merely that the range of sympathy extended only to those who were equals, and she could not imagine herself in the place of the peasants. In America, on the contrary, Tocqueville found a surprising display of charities of all kinds, as well as of good samaritanism among perfect strangers. For the same reason, tortures disappear as a means of punishment in modern society and there is a shift toward rehabilitation and general leniency toward criminals. This sympathetic attitude is not inherent in the culture of the Americans, Tocqueville argues, but is rather a product of egalitarianism. To prove it, he points to the inability of the white Americans to sympathize with the plight of the Negro slaves, whom they do not regard as equals: It is the limits of equality, and not the cultural outlook, that set the limits of sympathy. Tocqueville's principle is still illuminating today. It helps explain why Americans often aid each other in accidents on the street, whereas Asians or

Latin Americans are more likely to be indifferent to what happens to strangers in public.

On the negative side, Tocqueville noted the pervasive commercialism of American life. Equality, he felt, leads to ceaseless striving for social position. Where all are basically the same, it is debilitating to fall behind. Accordingly, everyone seeks to get rich quick. Tocqueville observantly points out that even though most Americans at that time were farmers, they were not farmers in the European sense. They did not grow food merely to live on, but rather, they developed land for profit. Indeed, much of the land was scarcely cultivated, but was bought and sold for speculation in land prices. Thus, even in 1830 the American farmer was less the virtuous rural citizen he always makes himself out to be and more the speculative businessman.

All this has a negative effect on culture. Business emphasizes practicality, not abstract truth or aesthetic style. As a result, Tocqueville argued, Americans become hazy and bombastic whenever they are forced to speak of any general ideas, for outside of the range of specific practical matters their minds have developed no refinements or distinctions. Culture in America thus is neither very high nor very low; everyone is well versed enough to get along, but there is no incentive or opportunity to stand out. Lacking the European aristocratic tradition in intellectual endeavor, America remains a land of comfortable mediocrity.

Also on the negative side, Tocqueville finds that the continual business dealings of America add up to a general monotony. The novelty of events stays on the same plane, and nothing rises above it. He found in America the general traits of conformity over a century before David Riesman and others popularized the idea. "I know of no country in which there is so little independence of mind and real freedom of discussion as in America," Tocqueville declared. He saw Americans' individualism as confined to economic competition and as entirely lacking in the world of ideas.

"We must understand what is wanted of society and its government," says Tocqueville.

> . . . If a clear understanding be more profitable to man than genius; if your object is not to stimulate the virtues of heroism, but the habits of peace; if you had rather witness vices than crimes, and are content to meet with fewer noble deeds, provided offenses be diminished in the same proportion; if, instead of living in the midst of a brilliant society, you are contented to have prosperity around you; if, in short, you are of the opinion that the principal object of a government is not to confer the greatest possible power and glory upon the body of the nation, but to ensure the greatest enjoyment and to avoid the most misery to each of the individuals who compose it—if such be your desire, then equalize the conditions of men and establish democratic institutions.[2]

But in fact, says Tocqueville, we have no choice. We will have equality whether we want it or not, and if its social consequences are neither very

[2]Ibid., Vol. 1, p. 262.

bad nor very good, the *political* possibilities it opens up are momentous. It is with these possibilities that Tocqueville is primarily concerned. Equality is not the same thing as freedom, he is quick to point out. It can result either in an excellent form of self-government or in anarchy and its concomitant danger, tyranny. As examples of the latter Tocqueville had in mind the bread-and-circus mobs of Rome preceding the Caesars' overthrow of the Roman Republic or the crowds at the guillotine in the Reign of Terror that prepared the ground for Napoleon's coup d'état in France. The events of 1830 in France again followed that pattern. The question is, *why* does equality sometimes lead to one, sometimes to the other of the results?

The United States (along with Britain) is Tocqueville's model of a good government based on equality; France is his example of its bad effects. He did not think of the United States as perfect, however. He objected to the electioneering, the office seeking, the patronage game, the personal attacks in the public press. But these are the inevitable side effects of egalitarian self-government. Despite them, the United States is favored by three kinds of conditions: the structure of its government, geographical and historical accidents, and the culture of its people.

Government Structure

Tocqueville found the main virtue of American political institutions to be their decentralization. He was impressed with the degree of local autonomy given to towns and counties in administering local matters such as roads, charities, schools, and taxes. By contrast, all such things in France were handled by a central bureaucracy in Paris. For the same reason, he admired the federal system, which gave the national government the powers necessary to control the currency, wars and foreign affairs, and national commerce, but which left all other matters to the states. He thought the principle exact: The national government should have full powers to take care of things affecting the nation as a whole, but not the power to intervene in what affected only a part of the country.

The effect of this system, Tocqueville believed, was to make Americans public-spirited. Tocqueville felt that the natural effect of equality was to make people individualistic and selfish, since they would be busy competing in business and thus uninterested in the affairs of the larger community. But decentralized institutions counteracted this, for they tied individual self-interest to public-spiritedness. If Americans wanted to get anything done, they could not rely on a government agency to do it for them; they would have to initiate the action themselves. Where cooperation was necessary, they would have to drum up support among their fellows, take part in local government, and contribute their own efforts to getting it done. The individual who wanted a road or a canal for his or her own use, then, would have to come up with a project that would appeal to others' interests as well. Thus, a decentralized government makes its citizens energetic, industrious, and prosperous; by contrast, the tone of a centralized autocracy is one of lifeless quiet.

Tocqueville also admired the way in which the authority that did exist was split up through its own internal balance of power. He liked the presidential and gubernatorial system that separated the executive from the direct influence of the legislature. Tocqueville, thinking of the radical shifts in mood in the French Assembly of the 1790s, considered direct control by the legislature (that is, the parliamentary form of government) unstable. It was liable to those moods in which the majority tries to impose its will by force on the rest of the country— "the tyranny of the majority."

Tocqueville was particularly impressed with the powers of the American courts to pass on the legality of the acts of the legislature, as well as to provide remedies for aggrieved citizens, thus making democracy into a rule of laws rather than merely a rule of politicians. But given the power of the courts in America, Tocqueville thought it important that their power was itself split up and restrained. In France, he declared, such courts would be an instrument of tyranny, for there the government exercised complete control over the courts, just as over any government agency. In America the courts were made independent through the tenure of the judges once they were in office, and the judges' power was itself circumscribed by the separation of prosecution and defense attorneys from the court. (Recall that Tocqueville himself was a professional lawyer, employed by the bureaucratic French courts, and that his visit to America was prompted by his difficulty in working for a regime of which he disapproved.) He also thought the jury system useful in balancing the power of the judges, as well as in educating citizens to participation in the orderly rule of law.

The effect of these balances was that the government could not be too strong or too precipitous in its actions, so that neither an emotional majority nor a would-be tyrant could easily enforce its will. Tocqueville was careful to point out that the United States was *not* a land of unlimited freedom where individuals could do whatever they pleased. Unlimited freedom, in Tocqueville's conservative view, was nothing but license for anarchy. On the contrary, he declared, "more social obligations were imposed on [the individual] there than anywhere else." America was full of agencies for group control over the individual, and Tocqueville cites with approval the New England ordinances that required citizens to go to church, prohibited drunkenness, and severely punished sexual improprieties. This great community power was restrained from creating a political tyranny, however, by being broken up through decentralization and balances of power, thereby making the government both less dangerous to the nation as a whole and more responsive to private interests. Tocqueville's observations on just what "freedom" means in America are pertinent today, as a struggle goes on between the rights of individuals and the public power to control individuals' morals. The "freedom" that is built into American political institutions is the freedom of local groups from unified central control, and there is very little built into the system to protect the individual from the tyranny of these groups.

Tocqueville also devotes some attention to freedoms that he thinks are dangerous in themselves, but that serve to counterbalance other dangers of the system. Tocqueville regarded freedom of the press and freedom of assembly as invitations to spread slander and extremist opinions and to form conspiracies to overthrow the government. This, at any rate, he believed to be the case in France. But in a country like the United States, where power was too decentralized to be easily swayed or overthrown by mass agitation, he believed these freedoms provided a necessary corrective to the other ills of the system. If elected politicians tended to be self-seeking and corrupt, the press could keep them in check by threat of exposure, and political parties created the competition that would publicize their failures in order to try to replace them in office.

Finally, Tocqueville remarked on the beneficial effects of the separation of church and state in America. Again his contrast is France, where the state-supported church made religion a bone of material contention. Religion was caught up in defending a particular political regime and hence added another source of political controversy. Political opponents of the regime became irreligious, and contending religions were driven into political opposition. The lack of a state church in America, then, strengthened rather than weakened both state and church.

Geographical and Historical Accidents

These political structures were the main features of stable self-government in America, but there were other contributing factors. For example, the United States grew up in the virtually empty continent of North America, with plenty of land for expansion and wide oceans between it and the warring powers of Europe. The result was that America had little fear of wars and no need to maintain a large standing army. This was important, for wars are the great centralizer. In wartime the central government assumes great powers over the nation, not only over local governments, but over the citizens themselves. The entire apparatus of government is directed toward providing the materials of war: People are conscripted, taxes are high, the economy is regulated. America was spared all this because it was protected by its geography rather than its army. Tocqueville was correspondingly pessimistic about the prospects for American-style decentralization in Europe, where the threat of warfare from neighboring states necessitated constant preparation by central governments.

Another accidental feature favoring stable democracy in America was the general equality of wealth. Accordingly, there were no overwhelmingly great differences among the people and no strong basis for revolutionary conflict. (The one exception, Tocqueville noted, was the existence of slaves, whose unequal condition provided the most explosive feature of American society.) Tocqueville thought it especially important that equality existed in America before the democratic government was established. By contrast, in France, where a war had to be fought against the aristocracy in order to create equality, the Revolution aided the process of centralization. The local institutions had been in the hands of the aristocrats, and hence the Revolution took away local autonomy in order to wrest control from the aristocracy; in doing so, it destroyed the decentralized bases of freedom.

American Culture

Democracy in America was also favored, in Tocqueville's view, by the unique social conditions of its people. They all spoke the same language, were mostly of the same Protestant religion, and had the same educational level of rough literacy. Again, here were few sharp distinctions, few bases for political conflict. Most important of all, he felt, was the strong hold of the Puritan religion. The church taught people discipline, moral order, and a belief in laws. Moreover, the Protestant churches in America were controlled by their congregations and hence provided a model of democratic self-government. All told, Tocqueville was inclined to view America as uniquely favored by its special characteristics to build equality into a stable form of democratic government, rather than to give in to its inherent dangers.

In the abstract Tocqueville was more pessimistic. Egalitarian society was dangerous to freedom, he felt; his views on the subject have become known as the theory of mass society. The abolition of the aristocracy resulted in there being no one strong enough to resist the tyranny of the central government and its head, whether he be king or dictator. Moreover, the equality of conditions tended to eliminate all independent sources of power that might check unlimited control. Equality among citizens makes them emphasize uniformity; as noted above, no one is willing to stand out against the strength of public opinion. The natural tendency of the public is to demand that laws and rules apply to everyone, without exception; the public feels that it should be allowed to oversee everything, and hence the state takes on the potential for exercising total control over the individual. Since everyone is equal, no one individual has any power, and people must appeal to the only thing above the individual—the state—to do things. The state becomes the only ideal outside of the private person; the overwhelming demand for loyalty is to the nation. Thus, the individualism of a mass society of equals goes together with the total power of the state. As the private individual seeks his or her personal gain in business or other purely private affairs, political interests are reduced to a desire for tranquillity—a government that will maintain order so that one can pursue one's own affairs. The individual of mass society is willing to give great power to the centralized state and in the process loses the freedom to oppose it.

The United States, in Tocqueville's view, had the uniquely favorable political structures, geographical circumstances, and customs to counteract these ill effects of equality. But France and most of the rest of Europe did not. On the Continent the governments were extremely centralized, controlling through their national bureaucracies not only armies, taxes, and public works, but charity and education, finance and workmen's savings, the regulation of manufacturing, and a large section of the public's employment. This centralization advanced irreversibly, through every revolution and restoration; there seemed to be no stopping it. Other conditions were unfavorable as well. France, Germany, and other European nations confronted each other across narrow boundaries and maintained their central governments to support a great war machine. Nor were the cultures of the people favorable to peaceful democracy: Great inequalities in wealth still existed, as did sharp cultural distinctions, religious conflicts, and a widespread absence of any religious faith at all. The prognosis for America was that there would be no more revolutions; only the unequal condition of the blacks, Tocqueville felt, could have that potential. For France and for the rest of Europe he feared more of the cycle of revolution and reaction.

Democracy in America proved very successful after its publication in 1835 (a second part came out in 1840). Of all the many visitors' accounts of America, Tocqueville's was by far the most famous. It's success was due partly to the fact that it said what people wanted to hear. Thus, it was most popular in England and America, whose institutions were praised, and least popular in France, which did not come off so well.

The book contains a very powerful theory of political institutions. Its main weakness is that it makes the United States seem a more perfect democracy than it really was, or is. From his aristocratic viewpoint, Tocqueville mistook middle-class Americans for poor people and hence concluded that the poor people in America were really fairly well off and, in any case, ruled the country. He saw more equality than really existed; in fact, there were poor people in the 1830s, just as now, but they were characteristically invisible, living in the remote parts of town and countryside.

This defect does not vitiate Tocqueville's insights, but it adds a new dimension to them. Indeed, it points us directly at the central dilemma of modern America: Democracy can operate and be very strongly entrenched and yet not serve all the people. As in Tocqueville's day, middle-class businessmen participate in local politics, but the poor are generally unable to do so. There is democratic bargaining for power, and in the process a middle-class majority is well enough served; in a country where the middle class is a majority, a democracy can easily ignore the poor. This is implicit in Tocqueville's analysis, for he saw that democracy could operate among the white majority even while excluding the black slaves. Tocqueville, the man of classical philosophy, would no doubt be willing to recognize his error and let his analysis stand even in that light. He would probably feel (as apparently do many people today) that a democracy of the middle class is better than no democracy at all and would consider the political exclusion of the poor as an unfortunate by-product, but a price one should be willing to pay for what freedom there is. As a conservative he would be unwilling to upset the balance of power in democracy as it stands in order to extend equality to the poor. That, in his terms, would be paying for equality at the price of freedom.

There is another side of Tocqueville, one that is generally ignored by his admirers and intellectual descendants. He has somber words on the subject of war as creating centralized power and thereby reducing the bases of freedom. For twentieth-century America, modern transportation and communications have ended geographical isolation, and World War II and its aftermath have created just the military megalith that Tocqueville predicted. Moreover, Tocqueville had some wise words on the tendency of military officers, who have a relatively low status in a business-oriented society, to seek wars in order to justify their existence and to give them chances of promotion. Another centralizing factor has also been operating, which Tocqueville missed: the growth of the business system to national and even international scale, which brings about central government regulation, especially in combating large-scale economic crises such as depressions. Such economic crises can have the same effects as wars in concentrating government powers, just as the growth of big business corporations has eliminated much of the individualism that Tocqueville found so much a part of the American scene. By the mid-twentieth century many of the bases of decentralization that Tocqueville thought important in upholding democracy in America had disappeared.

Tocqueville's own career showed how right he was about the structure of politics in Europe. In 1839 he was elected a deputy in the French legislature, representing the district of Vologne, where his ancestral château stood. He was continually reelected until his retirement from politics in 1851. In parliament he led the fight to abolish slavery in the French colonies and interested himself in the French colonization of Algeria. In 1848 he made a speech to the Chamber, which concluded with the words: "I believe we are sleeping on a volcano." The date was January 27, about the same time that Marx and Engels were finishing the *Communist Manifesto*. On February 16 riots broke out in Paris, and another revolution was under way. Tocqueville was elected to the Constituent Assembly, which was called to form the Second Republic; he led the monarchist faction. In 1849 he was named minister of foreign affairs in the government of the new president, Louis Napoleon.

Tocqueville lasted in office only five months. He came into conflict with his president, who was already preparing the coup d'état that in 1851 was to destroy the Second Republic and usher in the ill-fated Second Empire of Napoleon III. France's pattern was becoming set: Third, Fourth, and Fifth republics were in the offing, as well as a short-lived Communist commune in Paris in 1871, a Fascist regime collaborating with the German occupation during World War II, a Communist-based World War II underground, an attempted army coup in 1958, and a student-led near-revolution in 1968. Tocqueville's foresight was already becoming apparent.

After Napoleon's coup Tocqueville retired from government and attempted to search out the origins of France's calamities. The result was *The Old Regime and the French Revolution,* one of the greatest historical books ever written. Tocqueville broke new ground in several ways. Instead of relying on what other historians had said, Tocqueville went back to the files of provincial town halls for the original documents showing the operations of local government. He compared the development of institutions in France with the development of those in England, Germany, and elsewhere, in order to test his ideas against alternative sequences. The book is a model of good scholarship, scientific thinking, and beautiful style. Its results are still definitive.

It was not the Revolution that destroyed the decentralized institutions of France, Tocqueville found, contrary to what most conservatives held. Rather, it had been the French kings themselves. Back in the Middle Ages Tocqueville's class, the aristocracy, had jealously guarded their independence from the king. Parliaments and independent courts had been created by coalitions of nobles as a balance of power to resist the control of the king. Such institutions had existed all over Europe, even in Russia and Spain. The kings counterattacked and managed to destroy the power of the aristocrats by creating a royal bureaucracy, into which the courts were incorporated as subordinate agencies. The aristocrats were made royal officials, and their representative institutions were reduced to virtually nothing.

This process went furthest in Russia and the East and least far in England. In England, in fact, the courts and lawyers remained almost totally independent, and parliament won the final struggle with the king in the seventeenth-century revolution led by Oliver Cromwell. In France the struggle went on the longest. There the king built a mighty bureaucracy, but the aristocracy still held many powers, and the showdown did not come until the end of the eighteenth century, when a new commercial era had accentuated the trend to equality and created the massed population of Paris that would prove so important in French politics. The inefficiency of the French regime, balanced between an autocratic king and a parasitic aristocracy, led to the government financial crisis of 1789. In the temporary government deadlock the floodgates broke, and the masses attacked. The spirit of equality had been unleashed by the leveling bureaucracy and the growth of commerce, and the aristocrats who lived on with their old privileges but without their old powers and functions were to feel the vent of its fury. In the end the main effect of the Revolution was to strengthen and streamline the central government, something that could not be done as long as the aristocrats stood in the way. The Revolution merely consolidated the structure the kings had labored to create.

This account sharpens the irony of America in world perspective. The United States has the most protection against the instabilities of modern mass society because it derives its institutions—especially its decentralized courts and local governments—from the early period of British history. The colonists of the seventeenth century who founded American society were from the conservative, minor aristocracy of England, and they brought with them the institutions of decentralized feudal control. America thus escaped even from what centralization the English kings had managed to carry out. The United States, far from epitomizing the new era of politics, has come to have one of the oldest government forms in the world.

The United States, then, is not a hopeful model for the Third World, where, as if to follow Tocqueville's forebodings, revolutions destroy local autonomies in order to modernize and thus set the basis for total government control. For Europe Tocqueville's predictions have been only too true, as shown by the alternations of dictatorships and anarchical democracies in France, Germany, Italy, Greece, and elsewhere.

By 1815 the main outlines of the modern era had already emerged. Napoleon, the little corporal who brought in the army to stop the squabbling of politicians and restore order in France and then set out to conquer Europe for his system, foreshadows another little man with global ambitions, this time on the other side of the Rhine—Adolf Hitler.

Tocqueville's private secretary in the foreign ministry of Louis Napoleon was an aristocrat named Arthur de Gobineau. In the period after Tocqueville's death Gobineau was to become famous for his scientific theory of history as the conflict between superior and inferior races. History thus provides us with yet another ironic link between the old and the new.

CHAPTER FOUR

Nietzsche's Madness

Friedrich Nietzsche (1844–1900) was surely among the strangest of the social theorists. His intellectual journey too was one of the wildest, for he was the harbinger of the intellectual explosions that occurred in the twentieth century, and the explosiveness of his insights not only cracked the shell of contemporary nineteenth-century beliefs, but ended up destroying Nietzsche himself.

There is an enormous creative happiness in Nietzsche's work. His overflowing energy came through in the twenty books he wrote before collapsing at the age of forty-four; and every page, almost every line, has an intensity that must have gripped the author to his pen the way it holds the reader in his or her chair. "It is my ambition to say in ten sentences what everyone else says in a book," declared Nietzsche, "—what everyone else does *not* say in a book."

From modern depth psychology to existentialist philosophy; from modern poetry and literature to anthropology, sociology, religion, music, art, and culture; and in the tradition of revolt itself, Nietzsche has had an enormous impact. Some of this impact, such as the popularity of his ideas in the early Fascist movement, has seemed frightening, even though the interpretation of Nietzsche's ideas these forerunners of the Nazis made was virtually the opposite of what Nietzsche himself meant. Other parts of Nietzsche's work, especially concerning sociology and human freedom, are not yet fully unfolded. Max Weber said that one could judge the depth of one's intellectual seriousness by one's attitude toward Marx and Nietzsche. As yet only Weber and a few of his contemporaries have measured up to the challenge. The challenge still lies before us.

NIETZSCHE'S LIFE

Superficially, it would seem that Nietzsche had an uneventful, pampered childhood. His father, a Lutheran minister in eastern Germany, died when Friedrich was five, and Friedrich was brought up surrounded by adoring, puritanical females: his mother, sister, grandmother, and two maiden aunts. In this atmosphere of German Victorianism, Nietzsche received stern encouragement to work hard. He also acquired a deep-seated sexual inhibition, which later grew into a hatred and terror of women and an insight into the way religious sentimentality upheld a repressive emotional domination.

His family was well off, and the young Nietzsche was sent to an elite private school which had produced many famous German scholars, and then to the universities of Bonn and Leipzig. It was intended that he should enter the ministry, but he was drawn instead to the subject of philology (what might now be called historical linguistics), which at that time was just beginning to break new ground. Nietzsche impressed his professors enormously with his cleverness and energy. By 1869, when he was twenty-five, they had obtained a professorship in classical philology for him at the University of Basel, Switzerland. His promise was such that the formal requirements for the Ph.D. were waived.

Here, then, was the young Nietzsche, well on his way to a brilliant career in scholarship. But his energies were already overflowing the bounds of normality. His public opinions fluctuated violently. In 1866 he was ardently pro-Prussian, as the Prussians made the military moves that finally began to cast Germany into a unified state after centuries of fragmentation. Then in 1869 he renounced his German citizenship to become a Swiss. In 1870, when the Franco-Prussian War broke out, Nietzsche again became the enthusiastic patriot, and he volunteered for service with the Prussian army as a medical orderly. A few months later, Nietzsche was back in Switzerland. He was, however, bitterly disillusioned with the Germans and their war. Moreover, in caring for the sick at the front, he himself had caught dysentery and diphtheria, and he returned to Switzerland in bad health.

A pattern of illness during periods of stress was to stay with Nietzsche throughout his life. At age twelve, the time of puberty, he experienced severe difficulties with his eyesight; at age twenty his early fantasies of military greatness were ended by the realities of his first tour of duty, when he injured himself in a fall from a horse. Later, whenever personal or career strains blocked the easy path before him, he would always begin a withdrawal into another excruciating illness.

But for the time being the path was bright and Nietzsche was enthusiastic. In 1868 he met Richard Wagner, the flamboyant composer whose revolutionary ideas of musical tonality and orchestral color were beginning to take the European public by storm. Living near the Wagners in Switzerland, Nietzsche visited them as often as he could. He fell in love with Wagner's beautiful wife, Cosima. He became an enthusiastic member of the Wagnerian movement, and of the inner circle of disciples who took personal inspiration from the Master himself and who led the drive to bring his redeeming influence into the surrounding society.

At this time, the Wagnerian movement was not merely a musical experience—any more than the movement spearheaded by the Beatles and the Rolling Stones in the 1960s. Wagner's music was an attack on the decadence of formalistic, regimented nineteenth-century civilization. In his great mythological operas, Wagner rejected the bourgeois spirit of the time and put in its place the heroic figures of the German Middle Ages. For Nietzsche the theme meshed with a revolutionary possibility just emerging in his own scholarly studies as a classical philologist specializing in the language and literature of the ancient Greeks. At this time philologists were beginning to discover that the previous image of the Greeks as rational philosophers, mathematicians, and artists was only the surface of the picture. Behind the sculptural perfection of their white marble statues and the restrained symmetry of their temples lurked a more emotional, primitive Greece: a society wrapped in orgiastic rituals, strange sacrifices and frenzies, and, above all, intoxicating music and dancing that took people out of themselves and into a realm of magic and power. In his first book, *The Birth of Tragedy from the Spirit of Music* (1872), Nietzsche designated these two cultures under the names "Apollonian" and "Dionysian." In the former he discerned the controlled, rational spirit that dominated Christianity and modern European civilization; in the latter he discerned a deeper force, reemerging in his own time through the agency of Wagner and his music.

Nietzsche's book was poorly received by his more conservative colleagues, committed as they were to a narrower, more technical version of the field and unwilling to come to grips with the new spirit flowing through Nietzsche. At first Nietzsche fought back, publishing more attacks on orthodox thinkers and further expounding his enthusiasm for Wagner and his other heroes, such as the pessimistic philosopher Schopenhauer. By 1876, though, his health had deteriorated to such a point that he had to go on leave from the university. By 1879 he had resigned his job altogether on a small pension. From then on he moved from place to place in Switzerland and northern Italy, living at modest hotels in the most beautiful parts of the Alps, and taking long hikes when his health permitted.

And he was writing at an ever-increasing pace. Troubled by insomnia, migraine headaches, vomiting, and bad digestion, he would write for ten hours at a stretch, until his eyes burned. He lived on drugs: chloral hydrate, veronal, opium, and many others. Caught in a spiral of his own making, he pushed his mind as far as it would go, far beyond the limits of what anyone had hitherto dared to think. His frenzied writing, freed by his lack of official position and by his solitude, gripped him like a demon; his body paid the price.

Yet his illness also had its personal pattern. In the late 1870s, he began to break with Wagner and that circle, who were hitherto his main allies and friends. Wagner had moved to Bayreuth in Bavaria, where an admiring aristocrat had built him a lavish theater for his gigantic orchestra. In that atmosphere, Wagner's own megalomania reached its apotheosis, and he became an idol of respectable society. The final success affected his ideas: From the earlier revolutionary themes, he shifted to a sentimental reconciliation with Christianity, and he became the center of a movement of strident German chauvinism and anti-Semitism. Nietzsche, for his part, was going in the opposite direction, toward what he considered a new, psychological science—a hard but joyous wisdom that would break free from all surface conventionalities. During this split, Nietzsche underwent some of the worst pangs of illness. But at its end (around 1883, when Wagner died) the true voice of the philosopher had emerged.

Nietzsche's sexual life was also coming to a crisis during this time. Always exceedingly polite and repressed with women, he nevertheless proposed marriage several times during this period—and was refused. In 1882 he was introduced to a beautiful and idealistic young intellectual, Lou Salomé, then twenty-one years old, the daughter of a Russian general. Their ideas flashed; from intellectual intimacy they progressed to a very rhetorical, idealistic nineteenth-century courtship. Disavowing belief in marriage (as did Salomé), Nietzsche nevertheless proposed to her twice, each time unsuccessfully. Finally they hit on a plan to move to Paris in a platonic *ménage à trois* with another close intellectual friend. But Nietzsche's mother and sister heard of the plan and descended on him vengefully. At the age of thirty-nine Nietzsche could still quake at the moral imperatives of his aging mother. The plan was given up.

The next year Nietzsche's health picked up, and it remained good until his final collapse at the end of 1888. His productivity suddenly increased again, this time in a new poetic direction, with the composition of *Thus Spake Zarathustra,* followed by a series of outspoken works attacking Christianity and calling for a reevaluation of all values. No doubt the death of Wagner helped ease the strain; so did the resolution of his sexual hopes, enforced though it might have been. His sister Elisabeth, who was constantly meddling in his affairs, married an anti-Semitic politician named Förster and moved to Paraguay, where Förster was organizing a utopian colony. With the grounds cleared, Nietzsche was free to concentrate on his own thoughts. The torrent, already boiling, now broke all bounds.

THE BIRTH OF ANTHROPOLOGY AND THE DISCOVERY OF THE IRRATIONAL

Nietzsche's thought had its origin as part of a larger intellectual movement—modern anthropology. This might be described as the process of breaking away from a Europe-centered worldview, and away from belief in the universal validity of European standards of rationality and morality. Of course, since the voyages of discovery in the late fifteenth century, Europeans had been aware of the existence of other societies. Yet the tribes of the Americas and the South Seas seemed to most Europeans merely primitive, until an intellectual shift occurred that made them the subject of a new discipline. Intellectual impetus for this shift came from within the world of scholarship, and especially from specialists in the Greco-Roman classics and ancient history.

A number of developments in this area occurred in the 1860s. In England, for example, Henry Sumner Maine, studying ancient law, found that behind the legal contracts of the Romans there was a still more ancient form of law, based on the status of the persons involved in each case. One's membership in a corporate community came first; deliberate, rational decisions negotiated among individuals came later in history. At the same time in Germany, J. J. Bachofen thought he could discern behind the European patrilineal kinship system an older system of matrilineal descent and inheritance. This gave evidence of an era when societies were organized around women, with a female-centered religion and law that differed sharply from later, male-centered institutions. And in France, meanwhile, Fustel de Coulanges (who was Emile Durkheim's teacher) asserted that the Olympian religions of Greece and Rome were actually political cults. For example, the worship of Athena was the cult around which clans had united to form the city of Athens. And behind this stage of ancient religion was a still earlier form, the cult of the family gods, specific to each household, and a corresponding social structure in which each family was a fortified enclave, united by its own domestic religion, and owing loyalty to no one outside its own limits. Somewhat later the English classicist James Frazer would write in the same vein that behind the beautiful stories of love and jealousy among the Olympian gods was another religion of sacrifice to the underground gods, sacrifice designed to ensure fertility by magic means.

Nietzsche was part of the first wave of these discoveries. Trained in classical philology in the 1860s, just as these ideas were breaking upon the scholarly world, he devoted his first book to the subject of the two types of Greek religion, which, as he saw it, involved two styles of music and culture. On the one hand there was the musical cult (it was Nietzsche who discovered that music was originally religious, not a pastime) represented by Apollo and his lyre. This style, the Apollonian style, was serene, harmonious, and poised. It represented rationality, beauty in the form of perfect balance, and it was the source of the Greek ideal, which has descended to us as the notion that civilization is embodied in science, mathematics, philosophy, and classical art. The Apollonian style represented restraint—the golden mean between extremes.

On the other side was the Dionysian style, brought into Greece by a violently ecstatic group of dancers. They traveled from place to place, picking up new members who were willing to abandon their normal lives so as to chant and go into frenzies to celebrate their god Dionysus (Bacchus). This god was represented not in beautiful human form but as a satyr, a goat-man, and his province was the harvest, the wine, and the emotions connected with intoxication. In contrast to the Apollonian cult of restraint this was a cult of extremes, of emotional release of the basic life energies. Nietzsche discerned that the Dionysian movement became the basis for the Greek dramatic tragedies. The Bacchic chanters became the chorus, and their tale eventually came to be represented by actors. The theme was always the overweening pride of the hero, broken by the retribution of fate, as a kind of sacrifice to the endlessly fluctuating nature of life and death.

Nietzsche thus saw tragedy, that great stirring art, as capturing the Dionysian spirit within the limits imposed by Apollonian balance. At the time, he found both Dionysian and Apollonian styles important for a full human culture. But the balance would not remain stable. For Nietzsche came to see that all of Western civilization, including Christianity, had become an extension of the Apollonian culture. The Dionysian side, however, had been steadily buried; the Greeks had held it in some measure of balance, but the Christians repressed it. This was apparent above all in the nineteenth century, during which the mythological side of Christianity had been stripped away, leaving the underlying faith in rational controls and a calm belief in progress. More and more, Nietzsche came to see the creative, underground forces of life on the Dionysian side, and he began to launch a violent attack on the dominant forces repressing them.

THE ATTACK ON CHRISTIANITY

Nietzsche, like most intellectuals of the modern European era, was an atheist. In a sense the basic identity of the modern intellectual was formed in the movement for liberation from the dogmas of the church that had ruled Europe since the Middle Ages. Already in the seventeenth century the battle of the liberated minds against the authoritarians was symbolized by the new science of Galileo, which was condemned by the church that burned its opponents at the stake. By the time of the French Revolution, as we have seen in Chapter 1, the progressive intellectuals were solidly in revolt against dogma, and they were ready to set up a church of Reason on the ruins of Christianity.

But Nietzsche went a step further. He saw that only the overt political and intellectual repressions of the established church had been overthrown. Its deeper spirit lingered on in the dominating forms of nineteenth-century secular rationalism and Victorianism. What good did it do, declared Nietzsche, to detach oneself from Christian dogmatism if liberated intellectuals continued the very same values of emotional self-control and moralistic dedication to the community? They were merely substituting a belief in progress on earth for rewards in heaven. Nietzsche vehemently attacked the secularizers who portrayed Jesus no longer as the son of God but as a good man, the great teacher of morality, humility, and altruism. God was dead; but no one dared to see what that meant, what possibilities it opened up:

> Have you not heard of that madman who lit a lantern in the bright morning hours, ran to the market place, and cried incessantly, "I seek God! I seek God!" As many of those who do not believe in God were standing around just then, he provoked much laughter. Why, did he get lost? said one. Did he lose his way like a child? said another. Or is he hiding? Is he afraid of us? Had he gone on a voyage? or emigrated? Thus they yelled and laughed. The madman jumped into their midst and pierced them with his glances.

"Whither is God?" he cried. "I shall tell you. *We have killed him*—you and I. All of us are his murderers. But how have we done this? How were we able to drink up the sea? Who gave us the sponge to wipe away the entire horizon? What did we do when we unchained this earth from its sun? Whither is it moving now? Away from all suns? Are we not plunging continually? Backward, sideward, forward, in all directions? Is there any up or down left? Are we not straying as through an infinite nothing? Do we not feel the breath of empty space? Has it not become colder? Is not night and more night coming on all the while? Must not lanterns be lit in the morning? Do we not hear anything yet of the noise of gravediggers who are burying God? Do we not smell anything yet of God's decomposition? Gods too decompose. God is dead. God remains dead. And we have killed him."[1]

If God was now dead, Nietzsche asserted, we could no longer live in the hard shell left behind, stripped even of its magic. Humanity had only just begun on its hardest task: to live beyond this entire system of belief and control. "Is not the greatness of this deed too great for us?" asked Nietzsche. "Must we not ourselves become gods simply to seem worthy of it?"

Nietzsche's main attack was on the imperative of altruism, a principle brought from Christianity into modern culture almost without alteration. The Christian doctrine preached humility, imitating the suffering of Jesus on the cross, and giving charity to the poor. Salvation came through faith, suffering, and care of others. The ideal was epitomized by the monk who weighted himself with chains to exorcise the sexual appetites sent him by the devil; by the saint who washed the feet of lepers; and by the pious layman who gave food to the poor at Christmas and put something in the collection plate each Sunday. What difference was there if now the ideal was to be an upright citizen, living a respectable life, dedicating oneself to duty and to the grind of work? What difference was there if the altruistic imperative now meant that the meaning of life was to dedicate oneself to the State or the Nation, to liberal reform or mass socialism?

Nietzsche's argument was not just a negative one. Using his philological skills, he pointed to the history of language as a clue to an alternative morality. In modern language the contrast between "good" and "evil" was one between the moral, respectable, and altruistic on one side, and the selfish, hurtful, and egoistical on the other. But in the earliest Greek, the words meant something quite different. The "good" meant the good people, the aristocracy, those who had the energy, personal power, and grace to live well, win their battles, and dominate their situation. The "bad" meant not moral evil but people on a low level—those who failed, those with base and petty concerns, and those who lacked the vital energies and hence ended up on the bottom. If these conditions were the result of fate, then clearly there was nothing to be done about it but play one's part to the hilt.

From this Nietzsche concluded two things. On the historical level it was apparent that a reversal of values had taken place, that the slave morality of

[1]From Walter Kaufmann, ed., *Portable Nietzsche* (New York: Viking Press, 1959), p. 95.

the bottom had replaced the aristocratic morality of the top. And on the practical level, Nietzsche himself must undertake to launch a crusade to restore the creative forces to their proper place. We shall take up each of these in turn.

THE DYNAMICS OF THE WILL

Nietzsche's own theoretical position was now coming into focus. Based on a philosophy, it ramified into a strikingly modern social psychology—and a historical sociology as well. The basis of it was a theory of the will. The human essence, Nietzsche asserted, is will. (Indeed, he saw will as the essence of all life, and of all existence as well—much the way modern physicists declare that ultimately all is energy.) The true human nature is not consciousness, then, or logic, or mental categories, as Plato, Kant, and most other Western philosophers asserted. These things could only be derivatives of the will—modes of the will restricting and turning against itself. Such self-limitation by the will was not necessarily bad: After all, great thinking, art, and human action came from the molding of will into these conscious forms. But the vital energy came through these only because it represented transformations of the will itself, expressions of the selfish, untrammeled ego flowing out into the world, encountering obstacles—other wills—struggling and rebounding, and thereby establishing a self-reflection that issued in a creative civilization.

The early struggle of human wills in society, then, was essentially external. Out of these rival egoisms, a stratified society emerged. Those with the greatest energy, those most in tune with the flux of time, came out on top. From them came the creative works, the brilliant ideas, and the heroic actions. In their own unrestrained egos, they were the "good," or the "aristocracy." Those whose energy was weaker lost the battles and became slaves of the others. In the definitions of the time, they were the base, or the "bad." In the course of time, one might fall from high to low (the subject of the Greek tragedies), or even rise from low to high (like the mythological Greek heroes who became gods). If these shifts happened it was because of individual wills that committed the mistake of too much pride (*hubris*) or tapped a level of superhuman energy. The morality, then, was simple but dynamic. As long as people were able to act on it, there was no obstacle to their living on the highest level they could, in every sense.

Heroic morality survived only through the period of small, fighting, democratic city-states. At that point in history a fatal reversal set in. With the spreading Roman conquests almost everyone became a sort of slave. The slave class despaired of ever rising again, but its numbers were now so great that it could affect the ruling climate of thought and language. In the regimented society of the Roman Empire, the slaves' condition began to approximate that of the entire middle mass. The downtrodden will of the slave class reared its head in an insidious form. They resented being dominated and wanted revenge. They did not want to become dominant or free but to bring the dominators down to their own level. They instituted a revolution in the very standard of morality.

The successful dominators and their untrammeled wills now became defined as bad, or evil. Good was taken to mean the virtues of the slave—humility, self-abnegation, obedience, duty, and dependence on things above oneself. Ironically, these were what made good slaves, from the masters' point of view. The deviousness of this revolt of the slaves' will was in the slaves taking the lowest possible view of themselves, accepting even the worst demands placed upon them, and making these into a standard of virtue—with the aggressive twist, characteristic of the true will, expressed by applying these standards to everyone, masters included.

In this consisted the slaves' revenge; this was the great revolution of Christianity. Arising in a society where dominant, creative individuality had become impossible, it gradually spread to become the ideal of the entire world. Although slaves were freed and even other classes adopted Christianity, the old struggle for individual self-expression did not return. The entire society had adopted the slave morality. Altruism was its keynote, because this was the bond that linked the slaves to each other and subordinated the individual to the group.

Ironically, the professed altruism and egalitarianism of the humble did not produce a society of equality and justice, even in its own terms. Christian society, beginning with the late Roman Empire and proceeding through the Middle Ages into the period of modern European exploration and colonization, turned out to be just as stratified as the pagan society that had preceded it. Conscience and altruism, devious products of the repressed will to power, became tools of domination as soon as the opportunity presented itself. The new society was now dominated by priests, moralists, and respectable people who made the greatest show of their own humility and personal repression. Even the lot of the poor and the sick was not greatly improved by organized charity, for Christian society needed to have them always with it so that they might be ministered to. Suffering people were among the most precious possessions of the medieval Christian community, because it was through them that others' salvation could be assured. They were to be given charity, but by no means was their plight to be permanently alleviated by changing their conditions or encouraging their own energies.

Nietzsche charged the liberal and radical movements of his day with simply perpetuating this Christian interest in the sufferings of others. Now, however, it was disguised as a moral issue, through which the politicians could bring themselves to power.

Nietzsche's historical dynamic was also paralleled on the individual psychological level. Conscience, Nietzsche noted, was the repression of the primal, egoistical will by a devious will that struggled for a semblance of power by continuously appealing to the group that subordinated it. In this process not only the creative emotional energy but also the will to truth itself was repressed. I did this! declares memory. I did not! says will. At last, memory yields. Here again was more evidence of how will prevails over consciousness and allows the latter to form only on will's own terms. In this sense Nietzsche opened the way to modern depth psychology, just as his history of the will opened the way toward understanding Western Christian civilization.

THE REEVALUATION OF ALL VALUES

Nietzsche concluded from all this that life is only worthwhile as a clear, unobstructed expression of the will. All else is a turning away from life—a turning that, even on its own terms, cannot be successful, for only the will can do such a turning, and it expresses its will to power even as it negates itself. Thus altruistic, self-denying morality is doubly condemned: once, because it turns against creative life; and again, because it remains perverted even by its own standards—for it uses altruism and conscience only as slogans by which to dominate self and others.

The alternative, Nietzsche recognized, would be hard. It meant embracing a world of conflict, even of violence and cruelty. Yet it was the only realistic choice—especially for those who wanted some optimism about the future—and an escape from the grim vistas of endless mediocrity and individuality-destroying mass organization. This was the only route to personal health and cultural creativity. Nietzsche pointed to the great periods of history: the Renaissance, ancient Greece—these were times of great strife, uncontrolled ambition, and Machiavellian individuality. It was out of this strife, and the emotional extremes accompanying it, that life reached its highest point.

In a series of books, Nietzsche hammered out his position. Each title proclaimed his message more strikingly: *The Gay Science; The Dawn; Beyond Good and Evil; The Twilight of the Idols; The Antichrist.* In the midst of all this creativity, his own illness fell away, and he wrote his poetic masterpiece, *Thus Spake Zarathustra.* It is the portrait of his own prophecy, cast in the image of the ancient Persian sage Zarathustra (Zoroaster), and it is Nietzsche's own project for a new religion, if "religion" is indeed the word for something so individualistic. In it Nietzsche envisages a future after the death of God, one which holds a higher creature yet—the superman. The term is difficult to translate from the German; it is *Übermensch*, literally "over-human," a next level beyond the human type, and not yet in existence. In part this is the Dionysian individual resurrected from ancient Greece. But it is also an image of what cannot yet be stated but only created—an individual freed from social and psychological repression, and the product of struggles that have honed creativity and energy to a level beyond anything ever seen before.

How is the superman to be created? By freeing ourselves from the spirit of revenge, says Zarathustra: That is the bridge we must cross to get from human to superhuman. Nietzsche expressed not only an aim for historical liberation from the legacy of slave morality and psychological repression, but he also expressed a profound philosophy. For the spirit of revenge, he says, is an outcry against the flowingness of time; it is a harping back to what has happened, and a stubborn desire to make amends for what has passed and cannot be remedied. To wish to change the past is the height of pathology, but this is a motive that pervades Western society after the Greeks.

In place of this revenge spirit Nietzsche offers a strange doctrine of his own—eternal recurrence. Everything is destined to happen over and over again, he declares. This is in the spirit of the early Greek fertility cults like that of Dionysus, which celebrated the endless cycles of crops and animals, living and dying, and victory and defeat. The individual will to power that is oneself can only find fulfillment in this world of external conflict by willing the whole cycle. In other words, one makes the world one's own by willing it, repressing nothing, asking revenge for nothing, pressing continuously onward into a future that is fated to be like the past. It is a strange doctrine indeed, because at least superficially it seems to contradict our historical sense of what Nietzsche has told us of the ancient power morality, the slave revolt, the death of God, and even the prospective coming of the superman. Of all Nietzsche's ideas, this has been found to be the most unsatisfactory. Nevertheless, on another level, it too may have its sense and a meaning yet to be probed. In the language of the late twentieth century, we might put it thus: Is eternal recurrence the frame within which we are to see Nietzsche's own history, doomed to repeat itself? Or is that history, and especially the final phase of the superman, the frame within which eternal recurrence finally can emerge?

NIETZSCHE'S MADNESS

The year 1888 was one of Nietzsche's best. He was healthy almost all the time. He wrote five books, the biggest output of his life: two thunderous expositions of his ideas, *The Twilight of the Idols* and *The Antichrist*; two books attacking his old idol Wagner and holding himself up as Wagner's antithesis; and a bitterly sarcastic review of the importance of his own works, *Ecce Homo* (Behold the Man). The chapters of this last were entitled, "Why I Am So Wise," "Why I Am So Clever," "Why I Write Such Good Books," and "Why I Am a Destiny."

Nietzsche was beginning to become famous. For the first time he was attracting followers among important European intellectuals. The Danish literary critic Georg Brandes began lecturing about him. Nietzsche began to correspond with the famous French critic and historian Hippolyte Taine and with the great Swedish playwright August Strindberg. With these new connections Nietzsche became more demanding toward his older friends, wanting them to come out publicly in his favor instead of merely supporting him privately, and he cut off contact with them when they failed to do so. His letters, previously so polite, modest, and apologetic whenever he had a personal criticism to make, began to change in tone to megalomaniacal self-importance.

A new political note began to creep in as well, especially a violent anti-Germanism. His intellectual following was appearing in Scandinavia, Russia, Italy, France, Switzerland, and the United States, but in Germany there was still nothing but obliviousness or harsh reviews. Nietzsche began to predict an alliance of the European states against backward, authoritarian Germany. By the winter, the subject obsessed him. In December 1888 and January 1889 he began to invoke the anti-German apocalypse as well as predict it. He foretold a new era, a new antimoralistic religion of the twentieth century, to be ushered in by several world wars. And he himself was now calling together a convocation of the European powers to depose the pope and begin the battle in earnest.

Nietzsche began to appear in public smiling beatifically, in sharp contrast to the serious, even morose, expression that we see in earlier pictures of him. In January 1889 he was in Turin, Italy. He saw a coachman beating a horse on the street, ran to stop him, and collapsed with his arms around the horse. The next few days are unclear. A friend received a last postcard: "I am just having all anti-Semites shot. Dionysus."

From then until his death in 1900, Nietzsche was in the care of others. He wrote no more, neither books nor letters. He never spoke again of his ideas. He alternated between two moods. In one he was quiet, polite, capable of pleasant conversation, like the anonymous man one might have met by chance a few years earlier in a Swiss hotel dining room. In the other mood he would become Dionysus, smiling happily, laughing wildly, singing, emotionally ecstatic.

His sister Elisabeth returned from Paraguay to take over care of him from his mother. Her husband Förster had committed suicide in May 1889, when the anti-Semites' colony seemed to be failing. Taking up a greater cause, she moved her brother back to Germany and made a kind of shrine for him at Weimar, the famous old German cultural center. She arranged for the publication of his complete works, including the last and most violent, and she edited his notes under the title *The Will to Power*. Through her influence Nietzsche's work was popularized in Germany but with ironic results. The opponent of German nationalism and authoritarianism and outspoken critic of anti-Semitism was made into the hero of the nationalists. His anti-Christianity became a prologue for anti-Semitic propaganda; his insights into the nature of power and conflict were distorted into political tools, entirely alien to Nietzsche's own philosophy, but glorifying a militaristic German state. Nietzsche ignored it all, watched over by his sister and alternating between his moods of quiet and Dionysian outbursts.

There have been a number of attempts made to explain Nietzsche's erratic behavior and the physical ailments that plagued him, especially during his later years. A popular theory is that Nietzsche contracted syphilis during his student days or during the Franco-Prussian War in 1870, and that his deterioration was the onset of the syphilitic paralysis about twenty years later. Yet many crucial facts stand in the way of this theory. His health was good from 1889 until his death in 1900; there was none of the progressive physical and mental deterioration associated with syphilis. Nor is it very likely that he ever contracted syphilis in the first place given his extremely puritan character in sexual matters. There is, for example, an account of Nietzsche's being taken against his knowledge to a brothel during his youth. There he was so shocked at the sight of the prostitutes that he froze; finally he ran to a piano in the room, struck a chord, and breaking the spell, was able to flee.

Clearly Nietzsche's madness, like the physical symptoms that afflicted him throughout his life, was psychological or psychosomatic in origin. The syphilis theory is little more than an insult offered by those who wish to dismiss Nietzsche's ideas as the products of a diseased mind. But a psychological illness is not so easily dismissed. It reflects in the man the pressures of the real world and the self with which Nietzsche had to wrestle. Certainly, there is no one who used himself more as a laboratory and a wilderness for exploration than Nietzsche. Abnormally sensitive to strain, he nevertheless provoked himself by exploring his own wounds, uncovering the forces that produced his own terrors and inhibitions, his own self-punishments and driving ambitions. In the process, he uncovered the repressive, illness-producing forces behind Western civilization—religious morality and, beneath it, the dynamics of resentment by the powerless, as a subterfuge for their own will to power.

The strains that finally brought Nietzsche's collapse in 1889 seem to have been connected with finishing the intellectual phase of his life's work. He had discovered society's repressive forces, and he saw the need for a new culture—an emotional breakthrough for Western civilization. But he too needed the breakthrough, and though he thought he saw it coming in himself, the crucial weakness was still there—the long-standing terror of the opinions of others, no doubt stemming from his stern Teutonic, religious upbringing. Nietzsche was finally becoming famous, and this meant new dangers for him. After all, his writings were not merely an attack on respectable, bourgeois civilization, but they were undoubtedly the most violent and far-reaching attacks ever made on Christianity and religion in general. A few centuries earlier, people had been burned at the stake for much less, and even in Nietzsche's day the political power of the church was just beginning to crack in central Europe.

In the inner world of Friedrich Nietzsche's own mind and emotions, then, there may have been a personal danger that was even greater than this political one. He was becoming famous, and his mother would know at last what he had been writing and thinking all these years—that pious widow of a Lutheran minister, whose moral authority over her only son was still so great that she could interrupt his love affairs when he was thirty-nine. Perhaps it was this terror, mounting above the political and intellectual excitement, that pushed Nietzsche over the edge.

In a strange way, the whirlpool into which Nietzsche now fell was completely appropriate. His philosophy held the critical intellect to be a phenomenon of the tortured, self-reflective will; the duty and compulsion to write for others was part of this struggling world of moral repression. Cutting himself loose from all that, Nietzsche turned his back on the years of migraine headaches, burning eyes, and nagging illness. He turned instead toward the most immediate sources of happiness within. In his own world of supreme individualism he was a success; he had become Dionysus.

AN ASSESSMENT

To total the balance sheet of Nietzsche's work is still impossible. The currents from it have flowed far and wide in the twentieth century—the century that Nietzsche predicted would be his own—and they are flowing still. In sociology, Nietzsche had an immediate impact on Max Weber, alerting him to the role of the emotion-disciplining Christian work ethic in powering modern capitalist society and to the iron cage of bureaucracy that makes a slave morality appropriate for all. Nietzsche's depth psychology was taken up and explored by Freud, his colleagues, and his followers. Indeed, Nietzsche's ideas had become so famous in the early twentieth century that Freud declared he did not want to read Nietzsche, because he felt the ideas would contaminate his own researches; yet Freud himself was thereby acknowledging the pervasiveness of this atmosphere, in which the unconscious drives could now be explored. Other depth psychologists, such as Alfred Adler, explicitly developed the Nietzschean theme of the will to power. In philosophy, Nietzsche helped set off the existentialist movement, with its rejection of all specialized academic metaphysics and epistemology that does not derive from an immediate sense of one's own fully engaged life. In this philosophy, meaning is not given from outside, but must be constantly created from within.

On the other side, one cannot ignore the political uses that have been made of Nietzsche, at first by the German nationalists and the anti-Semites encouraged by Elisabeth Förster-Nietzsche, and later by the Nazis themselves. In the wake of fascism, Nietzsche was for a time in very bad repute in the West; Anglo-American intellectuals in particular have tended to repudiate him wholesale as a primary cause of Hitler's atrocities. Yet it can be said that almost every aspect of German culture has been attacked at one point or another as leading up to nazism. Thus do ideas become one of the casualties of warfare, even among the most well-meaning of intellectuals.

In recent times Nietzsche's true themes have engaged our attention again. Post-Freudian analysts like Fritz Perls have struck a Nietzschean note, breaking through their patients' intellectualism and moralism to force a stance of total self-assertion and total public honesty. Psychiatrist R. D. Laing asks if there is not a crucial element of repressed creativity that comes out, in the circumstances of most lives, only in madness. In this, Laing could have had Nietzsche's own life in mind as an example. And the psychedelic revolution of the 1960s reverberated the Nietzschean theme in yet another way—representing a struggle out of the bonds of nationalist militarism and bureaucratic career regimentation that characterized America at midcentury, into a life style of here-and-now high experience.

The social criticism and controversy of today seem to confront Nietzsche's issues more deliberately than ever before. The halo of altruism is beginning to be torn from the elite professions, in a manner that fits well with Nietzsche's own analysis. We are beginning to see the power interests (and financial interests) of medical doctors behind the elaborate public facade of service. We realize the investment medicine has in maintaining a continual supply of sick people to make scientific tests upon and peddle drugs to, and its resulting lack of concern with permanent cures and with preventing sickness in the first place. We are beginning to see the self-interests of teachers, administrators, and employers (and students, too) behind the liberal, service-oriented rhetoric of the educational system. And most recently perhaps, we are beginning to break free of the sexist domination that has been upheld by our romantic and familial conventions for centuries and has dictated the course of relationships between men and women. Ironically, Nietzsche's own attitudes were violently antagonistic to traditional women; but in cracking the facade of sentimental idealization and morality, he began to reveal the underlying system of domination.

On all these fronts, the ideas of Nietzsche still point us to the crucial paths toward liberation. Nietzsche's life itself shows the dangers of a mere halfway breakthrough. To uncover unconscious drives and attack dominant hypocrisy, one cannot afford to be cowardly in any respect. For there is the danger of being captured by just those repressing forces one is trying to become liberated from, just as Nietzsche in his madness was captured by the anti-Semites he had railed against. Yet we should remember Nietzsche as the first to tread this path, exploring the nastiest, most hidden parts of society and self. If he finally fell victim to what he uncovered, at least he had the courage to proceed in the first place, and what he revealed stands for others as guideposts to follow. In his explorations, as well as in his hardships and his ultimate tragedy, Nietzsche ranks among the most heroic of the discoverers of society.

CHAPTER FIVE

Do-Gooders, Evolutionists, and Racists

So far our history has dealt mainly with the thought of France and Germany. We take up now the third of the great intellectual cultures of modern times, that of the English-speaking world. It is not a world of towering individual thinkers like Marx or Tocqueville, with the exception of Charles Darwin, who is not really a social thinker at all. But it does produce some major ideas: the notion of society as organized around a market and the idea of man's continuity with biological evolution. It produces as well the characteristic political philosophy of Britain and America—liberalism, in both its right-wing (laissez-faire) and left-wing (welfare-state) versions. It develops the modern ideology of the application of science to the solution of social problems. For us today, concerned about the potentially dangerous consequences of science, there is a lesson in this. For it was out of the vogue of science, and especially of biology and statistics, that the ideologies of racism emerged. How this happens is still of some interest, for the mode of thought that produced racism has not disappeared along with that particular doctrine.

To begin, we must retrace our steps and return briefly to the eighteenth century. Medieval Christianity had held a monopoly on thought all over Europe, and Latin had been everywhere the language of the educated thinker. It was only in the eighteenth century, when thought broke out of its religious mold, that truly national differences in culture began to appear (although the Reformation paved the way for this by breaking up the Catholic Church into national churches). In France, as we have seen, the movement that we call the Enlightenment was a sharp revolt against religion, in the name of science. The *philosophes* of the Paris salons entertained their listeners with revolutionary principles cloaked over by witticisms. In Britain the break with religion came much more gradually, and the tone was mildly progressive, never revolutionary. Unlike the independent, secular French intellectuals, the British thinkers emerged first of all as university professors in Scotland, where they taught a branch of theology called moral philosophy. Originally this discipline consisted of practical advice on what the good Christian should do in specific situations to avoid sin, but it gradually became secularized into a consideration of how the good society is organized. From moral casuistry, it gradually turned into economics.

THE MORAL PHILOSOPHY OF FERGUSON AND SMITH

The agents of this transformation were two Edinburgh professors, Adam Ferguson (1723–1816) and Adam Smith (1732–1790). Ferguson began with the medieval idea that society is formed like a living body. The king is the head, his soldiers the arms, the church the heart, the artisans the stomach, the royal ministers the eyes and ears, and of course the peasants the feet. (This is a notion from which Shakespeare, a characteristically medieval thinker, drew many of his most elaborate metaphors.) Ferguson applied the model more seriously. If society does in fact consist of specialized parts forming a body, we must conceive of a division of labor among them and a system of exchange by which the services of one part are paid for by the services of the others. And given this natural exchange, one may draw a striking conclusion: that the social division of labor can carry on its exchanges very well on its own, without the interference of the government. The social body does not need the constant supervision of its head.

Adam Smith drew out the consequences of this in 1776 in *The Wealth of Nations*. The market, Smith showed, has laws of its own, the most basic of which is the principle of supply and demand, which regulates exchange for the benefit of the whole. No one could very long persist in producing what was not wanted, for one would get no return; the high returns for those who produce what is so wanted as to be scarce will attract other producers and thus reduce the scarcity. It is neither necessary nor desirable to interfere with this process, for there is an invisible hand that guides the results of people's labors, and in following their own self-interests, all may contribute to the general good. Smith thus at once founded the new science of economics and a new political philosophy, Liberalism.

LIBERALISM AND SOCIAL REFORM: BENTHAM, MALTHUS, AND MILL

The philosophy of Liberalism has two sides, which were united for a while, but later split into rival viewpoints. These two sides were organized respectively around the idea of rational beings and the idea of the natural laws of the market.

On the one side, there is the way of regarding humans as *homo economicus*, rational individuals who calculate profits and losses and act accordingly. This enlightened self-interest was all to the good of the system, as we have seen, and it became thought of as the principle around which all of society could be organized. The leader of this wing of thought was the lawyer Jeremy Bentham, who founded the school of *utilitarianism*, originally as a program of legal reform. The laws of England were a jumble of local and national statues, full of inequities and grotesque feudal punishments like hanging for stealing bread. Bentham argued that revenge and other sentiments were foolish bases for laws and proposed a set of reforms based on principles of reward and punishment that would induce people to be good. In the utilitarian philosophy the best action could be computed by a "hedonistic calculus," by which one arrived at "the greatest good for the greatest number." It provided a way of combining maximum individual freedom with the good of the whole society.

The other side of Liberalism was organized around the idea of the division of labor and the exchanges of the market, which follow their own natural laws. In the tradition of moral philosophy from which this model emerged, natural laws were regarded as the way in which God (or nature) had intended things to operate; they were laws about both how things work and how they *ought* to work. Thus, competition, through the principles of supply and demand, results in the production of just the amounts and kinds of goods that are needed and assigns them a fair price. All restraints on trade, whether business monopolies, government restrictions, or labor unions, are unnatural and hence must be opposed.

Sometimes the results of these laws seemed to be unfortunate. For example, in 1798 a country parson named Thomas Malthus published *An Essay on the Principle of Population* in which he stated that poverty was the result of a law of nature. As production increases, the population grows, he argued; but whereas the population increases by a geometric ratio (for example, 2:4:8:16:32, or some such *accelerating* curve), the production of food can only increase by an arithmetic ratio (1:2:3:4:5 or other *constant* increments), as new land is brought into cultivation only with effort, and even that approaches a limit of exhaustion. Accordingly, population will always tend to outstrip food supplies, and the less fit individuals will starve. This is not only inevitable, said Malthus, but even good for the system as a whole. Malthus and Smith used a labor theory of value and hence were confronted with the same paradox Marx grappled with: How is profit made, if the market ensures that one quantity of labor-value will be exchanged for an equal value? You will recall that Marx invoked labor exploitation as the answer; Malthus proposes population increase of the poor people as the saving element, for it ensures that there will be too many poor people for the available jobs and hence keeps wages low. Thus, the natural laws of the system are all to the good in the end, and in any case it is fruitless to interfere with them. Trying to save the paupers only enables them to reproduce, which makes the population problem that much worse. Parson Malthus even regarded this principle as evidence of God's moral retribution: Poverty is the punishment that humans bring down on themselves for their lack of sexual restraint.

Eventually, a split was to develop between the two wings of Liberalism, but they would retain much in common. They both believed in representative government, the capacity of rational individuals to rule themselves; in the civil liberties of freedom of speech, press, and assembly, which ensured that truth would arise from the free market of ideas; in religious tolerance and the separation of church and state; and in a minimum of government interference with the freedoms of individuals, as long as they do not use their freedom to infringe upon the freedoms of others. (Just where this infringement begins was to be a subject of bitter debate.) This implied a belief in private property as an individual right. The only way in which all Liberals agreed that one might interfere with others was through education (although not necessarily state-supported or compulsory education), which would enlighten people to see how their rational and moral behavior was best for themselves and for society. Liberals were uniformly opposed to revolution and believed only in gradual change and improvement.

The Liberal position was of course not the only one in England in the early nineteenth century; there were also conservatives supporting the rights of the aristocracy and other vested interests, as well as more radical movements among the workers. But for the educated middle class, Liberalism became a powerful force. At the same time, its two wings were coming more and more into conflict. Not only the harshness of Malthusianism but the evils of the industrial revolution were becoming apparent. Child labor, factory conditions, hordes of beggars and paupers, squalid poorhouses and debtors' prisons, periodic crises of unemployment—the same things that drove Marx to radicalism—moved one section of Liberalism into action. The utilitarian wing, with its belief in rational action and its principle of the greatest good for the greatest number, proposed doing something to correct these ills. Soon they were joining in the commissions that investigated conditions in the factories, proposing legislation on child labor, free schools (as a way to take the children off the market), workman's insurance, prison reform, public health, and a myriad of other worthy causes.

The intellectual rationale for reform was provided by the utilitarian leader John Stuart Mill (1806–1873). The "laws" of the market, Mill pointed out in 1848 in his *Principles of Political Economy,* are simply statements of how things will operate *if we let the market operate unchecked;* but there is no *necessity* for us to let it operate that way. Mill, in effect, destroyed the remaining assumption of moral philosophy, which saw "natural laws" as statements both of what *is* and of what *ought* to be. The market is only one system among many, Mill said. It is not God's single law, and if its results do not bring happiness, then we are free to modify it or to try another system.

This created liberalism with a small "l," the modern philosophy of reform that has led to the modern welfare state. The old laissez-faire Liberalism (with a capital "L") was put on the defensive. In Britain the bolder wing of the liberals went on to support not only legislative reforms but even trade unionism and eventually the Labour party. A mild reformist version of socialism was advocated by those liberals organized in the Fabian Society, whose membership was to include George Bernard Shaw. The consequences of liberalism were not merely political; they also began the tradition of empirical research in sociology. The investigating commissions in the factories were followed by tours of philanthropic individuals into the slums and poorhouses, resulting in such publications as Charles Booth's *Life and Labour of the People in London.*

SOCIAL EVOLUTIONISM: DARWIN AND SPENCER

Mill had given the reform wing some heavy intellectual ammunition. But just when the battle seemed won, the fading conservatives acquired unexpected help. In 1859 Charles Darwin published *On the Origin of Species*.

At a stroke, Darwin set the natural world in order, just as Newton had done two centuries earlier in physics. All the species of plants and animals could now be seen as evolving from common ancestors through the great principle of natural selection. Continual small variations in each generation resulted in gradual change, as those most fit to survive and reproduce in the available environments did so, and those less fit died out. The result was a series of branchings, as creatures evolved until they became adapted to stable habitats.

This was the great intellectual event of the nineteenth century, as its result was to put the capital "L" Liberals back in the saddle. Darwin's model of evolutionary advance through competition and survival of the fittest was strong justification for leaving social processes alone to take their course. Actually, Darwin's system had more than an affinity with laissez-faire, for Darwin had hit upon his great organizing principle in biology—natural selection—while reading Malthus on the dynamics of population. Darwin provided Liberals not only with support, but also with the right kind of enemies. The church conservatives naturally regarded evolutionism as contrary to the biblical account of Creation, and their outcry grew even louder in 1871 when Darwin published *The Descent of Man*, which carried out the evolutionary corollary that man must have a common ancestor with animals, most probably with the great apes. Liberalism, joining hands with evolutionism, once again drew the most progressive thinkers to its cause.

The most prominent of the social evolutionists was Herbert Spencer (1820–1903). Like Mill and Darwin, he was an eccentric, unsociable Englishman, although unlike Darwin he was poor enough to have to work for a living. Trained in science, Spencer began working as a railway engineer. He was always producing mechanical inventions, including a not-very-successful flying machine. The only invention that he actually made money on was a sort of early paper clip. By the time he was thirty Spencer realized that more money could be made by inventions in the world of ideas, but he continued to set up weird labor-saving devices around his own home.

Spencer's career was launched as a writer on scientific and political subjects for popular magazines, which were just springing up around mid-century to cater to the growing middle-class audience. To this public Spencer began to sell his combination of evolutionism and laissez-faire.[1] Evolutionism, Spencer argued, shows that we are subject to forces beyond

---

[1]Spencer was not a literal follower of Darwin, but it must be recalled that evolutionism was generally in the air at the time. From 1830 to 1833 Charles Lyell published his theory of geological evolution, which had already brought down the wrath of the church and popularized the subject. Darwin himself had formulated his ideas in the late 1830s, and they were privately known among leading scientists.

what we can see. Our actions, however well intentioned, will fail to achieve their aims if they attempt something contrary to the laws of nature. Spencer thus backed up the economic principles of laissez-faire with an evolutionist view of social stratification as produced by natural causes. Rich men have risen to the top by their talents, and the poor are at the bottom because of their inherent deficiencies. Accordingly, we should not expect reforms to work just because they seem to be reasonable and good.

For example, Spencer said, we need to determine the psychological differences between the sexes before deciding whether to give women the vote. Since all creatures adapt biologically to their environments, it is both useless and cruel to try to civilize the natives in the colonies or to allow criminals and mentally defective persons to produce their inevitably defective children. Spencer even questioned the value of universal education: To educate the intellect, he pointed out, does not change people's emotions or behavior.

Spencer thus claimed that we must know social science before making any changes. And where is that science? Spencer set out to produce it himself. Indeed, he produced not just a sociology but an entire encyclopedia. Between 1860 and 1896 Spencer turned out a massive series entitled *System of Synthetic Philosophy*. Volume 1 is *First Principles*, followed by Volumes 2 and 3, *Principles of Biology;* Volumes 4 and 5, *Principles of Psychology;* Volumes 6 through 8, *Principles of Sociology;* and culminating in Volumes 9 and 10, *Principles of Ethics*. There were volumes planned on *Principles of Astronomy* and *Principles of Geology*, but these were not finished before Spencer's death; these should logically have come first, but they were postponed because Spencer feared he would die before the main part was complete. We should recall that this was the era before radio and television, and the main leisure pastime of the middle class was reading. Spencer lived off this audience for most of his life, selling advance subscriptions to his works and also publishing them in magazine installments. *Principles of Sociology* began coming out in 1872 in *The Contemporary Review* in England and in *Popular Science Monthly* in the United States.

These volumes are full of interesting examples of different customs found around the world—child marriage, savage puberty rites, the forms of tribal kingship, and so on at great length. It is just the thing for a writer who gets paid by the page and whose readers have long hours at home in the evening to fill. Spencer hired three professors to gather together all the available data for his sociology, which he grouped under the headings of "Uncivilized Societies," "Civilized Societies (Extinct or Decayed)," and "Civilized Societies (Recent or Still Flourishing)." Thus we get our information especially from explorers like Captain Cook in the South Seas and Dr. Livingstone in Africa. Spencer supplied the unifying theory.

Basically, his model was like that of Comte, whom Spencer had read and appreciated. Society is like an organism, passing through various stages of development. Spencer updates this theory by showing that change is due not merely to progress in knowledge, but also to principles of evolutionary selection. He also emphasizes that society is different from an organism; it is made up of the actions of individuals and lacks a consciousness concentrated in one place. He also rejects Comte's conservative notion that society is a moral unit and, of course, Comte's political scheme for reorganizing the world under a "High Priest of Humanity." Instead, Spencer wanted to show how society develops structures that culminate in the invisible hand of the market, whereby individuals are given a maximum of freedom and yet contribute to the best functioning of the whole.

Spencer gave his system intellectual elegance by explaining all evolution—cosmic and biological as well as social—with a single basic principle: Matter begins as a homogeneous mass of simple particles and gradually becomes organized as the particles come together to form heterogeneous parts of a complex whole. In short, things move from the simple and unorganized to the complex and organized. Spencer took this idea from embryology: An embryo begins as a mass of undifferentiated cells, which gradually become specialized organs interacting with each other. Spencer stated the principle more abstractly and then applied it to the evolution of the solar system, the earth, biological species, and finally society. Evolution is the process of adaptation to the environment, and its long-term trend, from the lower and earlier adaptations to higher and later ones, is from simplicity to complexity.

Spencer thus arranges primitive, ancient, and modern societies in an order reflecting the stages of evolution. Societies build up as small tribes grow, are conquered, or otherwise combine with others. Size brings about a differentiation of structure. From the comparatively structureless tribes, we get first (a) a *regulative system* for dealing with the outside environment, analogous to the nervous system in organisms—that is, the state, which provides offense and defense against other societies; then (b) a *sustaining system* of economic production that provides life support for the regulative system; and finally (c) an *exchange and distribution system,* consisting of communications and transportation networks, commerce and finance, and so on.

As society grows, each of these sectors subdivides in turn. The state becomes more complex; the king must share his power with the royal bureaucracy and eventually finds himself relying entirely on his ministers. The economy becomes increasingly autonomous, as the market system alone is capable of coordinating the diverse productions. Spencer regarded religion as an archaic stage of development. Fear of the gods was based on fear of the spirits of the dead, he argued; society outgrows this sort of control over the individual, just as it outgrows the state. Thus one's mental capacities improve along with society. Humans become less emotional and more rational; ideas become more definite; lore is replaced by scientific knowledge; customs are replaced by laws.

Viewing the world around him, Spencer saw two main types of societies. One, the militant society, consists of societies in which the regulative system dominates the sustaining system. Cooperation is compulsory and enforced by the state; the society is autocratic, warlike, and religious. Such societies could be found in Germany and France. The other type, the industrial society, is peaceful and republican; cooperation is voluntary, through the means of the market. Here, the state exists for the benefit of its members and not vice versa. England was Spencer's prime example of such a society. He stuck by his principles, however, and denounced Britain's imperial conquests as a dangerous shift away from the industrial to the militant form of society.

LIBERALISM IN AMERICA

Both of these wings of L(1)iberal thought—the social reform and the evolutionist—spread to America not long after they arose in England. Spencer had a triumphant American tour. Lavish banquets were given in his honor by wealthy businessmen, grateful for the intellectual support he gave them in what was indeed an era of robber barons. The main home-grown exponent of laissez-faire evolutionism was the Yale professor William Graham Sumner (1840–1910). His tone can be gathered from an exchange with his students:

"Professor, don't you believe in any government aid to industries?"
"No! It's root, hog, or die."
"Yes, but hasn't the hog got a right to root?"
"There are no rights. The world owes nobody a living."
"You believe, then, Professor, in only one system, the contract-competitive system?"
"That's the only sound economic system. All others are fallacies."
"Well, suppose some professor of political economy came along and took your job away from you. Wouldn't you be sore?"
"Any other professor is welcome to try. If he gets my job, it is my fault. My business is to teach the subject so well that no one can take the job away from me."[2]

Sumner's system had some advantages over Spencer's in that it concentrated less on the overall form of social evolution and paid more attention to the particular "folkways" or customs that evolved to fit a particular historical situation. Sumner was especially astute in seeing that moral norms, which he called "mores," are simply customs that take on considerable emotional force. Sumner took a rather radical stance, considering that he was an ordained minister, as he detailed the varieties of moral beliefs and practices through slavery, torture, infanticide, cannibalism, monogamy, polygamy, public nudity, and sacred prostitution, in order to show that all standards are relative to the customs of the time. "The mores can make anything right," he asserted, thus claiming that there are no timeless verities, except of course the law of natural selection itself. Sumner, who retired from preaching in the pulpit in order to devote himself to preaching in the classroom, elevated natural selection to the status of the fundamental moral

[2]William Lyon Phelps, "When Yale Was Given to Sumnerology," *Literary Digest International Book Review*, III (1925), 661.

law. In fact, Sumner got into some trouble over this. He had a famous academic freedom controversy with the president of Yale, an extremely religious man, who objected to Sumner's assigning evolutionist readings to his students. But the tides were running for evolutionism, and Sumner emerged victorious in the end.

But if evolutionism was strong in America, reformism was even stronger. The reformers simply took what they wanted from evolutionism and ignored the rest. The reform mentality already had roots in America. The 1830s and 1840s witnessed a sprinkling of utopian communities, like the famous Brook Farm in Massachusetts, inspired by Henry David Thoreau and the transcendentalists. Some of them were modeled on the ideas of the Parisian prophets Charles Fourier and Auguste Comte. So when the British liberal reformers gathered in 1856 to form the British Social Science Association, the Americans were prepared to follow suit. In 1865 the American Association for the Promotion of Social Science was founded, with guiding advice from John Stuart Mill himself.

The American association was a mélange of reformers of all kinds, held together by a common quest for respectability under the guise of social science. Its diverse ingredients are shown by the groups that successively split off to form their own societies: the American Prison Association in 1870; the National Conference of Charities and Corrections in 1874; the American Public Health Association, the Association for the Protection of the Insane, and the American Historical Association in 1884; and the American Economic Association in 1885. From the latter were formed the American Political Science Association and the American Sociological Society in 1905.

Intellectually, these people were interested primarily in justifying their projects by whatever ideas supported them. But toward the 1880s academic factions began to form, and this stimulated a concern for intellectual coherence. What was happening was the great reform of the American universities, beginning with the foundation of Johns Hopkins University in 1876. The American colleges were adding graduate departments, expanding their student bodies, and offering electives and hence a variety of new courses. The universities were breaking out of the old classical curriculum and offering a place for new specialties in everything from modern literature to basketry. "Social problems" courses began to find their way into the curriculum, and gradually economics, political science, anthropology, psychology, and sociology got footholds in academia. The first sociology department in the world was founded at the new University of Chicago in 1892. Many of the Chicago sociologists had close connections with Hull House, a pioneering institute of social work ministering to the immigrants in the Chicago slums. Jane Addams, the founder of Hull House, began to do descriptive sociology by producing maps of social patterns on the South Side of Chicago. These maps became an inspiration for the urban sociology that later developed at the university.

There were no great intellectual figures among the early American sociologists, whose leaders were Lester Ward, Albion W. Small, Franklin H.

Giddings, Edward A. Ross, and William Graham Sumner. But they were all morally dedicated people. Many of them were sons of ministers, and quite a few had careers in the ministry themselves before becoming teachers. (This, however, was not unusual in the religiously oriented American college.) Only Ward, who was a paleobotanist with the United States Geological Survey, was not a college professor. Their one overriding interest was social problems and their main theoretical question (except for Sumner, who preached laissez-faire) was how to justify intervention in social problems, given Spencer's evolutionary case for laissez-faire.

Their arguments went generally as follows: First of all, they accepted the basic idea of gradual progress through evolution. The problem was to show that it was natural for men to lend a hand in the evolutionary process. The answer, in one form or another, was that evolution in its higher stages acts through human consciousness and volition. Lester Ward called this the "principle of social telesis." The state, then, was not an outdated impediment to evolution, but in fact acted as the conscious agent of the community as it planned its own advances. Sociology played its role in this advance by discovering the laws determining human behavior, so that society might intervene intelligently for human betterment.

What are these laws? A few sociologists advocated research to discover them, but most of them believed the laws were available through theoretical analysis. Comte and Spencer's notion of society as an organism would not do, for the Americans wanted to operate on the individual level, not to reform the entire society all at once. There was much discussion of the ways in which society was or was not like an organism, with the general conclusion being that since society consists only of individuals, sociology must provide an explanation of how the individual acts. Sociological theorists thus began with an effort to describe the basic elements of human behavior, whether these were to be called mental faculties, social forces, interests, instincts, or motives. Their theories consisted of long lists of them, such as desire for food, pleasure, sex, love, social belonging, and so forth. All social institutions, like the family or the state, were then explained as the results of combinations of these elements.

Actually, these were not explanatory theories at all. By the 1920s a researcher counted 15,789 different "instincts" listed in the sociological literature and concluded that this whole mode of explanation was useless. Merely giving something another name did not explain it; to try to explain social groups by the "instinct of social belongingness" told us nothing at all about why groups occur at certain times or in certain forms under different conditions. All the theorizing had merely served to give sociology a reputation for intellectual vacuousness.

But the sociologists were not greatly perturbed, for they were not seriously trying to build a real theory in the first place. They were not really interested in what determines social structures; they simply wanted a rationale for their efforts to reform the individual and solve social problems. They already knew the source of social ills before they started, and they wanted to get right at the solution.

What were these social problems? Recall that the sociologists were largely moralistic Anglo-Saxon Protestants from small-town or rural backgrounds. What they saw as a social problem was the growing industrial city and its immigrant population. Instead of containing clean, law-abiding, churchgoing, middle-class citizens, the city was dirty and crowded and full of crime, drunkenness, mental illness, illegitimacy, divorce, delinquency, unemployment, pauperism, radicalism, and political corruption. Sociology, then, consisted of describing these urban conditions and proposing what to do about them. Its answers fitted in precisely with the Progressive movement of the turn of the century (and incidentally, with the Prohibitionist movement too, as that rural movement built up for its last assault on the city just around World War I).

The answers consisted of social work and education on the one hand and legislation on the other. Social workers and schoolteachers could train immigrant workers to become good, clean, hard-working American citizens and thus raise themselves out of poverty and its attendant ills. Legislation could eliminate the conditions that bred these effects: reforming the structure of city government to take power from the corrupt immigrant politicians and put it back in the hands of the respectable middle class; encouraging healthy economic competition by breaking up monopolies and checking fraudulent business practices; reforming the penal system to rehabilitate criminals instead of merely punishing them. The most radical of the sociologists, Edward A. Ross, even went so far as to support the right of workers to form trade unions. As a result he got into a famous academic freedom fight at Stanford University with its wealthy benefactress, Mrs. Leland Stanford, widow of one of the great robber-baron railroad builders.

Neither the theorizing nor the research of the early sociologists produced any real advance in knowledge. They were convinced in advance that the "bad environment" of the city produced these ill effects; and they collected facts only to illustrate the conditions and to goad people into doing something about them, not to test their explanations or the efficacy of their cures.

Sumner, like Spencer in England, inveighed against all this. It would not do any good, he said. If you did not understand the historical forces that produced certain customary behaviors, your actions would not bring about the consequences you expected. Sumner himself was not immune to criticism. His own theory of natural selection was extremely general, and he tended to give a great many examples of different institutional forms, without developing a theory that explained just what conditions would produce what kinds of forms.

But in a large sense, Sumner was right. The reformers did not really understand how society worked, and hence their reforms were unsuccessful and full of unintended consequences. Their solutions were to rehabilitate individuals through education and social work and to legislate so that everyone would have an equal chance to compete in the world. In fact, their politics were naïve, and their rehabilitation sentimental. They were too individually oriented to understand how politics works, how power is bargained for, and how government bureaucracies really function despite the noble ideas that might guide them. They never did eliminate political corruption (except where the population of cities changed enough so that the middle class could be in control), or curb monopolies, or rehabilitate criminals. The modern therapy-oriented prison is no better than the old punitive one in end results. It serves primarily to introduce new inmates into a criminal culture, and it seems likely to do so as long as people with criminal records are kept out of all but the least respectable careers. Social work has become little more than bookkeeping for handing out welfare payments. The school system, the cornerstone of reformist hope, has expanded to include the vast majority of the youth population, but with paradoxical results: Instead of providing everyone with an opportunity for upward mobility, the mass school system has served mainly to push up educational requirements for employment, so that high-school graduates now search for the same low-level jobs that were once the lot of grade-school dropouts. And as the giant bureaucracies expand to include ever-larger segments of our lives, the rebellion and alienation found at the bottom of a competitive stratification system merely move into the school system. Instead of a solution to social problems in the outside world, the schools have become the containers and creators of their own problems. Observing all this, Sumner would have shaken his head and barked out something about "You can't change the folkways."

In retrospect the social-problems perspective is most revealing where its problems have disappeared. Divorce, for example, has dropped out of the catalog of concerns—not so much because there are no more divorces (there are even more than ever)—but because we no longer regard divorce as much of a problem. Without the old moralistic views of marriage, we have come to see divorce as a better thing for the individuals involved than an unhappy marriage. In the same way we are coming to see mental illness less as a purely individual condition and more as a term by which people label others who do not live up to their demands for social discipline and propriety; thus the "solution" can just as well be to change the social *demands* on the individual as to try to change the individual to fit those demands. In the long run the profound relativism of Sumner's "the mores can make anything right" is a far more sophisticated perspective than the moral absolutes of the reformers.

The chapter could end here with the admonition that rushing to eliminate social conditions that offend certain people's values, without really understanding the processes involved, leads to both intellectual and practical failure. But there is an even more sobering conclusion.

THE LIMITS OF SCIENCE

The great idea of the late nineteenth century belongs to the evolutionists: the insight into humankind's continuity with the animal world. This insight gave enormous impetus to scientific efforts to solve social problems, especially in Europe. If humans were a kind of animal, the reasoning went, then they could be measured, trained, or selected. A school of scientific criminology sprang up, following the Italian Cesare Lombroso's theory of the criminal type. Criminologists measured the cranial capacities of convicts and of "normal" people in an attempt to show that a hereditary degeneration was the cause of crime. The solution, they claimed, was compulsory sterilization. In England Francis Galton (whose own superior heredity was shown by the fact that his cousin was another gentleman-scientist, Charles Darwin) helped found modern statistics, which he used to demonstrate the family heredity of persons of genius and, conversely, of paupers, the mentally ill, and other defectives. On the Continent a large number of statistical studies attempted to show that the superior members of society rose to the top and the inferior ones sank to the bottom—and that superiority or inferiority was shown by differences in the sizes of heads and in their health, height, weight, vigor, and intellect. Gobineau had already written his scientific history as the conquest of weaker races by the strong; German historians and anthropologists developed military theories of social evolution, in which they argued for the beneficial effects of war in improving society.

This sort of biologism became the dominant (or at least the most popular) mode of social thought in Europe around the turn of the century. In the United States it was reflected in the writings of such figures as Sumner and Thorstein Veblen. Its main American impact, however, came during and after World War I, when the progressives finally became discouraged about reform and began to conclude that the only way to save American institutions was to cut off immigration from Europe. This was finally done in 1922. Ross, the most radical of the sociologists, typifies the shift. From supporting labor unions, he shifted to writing about the "yellow peril" of cheap labor from the Orient and about the degenerate paupers crowding in from southern and eastern Europe. On the other side of the Atlantic, racism focused into a growing wave of anti-Semitism, not only in Germany but in France, Russia, and elsewhere. The British, always a little aloof from Continental fads, were less concerned about inferior races than about inferior individuals. They turned their attention to such efforts as those of Francis Galton's Eugenics Society, dedicated to the breeding of only the best human stock.

What was the fallacy in all this? Partly, it was a matter of scientific interpretation. Some *individuals* are in fact constitutionally superior to others in intellect and other faculties, and certain societies have in fact conquered others. But society cannot be explained purely on the level of individual traits. Social institutions work according to principles of their own, regardless of the individuals involved, and the military strength of a society is due primarily to its accumulated culture and its form of organization. More careful studies show few discernible differences in intelligence or other abilities among races. On the individual level such differences undoubtedly exist. But the studies of Galton and his colleagues on individual heredity fail to control for social biases in measuring heredity's supposed effects.

The fact that poor people have poor parents, and rich people rich parents, is at least *partly* due to cumulative advantages and disadvantages in upbringing, education, and career opportunities, not to mention the inheritance of wealth. And, of course, differences in health, height, weight, and so on have something to do with the diets of children of different social classes.

But these are purely scientific mistakes, and if the object were merely to develop a correct explanation of the varieties of human behavior, they would eventually be corrected with the further testing of the theory. The damage is done, rather, because the theory is constructed only in order to solve a problem—and a "problem" is not an objective category at all, but a matter of *values*. If paupers are something to be eliminated as a burden on society, then a theory about hereditary degeneration will do very well as a justification. If one defined the problem from a different value standpoint— for example, a humanitarian concern for all people—then even if the hereditary degeneration theory were true, one would not want to eliminate people. Instead of judging poor people by their fitness to compete in society, one might try to fit society to them. In the same sense, arguments pro or con about racial inferiority are beside the point: It is an important question *only* if one is committed to a form of society that reserves all privileges for those on top, not if one cares about universal human rights.

Thus the scientific approach to social problems is often just a way of cloaking one's moral failings. An objective, scientific viewpoint treats people with detachment, as things to be analyzed to see how they run. This is a necessary stance for the advancement of theoretical understanding, and indeed modern social thought has advanced by transcending a naïve rationalistic model of humankind and coming to see the nonrational part of its nature. But scientific objectivity does not free us from moral choices. Lombroso, Arthur Gobineau, and the rest have been swept into the ashbin of history, mostly in revulsion against the Nazi regime that gave their ideas a bad name, as well as in scientific rejection of their theories. But the underlying attitude has not disappeared. Galton's eugenics survives more modestly in the IQ tests that govern people's passage through our educational bureaucracies. There is a new Machiavellianism that treats people merely as means to ulterior ends; because it understands some of people's weaknesses and susceptibilities, it is willing to treat their lives as humanly worthless. The technical planners of the CIA and their siblings in government bureaucracies around the world, with their kill ratios, public relations campaigns, and strategic population movements, are the spiritual heirs to Lombroso and Gobineau. Recognizing this, we enter the bitter world of twentieth-century sophistication.

THE SOCIOBIOLOGY REVIVAL

For all the bad reputation acquired by the nineteenth-century thinkers, biological sociology has made a comeback in recent years. Its leading practitioners have been biologists, not sociologists, but they have acquired a certain following within sociology itself. Edward O. Wilson, the curator of entomology at the Museum of Comparative Zoology at Harvard, is the founder of the new field of sociobiology, which he defines as "the systematic study of the biological basis of all social behavior."

The old nature/nurture issue in sociology, which traditionally favors the nurture, or learning, end of the continuum, is reversed by Wilson. His chapter on "The Morality of the Gene" stresses the comprehension of the evolution of social behavior through demographic factors and genetic structure. Wilson is a genetic determinist. According to his sociobiological hypothesis, nature is more critical in determining human society than nurture. A physicist once made a logical pun. Physicists are made up of atoms. Physicists study atoms. Therefore, physicists are the atoms' way of studying atoms. Thus, Wilson's view is that the organism is the genes' way for making more genes, and *Homo sapiens'* organic social structure is more influenced by biology than by socialization.

According to Wilsonian sociobiology, communication is genetically programmed to some extent by natural selection and consists of the *relation* of the pair of signal-and-response. Communication is a two-way street; it is neither the signal by itself nor the response. He notes that the great division between humanity and the ten million species of animals is our unique verbal system, which he uses as a measure to define the limits of animal communication. Wilson, unlike his contemporary, John Lilly, is no advocate of interspecies communication, because he sees human language as the most advanced system. Even the sophisticated waggle-dance of the honeybee cannot manipulate messages to provide new classes of communication, as is the case with science and its interdisciplinary spinoffs. Wilson's new science of sociobiology is an attempt to bridge the gap between the natural and social sciences through a creative synthesis.

Two modes of metacommunication, which Wilson defines as "communication about the meaning of other acts of communication," are status signaling and play invitation. He uses the model of dominance and submission as a heuristic device, and takes the case of the brisk gait, erect-tail posture, and calm manner of the dominant male rhesus monkey and the opposite set of signals displayed by the subordinate male as an example of status signaling. He analyzes the "let's have fun together" attitude of humans and other mammals as examples of play invitation. Taking the social insects as a select sample, Wilson observes that their most highly organized communication systems are incommunicable from individual to individual but only arise between groups. A sociological example within the context of our species' interacting macrosocial units is that of nations and multinational corporations.

Wilson is a human chauvinist, who ranks humankind as the fourth and peak pinnacle of social evolution above the nonhuman mammals, the higher social insects, and the colonial invertebrates. The latter category includes such zooids as corals and jellyfish, whose individual members are, in most cases, fully subordinated in function and physical interdependence to the group. This society or colony he defines as an organism. Such higher social insects as ants, termites, and certain wasps and bees recognize castes rather than individual nest mates, and their societies succeed because of their ability to dispatch food gatherers that return on a regular basis to home base. Conflict arises in bumblebee society through the constant struggle between queens and workers to produce sons, and the queens exercise social control by attacking their daughters who attempt to lay eggs.

Wilson notes that such cold-blooded vertebrates as fishes, reptiles, and amphibians are the equal of mammals and birds in the social organization of parental care, territoriality, and courtship patterns of behavior. However, the main evolutionary trend within the higher mammalian order is its females' ability to provide milk. The universal nuclear unit of mammalian societies is the mother–offspring association and the biosocial fact of prolonged child dependency on the mother. Mammals have diverse social systems with male–female pair bonding as the universal unit in monogamous and polygamous modes. The most complex social systems in each of the nonhuman mammalian orders (e.g., the marsupials, carnivores, rodents, primates, and ungulates) occur in the physically largest member. The highest status humans have given to the carnivores among the nonhuman mammals in our folklore is "king of the beasts"—the lion. A group of lions is defined as a pride, the core of which consists of a closed sisterhood of several adult females who are at least cousins and have inherited fixed territories of association over several generations.

Wilson is akin theoretically to H. Spencer and W. G. Sumner in his Social Darwinism and his assertion of the superior complexity of human social organization as the fourth pinnacle. Human societies vary more than the nonhuman ones in group size, gene exchange rates, and hierarchy properties because of the inequality of their members in behavior and achievement. He explains the great variation in human social structures, from the savage customs of the old slave society of Jamaica to the civilized legal codes, folkways, and mores of modern societies as a lack of competition from other species. He observes that due to this "ecological release," humans have been so successful during the past ten thousand years in dominating the environment that any culture can succeed for a time which has internal consistency and maintains reproduction. Human altruism notwithstanding, Wilson fails to account for the major political consequences of the scientific revolution, the increasing likelihood of mass destruction or species decimation with our overkill arsenals of nuclear weapons and biochemical warfare agents.

Wilson's sociobiology has been regarded by many as reactionary in its political implications. A number of other sociobiologists have drawn conservative conclusions regarding sex roles, which have been strongly attacked by feminists. Wilson and his colleague, Lumsden, have come very close to old-fashioned racism in their theory of biological bases of cultural differences among groups. Interestingly enough, Wilson's approach to evolution has been challenged by another type of biological/social research.

According to the dolphin researcher John C. Lilly, our society and science have been human-chauvinist in their orientation and tendency to consider other species inferior in mind and primitive in group relations. Lilly defines our generalized other of human chauvinism as "interspecies deprivation," and we suffer the consequent loneliness of a species with a superiority complex. The symbolically interactive mode of Lilly's research agenda puts him squarely in the Meadian camp, and the biosocial fact that dolphins have large brains and minds gives human beings the opportunity to discover the society and culture of a twenty-five-million-year-old terrestrial life form. The dolphin's major mode of perception of the world is acoustic compared to the visual orientation of the human being. The dolphin has a sophisticated sonar detection system and is able to communicate with other dolphins through a series of clicks, whistles, and buzzes, which Lilly calls "dolphinese."

The research resulting from the emergent, mutually consenting human–dolphin community indicates that the dolphins show the beginnings of understanding a computer-generated vocabulary by responding correctly to sonic cues or tones. Full communication with humans has not yet been achieved, but the establishment of an ongoing symbolic interaction would amplify the dimension of the collective consciousness of humanity into a more expanded *we* feeling and create a context for intraplanetary communication with another intelligent species.

Whatever its outcome, research of this sort shows an alternative to the reductionistic genetic approach of sociobiology. There is a biological dimension to human society, but it may well be that the ecological rather than the genetic side will turn out to be its crucial aspect.

DARWIN'S CONSEQUENCES

The great idea of the late nineteenth century belongs to Darwin. And if its consequences were sometimes frightening, they could also be extremely illuminating. Darwin's vision of humankind in the perspective of animal evolution sets the starting place for a sociology that could finally begin to become a science. It gives us a vantage point, detached from our immediate concerns, from which to see just what it is we should be explaining: the behavior of a smart, hairless monkey, who walks upright and is able to communicate and cooperate in extraordinarily intricate ways. The implications of this vision are carried out by those thinkers referred to in the next section as the makers of the great breakthrough. The symbolic nature of the social world this creature inhabits and the way in which it affects the consciousness of the human animal were to be exposed by Cooley and Mead. Freud was to explore the human animal's instincts and the ways in which they interact and conflict with the pressures of society. Weber was to unravel the complexities of struggle for domination in this human, symbolic world. And Durkheim would grasp the nature of the invisible social structure through the rituals that sustain it. As American social thinkers were complacently refining their technical apparatus for measuring social problems and as Europeans gathered ideological ammunition for a military bloodbath, an intellectual revolution was shaking the world of social thought at its core.

PART II

The Great Breakthrough

CHAPTER SIX

Dreyfus's Empire: Emile Durkheim and Georges Sorel

1898: Paris in turmoil again. The issue: the Dreyfus affair, a scandal in the French army blown up into a political cause célèbre between the contending factions of France. Dreyfus, a Jewish captain in the French army, had been the victim of an effort to cover up a spy scandal. Secret military documents were recovered from the German embassy. The real culprit seemed to have been an aristocratic debauchee named Esterhazy, but the investigation arbitrarily seized on Dreyfus, an outsider to the army tradition, as scapegoat. He was degraded with full ceremonial regalia. Troops lined up on the parade ground, resplendent in gold braid and red-striped trousers; Dreyfus stood at attention while his commander tore the epaulets from his sleeves and his medals from his chest, and broke his sword across the knee. The dishonored Dreyfus was sent off to the inhuman labor colony at Devil's Island, and the army, its honor restored, returned to its arms race with the enemy across the Rhine.

But the case would not stay covered up. Emile Zola, the most famous novelist of France, penned a famous open letter to the president of the republic. *"J'accuse!"* it began, and it charged the government with deliberate complicity in a miscarriage of justice. Zola was himself arrested and tried for crime against the state. The trial aroused the nation, both left and right; crowds fought outside the courtroom. Zola's ringing speeches had no effect on the court, a sort of Warren Commission of its day; he was found guilty and sentenced to prison. He escaped to England, where he continued to rally the cause. The scandal could not be contained by the ritual of the courtroom. Ministers were forced to resign, fights broke out in the Assembly, students battled in the streets. There were more trials as the army took its revenge on an officer who had dared question the nonexistent evidence against Dreyfus. Unfortunately for the army, the evidence in the new trial was exposed as a forgery. The conservatives had gone too far, and their enemies closed in ruthlessly. The army, the Catholic Church, the wealthy bourgeoisie, and the peasants all fell back under the pressures of a revengeful left—the anticlerical civil servants, teachers, students, and workers.

The victory proved short-lived. The conservatives eventually benefited from a mood of reaction to the changes proposed by the victorious liberals, a series of confrontations with Germany brought chauvinism back to the fore, and France settled down again from the acute to the chronic phase of social conflict. The battles would all be fought again, many times, throughout the decades to come.

The students of the University of Paris were in the center of the battle as it dragged on through the first decade of the twentieth century, and some of their professors were rallying points of the Dreyfusard cause. Battles between radicals and conservatives often raged in the streets of the Latin Quarter, and the students were organized in an elaborate system of shock troops, spies, and messengers on bicycles to alert their fellows when a conservative gang tried to break up the lectures of popular republican professors. Among the most eminent of these professors, the holder of the first chair of sociology ever established at the French university, was Emile Durkheim (1858–1917), one of the intellectual giants of modern times.

Durkheim's sociology, more than any other, began to make sense of the events that swirled around him: the heavy silence of the parade ground as Dreyfus's epaulets were stripped off, the impact of Zola on the stand at his rigged trial, the waves of public hysteria breaking across France, now in one direction, now in another. Durkheim penetrated these events with a vision of the nature of society that revealed what the rationalist thinkers of the nineteenth century could not see: Society is a ritual order, a collective conscience founded on the emotional rhythms of human interaction. At the peak of scientific and industrial progress, Durkheim broke through into the intellectual world of the twentieth century and its deepest problem: the nonrational foundations of rationality.

DURKHEIM: THE DIVISION OF LABOR IN SOCIETY

Durkheim's basic concern was the instability, violence, and decadence of modern society, at least as it displayed itself in France. The optimistic predictions by Comte and Spencer of continual progress in industrial society had not come true. But Durkheim could not accept the Marxist idea that the modern industrial division of labor is inherently self-contradictory and self-destructive or the conservative idea that we must return to the old order of religion and authority. Durkheim was a bourgeois liberal, a self-conscious member of the rationalistic educational bureaucracy, neither a radical nor a conservative. He identified with the French Third Republic, which had succeeded Napoleon III's Second Empire after the disastrous war with Prussia in 1870. He was a modernist and nationalist, an ardent believer in science and in republican France. He took as his task to defend the modern division of labor without being a naïve optimist. The purpose of sociology was to explain how to make modern society work.

Durkheim was also an ambitious man. He was born the son of a Jewish rabbi in a province of eastern France and made his way to the elite Ecole Normale Supérieure in Paris by his high intelligence and hard work in the competitive exams. The Ecole was the training ground for teachers and scientists. Most graduates went to the schools of the provinces; the best captured the few prominent positions in Paris. Durkheim's chances lay in the realm of social science, and he played his cards well. In 1885 he paid a visit to the laboratory of Wilhelm Wundt in Germany, who had just created the science of experimental psychology out of an old philosophical field of speculation. But psychology in France was overshadowed by conservative crowd psychologists like Gabriel Tarde and Gustave Le Bon. Durkheim, instead, adopted the sociology of Comte and Spencer, which emphasized a realm of phenomena above the psychological level. Here one could create a science of social order and could defend the republic and industrial society. The only problem was that sociology remained largely speculative, as well as intellectually naïve. Durkheim set out to do for it what Wundt had done for psychology: to take it out of philosophy and establish it on the research methods of empirical science. The strategy was sound, and Durkheim's brilliance made it work. By 1902 Durkheim was back from the provinces and teaching his new science at the Ecole Normale. The modern era in sociology had begun.

Bald, bespectacled, wispy-bearded, intensely serious, Durkheim applied himself to sociology with rabbinical devotion. His fellow students at the Ecole had called him "the metaphysician." His logical mind turned itself to the task of finding a scientific basis for social order. His fundamental hypothesis came from Comte—the basis of society is a moral order. His first great work, *The Division of Labor in Society* (1893), attacks the problem rigorously from several angles.

First, Durkheim gives a deductive argument. Society cannot exist simply by rational agreement, he states, because agreements are not possible unless each partner trusts the other to live up to them. Think of economic contracts, which Spencer and the utilitarians and economists before him thought of as the basis for modern social cooperation: I'll agree to work for you for a week, if you'll agree to pay me out of the proceeds of this work at the end of the week. But notice: We are agreeing not only to exchange labor for pay; we are also agreeing to uphold the agreement. The second agreement is implicit rather than conscious, but it is absolutely crucial. Without this implicit mutual trust, no specific contracts would be possible; for if this trust does not exist, the truly rational individual will not live up to his or her contracts. If I trust you but you break the contract, then you have a week of work from me for nothing. On the other hand, if you trust me and I break the contract, I can perhaps collect a week's pay for little or no work. In the absence of mutual trust, then, the rational individual will never live up to his or her contracts and will never trust others to live up to theirs. Modern game theory would put it as shown in the accompanying table. The rational choice for both game players is always to cheat, since each then stands a chance of winning everything (if the other follows the contract), and at least they will not lose anything (if both cheat). To follow the contract without being sure that the other player will follow it too is to risk losing everything for a moderate gain.

What this proves, says Durkheim, is that a "precontractual solidarity" must exist before contracts can be depended upon. The facts seem to bear out his analysis. In a factory in which boss and employees do not trust each other, the boss must spend all his time making sure that his employees are working, and his employees do their best to get as much pay as possible for the least amount of work. Sheer economic rationality reduces cooperation to the amount that can be produced by immediate control of one party over the other. On the other hand, tremendously productive cooperation is possible if everyone identifies with a common goal.

This is Durkheim's logical argument that society is based on a common moral order rather than on rational self-interest. The "social contract" of Thomas Hobbes, Jean-Jacques Rousseau, and others is thus revealed to be an impossible fiction; contracts are only possible after society has been established, not before.

An objection that might be advanced is that people live up to their contracts because they are forced to. If a man does not pay me for my work, I can sue him, and the state will force him to pay. This argument is open to the reply that governments have only recently in history come to enforce contracts for private citizens and that exchange before that had to be built up on some other basis. Moreover, Durkheim argues, the state itself exists only because people have banded together and agreed upon certain ways of exercising force; the king did not rule because he personally was stronger than everyone else put together, but because he led a group of followers. The collective use of force, then, depends just as much on a prior solidarity as anything else does.

What creates this fundamental solidarity, then? It is not an intellectual agreement, says Durkheim, but a shared emotional feeling. People in society have a "collective conscience" (or "collective consciousness," since the work in French means both these things): a sense of belonging to a commu-

		B	
		Follows contract	**Cheats**
A	**Follows contract**	Both share gain.	B wins everything. A loses everything.
	Cheats	A wins everything. B loses everything.	No one wins or loses anything.

nity with others and hence feeling a moral obligation to live up to its demands. We share feelings of right and wrong, and these are inseparable from our feelings of belonging to a group, whether it be the human race, one's country, or one's family. The collective conscience does not mean that there is a group mind hanging over our heads, but rather that people have feelings of belonging to a group.

Where do these moral feelings come from? Durkheim proposes that they come from forms of social interaction between individuals, especially in ways that we would now call "rituals." Roughly, he proposes the principle (taken from the crowd psychology of his day) that as people come together and focus their attention on a common object, thoughts and feelings passing back and forth among them become strengthened until they take on a supraindividual force and seem to be detached from the individuals themselves. Thus, the members of a crowd watching a flag being raised and singing a national anthem together focus their attention on these objects and, knowing that others are focusing their attentions too, they come to feel that they are in the presence of a principle or force greater than any of them individually—the nation. Ideas held in common thus become transformed into a world of their own, the world of moral norms.

If moral feelings are the result of social interactions, Durkheim can apply and test his theory in another way. He can go to the historical evidence and see if moral norms change as the result of changes in social conditions. This second argument, an empirical one, makes up the bulk of *The Division of Labor*.

As an indicator of moral norms, Durkheim uses laws. Laws are not a precise indicator of the moral feelings of a society, he says, since they may lag behind or run ahead of public sentiments; but they give at least a general indication of how people conceive of right and wrong. There are two kinds of laws: criminal laws and civil-administrative laws. Criminal laws express a strong state of the collective conscience, for they provide that an individual who disobeys society's law incurs society's anger and must be punished. Looking back through history, Durkheim points out that this collective conscience must have been very strong indeed, for it often prescribes violent punishments for violations of taboos, even when the violations do not involve harm to persons or property. On the other hand, civil and administrative laws express a much milder sense of community conscience, since they carry very different penalties. Whereas criminal laws call for punishment regardless of what damage has been done, civil laws call only for offenders to make amends for what they have done: If they have failed to pay, they must pay up; if they hold someone else's property, they must give it over. On the one hand, the law demands *retribution*; on the other merely *restitution*.

Durkheim then shows that the proportion of these kinds of laws has changed with the type of society. In smaller, earlier societies, most law was *retributive*, punishing almost all offenses with torture, mutilation, or execution. In the larger, modern societies law becomes mostly *restitutive*. Not only do the pages of the law books come to be made up largely of civil-administrative laws, but also there is an absolute decline in the number of things that penal laws control and a diminution in the severity of the punishments.

The connection between these societies and their laws, Durkheim finds, is the changing division of labor. Retributive law is found mostly in societies with little division of labor, restitutive law mostly in those with a high division of labor. The former societies are based on what Durkheim calls "mechanical solidarity." By this he means that in a tribal or peasant society like the Hebrew tribes of the Old Testament (which he had studied thoroughly), most people are like each other. Almost everyone is a farmer or a warrior. Accordingly, there is a very strong collective conscience, since people have many ideas in common from their common experiences. Any violations of this collective conscience find crushing punishment from the laws; the individual, being like others, is given no leeway to depart from their collective practices. The individual is integrated mechanically and by force.

Societies with a high division of labor, on the other hand, Durkheim refers to as bound together by "organic solidarity." People have a great variety of different occupations; they come into contact only because the worker, the farmer, the shopkeeper, the carpenter, the engineer, and so on exchange services with each other through a complex economic market. People experience very different life circumstances and thus have much less in common with each other. But they do acquire some knowledge of each other's viewpoints by repeatedly coming in contact with others while making exchanges; hence a newer, milder form of collective conscience appears. This is expressed in the restitutive laws that regulate civic commerce, which provide only enough social control to keep the complex society operating and do not impose the collective outrage of the whole community on violators of a private contract touching only a few individuals. Durkheim calls this organic solidarity because it is the exchanges themselves, like those between the different organs of a body, which provide the basis of collective belonging.

The historical argument bolsters Durkheim's deductive argument about the necessity of precontractual solidarity. Not only must nonrational solidarity come first logically, but it does in fact come first in history. As Durkheim had learned from his teacher Fustel de Coulanges, ancient civilizations like those of Greece and Rome grew up on the basis of religious rituals that regulated virtually every aspect of everyday life; the rational economic contracts came later, after the society already existed. Nor does the collective conscience disappear after the modern division of labor is set up; it merely changes its form. Thus, societies begin in small groups that maintain order through a strong and repressive collective conscience. As societies grow, a larger population presses down on the available resources for living, and individuals begin to specialize. The division of labor begins to grow more and more complex. Thus, some individuals become different from others they come into contact with and are bound together through economic and political ties across longer distances. The collective conscience has fewer things to build upon, for there are fewer things that all members of a society have in common. Its contents gradually become more abstract. Rather than sanctioning specific local customs and taboos, it begins to uphold only the more general and abstract principles of fairness, justice, honesty, and so on. The collective conscience becomes simultaneously less powerful and more principled; its tone is less violent and more humanitarian. Durkheim thus manages to give a theoretical explanation of the phenomenon that both Comte and Tocqueville had noticed without being able to explain: that the scope of human sympathy expands with the progress of civilization.

All in all, Durkheim hoped with this demonstration to prove that modern society is good. A complex division of labor is inherently orderly, for it contains within it its own moral principles. The decline of traditional religion is nothing to worry about; on the contrary, the modern morality that replaces it is more humanitarian and tolerant. The complex division of labor creates individualism, since people must follow specialized life patterns of their own, but there is nothing to fear from individualism, for it does not mean that individuals no longer have any social ties. On the contrary, individualism is socially produced and expresses only the way individuals relate to each other through exchanges, rather than via the repressive similarity of mechanical solidarity.

As we shall see, Durkheim was not entirely successful in arguing that all is basically well with the modern division of labor, and he kept returning to the subject again and again as his researches kept turning up evidence that could just as well be interpreted to mean that modern society is self-destructive. But Durkheim was not yet through with his main theoretical task: to show how moral feelings of solidarity underlie social order. To his logical and historical arguments, he added an empirical proof based on observations of the society around him.

The collective conscience is a social fact, says Durkheim. And indeed, you can experience it yourself when you are in a group. It is a feeling of contact with something outside yourself that does not depend precisely on any one person there, but which everyone participates in together. "An atmosphere so thick you could cut it with a knife." What can produce such a feeling? For Durkheim, examples were all around in the still-smouldering political tradition of France: the tense stillness surrounding Dreyfus on the parade ground, the vengeful excitement of the crowd at the guillotine. What provided the power of these collective situations was that people were gathered, focusing their attention on the same thing, and generating a contagious emotion. From these extreme and powerful instances of a collective conscience existing where people play the role of the Public at its most awesome, we may see a continuum that shades down through the shared moods of football crowds and theater audiences to parties, committee meetings, and finally to the most casual conversations.

The stronger states of collective feeling are the easiest to notice; the subtler ones we take for granted. But for every case Durkheim provides a method by which a state of collective conscience can be made clearly observable: You know a social norm is there because you encounter resistance to violating it. The sentiments behind minor rules of politeness and deference show themselves most clearly in the uneasiness that occurs when someone breaks them; the invisible barrier of social conventions is never so apparent as when someone utters an obscenity at a polite gathering. The standards of just what the polite rules are can change between different times and between different groups, of course. But where the norms are strong, whatever they happen to be, the invisible order of a collective conscience can be clearly seen. This was all the more noticeable in the heavy formalities of nineteenth-century bourgeois France.

Deviance and Social Solidarity

Durkheim was especially interested, then, in acts of deviance, because it was here that society's norms could be seen most clearly in operation. Crimes and their punishments, he felt, were among the central features of a society. When one man commits a crime—a murder or a rape, for example—there is a widespread sense of public outrage, shared by people far beyond those who are personally damaged or threatened by the criminal. People show their nonrational, non-self-interested attachment to society in general by their reactions to events that have nothing to do with themselves personally. The fact that this is not a feeling of personal interests is shown when the same sort of public outrage occurs over purely symbolic issues, in which no one is damaged at all—for example, cases of public obscenity (the showing of a nude play or movie would be a modern example) or symbolic political acts, like Zola's letter to the French president. What is violated, in all these cases, is not someone's personal interests but the collective conscience itself. A ritual order has been defamed, and ritual punishment is necessary to restore its purity. This is why there is so much public concern with ceremonies of punishment such as court trials and executions. It also helps explain why there is so much sentiment favoring capital punishment, in the face of overwhelming evidence that it has no deterrent effect on crimes of violence: The punishment serves a ritual function, not a practical one, and hence it is supported by people who attach themselves to a certain kind of ritual order.

Durkheim even went so far as to argue that crime is functional for holding society together. Without crimes there would be no ceremonies of punishment; and without such periodic ceremonies to bring people together in a ritual reaffirmation of their solidarity, society would gradually fall apart. The argument is overstated to make the point, of course. Durkheim himself later pointed out that there are positive rituals as well as negative ones, which also serve to create a sense of solidarity. The rituals of church services, patriotic holidays, and even family festivities like birthday parties all serve this function. The entire functionalist school in anthropology follows up on Durkheim's basic insight. Thus, Marcel Mauss (Durkheim's nephew), Arthur Radcliffe-Brown, Bronislaw Malinowski, Claude Lévi-Strauss, and others have shown how marriage ceremonies, funerals, rites of passage, and gift exchanges all function to reaffirm social bonds especially when the bonds are disturbed by the loss or gain of a member in a group. In sociology W. Lloyd Warner and Erving Goffman have made the most important applications of Durkheim's perspective to the rituals of modern American society.

Durkheim went still further in his study of deviance and solidarity. In addition to his general observations, he produced a study of statistical data which remains a model for scientific research in sociology. This was his great work *Suicide,* published in 1897. Durkheim was not entirely original here. He drew on a tradition that went back to the 1830s, when the Belgian statistician Adolphe Quételet pointed out that the rates of births, deaths, marriages, murders, suicides, and so on remained fairly constant from year to year, even though each of these rates was the result of many independent individual actions. Quételet thus argued for the existence of a realm of social facts independent of the individual and proposed a science, which he labeled "social physics," to explain these facts. But Quételet was only a statistician, and he came up with no explanation beyond a notion of an "average person" who is likely to act in given ways. This line of research was ready-made for Durkheim, for it dealt with acts of deviance—especially suicide—for which he did have a sociological theory. He now had an opportunity to test his theory in a rigorously scientific way.

Suicide was the first really good piece of large-scale data analysis in sociology. Throughout, Durkheim applied the basic methodological principle of all good research: If you want to know the cause of something, look for *the conditions under which it occurs* and compare them with *the conditions under which it does not occur.* This is akin to Durkheim's principle of how to observe social norms by looking for the cases where they are violated. Behind both principles is the strategy of understanding through opposition: Explanations are revealed by contrast and comparison. It is this principle that was behind the insights of Tocqueville as he compared France and America, and it continues to provide the basis for virtually all important advances in modern sociology.

Durkheim, for example, began with the popular theory that suicides are due to individual psychopathology. This was the sort of explanation he wanted to dispose of, since he was engaged in an academic battle for recognition in which psychologists were his major competitors, and he wanted to show that social factors are on a separate and more important level of explanation. In short, Durkheim was opposed to psychological reductionism, which saw events only through the actions of individuals instead of penetrating to the social conditions that moved the individuals. He attacked the psychopathology theory of suicide by comparing the regions of Europe having the highest suicide rates with those having medium and low suicide rates and then showing that there was no correlation between rates of suicide and rates of psychopathology. In a similar fashion he tested other popular theories that attributed suicide to ethnicity, climate, or geography. In each case Durkheim showed that on close examination the variations in ethnic composition, average temperature, and so on did not correspond to variations in the suicide rate.

Having disposed of these competing explanations, Durkheim proceeded to advance his own. The suicide rate did vary by social condition, he found. For example, Protestants had higher suicide rates than Catholics, who in turn had higher rates than Jews. This could not be explained just by differences in theology, Durkheim argued. If Catholicism made suicide a more serious sin than did Protestantism, Judaism nevertheless made no special prohibition of suicide and yet had the lowest suicide rate. The difference among these religious groups, rather, was in the social environments they provided for their members. Judaism was the most close-knit religious community, Protestantism the least, with Catholicism intermediate in surrounding the individual with a round of ritual activities. In general, Durkheim argued, the more tightly integrated into society the individual is, the more he is prevented from committing suicide.

Durkheim backed up this interpretation by looking at further variations within these categories. In every religious group most suicides are among men, since women have the greatest day-to-day religious participation and are more tightly integrated into the close community of the family. Among the Protestant churches, the Anglicans had the lowest suicide rate, and they were the most ritualistic and Catholic-like of the Protestant denominations. Durkheim went on to point out, rather ingeniously, that the regions of Europe with the highest levels of education have the highest suicide rates, except among Jews. This corroborated the general argument that the lack of social integration caused suicide, since education was an indication of a secularized, individualistic, nonreligious society except among Jews, for whom education of laypeople had been a key part of the religious tradition.

From different angles Durkheim corroborated his general theory: Society is what gives meaning to individual lives; it is when individuals are cut off from society that they kill themselves. Not only did the evidence on religion point to these conclusions, but also the fact that suicide rates declined in times of war, revolution, or other periods of great social crisis that drew everyone together into a common sentiment. The evidence also showed that married persons were less likely to kill themselves than unmarried persons; that widowhood and divorce increased the chances of suicide, but that this was mitigated the more children there were remaining. The more social bonds surrounding an individual, the less the chance of suicide; the fewer the bonds, the more danger of self-destruction. From all of this emerged one of Durkheim's key concepts: the idea of a state of "anomie" or lack of norms that give a clear direction and purpose to the individual's actions. In this concept Durkheim sums up a major cause of the ills of modern society.

Durkheim's *Suicide* is a classic work, and it survives as a model of how to use empirical analysis to corroborate a general theory. It does have various shortcomings. The data are not entirely reliable, and there were mistakes in the analysis. Moreover, Durkheim did not fully explain suicides. After all, not everyone who is Protestant commits suicide, even if he or she is unmarried, highly educated, and so on. The full explanation of any individual case of suicide must involve just the kind of psychological factors that Durkheim wanted to exclude. But Durkheim was less interested in providing an exhaustive explanation of suicides than in showing that social integration and social anomie have important effects on the individual's behavior. He was less interested in suicide itself than in what it can tell us about the structure of society.

Suicide remains an important book in the history of social thought, whether it is precisely valid or not. It not only helps to support Durkheim's general analysis of the importance of ritual interaction for social solidarity, but it also lays down the model for sociology as a science: to treat general theoretical principles in terms of variables and thus to test them by systematic comparison with the supposed causal conditions. Durkheim thus moved from the methods of nineteenth-century speculation to the sophisticated analysis of the twentieth century.

Religion and Reality

These might seem enough major contributions for one man, but Durkheim was not through yet. He organized the first French sociological journal, the *Année sociologique,* and around it a school of researchers to carry on the new tradition. Out of this group came a major school in modern anthropology, which constituted Durkheim's main following in France. Durkheim himself became increasingly interested in ethnographic reports on primitive tribes, some of which material he analyzed in collaboration with his nephew Marcel Mauss, who had done much of the statistical compilations for *Suicide.* In 1912, a few years before his death, Durkheim published his final work, perhaps the greatest single book of the twentieth century. It was entitled *The Elementary Forms of the Religious Life.*

In this work Durkheim carried through to another level the revolution in our view of reality begun by Karl Marx. Every class has its own view of reality, its own consciousness, Marx had argued. Durkheim went even further, to demonstrate the social relativity of even our most general and taken-for-granted ideas. Time, space, causality, God, the self—all these could now be seen as creations of society. In place of the old absolutist view of reality "out there," Durkheim shows us that the natural world is only a backdrop for the symbolic creations of humans and their social rituals. As we have come to see through the applications of this perspective by Erving Goffman and other recent sociologists, there is not one reality by many, and they exist only by virtue of being enacted by human beings.

Durkheim carried out this revolution in our perspectives by analyzing data on the aboriginal tribes of Australia, plus some other tribal societies, in an effort to understand the basis of religion. But since religion was all-pervasive in the worldviews of these peoples, Durkheim had an opportunity to explain the basic modes of thought in a society.

He began by trying to define religion. What is it that all religions have in common? Not the idea of gods or spirits, since religions such as Buddhism and Confucianism lack these. Not the idea of a supernatural realm set apart from the world of nature, since primitive societies have not developed the idea of a realm of nature and hence make no such distinction. In fact, says Durkheim, we cannot find the key to religion in the realm of ideas at all. The only thing that all religions contain is a set of "sacred objects" that are set off from all other objects and toward which humans must act with ritual care. Ritual objects in Christianity, for example, include Bibles, altars, rosaries, holy water, and consecrated bread and wine; in the aboriginal tribes that Durkheim analyzed the main sacred object was the tribal totem. A totem is an animal, such as a fox, snake, grub-worm, or kangaroo, which tribe members are forbidden to kill or eat; and periodic ceremonies are held in which the tribe comes together to pay respect to this sacred object.

It is impossible to understand this treatment of a totem from a practical point of view, says Durkheim, but if one views it socially, its significance becomes obvious. The totem functions to hold the tribe together. Without it, there would be no tribal unit at all, for it is by sharing a common totem that its members identify with each other. The totem is thus the basis of kinship and of social membership. The whole tribe is assembled only at the periodic totem ceremonies, and it is at these rituals that its members create and re-create the sense of emotional solidarity that Durkheim had argued was so important for social order. The totem thus creates a social and moral order. Since it is forbidden to kill the totem animal, it is also forbidden to kill those who name themselves after the totem, one's fellow tribesmen. The totem, in effect, symbolizes the society and its moral demands on the individual.

In the same way, one can see more modern religions as functioning primarily to maintain a moral community. The church service of a nineteenth-century American village, for example, brought the community together once a week—perhaps the only time the community regularly assembled. The rituals of the service, from the reading of the sacred book to collective hymns and prayers, functioned to create a feeling of moral order. In general, Durkheim argues, the moral commandments of a religion—its Golden Rule, Ten Commandments, restrictions on self-indulgence in the pleasures of the flesh—are fundamentally *social* rules. They regulate humans' behavior toward each other and serve to keep up the sense of social unity and restraint on self-interest that make society possible.

Why do people live up to such moral rules, at least to some degree? Not really because of fear of supernatural sanctions like heaven and hell or of the sacred power of the totem; these rationalizations for religious customs come and go, but the power of social controls remains. Rather, suggests Durkheim, it is because the supernatural sanctions *symbolize* society and its acceptance or rejection of the individual. The people who live up to the

moral commandments and participate wholeheartedly in the religious rituals get a great feeling of solidarity with the countless generations who make
up their society, and they represent this feeling to themselves as being
"saved." Those who break the rules and avoid the rituals cut themselves off
from this feeling of belonging and suffer the consequences of their own self-
centeredness. As theologians put it, to be cut off from God is the sinner's
self-inflicted punishment. Durkheim would agree, but with the added sociological proviso: God is only a symbol for society.

Durkheim thus brings to a close a chapter that began in the Enlightenment with the attack of science on religion. But religion must be more than
superstition and error, Durkheim had pointed out, for how could it have
survived so long if it were only this? Durkheim at last enables us to understand beliefs about the supernatural, by showing them for what they really
are: symbols generated by social behavior that is at the core of every society. God is revealed to be not exactly what believers think, but something
real nevertheless: the collective conscience of a community. And if this collective conscience changes its symbolizations from the sacred totem animals
to more universal gods, until finally even the remote Christian God with his
transcendental heaven and hell disappears into the memories of the past,
this is only what we would expect from Durkheim's earlier demonstration,
in *The Division of Labor*, that a society's moral order changes with its social
structure. Sacred objects like totems, altars, and books are only displaced by
new sacred objects like flags, which represent the worship of the state. By
implication, much that seems bizarre in the behavior of avowedly atheistic
and materialistic Russian and Chinese Communists becomes clearer when
we see that communism has been organized as a political religion, now split
between competing orthodoxies. In general, Durkheim's theory proposes
that the historical trend is toward a more and more abstract and general
collective conscience; concrete symbols of God disappear into a generalized
moral belief about the brotherhood of humanity.

Durkheim's sociology of knowledge thus manages to explain humans',
fundamental religious ideas in terms of their social interactions. In addition,
Durkheim shows that society determines even the basic categories of our
thought. We live in a world of time and space, but how we conceive that
time and space is socially determined. It is Friday; it is eleven o'clock in the
morning; it is the year 1992: Implicitly this puts me in a world held in common by most other people in our clock-watching, post-Christian civilization. But there is nothing *absolute* about these units. There is no reason that
time must necessarily be broken up into seven-day weeks or twenty-four-
hour days; we could just as well have ten-day weeks or no weeks or hours
at all (as is the case with many primitive tribes). We divide time into units
only because we need to coordinate our activities with others in our complex modern civilization, not because hours and weeks really constitute the
framework of nature. But as we continually act upon them, these units become part of the framework of our minds, and we make them subjectively
into an absolute reality. In just this way, society implicitly furnishes the

bases of our worldviews. The year A.D. 1992 puts us directly in the context of a *Christian* view of history, since the anno Domini orients us in relation to the year 1 of the mythical birth of Christ. The Chinese, whose calendar would stand at the year 4690, inhabit a fundamentally different historical universe.

Time concepts, Durkheim shows, derive first of all from the scheduling of religious ceremonies. Space, causality, number—all these abstract ideas can also be traced to social origins and continuing social uses. Space is the area the tribe inhabits; this has grown immensely from the wanderings of aborigines in the Australian desert, through the voyages of Columbus and Magellan, but it still has a basic social meaning for us, as the effects of space travel on our thought about the universe continue to illustrate. Our fundamental concepts all grow from a social matrix in a similar way, and our very idea of objective knowledge ultimately refers to things that we can reliably communicate to others. Durkheim tears away another illusion that keeps us from seeing the world as it is: We mistake our socially given images of reality for the reality itself. Only by seeing the social relativity of our ideas are we on the path to understanding ourselves.

It is a powerful intellectual performance that Durkheim puts on, indeed one of the most impressive of modern times. But what about the social issues with which he began, the effort to cure the social strife of modern France? Here Durkheim was less successful. He tried to use sociological functionalism as a basis for a scientific diagnosis of society's ills: not to impose any particular values on how society should operate, but to ascertain the "healthy" state of the social organism and thereby to understand its "diseases." He tried to show that a modern division of labor is basically healthy and well integrated and that when it is not, it must be because of special conditions. Thus Durkheim believed that strikes, political conflict, and labor violence were forms of the "abnormal" division of labor. But he was never able to propose a clear solution. His theory told him that the problem must lie in a lack of sufficient integration of the individual into the moral order of a social community, and in his famous *Preface* to the second edition of *The Division of Labor*, Durkheim proposed that the lack of solidarity could be cured by organizing individuals into occupational guilds.

The solution was not convincing, for there is no reason to believe that such occupational communities would not continue to conflict with each other. Durkheim's main shortcoming was that he never came to grips with the existence of stratification and the realities of political conflict; he concentrated on the bases of social solidarity to the extent that his image of society excluded all nonsolidarity features. Durkheim would have been more successful in his search for political solutions if he had followed Tocqueville's lead on how political organizations can intensify conflict or limit it.

In general, Durkheim's optimistic argument that modern industrial society is *normally* well integrated is not convincing. His own theories tend to refute it. If humans are emotional animals who derive their sense of purpose from the rituals they perform with others, then the gradual suppression of emotions and the elimination of ritual in our highly bureaucratic society should produce considerable malaise. Such, in fact, were the more pessimistic conclusions of Weber and Freud. Although Durkheim did not want to draw this conclusion, his evidence on anomic suicide resulting from the loosening of ritual social bonds supports a pessimistic interpretation.

THE REVOLUTIONARY PHILOSOPHY OF GEORGES SOREL

One of Durkheim's compatriots drew the implications better than he did. This was Georges Sorel (1847–1922), a retired engineer, whose values and politics were as far removed from Durkheim's as possible, although both men held each other in considerable respect. Sorel was an acquaintance, among others, of V. I. Lenin, Benito Mussolini, and Fritz Ebert (the Socialist who became the first president of Germany after World War I). His politics seemed an equally bizarre flux, from monarchism on the far right to anarcho-syndicalism on the far left. But there was a basic principle underlying Sorel's shifting political sympathies. He regarded modern society as completely decadent, lacking in any real virtue, dedication, or brilliance. He despised the petty squabbling of the academics, and saw the business world as entirely self-seeking and corrupt and politicians as equally contemptible. The failure of the Socialists to take a stand on the burning moral issue of the Dreyfus affair at the time when Zola was putting his life on the docket convinced Sorel that the organized left was equally decadent. By 1907, when he wrote *Reflections on Violence*, Sorel had come to identify with ultrarevolutionary anarcho-syndicalism.

Reflections on Violence takes up the anarcho-syndicalist idea that a general strike of all workers will someday bring down bourgeois society and usher in the new era of the revolution. This revolution, says Sorel, is a myth. It will never be, for society after the revolution would not be greatly changed, and in any case the chances of victory are nil. But—and here is where Sorel parts company with most other "practical" thinkers—the myth of the general strike nevertheless serves a purpose. It unifies the group of workers and gives them a feeling of participating in a moral cause. In the same way, violence has an important value, for it unifies individuals in a struggle for their common ideals and against their common enemies. In modern society, says Sorel, only social movements in battle have this high moral tone, a sense of joyous spontaneity as individuals feel themselves dedicated to something greater and higher than themselves. For this reason, such revolutionary movements are the only source of value today, even if they are doomed to fail. It is not the actual goal that counts, but the feelings that go along with struggling to attain it in the company of others.

Sorel throws light on the appeal of violence in modern society, although his analysis applies just as well to nonviolent movements. The civil-rights movement and its succeeding peace and student movements of the mid-1960s often had much of the sense of euphoria among their participants that Sorel describes as the main value of such movements. And if these movements have generally failed to bring about their goals, that does not make them any the less worthwhile. Sorel's lesson foreshadows later existentialist insights: that in a world of dilemmas and well-entrenched injustices, the value of an action is to be judged less by consequences than by its intrinsic rightness.

Sorel has always been a puzzling figure, since his point of view lends itself to many interpretations. Sorel himself defended the Communist revolution in Russia, while Mussolini praised him as a source of Italian fascism. But Sorel was not really a Fascist. He did not want a society that tries to impose an imitation of old-fashioned order by brutal suppression; his values, rather, were for the spirit of perpetual movement. More than anything else, Sorel was a true anarchist. And whatever the political implications that could be drawn from his work, Sorel clearly pointed out two characteristic phenomena of modern society: its emotional starvation and the irrelevance of its ideals to workaday reality. This was more than Durkheim allowed himself to see, although he spent most of his life probing the conditions of the same feelings of solidarity.

Durkheim wanted very strongly to believe in something, and in the end it cost him his life. World War I turned his ardent French nationalism into a paroxysm of anti-German sentiment. When his son André was killed at the front, defending the flag that Durkheim considered the modern version of the most sacred object, Durkheim went into a depression that culminated in 1917 in his death. It was not the first time that an individual's insights, so valuable to others, had gone unused by himself.

CHAPTER SEVEN

Max Weber: The Disenchantment of the World

Max Weber (1864–1920) has exerted more influence than any other social scientist except Marx and Freud. His ideas had wide currency, first in Germany and then throughout the scholarly world. His term "charismatic leadership" has passed into general usage, and all of social science knows something of the concepts of legitimacy, bureaucracy, rationalization, *verstehen*, ideal types, value-free science, the three-dimensional approach to stratification, and the Protestant ethic with its links to the origins of capitalism. Yet Weber's general sociology and his vision of world history are as yet barely known; they remain hidden behind isolated selections and popularizations, and we are continually surprised as more and more powerful portions of Weber's worldview are brought into the light. Weber himself is partly to blame. His works are voluminous but unfinished and scarcely succinct, and even a superficial acquaintance with them turns up notions of such utility that one is tempted to inquire no further. In recent years, as the fuller discovery and development of his sociology go on, Weber increases his hold on our attention. The most commanding figure of the great period of German social scholarship, Weber still towers over the world scene more than seventy years after his death.

Like many other great sociologists, Weber (pronounced "Vay-ber") was a man at the center of things, pulled loose from illusion by constant exposure to contradictory points of view. Born in 1864 into a prosperous family of German industrialists, he grew up in Berlin where his father was a judge and a successful politician. Backstage acquaintance with the *realpolitik* of Bismarck's empire made Weber a political realist from his childhood. His father sat in the Reichstag with the National Liberals, representing the interests of the big manufacturers and standing between the Junker aristocracy on the right and the Social Democrats (socialist labor unionists) on the left. It was not a propitious time for liberals in Germany (indeed, it rarely ever was, except during the short-lived revolution of 1848). The landowning aristocracy and the army took a rigid stand against democracy, and the Socialists preached revolution according to Karl Marx. The liberals had no one to turn to except the state bureaucracy, and their ideals went down the drain as their nationalism increasingly became their only political resource. From an early age Weber scorned the unrealistic claims of left and right, but found himself increasingly uncomfortable with the center. Throughout his life an ardent nationalist, he nevertheless saw Germany blundering steadily into a war that would destroy it. His sociology confirmed his fears of imminent disaster, and Weber came to see himself as a twentieth-century Jeremiah, prophesying doom.

He began a career like his father's, studying law at Heidelberg and Berlin. But his pessimism about politics and his own overpowering urge to exercise his independent intellect steered him into an academic career. Germany in the nineteenth century led the world in the eminence of its universities. It was especially prominent in the historical fields. It had been here that Leopold von Ranke and Friedrich von Savigny transformed history from the status of antiquarian chronicles into a science, with its canon to tell things "as they really were." With German thoroughness, the Herr Professor Doktors had produced detailed accounts not only in conventional military and political history but also in economic, legal, and cultural history and in archaeology, ethnography, and linguistics. German philosophy, too, since the days of Hegel had a strong historical flavor. Weber trained himself in virtually all these fields, with the result that his knowledge of world history probably exceeded that of any other person who had ever lived.

In an age of growing specialization Weber's feat was the mark of an extraordinary individualist. But Weber was nothing if not extraordinary. Tall, stout, black-bearded, and moody, he impressed all who met him. His colleagues viewed him as a towering intellect. At the end of Weber's doctoral exam Theodor Mommsen, the most eminent historian of his day, rose and said that he knew of no man better qualified to succeed him "than the highly esteemed Max Weber." But Weber stood in an intellectual circle even wider than the world of German historians and philosophers. At his father's house he had met the eminent politicians and academicians of Berlin. In his own house at Heidelberg the leading intellects in all fields, as well as artists and musicians, met. Among his circle would be found such men as Karl Jaspers (the future existentialist psychiatrist), Ferdinand Toennies, Georg Simmel, and a young radical who could not get a university position despite Weber's intercessions on his behalf, Robert Michels. Weber was fully acquainted with Marxist underground thought. He read many languages, traveled broadly, and knew the English evolutionists and the French positivists as well as the German historians. He was a one-man crucible for the intellectual currents of the nineteenth century, and from his central position he forged a viewpoint for sociology as both a science and a study of meaningful human creations. His twin methods of *verstehen* and ideal types emerged from his position at the center of intellectual crosscurrents: Social reality is not merely to be explained by mechanical analogies to the natural world, but must be understood (in German, *verstehen*) by imagining oneself into the experiences of men and women as they act out their own worlds. Ideal types, as we shall see below, are the tools for making scientific generalizations out of our understanding of this infinitely complex and shifting world.

Sociologists must sympathetically understand the people around them—indeed, also those who have been dead for centuries—and they are bound to feel acutely what is closest to home. Here, too, Weber was at the center of powerful antagonisms. Beneath the surface of a proper German bourgeois family, Weber's father and mother carried on psychic war. His father—harsh, self-righteous, and authoritarian—clashed incessantly with his altruistic, self-denying, and religious mother. Between the two poles Weber may have discerned the remnants of a rigid Protestant ethic whose discovery is his most famous contribution. Certainly Max Weber himself was a prime example of the ethic. Immensely hard working, impeccably honest, dedicated, serious, methodical, he drove himself with an inner vehemence that left him an insomniac for years and dead at the age of fifty-six.

The family conflict finally took its toll. In 1897 when Weber was thirty-three and just beginning his career as a professor of economics at Heidelberg, he became involved in a quarrel while visiting his parents. Years of suppressed bitterness broke through the respectable patrician formalities, and Weber angrily threatened to break off all contact with his father if he did not change his treatment of his mother. Not long after, he heard the news: His father had fallen dead of a stroke.

Depression set in. A powerful, even charismatic, lecturer, Weber found he could no longer teach. When he tried, his arms and back became temporarily paralyzed. He found it difficult to speak; serious thinking was impossible. He took a leave of absence from his job, finally resigning it entirely. He traveled incessantly, yet spent hours in hotel rooms staring at his fingernails. He spent several weeks in a mental institution. The experience opened a new side in him. "Such a disease has its compensations. It has reopened to me the human side of life," he wrote his wife. "An icy hand has let me loose. In years past my diseased disposition expressed itself in a frantic grip upon scientific work, which appeared to me as a talisman. . . ."

Slowly he began to recover, and in 1904 he was back at work. He took a trip to America on an invitation to speak at the St. Louis World's Fair. The loftiness of American ideals and the corruption of American capitalism fired his imagination, and he returned to Germany to finish his first famous work, *The Protestant Ethic and the Spirit of Capitalism*. From then on his production never flagged, although he was unable to bring himself to teach until the end of his life, after the close of World War I. He had lost seven years. The work of the next sixteen has never been surpassed.

Weber's sociology is often obscured behind the maze of crosscutting definitions that make up the opening chapters of *Economy and Society*, his major work. Clear and distinct concepts are essential to make sense out of a subject as complex as the workings of society. But concepts are easiest to grasp if we can see them as they are actually put to use. Weber set himself the task of explaining the greatest development of world history: the rise of modern industrial civilization. In order to do this he had to push his sights progressively back from economics to law, politics, and religion; to chart the interconnections between kinship and stratification, bureaucracy and warfare, until every institution was connected with every other, and the web of explanation stretched from the present to the beginnings of human life on earth. In exploring the question of economic development, Weber created nothing less than a sociology of world history. His contributions to general sociological theory consist of the models he developed in an effort to grasp the key processes of society without doing violence to the complexities of history as it actually occurred. Weber had nothing but contempt for evolutionist or cyclical theories that blindly simplified the facts to fit a few preconceived principles of growth. In his tightrope walk between vague or inaccurate generalizations and the myriad particular forms of world civilization, Weber moved toward a comprehensive theory of humankind's social behavior and of the institutions humankind creates. We shall take up first Weber's general sociology, then his vision of world history.

WEBER'S SOCIOLOGY: STRATIFICATION, ORGANIZATIONS, AND POLITICS

Stratification: Class, Power, and Status

Weber's sociology centers around three interrelated subjects: stratification, organizations, and politics. Of these, stratification provides the core theory of society, to which all else is related and within which may be found the forces that move society. Weber was a thoroughgoing nominalist; for him, real people in real physical places are the subjects and movers of all that exists and happens in society. To be sure, cultural ethos (such as the Protestant ethic), legal systems, and large-scale organizations all have their own logical structures and laws of development. But they never develop by themselves; they develop through the thought and action of real people.

Weber might well have adopted Marx's slogan as his methodology: "Men make their own history, but they do not make it just as they please." Weber could not accept a reified abstraction like "Society" as it appeared in organic analogies, nor the *Weltgeist* (world spirit) of Germanic cultural theorists. We never see society, but only groups of men and women. Furthermore, these groups are very different, even within one society. It is an error to suppose that the ethical philosophies of the upper classes express the beliefs of middle-class shopkeepers or peasant laborers. India cannot be summed up in Brahmin philosophy, nor Germany in Hegel. If we are to understand society and culture we must begin with the actual diversity of separate groups, not with some easy generalization based on a single perspective. Stratification, for Weber, provided the link between the diverse groups we can actually observe and the invisible order through which thousands and millions of individual actions add up to results that individuals neither intend nor control.

What kind of order is it that ties people to others whom they may never see? Weber found three such orders: economics, politics, and culture. A man sells his labor in a factory that exists only because of a nationwide division of labor, and he affects the price of goods by the ways he spends his wages; he pays taxes and is killed on a distant battlefield because far-off government ministers struggle for power; his family walks in a funeral ceremony elaborated long ago by a hierarchy of priests and changed slowly from one repetition to another. Each order affects humans' behavior, lays down the conditions within which they must make their lives, determines both their views of the world and which people they will associate with. But not all people are affected alike. The life chances of the financier's son are not those of the farm laborer's; the ordinary citizen's worldview is not that of the party leader; the pious housewife does not inhabit the social milieu of the intellectual. We can see the social order comprehensively if we think of it as a stratification of individuals into groups based on similar economic, political, or cultural positions. Groups of people who associate together are the basic units of society. Much research since Weber's day has shown that it is in such face-to-face groups that people acquire their identities, their values, and their worldviews. Thus the diversity of society is produced by its major institutions—businesses, states, armies, churches, schools. At the same time the members of the various groups are tied together through their positions in these institutional networks.

Weber did not find it necessary to ask the general question of what holds society together. He saw that societies over the sweep of history were always coming together and falling apart, shifting and changing from one set of institutions to another. History shows nothing permanent but continual war, conflict, and change: states conquering and disintegrating, trade and finance spreading and shrinking, religions and arts slowly shifting from one theme to its opposite. What does remain beneath the change, the concrete basis of human society, are groups of people bound by ties of common feeling and belief: families, households, kinspeople, church and cult members, friends, communities. The core of Weber's view of stratification is thus a theory of group formation, a set of hypotheses about the conditions that bring people together into solidaristic groups. These conditions are found in the way people relate to the institutional orders that link groups together into a society.

Weber accepted certain motives as a basis for an explanation of human behavior: need for food and material comfort; fear of death and avoidance of physical pain; desire for sexual gratification, for membership and status in a social and moral community, and for a meaningful view of the world. Weber did not attempt to explore the psychological dynamics of these motives or to account for individual differences in motivation; in these respects his theories may be complemented by the insights of Freud and Mead and by the social theories concerning group solidarity of Durkheim and his followers. Weber took these motives as given because he found them manifested throughout human history. They enter his theories as the three main sanctions by which people influence each other's behavior: offers of economic gain, threats of physical coercion, and appeals to emotion and belief. Economics, politics, and culture are corresponding institutional realms; class, party ("power group" might be a preferable term), and status groups are the groups formed on their bases.

Weber's central hypothesis is that people who share common positions and interests in the economic arena, in the political struggle, or in the realm of culture are likely to act and associate together and to exclude all others from their company of equals. In the economic market classes are formed as people come together with others who experience similar work conditions. Here Weber follows Marx's discovery: The peasant laborer, the factory worker, the skilled craftsperson, the rural landlord, the industrialist, the merchant, the stock-market speculator all inhabit distinct social worlds. Material conditions have a powerful effect on people's lives, throwing factory laborers together in urban tenements and drawing country gentry together in their round of visits between estates. Economics shapes not only how people live and in whose company, but also how they see the world and how they will act. Economic position gives people distinctive interests: The worker sees an advantage in demanding higher pay, forming a union, or supporting a Socialist party; the peasant tries to keep down his duties to his lord and his taxes to the king; the industrialist opposes unionization and socialism; the financier is concerned about the price of gold and the prevailing rate of interest on loans. People are thus moved to act on their economic interests, and the resulting conflict draws individuals of similar economic position closer together and isolates them from those of opposing positions. How many such opposing groups there will be and how extensive the conflict among them depend on the nature of the economic system in that particular society and on the relationships between economic stratification and political and cultural stratification. Weber incorporates Marx's basic model into his theory of stratification, but he sees economic determinism as only one of three factors.

Weber viewed politics, like economics, as a realm in which struggle is widespread. History, after all, reads most obviously as a record of military conquests and feudal rivalries, palace intrigues and coups d'état, peasant revolts and urban insurrections; the activities of peaceful eras consist of the ups and downs of politicians' careers, the shifting authorities of officials, and the power play of interest groups in voting and lobbying. Thus, individuals may be stratified by their political interests as well as by their economic interests. Minor government officials are drawn together in a distinct group, as are military officers, independent feudal knights, modern party politicians, or municipal judges. Coercive power is a scarce good; many people are concerned with getting as much of it for themselves as possible, and virtually all people wish to make it bear on themselves as little as possible. As we shall see below, politics may be analyzed as a continual struggle to gain authority for oneself and to evade subjection to the authority of others. Political interest groups may overlap with economic interest groups—feudal knights may represent the landowning class; politicians, the classes of industrialists or workers. But power is a separate pie to be carved up, capable of inducing alignments of its own. The kinds of political stratification and political group formation in a particular society depend on the nature of its political institutions.

It should be apparent by now that Weber saw society as a complex and ever-shifting interplay of forces. Political stratification is influenced by economic alignments and vice versa; both of these interact with cultural stratification. Weber was forced to devise a strategy for talking coherently about this world in which nothing ever stays put long enough for us to pin a label on it and in which our labels always oversimplify what is going on. For this purpose he conceived the notion of the *ideal type*, by means of which he could abstract from reality a form of social action that is rarely or never found by itself. We can discover the dynamics of stratification, for example, if we mentally decompose it into its constituent elements—the ideal types of class, power group, and status group. We can thereby discover the dynamics of economic class formation without having to bear in mind the processes of power politics. Having done this, we can successively take up political struggles and the status-producing effects of culture. Finally, we can apply these insights to the overall stratification of any society resulting from the interaction of these three processes. The technique is similar to that of the chemist, who explains the properties of a compound first by identifying its constituent elements and then by noting their interactions. The modern sociological research method called the "multivariate analysis" of survey data reflects the same general strategy.

The interaction of culture with economics and politics is especially subtle. As already noted, economic and political positions have considerable influence on the values and beliefs of their occupants. Marx was the first to notice this for economics, and Weber carried out a parallel analysis of politics. We can speak, then, of economic and political determinants of culture. But there is a third way in which culture enters stratification, a discovery of Weber's own. If culture were merely the result of economic and political position, one could not say that culture was important for stratification. People would be stratified by their income or their power; and whatever deference they received or had to give, whatever boundaries were drawn between them and people who would not deign to associate with them (those ranking above them) and people whom they did not care to associate with (those ranking below) would be based on money or power, not on anything to do with their culture. Weber saw that this was not so: that in addition to the stratification produced by class and power, there were numerous possible hierarchies in the realm of culture. Historically, the most important of these cultural hierarchies have been based on religion. There is a definite stratification within every religion: At minimum there is a difference in status between believers and nonbelievers. The former consider themselves more virtuous and enlightened than the latter, regardless of their respective wealth and power, and such cultural strata are just as likely to associate together and exclude outsiders as are economic classes and power groups. Most religions have much more than this minimum stratification. There are hierarchies from popes, gurus, and high priests on down through minor ceremonial assistants, devoted worshipers, merely formal members, and intermittent sinners. Admittedly, this is not necessarily an exclusive basis of stratification; churches often have property interests and political connections, and clergy may associate socially with correspondingly wealthy or powerful laypeople.

Cultural stratification is important especially because it is closest to the way most people actually view their worlds. We feel that we associate with certain people and not with others, not usually because we see ourselves as economic or political allies, but because we like and respect certain people and not others. If we analyze that liking we find that it usually involves cultural stratification. Respectable churchgoing people in general prefer others like themselves, not hard-drinking denizens of bars and pool halls; hostesses who practice gracious etiquette and converse about the arts do not invite the backyard barbecue set.

It is here that Weber's philosophical background plays a key role in his sociology. In his introductory methodological writings, Weber emphasized that the proper subject of sociology is *meaningful* human actions. It is not a meaningful social action when all people put up their umbrellas at the same time, if they are simply reacting to an external stimulus—rain. Rather, what sociologists are concerned with are actions that people understand as having social significance. Work is significant because people understand it as a path to social success, or as too degrading for the gentry, or as an assurance of salvation in the afterlife. Leisure, too, is a field of meanings: One lives in a noble style of display and consumption, or one eschews the external world for the sake of one's ascetical enlightenment, or one competes with one's neighbors to show one's respectability. There are many such possibilities, and these make up the field of cultural stratification. They were so important in Weber's overall model of society that he continually emphasized the subjective side of life. For Weber, sociological analysis had to always involve *verstehen*—an empathic understanding of what people's subjective meanings are. Whether we deal with our contemporaries or with people in the past, we must always make the effort to put ourselves emotionally and intellectually in their places. Only thus do we understand the struggles involved in stratification and the rest of human social life.

Cultural stratification is thus the most complex and subtlest of all the forms of stratification. There are relatively few distinct political and economic groups in any society, but the varieties and ramifications of cultural hierarchies can be enormously refined, especially in a modern industrial society. Indeed, cultural stratification can subdivide the lines of status distinction to such a degree that virtually every group or individual may have a status of its own. In addition to religion, cultural hierarchies can be based on secularized religious ideals like honesty, hard work, ambition, and self-control (Weber's Protestant ethic); on achievement or understanding in science, literature, music, and art; on good manners, tastes in decoration and clothes; or even prominence in sports. Cultural stratification may be formally recognized in a society, as in the Hindu caste system based on ritual acts that keep members of the "higher" religions from coming into close contact with those who once belonged to "lower" religions. The ranks of European aristocracy, with their elaborate etiquette and code of honor, illustrate a similar development on a nonreligious basis.

Cultural hierarchies are the substance of the world as most people experience it, but their significance comes from the ways in which they are connected with the rest of the social order—with economics and politics and their corresponding forms of stratification. This connection can operate in two ways. First, cultural stratification can be the basis for economic and political stratification. The New England colonies are one of the best examples of this. The church leaders were also the political authorities, and only members in good standing of the church congregation—a minority of the people—could participate in governing the community. Moreover, the religious upper class took the lead in organizing commerce, farming, and fishing and thus became an economic upper class. The religious, political, and economic hierarchies began to separate in the eighteenth century, but even today Americans (especially middle-class, white, Anglo-Saxon Protestants) tend to judge people's status according to their "respectability" in religious terms—essentially, according to how well they live up to the vestigial norms of the Protestant ethic.

Second, economic and political stratification tend to turn into cultural stratification. The cold realities of wealth and power are too blatant for most people, no matter what their status. There is a widespread need to feel that those on the top merit their good fortune; thus people who rise in wealth or power attempt to cloak themselves in cultural respectability. The conquering tribesmen of antiquity called on priests to sanction their conquests, just as Charlemagne had himself crowned by the pope after building a kingdom by war. Later, the way to the top is forgotten; the aristocracy claims that it rules not by force but by hereditary right and by the merits expressed in its code of honor and its patronage of the arts. Just such a mutation has occurred between the robber barons of nineteenth-century finance and the high society of today.

Economic, political, and cultural goods can be traded off for each other, and Weber postulates a tendency for the three hierarchies to come together in times of social tranquillity. The wealthy try to become powerful and cultured; the powerful use their influence to become rich and surrounded with high culture; cultural elites try to use their prestige to acquire wealth and power. But changes and competition within the realms of economics, politics, and culture periodically upset the composition of classes, power groups, and status groups, and we find the three hierarchies consolidating, breaking down, and rearranging again and again. History is a continuous battle, not only of knights against officials, bureaucrats against politicians, landowners against financiers, industrialists against unionists, and priests against scientists and intellectuals, but of each of these orders against the others. The processes of stratification not only make up the fabric of our everyday lives, but as we shall see shortly, they turn the engines of history as Weber saw it.

Organizations: Patrimonialism and Bureaucracy

Surveying world social forms, Weber noted that there are two general ways in which people can stabilize their relationships: either by establishing strong personal ties or by setting up general rules. These were ideal types, of course. Reality is always a mixture of them, although the organizations of traditional societies have usually fallen near the personalistic pole, and modern organizations near the abstract rules pole. Weber often speaks of the former type of organization as patriarchal or patrimonial and of the latter as bureaucratic. The distinction follows broadly from that which Weber's older colleague Ferdinand Toennies made between *Gemeinschaft* (community) and *Gesellschaft* (society).

Personalistic organizations usually begin with the family household. We find the lord in ancient China or Assyria, or the citizen in Athens or Rome, or the baron in medieval Europe running his estate and his politics like a great family enterprise. Sons and brothers are his most trusted assistants, whether in supervising farming or trading expeditions, fighting a war, or collecting taxes for a higher authority. Servants and slaves are like part of the family, subject to the same loyalties and jealousies and to the same patriarchal whims. No distinction is made between public and private, between the official finances and the domestic purse. The king collects taxes equally for his troops and for his wine cellar, and his subaltern lord pays his own expenses and profits out of what he can collect before passing it on up. This form of organization can be extended across large numbers of people by linking together chains of masters and followers. In a patrimonial regime the king has trusted lieutenants who administer distant sections of his realm; they in turn assign their trusted followers to various areas and tasks; and so on down to the lowest official, whose job it is to coerce the peasants to give up their produce. Premodern trading companies and factories were organized in the same way, but on a much smaller scale.

The main disadvantages of the personalistic form of organization are that it is neither very efficient nor very easy to control. Lines of communication from top to bottom are virtually nonexistent, and orders from above are likely to emerge as rumors below, if indeed they are passed on at all. How tasks are carried out depends almost entirely on the energy and initiative of the individuals involved. Under the circumstances such organizations tend to fall back on tradition—to do a job as it was done last time and as far back as anyone can remember, since there are no other guidelines and it may not be safe to do anything that a vengeful superior could criticize. At the same time, such organizations continually slip from the control of their founders. Again and again in history a lord conquers a large territory and appoints his most trusted followers to collect the spoils, and they in turn appoint their assistants. By the time the conqueror dies, and sometimes before, the central authority begins to dissipate. Only a small portion of the taxes or booty collected comes through to the king. Eventually the more powerful lords may make themselves totally independent. Sometimes the process continues until the jurisdictions are fragmented down to the lowest level (as happened in medieval Germany); sometimes it is arrested halfway in a feudal compromise splitting authority among the levels; sometimes it is reversed by another conquest.

These political disadvantages provided the impetus for developing the other main type of organization: bureaucracy. Kings and lords long ago found that they could arrest the dissipation of authority not merely by setting servants to spy on each other (which tended to make an organization secretive and clique-ridden) but by laying down general rules. Instead of leaving procedures to the discretion of subordinates, the ruler himself could control matters from afar by selecting, training, and checking up on persons whose only job was to follow the rules. Instead of having general authority over a territory, an official could be confined to one specialized kind of job; power was thus split up and controlled from above. If abuses came from the lack of distinction between personal property and the king's property, a rigid line between public and private could be drawn. Instead of tasks being performed intermittently by local barons, they could be handled by officials recruited for full-time careers and paid specified salaries.

Weber found elements of this type of organization in cultures as far back as ancient Egypt and China, but its main development occurred only in Europe as the absolutist monarchies emerged on a bureaucratic basis, ending the period of medieval feudalism. The first great bureaucracies (after the Catholic Church of the Middle Ages) were developed in France, Prussia, and Russia in the seventeenth and eighteenth centuries. By the nineteenth century the form was widely imitated, not only by governments but by industrial enterprises that needed an efficient form of control over a large and complex division of labor. Since then bureaucratization has spread to all forms of social life—so much so that Weber regarded it as one of the main currents in modern history.

Considering its advantages, why did full-blown bureaucracy develop so late? Weber pointed out certain social and material prerequisites. The development of writing and then of a large group of literate officials was necessary for an organization carrying out specialized rules and keeping records of its activities. A money economy was needed if officials were to be paid in salaries instead of in land or booty. Improved transportation and communication (roads, navigable rivers and canals, a courier system) were necessary if a king was to keep track of what his officials were doing in distant realms. Changing material conditions aided the development of centralized administration. Firearms made the self-equipped knight obsolete

bureaucracy

and aided the rise of the large, bureaucratic army of foot soldiers. Similarly, the invention of industrial machinery helped replace scattered handicraft production with the bureaucratic factory. But the bureaucratic form itself is historically primary; without its development through the struggles of politics, modern industrial innovations could never have been used and hence would never have been invented.

Moreover, bureaucracy is hardly utopian. The kings who created it in order to control their errant knights soon found that their new machinery was slipping from their hands. Once established, the bureaucracy could do its work of administering regulations without a ruler and could even make up new rules as the occasion provided. Indeed, rulers soon began to get in the way of its smooth functioning, and hereditary monarchs grew progressively weaker until they fell in revolutions or degenerated into figureheads. Nor is bureaucracy the epitome of efficiency. Cabinet ministers and industrialists often have little more control over it than do kings. Weber saw in the world around him all the phenomena that have become famous under the labels "red tape" and "Parkinson's Law": the tendency for officials to see rules as ends in themselves rather than as means to ends; the difficulty of finding responsible decision makers amid a maze of rules and regulations, the tendency for organizations to drift, to expand mindlessly, to make their own survival the highest value. Many of these themes have been explored in subsequent research by such sociologists as Philip Selznick, Peter Blau, and Michel Crozier.

Always a political man, Weber discovered organizational politics even in the supposedly neutral instrument of bureaucracy. As was noted with regard to his theory of stratification, Weber saw how individuals' views and interests develop from the positions they hold, and he saw how rules and regulations could be used in the continual jockeying for authority and autonomy that human beings carry on. What American sociologists have since come to think of as "informal organization" within "formal organization," Weber saw as part of the implicit dialectic of the struggle for control. Personalistic and bureaucratic forms of organization, after all, are ideal types, and reality is always a mixture. As the Weberian scholar Guenther Roth has pointed out, the clever administrator uses *both* strategies of control—a mixture of personal loyalties and bureaucratic impartiality and the use of special emissaries with diffuse authority to carry out tasks that the rules and regulations impede. Franklin D. Roosevelt and John F. Kennedy were masters of the technique of mixed strategies. Both methods have their drawbacks, but only by tireless juggling between them can an organizational leader actually lead.

Politics: Traditional, Charismatic, and Rational-Legal Legitimacy

Politics is conflict over who shall control the state, the apparatus of coercion in a society. To call the state an apparatus of coercion means only that its ultimate appeal to force is the one thing that all states have in common; it does not mean that all states necessarily coerce most of their members most of the time. A democracy is a type of state in which power is split up among contending parties and separate jurisdictions, so that in fact the state does relatively little coercing. That perhaps is an ideal, and Weber would agree with Hegel's verdict that "history is the chopping-block at which the happiness of peoples, the wisdom of states, and the virtue of individuals have been victimized."

Politics is made up of three components: the groups contending for power, the organizations through which power is sought and exercised, and the ideas and ideals that legitimate authority. We have already considered the first two: The contending groups are found in the stratification of a society and may consist of economic classes, existing power groups, or status groups—each interested in manipulating the state to further its ends. We can have various kinds of political movements: those interested in economic policies and the state protection or control of property; those interested in power for its own sake or in extending the power of an organization (whether it be a party, welfare bureaucracy, army, police force, or court system); and those interested in having the state sanction some particular culture with official status (those interested in or opposed to school prayers, abortion, the prohibition of alcohol, explicit sex in movies, psychedelics, and so forth). We have also seen the various kinds of political organizations that have existed and noted some of their preconditions and dynamics.

There remains the dynamics of legitimacy. Weber saw that people have material and power interests, but that they also see the world in terms of ideas and ideals. Individuals will fight and die for worldviews as well as for money and power. The difference between Weber's view and the naïve conservative view that sees the state as a spiritual unity is that Weber realized that people's ideals *differ* within the same society. As Weber put it, people have both material and ideal interests, and their interests often conflict. As Weber noted, a society cannot be held together by force alone. Obviously, an army can control an unarmed populace. But within the army the general is not necessarily the strongest man, and he may not even carry a gun. Why then are other men afraid to disobey him? Because if one man disobeys and the others obey, the single dissenter will be shot. Why don't all the men disobey together? Because if they want to act together, they must have some sort of organization, and that again raises the question of who shall lead and how his authority will be enforced. To the old philosophical question "Who shall guard the guardians?" Weber replied that organizations can be based on force provided widespread beliefs about legitimacy exist. The general's orders are obeyed because each man expects others to obey him, and this expectation is based on the widespread *belief* that the general has legitimate authority.

Weber was well enough acquainted with history and with the daily newspapers to know that orders are not always obeyed, that the legitimacy of a leader or regime can rise and fall. Accordingly, he was interested in the dynamics of legitimacy. Out of his historical perspective, Weber produced

charisma
tradition
rational—legal

three ideal types of legitimacy. First, authority could be based on tradition: A king rules because his family has always ruled (so he says), because he is chosen by the gods, or because the tribal council selected him through traditional ceremonial methods. Second, authority could be based on personal charisma: "It is written . . . , but I say unto you . . . ," proclaims the prophet, the hero, the dominant personality, discarding tradition in favor of his own revelations. Third, authority could be rational-legal: The laws provide the procedure for selecting legitimate presidents and chancellors; bureaucratic regulations delegate authority to the police and the passport clerks. Each of these forms of legitimacy has a corresponding form of organization. Traditional rulers are found primarily in patrimonial and patriarchal organizations; charismatic leaders usually have a personal retinue of disciples and a large unorganized following; rational-legal officials are found in bureaucracies.

Each form of legitimacy has its advantages and drawbacks. Traditional leaders seem to have little to worry about. Tradition says they are kings or chiefs, and there is nothing anyone can do about it (except of course their enemies in other kingdoms and tribes). Still, Weber points out that political struggle is never entirely absent, although it may be underground. Traditional rulers are often limited by the very tradition. Their advisers, noblemen, and priests are seldom idle about interpreting tradition to their advantage and against the powers of the ruler. If they want to do things their way, they must continually struggle to interpret traditions to *their* advantage. But there are dangers in success, too; if they extend their power too far beyond tradition, they may lose their traditional legitimacy. Ancient history (and modern, too) is full of kings turned tyrants who were overthrown and replaced by one of the noblemen waiting in the wings.

One possibility for the ambitious traditional monarch is to mix traditional authority with personal charisma. But this has its difficulties and dangers too. First, in order to be charismatic, one must have some extraordinary personal qualities. To be sure, these can often be evoked by stagecraft and public relations, but the charismatic leader has entered an arena in which the pressure is on, and he or she must live up to the billing or disappear into that special obscurity reserved for has-been charismatics. Every emergency—famine, riot, invasion, or special omen—calls for a corresponding miracle. If the charismatic leader does not live up to his or her own reputation, he or she soon loses legitimacy to a rival charismatic or to an "I-told-you-so" traditionalist. The tides of legitimacy can ebb and flow with startling rapidity, as the history of modern coups d'etát demonstrates.

Finally, authority can be rational-legal. But rationalization is another dangerous beast to ride. Once this force is unleashed, there is no individual who cannot be found dispensable. The European monarchs who tried to consolidate their traditional authority by building a purely legal state found in the end that there is no justification for kings in a rational-legal code. The descendants of Louis XIV and Frederick the Great paid for the power they built. Rationalization attempts to remove the arbitrary, to provide a clear and sufficient reason for every social act. Not only kings, but party leaders, prime ministers, dictators, and individual bureaucrats themselves can be found wanting by the standards of the rational-legal regimes they control. Every regime that proclaims its principles—whether in the ideals of social-ism, the United States Constitution, or the Declaration of the Rights of Man—is subject to the judgment of its people. Of course, regimes can get away with considerable deviations from their avowed ideals, since they control powerful organizational and material resources, including the com-munication facilities, which can define much of the reality its people ob-serve. Still, ideals create a rallying point for potential opponents (like the dissident writers in the Soviet Union or the antiracist and antimilitarist movements in the United States) and constitute the weak link in the author-ity structure of a regime weakened by defeat, economic crisis, or internal conflict among its power holders. The traditional ruler, at any rate, did not have to spend much effort in justifying his or her actions. Thus, even where they are not lived up to (that is, almost everywhere), rational-legal princi-ples of legitimacy set the basic context in which political dispute goes on.

WEBER'S THEORY OF HISTORY: THE RATIONALIZATION OF THE WORLD

The great transformation in history was that unmistakable phenomenon called "modernization," which turned a world of peasants, lords, and priests into a buzzing hive of organization, machinery, and movement. Weber found the core of that change in the new industrial economy. An ex-planation of the emergence of modern capitalism would thus be an expla-nation of modernity, and Weber's search for its roots led him to describe the social outlines of world history.

Weber began by analyzing the modern economic system. The key at-tribute is predictability. There is no point in manufacturing large amounts of goods unless you can be sure of a regular market for them, and you can-not get the benefits of modern machinery and specialized division of labor unless you can continuously produce large amounts. Moreover, you cannot run a factory unless you can depend on having a regular supply of workers to hire and unless you can borrow money for capital expenses when you need it, and under fair and reasonable conditions. In short, modern indus-try depends on large and stable markets, a dependable and economically motivated labor force, and a trustworthy financial system. Weber saw that these preconditions were missing throughout most of history and that a long chain of prerequisites had somehow to emerge before the modern economy could take off.

Markets, for example, had been mostly local—peasants producing their own necessities and bartering or selling the rest in nearby towns. Of the many factors that limited larger markets, three important ones were: (1) the riskiness of transporting valuable goods in a world of continuous warfare and conquest, where robbers and barons were equally dangerous and civil order existed only within the walls of one's town or sometimes only in one's house; (2) the general lack of a widespread system of money and credit to facilitate large-scale trading; and (3) distrust of strangers—from other lands, other religions, other villages—which made trading a matter of crafty haggling and merchants often indistinguishable from pirates.

Labor, in the modern sense, was also a historical rarity. Industries cannot run efficiently and competitively if workers are not available who will move from job to job as demand for products changes and who can be attracted to the areas of greatest profit by offers of commensurate wages. (As we see, Weber's economics is in the classical English tradition.) But workers in traditional societies are for the most part not free economic agents. Peasants are often bound to the land as serfs; industrial laborers are usually family members, household servants, or slaves, bound to the enterprise, and a continuing expense whether they are overworked or underworked. Guild monopolies control most of the remaining labor supply. All these various obstacles had to be broken down before the industrial labor force could be brought together in the factory system.

Finally, modern finance is also a recent development. Only in the large kingdoms and empires did a widespread system of money exist at all. Even then, there were many obstacles to a dependable system of loans. Widespread literacy was necessary before the more complex forms of credit—such as the stock market—could arise. Money was lent only at exorbitant rates of interest as long as the risks of nonpayment and failure were great—as they were in an era when courts and police did not exist to back up contracts and when every business enterprise was risky. Not the least of the danger came from the state itself. Taxes were capricious and often little more than robbery; if a banker lent money to a king, there was no guarantee that he would ever get it back. Thus several great German banking houses—including the famous Fuggers of Augsburg—were wiped out in bankruptcies of the kings of Spain during the fifteenth and sixteenth centuries. In such a world the life of a businessman was a precarious one. If by chance he was successful and amassed a fortune, he did not reinvest it in expanding his business, but made every effort to buy himself some land and a title of nobility and thus get out of the business world entirely.

Weber's task was to trace back through history to find out where and how each of these obstacles fell—to determine the one time and place where all the circumstances were right and where the industrial takeoff could begin. The story begins in remote antiquity in a world of tribal societies—some agricultural, some made up of nomadic herdsmen and hunters. Religion played a key role in their social structure and in their worldviews. People lived and worked almost entirely with their kinspeople, and the kinship network and the community were united by a common set of ceremonies surrounding all aspects of life. Gods and spirits were everywhere—in the sky and the trees, guarding the hearth and the door of the house, and legitimating the authority of the patriarch-priest-chief. Like Durkheim, Weber recognized the integrating force of religion in primitive society.

Change came about especially by political struggle. Hunting tribes conquered agricultural tribes, creating two-class societies of peasants and warrior-aristocrats. Conquests went wider and wider; empires rose and fell; kings emerged; complex stratification grew within the ranks of the aristocracy; and royal administration (primitive bureaucracies) came into being. The familiar pendulum swings of world political history began: Overextended patrimonial regimes disintegrated into feudalism and then reconsolidated under a new conqueror. In these larger, more complex societies, wealth became concentrated. A division of labor developed around the royal courts, as artisans, servants, scribes, and merchants specialized to satisfy royal tastes. Priests developed separate hierarchies of their own, amalgamating war gods and nature gods into new syncretisms and pantheons.

In a number of these large societies—notably China and India—and in independent cities and small states on their peripheries—notably in Greece and Israel—a great change took place in the realm of religion between the sixth and fourth centuries B.C. Talcott Parsons, a leading interpreter of this phase of Weber's work, calls this change the "philosophical breakthrough": the rise of the great world religions. In each of these—Confucianism, Brahminism, Buddhism, Greek ethical philosophy, monotheistic Judaism and its later offshoots, Christianity and Islam—the nature of humankind's relationship to the physical and social worlds changes. The change consists of *separating* the idea of the natural world from the idea of the spiritual world. Instead of gods and spirits routinely intervening in the world around us (as in Greek mythology), there exists another, very different realm: heaven and hell, another sphere of reality, a world of ideal principles.

The consequences of this change were far-reaching. As long as the world is in the play of gods and spirits, it cannot be taken as a very predictable place. One can only try to placate its invisible rulers by ceremonies and sacrifices or to control them by magic. But once the spiritual realm becomes separate, both nature and society can be treated in a stabler way.

First, by removing animistic entities the world becomes open to rational explanation. The door is opened to scientific investigation and explanation. This new-found rationalism can spill over into the social realm as well. People can think of laws based on consistent general principles, instead of bowing before the eccentricities of sanctified tradition. Political and social arrangements, too, become subject to a rational critique—although this latter implication was not really seized upon until the French Enlightenment of the eighteenth century.

Second, religion itself can develop in new directions. Primitive religions merely describe an accepted if invisible side of the ordinary world. One placates the gods in order to kill one's enemies and make one's crops grow; one does not worry about being good or going to heaven. (Think of the heroes of the *Odyssey* or the early part of the Old Testament.) The philosophical breakthrough opens up two new possibilities: (1) The spiritual realm can now be a place to which one escapes from the trials and tribulations of the world. If the righteous individual—the one who follows all the rituals and does all his or her duties—nevertheless has bad fortune in the world, it does not fundamentally concern that person. In fact, the material world can now be seen as a dangerous temptation, for the truly holy person concentrates only on salvation. (2) The ideas of good and evil can develop separately from the ideas of worldly success and failure. For the primitive person sin simply means misfortune; as long as one is prosperous, healthy, and powerful, one has a clear conscience. The philosophical breakthrough puts a new ethical obligation on human beings. They are now to be concerned with justice and injustice toward their fellow human beings; conscience becomes its own reward and punishment.

These new possibilities, especially the second, are potential forces for great changes in society. The new ideas of good and evil and the concept of a world of perfection can provide tremendous leverage for changing the world to make it live up to these ideals. Here in antiquity we find the basis of Weber's Protestant ethic, which was to play a powerful role in the takeoff of industrialization 2,000 years later.

There is one more crucial attribute of the religions of the philosophical breakthrough: They are all *universalistic*. Earlier religions are limited to the members of one family, one tribe, or one ethnic group. The world religions, emerging in or near empires with unlimited ambitions of conquest, exclude no one. Indeed, earlier religions are tolerant; they conceive of a pluralistic world of many peoples, each with their patron gods. But for Confucianism, Buddhism, Christianity, and so on there is only *one* god or spiritual reality; all else is false, illusory, or subordinate. This shift is crucial because religions mark the limits of solidarity in society. In primitive and traditional societies, people are bound together with those who share a religious community. One can and must trust people who worship the same household or tribal gods. But strangers—people with different gods—are alien beings who cannot be trusted. One result of this setup was a widespread prohibition on usury—lending money at interest to other members of one's own religious group. Outside the group one could bargain in as cutthroat a fashion as possible, since there were no ethical obligations toward outsiders. Thus, to universalize a religion was abruptly to broaden the community within which peaceful social transactions could regularly be carried out.

The philosophical breakthrough opened many of the doors to industrialization: laying the basis for a moral community of trust underlying peaceful commerce; rationalizing the legal system; motivating people to remake political, social, and economic institutions in keeping with an imperative to transform the world more closely to the ideal. But these implications took a long time to work themselves out, and not all the world religions opened up just the right path to the transformation of society.

Weber's first major writing, *The Protestant Ethic and the Spirit of Capitalism*, is on this subject. It selects for careful study only one thread in the complex tapestry that was rising capitalism—the role that religious beliefs played in motivating the businessmen who developed capitalism in the seventeenth and eighteenth centuries. Weber points out that the attitude of the modern capitalist is not simply the drive for economic gain; this acquisitiveness is found everywhere in world history without resulting in a mass-production economy. What is significant for a large-scale, profit-making system, rather, is the methodical attitude: the making of a continual series of small savings and small profits that gradually add up to a long-term, mass-production economy and, ultimately, to far greater profits than the greedy, one-shot businessperson could ever attain. Weber saw this methodical, "rationalized" attitude emerging first in another sphere—the religious ideas of the most radical Protestants soon after the Reformation. These were especially the followers of Calvin, who were prominent in the most commercialized areas of the Netherlands, France, Germany, and, above all, England and America. They no longer believed in salvation by prayers, charity, or religious rituals; they believed that God was an omnipotent, inexorable power, who had already picked out those who were to be saved and those who were damned. The psychological effect of this doctrine of predestination, Weber declared, must have been to put a tremendous strain on the believers. Was one saved or not? One could do nothing specifically *religious* to help oneself; priests and monks were no better than anyone else (and quite possibly worse, since they could do no honest work); hence these radical Protestants eliminated monasteries and tried to make priests as much like lay persons as possible. What one could do, though, was to work—hard, methodologically, without coveting gains but continually pressing on, until by one's own success one felt that one did fit into God's scheme of predestination, and that one was one of the elect. In this way, the religious beliefs of radical Protestants helped produce just the attitudes that made successful capitalists and thus fostered the industrial revolution.

This theory, known as "the Weber thesis," has been argued pro and con ever since it first came out in 1904. Unfortunately, it has become so famous that many scholars have attempted to refute it (or support it) without knowledge of Weber's later work on the other world religions, or of his general sociology, in which he ties religious ideas to organizational forms, status groups, and political struggles. Weber's theory of capitalism has been interpreted narrowly as an argument that ideas determine social change. Probably the reason it has been so popular is that it apparently refutes Marx, showing that religion is the cause of material conditions instead of vice versa. This position has been especially fostered in the United States by Talcott Parsons, who translated *The Protestant Ethic* in 1930, which was years ahead of translations of any of Weber's other major works.

Now, however, we have a wider picture of what Weber actually discovered. The study of radical Protestant beliefs was just a preliminary analysis of recent Western religious history; later he would develop a massive world comparison of all the great religions and their social effects. Weber completed *The Religion of China, The Religion of India,* and *Ancient Judaism;* he died before he could begin his studies of Islam and early Christianity. His broad conclusion was that only a certain kind of breakthrough—the mixture of the ethical and scientific rationalism of Greek philosophy with the Judaic-derived legalism and world-changing activism that went to make up

Christianity—gave the impetus for rationalizing social institutions and changing the world in the economic and political upheavals of modernity. Confucianism, Brahminism, Buddhism, and Islam he found entwined with the patrimonial order of stratification in such ways that they strengthened the unpredictable, irrational aspects of their societies rather than weakened them.

In Europe the key story concerns the growth of the Christian Church—the first large-scale truly rationalized bureaucratic organization in history—and its growing consolidation with the remnants of the Roman Empire, itself legally rationalized under the influence of Greek culture. The age-old pendulum of political consolidation and disintegration swung on, but was nearing the end of its monotonous cycle through time. By the sixteenth century kings began to build the bureaucracies—using priests as their first bureaucrats—that would eventually destroy the fragmented and conflict-ridden feudal system, establish a predictable set of laws and a trustworthy monetary system, bring peace and order to large expanses of territory, and carry out regular tax policies. Commerce spread; mechanical inventions were sought and made; and handicraft industries developed. Western Europe perched on the brink of industrialization, held back only by government mercantilist policies of establishing monopolies and by the feudal bondage of labor to the soil.

The final obstacles fell in England—ironically, the Western European country in which the feudal gentry had fought the most successful battle against the king and in which royal absolutism was least far advanced. After the civil war of the seventeenth century the small gentry class gained control of the state bureaucracy and used it to further their economic interests—moving the peasants off the land, thereby creating a labor force for the textile mills, and establishing an economic policy that would remove restraints on competition. The battle was fought and won by radical Protestants: men who felt that work, honesty, and rule following were the commandments of God and who were further impelled by a powerful vision of the ideal world of heaven and hell. Their emergence at this propitious time in history is not yet understood, but the tradition from which they emerged is clear: They revived the early spirit of Christianity and brought to fruition the world-transforming potential of the religious breakthroughs of antiquity.

Once the industrial revolution was in full swing, its progress was unimpedible. New social classes appeared, transforming politics from the exclusive province of military aristocrats and court cabals to an object of mass movements and bureaucratic manipulations. Science, education, and mass communications were unleashed, to transform again and again the nature of stratification and of industry. England rose to wealth and world power. The rulers of other nations, however fearful of modernization's destructive effect on the old order that supported them, were forced to emulate England in order to keep pace militarily; otherwise, they faced the risk of becoming colonies of the modernized states.

From his towering intellectual vantage point, Weber watched the panorama of events flow through the centuries. *Die Entzauberung der Welt*, he called it—the disenchantment of the world, the master trend of history. Rationalization steadily pushes back the uncertain, the mythical, the poetic. Once all the world was seen through a veil of ritual and ceremony, goddesses and fire-breathing dragons, and the thousand fearful chances of everyday life; now daily railroad trains bring tourists to the castles of Transylvania. Even the God-fearing Protestant entrepreneur has disappeared, replaced by the bureaucratic employee. Since the modern system is established, it runs of its own accord. But the Protestant ethic is not dead, it is merely secularized. Its spirit hangs on in the very institutions of modern society and in the tightly controlled personalities of people who work in a world of rules and regulations, merit ratings, and bureaucratic security. In an America split in cultural war between a white middle-class generation still deep in the Protestant ethic and that generation's own sons and daughters, who have rejected the "uptight" world in alliance with the members of a black culture that escaped such a world only by being kept at the bottom, Weber's sociology strikes the central theme. No one saw more clearly than Weber the ways in which our lives are "haunted by the ghosts of dead religious beliefs."

For all his voluminous writings Weber was first and foremost a political man. From his early career he was active in the law courts and government agencies of Berlin. His interest in economics was first stimulated when reform groups commissioned him to study the problems of labor immigration in East Prussia and stock-market manipulations. He began with his father's upper-class imperialist loyalties, but increasing exposure to the hardships of the lower classes shifted his sympathies gradually to the left. Nevertheless, he had no illusions about the costs of reform. He regarded the Socialist utopia as an ideology with which the leaders of the Social Democratic party kept their followers in line, and he was in accord with his young friend Robert Michels' analysis of the "Iron Law of Oligarchy" in party politics.

The Marxists' flaw was that they failed to see the bureaucratic nature of the modern economy, whether it be capitalist or Socialist. Weber became interested in Russia during the abortive revolution of 1905 and learned Russian in order to follow the events firsthand. His analysis was a remarkable foresight into the Soviet period. Should Russia lose a major European war and the revolutionary left come to power, he predicted, Russia would experience a bureaucratization of the entire social structure such as the world had never seen. Considering Weber's views on the quality of life in a bureaucracy, his expectations were anything but optimistic. "The dictatorship of the official and not of the proletariat is on the march," he wrote.

The situation in Germany was scarcely more hopeful. Weber's growing disillusionment with conservative nationalism came as he watched Germany's inept foreign policy, losing allies and progressively isolating itself while at the same time carrying on an arms race and an increasingly strident campaign of nationalist self-glorification. He placed the blame on Germany's political structure: an impotent parliament incapable of controlling an irresponsible state bureaucracy; an army staffed by the defensively arrogant aristocrats of a bygone era; and a foolish hereditary monarch initiating policies that trapped the rest of the nation in their wake. In the 1890s Weber took part in efforts to create a responsible democratic party, but he dropped out when its hopelessness became apparent.

When World War I finally broke out, the release from years of tension came as a relief. Weber was at first enthusiastic. "In spite of all," he declared it "a great and wonderful war." As a fifty-year-old reserve officer in the German army, he was called to duty as the director of military hospitals in the Heidelberg area. A year later he retired and went to Berlin to wield what political influence he could to end the war. After his first enthusiasm had worn off, Weber quickly realized that Germany's military and political leadership was incapable of carrying out a victorious policy and that a prolongation of the war could only result in the destruction of German—indeed, of European—power and the turning over of world domination to America. By 1918 his last loyalties to the Kaiser were gone, and he published a series of newspaper articles calling for a democratic constitution for postwar Germany.

The fall of the old regime seemed to take a personal weight from Weber's shoulders. From the Versailles peace conference, where he served on the German delegation, he wrote that he slept soundly at night for the first time in many years. Even his inability to teach was overcome. He accepted a professorship at Munich, where he lectured to enormous crowds of students, intellectuals, and public dignitaries. Politics suddenly showed opportunities. Weber became the leader of a new, liberal, democratic party. An archrealist, he nevertheless saw a ray of hope. Political parties might be corrupt oligarchies, but only within free parliamentary competition might leaders arise capable of controlling the recalcitrant state bureaucracy and giving the nation intelligent policies.

But time had run out. In 1919 Weber fell ill of pneumonia, and he died the next year at the age of fifty-six. His party collapsed; the first of the German republic's many economic and political crises was upon it. Responsible leadership would not be forthcoming; the irresponsible leaders were already gathering in the beer gardens of Munich. Politics is a dangerous and morally taxing vocation, Weber had told his students in one of his famous last lectures. The idealist as well as the cynic is caught in webs of consequences far beyond those intended in his or her acts. Ideals alone are not enough; they must be accompanied by hard realism, sympathetic imagination, and an unyielding sense of responsibility. The following might have been his own epitaph for his accomplishments in the realm of knowledge as well as his failures in the realm of politics:

> Politics is a strong and slow boring of hard boards. It takes both passion and perspective. Certainly all historical experience confirms the truth—that man

would not have attained the possible unless time and again he had reached out for the impossible. But to do that a man must be a leader, and not only a leader but a hero as well, in a very sober sense of the word. And even those who are neither leaders nor heroes must arm themselves with that steadfastness of heart which can brave even the crumbling of all hopes. This is necessary right now, or else men will not be able to attain even that which is possible today. Only he has the calling for politics who is sure that he shall not crumble when the world from his point of view is too stupid or too base for what he wants to offer. Only he who in the face of all this can say "In spite of all!" has the calling for politics.[1]

[1]Max Weber, "Politics as a Vocation," in H. H. Gerth and C. Wright Mills (eds.), *From Max Weber: Essays in Sociology* (New York: Oxford University Press, 1946), p. 128.

CHAPTER EIGHT

Sigmund Freud: Conquistador of the Irrational

The cataclysmic twentieth-century wars had yet to burst upon the face of humankind; Darwin's *Origin of Species* was three years away from publication, and Einstein's birth lay twenty-three years in the future, when Sigmund Freud (1856–1939) was born in Freiburg, Moravia. Western civilization was intact. Europe enjoyed an uneasy peace, while America was on the verge of civil war.

In modern times Freud has become a legendary figure in the history of science. He is remembered as the founder of psychoanalysis, a method for understanding human motivation and a technique for healing the psyche. He presented himself in his autobiography as a scientist; yet he opened a crack in the scientific edifice of Reason, which had dominated the intellectual scene since the Enlightenment. The social philosophers of that period, including Montesquieu, Diderot, d'Alembert, Rousseau, Condorcet, and Turgot, subscribed wholeheartedly to the Aristotelian dictum that humankind is composed of rational animals. The philosophers' vision, which the founding fathers of sociology attempted to put into practice, was of free rational humans emerging from centuries of ignorance, fear, and superstition into a bright new dawn of Reason, science, and unlimited progress. Humankind, the moving force of society, was to be guided by rational knowledge in a conscious attempt to remake the world in its own image and thereby shape its planetary destiny.

Freud's greatest discovery was the systematic unearthing of the vast and hidden continent of the human unconscious. Via the method of psychoanalysis he probed the depths of the psyche and uncovered the irrational side of human nature. It is one of the paradoxes of Freud's life that the work of this eminent scientist and man of reason should have heralded the end of the Age of Reason. The Enlightenment dream of the eighteenth-century philosophes died in Freud, a child of that Enlightenment. No longer could the Western individual trust solely and naively in Reason to solve the problems of collective living. Freud showed that the individual is basically a nonrational being, driven by such emotional forces as "sexual instincts" and "repressed wishes."

Although Freud did not discover the unconscious, he was the first to give content to what had previously been an unfilled form. The idea of the unconscious had been brewing in the German intellectual climate since the publication of Eduard von Hartmann's *The Philosophy of the Unconscious* in 1859. But the metaphysician von Hartmann did not claim to have explored the region of the unconscious; rather, he arrived there by a process of abstract reasoning and found "will" and "intellect" (parallel to Freud's formulations of "id" and "ego") in a state of conflict. Nor was the nineteenth century the first age in the history of Western thought to have conceived this idea; it may be traced back to antiquity. The idea of an unconscious in humankind lurked in Plato's parable of the cave more than two millennia prior to Freud.

EARLY LIFE AND WORK

As a child, Freud was the center of attention in his Viennese family's household. He was so much his mother's favorite that she discontinued his younger sister's piano lessons because the ten-year-old Sigmund complained that the noise disturbed his studies. Freud was a child prodigy who began reading Shakespeare at age eight and was later fascinated by Thiers' *Consulate and Empire.* A hero-worshiper during adolescence, he dreamed of becoming a great general. He was so taken with the romance of Napoleon that he pasted onto the backs of his toy wooden soldiers little labels bearing the names of the French emperor's marshals.

Freud graduated summa cum laude from high school. During the last six of his eight years at Sperl Gymnasium he ranked number one in his class and occupied such a privileged position that he was hardly ever questioned in class. His choice of profession was determined to a great extent by his social position as a Viennese Jew. The alternatives open to him were those of industry, business, law, and medicine. His intellectual bent eliminated the first two, and he considered taking up the study of jurisprudence. However, although he felt no direct attraction to medicine, he was motivated by the sort of curiosity that is directed more toward human concerns than toward natural objects. It was a period of indecision. On the one hand, he was influenced to study law by a school friend who was later to become a famous politician; on the other hand, he was attracted by the then topical evolutionary theories of Darwin, which offered hopes for an extraordinary advance in understanding the world.

Freud reached his decision to enter the field of medicine upon hearing a dramatic reading of Goethe's essay on Nature. His youthful idealism was given direction by the old master's romantic picture of Nature as a bountiful mother, who allowed her favorites the privilege of exploring her secrets.

Freud had come to believe that the secret of power lay in understanding rather than in force. Swayed by the late-nineteenth-century *Zeitgeist*, he questioned humankind's relation to itself as well as its place in Nature.

With his father's blessings and financial support, Freud embarked on his career as a medical student at the University of Vienna in the autumn of 1873. His work load averaged over twenty-five hours per week, including lectures and laboratories, in such broadly diversified fields as anatomy, chemistry, botany, microscopy, mineralogy, physics, spectrum analysis, biology, histology, Aristotelian logic, physiology, and zoology. The budding genius thereby acquired a solid scientific background in addition to the habits of hard work and self-discipline. During this academically successful period Freud began to recognize the limitations as well as the capabilities of his intellectual gifts. He learned also the truth of the Mephistophelean dictum: "It is in vain that you range round from science to science; each man learns only what he can."

After receiving his first grant in 1876 to study the gonadic structure of eels, Freud found a temporary home in Ernst Brücke's physiology laboratory. Brücke was for Freud a role model as well as an intellectual mentor. He was an exemplar of the person of science—uncompromising, ascetic, disciplined. An austere German Protestant professor with a Prussian accent, Brücke represented the antithesis of the Viennese *schlamperai* (or "sloppy thinkers") with whom Freud was already familiar.

Brücke's Institute of Physiology was part of a far-reaching scientific movement known as the Helmholtz school of medicine, whose teachings made a lasting impression on Freud. Its founders, all to become famous scientists, had sworn a youthful oath to uphold the principles:

> No other forces than the common physical-chemical ones are active within the organism. In those cases which cannot at the time be explained by these forces one has either to find the specific way or form of their action by means of the physical-mathematical method or to assume new forces equal in dignity to the chemical-physical forces inherent in matter, reducible to the forces of attraction and repulsion.[1]

By 1870 this current of thought had achieved complete dominion over the minds of the German psychologists and medical teachers; it stimulated research everywhere.

Helmholtz's mid-nineteenth-century mechanical view of the universe, which reduced all natural phenomena to the forces of attraction and repulsion, was incorporated by Brücke into his *Lectures on Physiology* (1874). The student Freud was captivated by his teacher's account of physical physiology. Brücke defined physiology as the science of organisms. He distinguished between organisms and machines; the latter were mere dead material entities in action, while the former possessed the faculty of assimilation.

---

[1]Ernest Jones, *The Life and Work of Sigmund Freud*, edited and abridged by Lionel Trilling and Steven Marcus (New York: Doubleday Anchor Books, 1963), p. 29. Reprinted by permission of Basic Books, Inc., Publishers, New York, 1961.

However, both were considered to be phenomena of the physical world. According to the principle of the conservation of energy, organisms and machines were similarly composed of systems of atoms and driven by forces. In science the real causes were symbolized by the word "forces." The less scientists knew about these causes, claimed Brücke, the more kinds of forces they had to distinguish: mechanical, electrical, magnetic, light, heat, and so forth. Progress in knowledge had reduced these forces to two—attraction and repulsion. Brücke extended this line of reasoning to the human organism. He incorporated this nineteenth-century image of humankind into two volumes of what was then known about the interplay of physical forces inside the living organism. That Freud was influenced strongly by the content and spirit of these ideas is revealed in his 1926 characterization of the dynamic aspect of psychoanalysis as forces that assist or inhibit one another and combine with and enter into compromises with one another. His image of the human being, as we shall see, was tinged heavily with the mechanistic view, which he absorbed as a student at Brücke's institute.

With the aid of a photographic memory Freud passed his final medical examination in 1881 with flying colors. During that year he found Theodor Meynert's lectures on psychiatry of particular interest because of their non-laboratory approach to medical science. Although he wanted to pursue a theoretical career, his financial situation upon receipt of his M.D. was so shaky that he accepted Brücke's advice to abandon this ambition. He served as doctor in residence at the Vienna General Hospital, where he gained three years of experience in surgery, internal medicine, dermatology, and psychiatry.

One year before his marriage to Martha Bernays in 1886, the twenty-nine-year-old Freud was seeking the professional recognition that would enable him to establish a private practice and to start a family. He hoped that his discovery of the clinical use of cocaine as a local anesthetic would earn him early fame. Using himself as a guinea pig Freud observed that cocaine produced exhilaration and lasting euphoria; it increased his capacities for self-control and intensive mental work. Although it aided him in controlling the contents and flow of his consciousness, preoccupation with the magical rather than the medicinal properties of the drug cost him credit for the find. A younger colleague, Carl Koller, won the distinction of inaugurating the use of cocaine on the sensitive eye surface. Freud had yet to prove his worth.

The Interpretation of Dreams

Prior to Freud the field of psychiatry was relatively virgin territory. The great French scientists Jean Charcot and his student Pierre Janet had established a lone outpost with their work on hypnosis and hysteria.[2] The relationship between Charcot, with whom Freud studied during the years 1885–1886, and Janet was akin to that between Saint-Simon and Comte.

[2]Hysteria may be briefly defined as the experiencing of mental anxiety and/or bodily pain without an apparent physical cause.

Saint-Simon and Charcot were the inspirational thinkers, while Comte and Janet, their disciples, were the systematizers. It was Janet who delved deeply into the psychic process of hysteria and found, according to the theories of heredity that dominated *fin de siècle* French psychology, that the disease was a form of degeneration of the nervous system that manifested itself in congenital "weakness." Since Freud's pioneering psychiatric work, forms of mental illness (including hysteria) have come to be viewed largely as socially conditioned, although organic causes can combine with social ones. The background role of heredity in mental illness remains obscure, even after almost a century of research.

Upon publication of *The Interpretation of Dreams* in 1900 Freud began to emerge from obscurity. He had been practicing neurology and psychiatry for a decade in Vienna. In 1897 he began an arduous self-analysis, which gave him greater insight into the resistance of his patients and laid the foundations for his system of psychoanalysis. His revolutionary scientific work examined for the first time in a comprehensive and systematic manner the previously unsuspected notion that the fulfillment of a wish was the essential motive of a dream. The conquistador of the irrational had struck ore in an unexplored land.

His first great discovery on this hidden continent was the "dirty little secret" that people lust and hate. Although this came as no surprise to the lower classes, the established middle and upper classes, including their learned scientists and scholars, were shocked by such a picture of themselves. The mere mention of Freud's name was considered impolite and risqué in the genteel drawing rooms of Viennese society. Respectable society followed the leaders of nineteenth-century European intellectual life in considering *their* civilization the summit of human progress. The social evolutionary trend of nineteenth-century sociological and anthropological thought, including the work of Comte, Frazer, Morgan, Tylor, and Spencer, had convinced modern Europeans of their cultural superiority to the so-called barbaric or primitive peoples. These modern Europeans, secure in their conversation parlor, stereotyped native tribespeople as packs of painted savage, drum-beating cannibals, and promiscuous sexual libertarians. Since the nineteenth century had a way of turning Victorian moral absolutes into hereditary categories, Europeans came to believe the myth that they were racially superior to black Africans. The latter were considered to be subhuman, abnormal, and sexually unrestrained. Freud disturbed Europe's sleep by showing in his case studies and dream analyses of respectable society matrons that the moral barrier between "normal" and "pathological" scarcely existed and that the sexual underground was much bigger than anyone was willing to admit.

Repression

Freud's greatest discovery on this new continent was the phenomenon of repression. The entire structure of psychoanalysis is based upon the foundation of repression as it operates in the human being. According to Freud, random thoughts, dreams, slips of the tongue, neurotic symptoms, and daily mistakes all have meanings (that is, express intentions or purposes) that are unknown to the person. They are what he calls "unconscious ideas." The individual who is undergoing psychoanalysis resists becoming aware of unconscious ideas that may threaten his or her established sense of self. The individual's rejection of an idea or a desire that he or she nevertheless possesses is repression. It functions to keep things out of consciousness; its consequence is that the individual refuses to recognize the realities of his or her human nature.

In his first major work Freud divides the mental apparatus into three components. He compares the unconscious system to an anteroom, which houses the various excitations, desires, ideas, drives, and instincts. These elements push forward to gain admission into a second and much smaller room that houses consciousness. A doorkeeper or "censor" stands between these two rooms in the parlor of the preconscious, so to speak. The doorkeeper scrutinizes ideas and excitations that seek admittance, and those that are turned back at the threshold are repressed. Freud found in numerous clinical cases that repression occurred where there was a conflict between opposing wishes and desires. In addition, he found that experiences that were the occasions for such conflict almost invariably had sexual content.

Freud relates the case of a girl who felt great relief upon her older sister's death. Since she could not recognize consciously the envy of her deceased sister, whose husband was now available to marry *her*, the girl became hysterical. She had repressed the thought, "Now he is free and can marry me." During the course of psychoanalysis she was able to remember the thought and to reproduce the intense excitement that she had experienced upon the occasion of her sister's death. In a burst of emotion, her conscious mind had suddenly recognized the unconsciously repressed material. By reliving that trauma from her past, she effected her own cure.

Next came one of Freud's keenest insights: that people with the highest ideals tend to have the greatest repression of strong aggressive and sexual desires. This empirical generalization, based on his observations of patients, suggested that ideals were *founded* on repression and that they took their vitality from the suppressed feelings themselves. In short, uptight, honest, hard-working, righteous, authoritarian believers in the Protestant ethic derive their energetic tension from love and hate turned in upon themselves. Freud later cited Woodrow Wilson's intense moral idealism as an example of this character type.

A third discovery, one that stemmed directly from the theory of repression, was that children have sex lives. The seemingly obvious notion that children are sexual creatures so roused the ire of his contemporaries that they ostracized him. However, Freud stuck to his empirical guns. In analyzing dreams and neurotic symptoms, he found that they contained a core that represented a return or regression to early childhood experiences.

Assuming the validity of the hypothesis of the unconscious, it follows that children learn to repress their emotions. At one point they are innocent and unrepressed. The unconscious and conscious are not yet separated. Wishes to play with their orifices, genitals, and feces are freely indulged. It is only through the process of socialization, when the child begins to internalize the parents' values of cleanliness, propriety, and order, that the child learns to behave in a "proper" manner and to tailor himself or herself to society's norms.

FREUD'S EXPLANATORY SYSTEMS

Freud evolved several major explanatory systems during the course of his career: (1) the theory of primary and secondary process; (2) the theory of stages of sexual development; (3) the libido theory; (4) the trinitarian theory of the psychic apparatus; and (5) the theory of Eros versus the death instinct. Although none of these systems is self-contained and discrete from the others, we may isolate each for the purposes of analysis. The fabric of Freud's thought is sewn with many threads, and in order to unravel the whole, it helps to proceed from earlier to later systems.

Primary and Secondary Process

Freud's earliest system began with the act of repression itself, which he explained in terms of the "primary process," as expressed in wishes, symbols, and fantasies; and the "secondary process" of our socialized awareness, which censors and controls the former. Each concept may be used to refer to either ways of thinking or ways of managing energy. Freud contends that humankind transcends its animality by undergoing a basic change from primary process, ruled by the unconscious system and the vicissitudes of the id instincts, to secondary process, dominated by the conscious system and the demands of the ego. Although primary process persists into adulthood, the mature ego is able to control the childlike id by denying gratification, restraining pleasure, working to achieve rational goals, and remaining secure from irrational passions. Freud describes this dynamic shift within the human psyche as the transformation of the pleasure principle into the reality principle. Beyond seeking mere instinctual satisfaction, human beings develop the faculty of reason and learn to test reality; they discover that making distinctions, such as good from bad, true from false, and useful from useless, is the beginning of wisdom.

Human beings thereby metamorphose from pleasure-loving babies into conscious, thinking subjects located within a social system that demands that they function properly in their economic roles. Of course, they are free to have a fantasy life; however, they must ultimately subordinate their mentality to the reality principle (that is, they must obey society's norms and live according to its values). They may have strange dreams, weird thoughts, irrational wishes, powerful desires, or immoral fantasies, but they must not let the imagination run away with itself to the point of excluding external reality. For example, James Thurber's beloved character Walter Mitty imagines himself to be a famous brain surgeon in the act of performing a crucial operation on a millionaire banker who is a close personal friend of Roosevelt, only to have a parking lot attendant shout at him to stop his car before he slams into a Buick.

The Stages of Sexual Development

One of Freud's major hypotheses is that the first five years are crucial in the further psychological development of the person. It is during this phase of life that the link between the individual and society is forged. Talcott Parsons later interpreted this to mean that the child acquires a superego (or conscience) during this period by identifying with parental values. Since the parents are society's cultural agents, the child will learn the dominant values from them. If cultural values are success oriented, as they are in America, the child will be encouraged to gear its organism toward the achievement of such desirable goals as position, power, and prestige. The will toward acquisition of goods, from soap to status, is thereby built into the individual by society from an early age.

From his observations of patients and their neuroses Freud developed a model of five overlapping stages of psychosexual development: oral, anal, phallic, latent, and genital. During the earliest stage infants derive gratification from sucking the mother's breast. The erogenous zones of the mouth and lips are the first to come into play in deriving sexual pleasure. During this oral, or cannibalistic, phase the amoral baby makes no distinction between taking food and sexual activity. The suckling aims to incorporate the object (mother's breast) into its own body; it still lives according to the primary process of striving for instant gratification and has not yet developed the secondary process by which it distinguishes itself from the world and separates subject from object. The baby *is* the universe; it is at one with the environment. During the latter part of this stage the child begins biting; it becomes oral-sadistic. It begins to objectify and to differentiate itself from its surroundings. Although it does not yet know their names, it begins to locate such objects as the breast, the nipple, the blanket, the rattle. It encounters its first significant "other"—mother. It is cutting its first teeth and it explores the world by grasping things, shoving them into its mouth, and chewing on them. It is not sure whether to bite or suck. It is ambivalent. This primeval uncertainty, Freud argues, is the prototype for the polar emotions of love and hate.

During the anal phase of the organization of the libido the child concentrates its energy on the anus as a source of gratification. The child becomes fascinated with its feces and enjoys playing with them. Excrement is viewed as an extension of itself without any connotations of good or bad; it is neutral waste. Through the mother the child learns, via the diaper change, that excrement is bad. This routine is a rather unpleasant task, however loving the mother. The helpless nursling, who is emotionally sensitive to even the subtlest nuance of facial expression and tactile sensation, sees and feels the parent's distaste at this daily ritual. The role of this early memory trace or psychic imprinting upon the baby can hardly be overestimated in the course of individual development. Excrement becomes negative, associated in the child's mind with the smelly, dirty "bad-me." The clean "good-me" of the child is rewarded with parental smiles and verbal acclaim for not soiling its clothes. Toilet training is the beginning of civilization in the individual. The seeds of society and repression are sown by teaching the child self- (that is, bowel) control.

During the phallic stage of psychosexual development the individual discovers the genital erogenous zone as a source of pleasure. The penis for the male and the clitoris for the female become the primary organs of sexual excitement. Freud understood the initial sexual instincts of childhood to be largely objectless, or "autoerotic." The key stage of development is the phallic, at which the Oedipus complex emerges, for this is the point at which sexual drives become firmly attached to an external object. Harking back to the Greek myth of Oedipus Rex to find an archetype for his clinical diagnoses, Freud theorized that the young male desires his mother and hates and fears his father. (For the female child, he expected the process to be the reverse.) The male child resolves this conflict by repressing the wish to kill his father; he identifies with him instead and makes him his personal ego-ideal. Thereafter, the internalized father (or superego) punishes the child by making him feel guilty whenever he wishes for something forbidden. The external punisher has taken up residence inside the child's own mind.

According to Freud, sexual interests are submerged during the latency period between the ages of five and twelve, to reappear again at puberty in the genital or adult stage of sexual organization. During these years between the phallic stage and puberty, the child learns from its initial social environment, its family and school, how to channel its sexual feelings into socially acceptable behavior.

Although Freud postulated the Oedipus complex as sociologically universal, ethnographic work by Malinowski and other cultural observers has disconfirmed this hypothesis. The concept does, however, provide the student of humankind with a heuristic device for understanding the individual's advance from bondage to freedom. As long as the individual remains attached in an emotionally dependent way to the parents, personal independence has yet to become a reality. Freud based his encompassing theory of neurosis upon fixation at the oedipal or one of the preoedipal stages, due to some conflict over gratification. In addition, some personal trauma in adult life may bring about temporary neurotic regression to an earlier mode of gratification.

The Theory of Libido

Freud's image of humankind reflected the mechanistic bias of his contemporaries. For Freud, as for other middle-class thinkers of his time, humans were perceived as primarily isolated and self-sufficient. They were alone in a universe not of their making and found themselves, somewhat akin to Hobbes' imaginary atomic individual, surrounded by others in the same predicament. Uprooted from the medieval context of soil, hearth, and community, nineteenth-century urban individuals' needs for commodities drove them to the marketplace, where they encountered other individuals who needed what they had to sell and who had to sell what they needed. Society's cement consisted in this mutually profitable exchange. The wheeling and dealing for the material advantages took place on the vast stock-exchange floor of life under the guidance of Adam Smith's "invisible hand" of the self-adjusting market. Freud's libido theory, as we shall see, expressed the same idea in psychological rather than economic terms.

The French aristocrat and *homme de belles-lettres* La Mettrie argued cogently in 1748 that humankind is a complicated machine. Although Freud probably never read La Mettrie, he did pick up this theme. Freud's mechanical human was driven by libido (basic sexual energy) and regulated by the need to reduce tension to a certain minimal threshold. Pleasure consisted in an unwinding or reducing of tissue tensions and in the avoidance of pain. The barometer of well-being was a kind of tepid mean between ecstasy and depression. Males and their mechanical brides sought each other out in order to arrive at mutual satisfaction of their libidinous needs. Nevertheless, they remained as fundamentally alienated from one another as seller and customer on the market. Despite their mutual attraction, they remained at opposite magnetic poles and could never transcend their separateness. According to Freud, humankind's nature is fundamentally aggressive and asocial, and humans are social animals only by virtue of the necessity to satisfy the ravenous libido.

The concept of libido is essentially a nineteenth-century economic idea in psychological dress, in the sense that it is conceived of as a fixed quantity subject to the laws of matter. One may spend it as one pleases, but once it is spent it cannot be recovered. In the same way, Freud treats love as property or capital. Love was considered as a valuable commodity to be invested wisely and not merely to be frittered away on every passing stranger. Hence, Freud despaired of the possibility of altruistic love, except among the psychoanalytic elite; he ridiculed the commandment to "love thy neighbor as thyself" as an absurdity.

Ego, Id, and Superego

Freud's mature system emerged as a three-element conception of the psychic topography. The ego (cognition of the external world), the id (the emotional or instinctual being), and the superego (identifications and social ideals) were portrayed as dynamically interrelated regions or "psychic localities" within the mind of humankind. These concepts are ideal types in the Weberian sense. They function as diagnostic categories, which are neither separately observable entities nor physical portions of the brain;

rather they are interactive mental principles that are always found in mixed form. For example, the primitive id drives become fixed on (or "cathected to") certain objects, such as mother, father, or self. These object cathexes are incorporated by the unconscious system of the mental apparatus and act as the building blocks of the emerging character structure of the individual.

The ego is a structure or organization of the mental process by which the human being stays in contact with social reality. It represents the viewpoint of Reason, which constrains the limitless passions and impulsive desires of the irrational id. The ego simultaneously draws energy from and acts as the agent of the id. The outpouring of "how to" books for single men and women—how to find a mate or how to seduce a member of the opposite sex most effectively and deliciously—illustrates this point.

The superego emerges as a function of the ego. It arbitrates the relationship between the ego and the external world and even punishes the ego. The superego is the interior judge, which represents the moral demands of society and reinforces the authority principle as it operates in the affairs of human beings.

One of the major fruits of this tripartite system was Freud's essay "Group Psychology and the Analysis of the Ego," in which he set forth an explanation of the foundation of social unity and its dissolution. Taking Gustave Le Bon's treatise on *The Crowd* as a springboard for analysis, Freud sought to fathom the willingness with which the ordinarily civilized individual subordinates his or her ego to the mindlessness and destructive tendencies of the group (that is, individuals en masse). Since Freud's basic premise was that social cohesion is based on sexual organization, it followed that the libidinal bond, rather than a community of interest, was the power that cemented the group.

Beyond sex, what held society together was the dynamic psychic mechanism of identification, whereby a number of separate individuals join together by substituting a common object for their ego ideal. Freud interpreted the ruler as a father image, an answer to people's wish to be led. Thus, the persecuting primal father becomes the "cultural superego," or what Comte called the "Great Being of Humanity," who is incarnated as the totalitarian dictator and invested by the people with supreme temporal power. Charismatic leaders, as Weber reminds us, derive their domination from neither legal nor traditional sources; rather, their authority and power to command are founded in the collectivity's perception of their possession of extraordinary, unique, and magical qualities. Alexander the Great, Caesar, Charlemagne, Genghis Khan, Ivan the Terrible, Napoleon, Lenin, and Hitler are examples of such politically charismatic personality types. Louis XIV, the divine-right monarch of seventeenth-century France, epitomized the secular sanctity of this administrative function in the famous historical aside, *"L'état, c'est moi"* (I am the state). The absolutist political leader thereby places himself or herself in the stead of the subjects' parents, and the subjects tend to obey readily and even to worship that leader.

Eros Versus the Death Instinct

Freud's culminating explanatory system seeks speculatively to understand the individual and history in life-and-death terms. In the history of culture Eros may be distinguished from Agape; the former recalls the Greek ideal of passionate love between human beings by means of which each overcomes the sense of separateness, and the latter refers to the concept of altruistic love, according to which we are all one. Freud treats the two of these together in contrast to Thanatos, which represents the personification or mask of death in Greek mythology; it is the harbinger of suicide, war, pestilence, and famine. Like elliptic cycles, each of these heavenly powers, as Freud called them, recurs periodically in the rise and fall of civilizations and individuals.

Transsexuality is a recent gender category in the sociology of sex; and despite Freud's scientific metholology and tolerant attitude toward *homo sexualis*, he had no transsexual clients in Victorian-era Vienna. Hence, his theory was consequently void of their mention.

In the life of individuals Eros stands for the sexual instincts. More specifically, it points toward those modes of human sexuality that have been categorized as heterosexual, homosexual, bisexual, and transsexual. Whereas the dominant social value of heterosexuality may be understood as the attainment of genitality, and homosexuality as oedipal identification with the wrong sex, bisexuality gained little or no stature in Freud's psychomorphology, except for the indication that polymorphous perversity might be a characteristic of early childhood. However, one of the most revolutionary implications of Freud's psychology of sex is the postulate of the universal bisexuality of human beings. In seeking to explain neuroses and perversions, Freud borrowed his colleague Wilhelm Fleiss's concept of constitutional bisexuality. Fleiss contended that this condition is biologically based in male and female characteristics, which are present in both men and women. Although Freud rejected the organismic in favor of the psychological viewpoint, he accepted the validity of the theory of bisexuality as explaining many traits of human behavior. Freud's brilliant and wayward disciple Carl Jung picked up this theme of male-in-female and female-in-male, translating it in terms of archetypes of human consciousness rather than biological fixtures or psychological entities. Whatever the individual's mode of conduct, the theory of bisexuality sheds light on Agape as well as Eros, for it shows the human being as capable of expressing tender as well as aggressive emotions.

Looming in the Freudian unconscious are death and sexual instincts. Drawing upon August Weismann's heuristic division of the living substance into mortal (or "somatic") and immortal (or "germ plasmic") parts in multicellular organisms, Freud deals with two forces operating in the substance. While the sexual instincts perpetually strive to renew life, the death instincts seek to lead the living toward death. In *Beyond the Pleasure Principle,* Freud postulates the "nirvana principle," according to which "the dominating tendency of mental life, and perhaps of nervous life in general, is the effort to reduce, to keep constant, or to remove internal tension due to stimuli." This proclivity in the life of human beings finds partial expression in the pleasure principle, which strives to reduce the tension of desires by satisfying them. In addition, Freud uses the nirvana principle as a basis for believing in the existence of death instincts. He assumes that life is striving to return to an initial state of things from which it originally departed. Thus, "the aim of all life is death."

On the supraindividual or historical level the death instinct manifests itself in periods of cultural degeneration, civil war, and international antagonisms. Indeed, the present age has been characterized by Raymond Aron as "the century of total war." Of course, history is replete with wars, plagues, famines, revolutions, crumbling civilizations, and the like. It was Hegel who once remarked that "what we learn from history is that we learn nothing from history." The radical difference between today and yesterday is that with the technological development of nuclear weapons and sophisticated methods of chemical-biological warfare, our species now has within its power the means to extinguish itself entirely. Freud was a pessimist with regard to human affairs. He recognized a death wish in the collectivity as well as in the individual. But he had not completely given up hope. In the concluding paragraphs of *Civilization and Its Discontents* Freud invokes the life force, Eros, as the other heavenly power to rise up and defeat its equally immortal adversary, Thanatos.

LATER CAREER

In his later years, Freud turned to the elder-philosopher role and began to comment on the issues of war and peace, the drift of modern secular history, and the place of humankind in the biological cosmos. To the end of his days in 1939 Freud wore the mantle of scientist-explorer. In a lengthy letter to Einstein in 1932 Freud expressed the hope that a combination of the "cultural attitude" against war and the fear of the consequences of a future war might result in its elimination as an outmoded institution.

In *Civilization and Its Discontents* he posed the key question of the modern era: Is not civilization founded upon repression, and, if so, is not the universal neurosis of humankind its price? Unlike Marx, who sees the historical deck as stacked against the collectivity, Freud sees it as stacked against the individual. In lieu of *homo economicus* Freud presents us with an image of humankind as *homo sexualis*, whose irrational drives must be channeled into productive labor in order for civilization to carry on. Society sublimates sex into the striving for success.

As a champion of the Enlightenment, Freud was highly suspicious of any notions that would contradict his famous dictum, "Where id is, there shall ego be." Although he was not blind to suffering and to the sources and means for overcoming it, he maintained his rational posture and dismissed religion as a consolation for the person who possesses neither art nor science. In *The Future of an Illusion* he psychoanalyzes religion as a projected superego of the helpless individual who identifies with an omnipotent and omniscient God, the father-king. Like the skeptical Voltaire, Freud wanted to live without illusions and preferred to cultivate Reason's garden.

THE FREUDIAN MOVEMENT: ADLER AND JUNG

Within the span of a half-century, the psychoanalytic movement gathered disciples, both wayward and orthodox, and established professional associations in countries around the globe. Psychoanalytic thinking has penetrated the social sciences as well as the humanities. Whole societies have been explained by a cultural "unconscious," and studies on the sexual customs and habits of populations have been published. No longer is a classic appreciated on the sole basis of art for art's sake; nowadays, we inquire à la Freud into the artist's early childhood secrets or sexual hangups to see what really makes him or her tick.

By 1909 Freud had achieved international recognition. In that year he journeyed to America to deliver a series of lectures at Clark University in Worcester, Massachusetts. He gave five talks in German to large audiences on the fundamental techniques of psychoanalysis and was generally well received by such American psychological luminaries as Adolf Meyer, Edward Titchener, and William James. The lectures were published as *The History of the Psychoanalytic Movement*. In this polemic he explained his revolutionary ideas, sketched the movement's history, and castigated Alfred Adler and Carl Jung as heretics.

Adler was more concerned with the phenomenon of power in society, and he based his psychotherapy upon the patient's neurotic sense of powerlessness or inferiority. The thrust of his teaching was the attempt to understand and to cure this condition by the psychotherapeutic reawakening of social interest. Adler comprehended sexual conflicts more as products of the individual's maladjustments in his later social milieu than as reflections of early childhood difficulties. Adler, Karl Menninger, Harry Stack Sullivan, and Carl Rogers emphasized social more than sexual factors in the etiology of mental illness. Notwithstanding Freud's early indignation at this line of approach, their work has made the greatest impact upon the practice of psychotherapy in America.

Carl G. Jung (1875–1961), Freud's most influential disciple, was born in a suburb of Basel, Switzerland, the son of a Protestant minister. Religious experiences in early childhood helped Jung to transcend the psychic ropes of the conventional piety of the Church, which he observed to be more concerned with rituals, rites, and roles than with considering Jesus Christ and the spirit of God as a living reality. He was a lonely youth, read everything he could, and chose the study of medicine as a compromise between the sciences and humanities. He was attracted to psychiatry as the study of "diseases of the personality," became interested in psychic phenomena, and wrote his thesis "On the Psychology and Pathology of So-Called Occult Phenomena."

Jung did his internship at the Burgholzli Medical Hospital in Zurich, which became his permanent home. He studied with Pierre Janet, the famous French psychiatrist, in 1902, set up an experimental laboratory at the Psychiatric Clinic, and invented the word-association test for psychiatric purposes. He became a lecturer and senior physician there in 1905 and sent copies of his articles and his first book, *The Psychology of Dementia Praecox*, to Freud. His intellectual mentor invited him to Vienna and the pair of great psychologists talked non-stop for thirteen hours in their first dialogue. Weekly correspondence followed, and Freud came to regard Jung as his

Jung's Structure of the Psyche

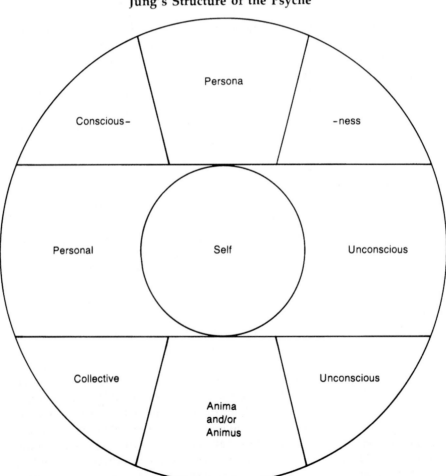

successor because of the disciple's deep insight as well as his scientific connections in the Christian society of early-twentieth-century Europe.

Although they maintained a close friendship, the founding fathers of psychology had basic disagreements. Freud insisted that the causes of repression are always sexual trauma and Jung disagreed. He saw humans as more than biological and sexual beings and took an interest in the way occult, mythological, and spiritual phenomena were interwoven throughout daily life and the case histories of his patients. Jung published *Symbols of Transformation* in 1912, which analyzed the Freudian concept of libido as generalized psychic energy and contained other ideas that varied from Freud. Jung's increasing self-reliance caused a break between himself and Freud, but Jung stood by his own convictions despite the pain of the split from his guru. Unlike Freud, who traveled little, Jung was more cosmopolitan; he visited Africa, India, and the Pueblo Indians, and studied non-European cultures while developing his own theories of the unconscious and religious symbolism. When their collaboration ended in 1913, Sandor Ferenczi, an associate of Freud's, quipped, "The Jung no longer believe in Freud."

Jung is in accord with Weber, Durkheim, Simmel, Sumner, Cooley, and Mead in the assumption that society precedes the individual in the interconnectedness of mind as well as the ways in which the individual expresses in his or her personality the characteristics of the culture as a whole and the qualities of the historical phase in which we live. The following interrelated concepts are relevant for the comprehension of Jung in sociological and historical terms: the psyche; psychic energy; archetypes and history; the persona; anima and animus; the attitudes and functions; and the collective unconscious.

The circle motif pervaded Jungian psychology and the self is portrayed as the central archetype of the total personality. Jung conceived of an archetype as a form or image of a collective nature which occurs cross-culturally. In the individual product it is unconscious. The concept of the unconscious in the Jungian topography of the psyche occupies a much vaster space than that of the conscious. The unconscious includes the nonwaking stages of dream and deep sleep and is divided into personal and collective aspects. The personal unconscious contains psychic contents which have been repressed or forgotten and drives which have not reached the layer of consciousness. It contains material which has been in consciousness or may be potentially in consciousness and is related to a particular individual.

The psyche is the functional starting point for analyzing the framework of Jung's thinking. It is a container, and when he asks what moves in its "space," he discovers "energy." He borrowed the Freudian term *libido* for instinctual sexual energy and redefined it as psychic energy, or the energy of the processes of life. Jung had a larger and more flexible concept of energy than Freud, as the energy is expressed on the cosmic level of life in the sociological network of relationships, and on the individual plane of the psyche of the human being. Jung takes a dialectical orientation based on the idea that all forms of life may be understood as a struggle of contending forces. Male and female, yang and yin, destruction and creation, death and rebirth, cold and hot, suffering and joy, damnation and salvation, pain and pleasure, doubt and faith, despair and hope, hate and love are all examples of the constant dance and drama of the pairs of opposites. Jung saw all life as energy and the principle of opposites is an integral part of his conception of the psyche. Yet he always remained aware that the map is not the territory. According to Jung, the amount of psychic energy generated varies directly with the intensity and depth of a conflict, and he stated that the greater the tension between the pairs of opposites, the greater will be the energy that is set loose.

The psychic energy that is generated by the dynamic interplay of the pairs of opposites is the moving force of society. The process of self-indication and the interaction of selves in institutions and organizations are driven by the libido and psychic energy. Just as the central archetype of the personality is the self, which functions as the nucleus from which the ego and persona radiate, so the primal archetypes of religious symbolism are God and the Messiah. All world religions have names for God, and the most sacred object, in the Durkheimian sense, is the legend and myth of the Messiah as the expectation of the Coming One. This empirical phenomenon is a matter of comparative religion and not mystical wish-fulfillment. The archetypes and history converge at a deep level of the collective unconscious as the panorama of a world historical age in themes such as the Second Coming of Christ, the Advent of the Messiah, and the return of the Mahdi in Christianity, Judaism, and Islam. The rise of Panduranga Vittala and the Coming of the Maitreya Buddha appear in Hinduism and Buddhism. This arrival of a Great Savior has been forecast by all world religious scriptures, tribal story-teller sages, mythologies, and folklore of the human race. The Messiah archetype may be another name for a highly refined and infinitely renewable energy.

Jung's concept of the persona is similar to the Mead–Cooley theory of the social self. The persona is the way we present ourselves to one another in daily life, and Jung referred to it as the mask individuals wear for social intercourse. The life process is conceived of as a theater of social encounters in various milieux, and the ego projects images of a persona that is suitable to the situation as it emerges. Thus, the persona includes social roles, the clothes and costumes we wear, and our styles of self-expression in ideas, speech, facial gestures, and body language. The persona functions as a cover for the inner life of the individual in the stage play of society, which requires easily identifiable occupational categories and basic attitudes, such as amiability or harshness.

While Freud postulated the constitutional bisexuality of human nature, Jung recognized that in every man there is a woman and within every woman there is a man. The Jungian psyche is balanced by the feminine side in men, which he called the *anima,* and by the masculine side in women, which he called the *animus.* The feminist movement owes a good measure of its success to the growth of the animus factor in the female population, while the gay liberation movement has been partially fueled by the rise of the anima element in the male population. Jung even asserted a biological basis for these sexual opposites within the personality. Although Jung's biological claim has not been demonstrated, the concepts of the anima and the animus play an important role in the social psychology of sex.

Notwithstanding the androgynous person's mode of integrating the anima and animus, Jung explains introversion and extroversion as the attitudinal types which symbolize the inward and outward movement of the reservoir of psychic energy. They are ideal types, in the Weberian sense that no individual conforms all the time to either an inward or an outward orientation but tends in one direction or another depending on will and circumstance. The psychic energy is constantly expressed in four functions, two of which are termed rational and two nonrational. Thinking and feeling are defined as rational functions of the psyche because they involve the individual taking a deliberate attitude and action toward an object. The thinker interprets an object; the feeler judges it. Sensation and intuition are considered nonrational because they are not purposive. Jung saw the sensation function as passive because the object is experienced by the individual instead of acted upon. The function of intuition is such that during the nature of the process the individual does not seek directly to understand the object. An idea, an answer, etc., just "comes" to you, and is therefore nonrational. One should see the overlaps and variations in these functions and attitudes and not analyze them as neat and separate categories. They are heuristic devices for understanding psychological types and trends in society and history. For example, Jung contrasted Immanuel Kant, an introverted-thinking type, with Charles Darwin, an extroverted-thinking type. Both theoreticians developed thinking as their dominant function, but Darwin turned it outward and Kant inward. Jung said, "Darwin ranges over the wide fields of objective facts, while Kant restricts himself to a critique of knowledge in general."[3]

The Collective Unconscious

Jung borrowed Freud's bimodal paradigm of the structure of the psyche by portraying a division between the conscious mind and the huge realm of the unconscious. According to Jung, the human infant is born with a psychological, as well as a biological, heritage. The neonate inherits more than a human body with a long evolutionary past and the genes of its parents; the baby comes equipped with a kind of psychic receptacle Jung called the collective unconscious, which is filled with archetypes. He used the word "collective" to differentiate it from "personal" and to indicate its priority to the individual personality. It is not collective in the ordinary sociological meaning of joint possessiveness; rather, it is collective in the sense that it is something generically present in humans and collectively held by all people. The unconscious is not a negative concept, as in Freud. Jung refers to the unconscious as that vast reservoir of psychic energy out of which all the

[3]C. G. Jung, *Psychological Types*, trans. by H. G. Baynes (New York: Harcourt, Brace, 1923), p. 484.

materials of consciousness emerge. Although the idea is amorphous and difficult to analyze, it is theorized as a positive and creative entity which supplies the symbols and other psychic contents which are brought to the surface of waking-state consciousness in daily life.

Jung went beyond the psychological to the archetypal self in *Modern Man in Search of a Soul.* Jung understood that we live in anomic times, in an historical transition period from an old to a new order of society, and recognized that individuals have spiritual needs which transcend the economic marketplace, social status, and the political arena. As a psychiatrist, he assisted his patients on their paths of growth to individuation; he also explored the collective unconscious and pointed to the cross-cultural archetypes, such as the eternal wonder child (e.g., Jesus, Hermes, Moses, Zeus), the universal mother as earth goddess in Hindu, Greek, and Roman religions, the grandmother of the American Indians, and the hero cycles in world mythologies. Jung had a marvelous way as a therapist of bringing people to their creative selves in the individuation process of his analytic and depth psychology. Through the interpretation of dreams, myths, and symbols, he brought people to a higher level of awareness of their fund of psychic energy that is the source of self-fulfillment, worldly prosperity, and the ongoing symbolic interaction of society.

And yet, Jung was aware of the shadow side of human nature, of the irrational element in the collective unconscious of civilization, represented by such death archetypes as Yama-Raj (God of Death in Hinduism), Thanatos (the Death Wish in Greek), and the Grim Reaper. Equating the archetypal self with "spirit" and "Christ" is counterbalanced in Jung's dualistic pairs of opposites schema by the shadow side of the inner executive ego, portrayed as a demon or the devil. Dr. Jekyll and Mr. Hyde are built into the psyche and its social manifestations. The causes of World War II may be explored through a social orientation of Jung's psychology. Nazi Germany can be seen as a classic example of demons and the Wotan symbols (e.g., primitivism, violence, and cruelty) of pre-Christian Germanic mythology arising from the historical depths of the collective unconscious into the national character and social psychology of a modern warlike state. Speaking generally, Jung says, "It is—and always was—my opinion that the political mass movements of our time are psychic epidemics, i.e., mass psychoses."[4] Jung thus made the connection between the archetypes, the collective unconscious, and history.

FREUD'S LAST TESTAMENT

Freud continued to live in his beloved Vienna until the situation there became intolerable. With the rise of Hitler to power in Germany the predicament of the Jews worsened. Psychoanalysis was "liquidated" in Germany.

[4]C. G. Jung, *Essays on Contemporary Events* (London: Kegan Paul, 1947), p. 79.

Freud's and other psychoanalytic books were burned in Berlin in 1933, and Jews were forbidden to serve on any scientific council. The Nazis seized control of the German Society for Psychotherapy, renamed it the International General Medical Society for Psychotherapy, and required all members to make Hitler's *Mein Kampf* the basis for their work. Several official Nazi psychotherapists met with representatives of the society and informed them that psychoanalysis could continue only if Jews were excluded from membership. Threats accompanied pressure, and the leveling process continued as the various branches of science were "nationalized," brought under a central control, and geared to serve National Socialist aims. In lieu of Freud's psychoanalysis and Einstein's theory of relativity, Nazi science adopted the doctrine of Aryan racial superiority.

With the Nazi invasion of Austria in March 1938, the streets of Vienna were lined with roaring tanks and trainloads of patriotic "extras" shouting, "Heil Hitler!" Freud was surprisingly reluctant to leave his native land; but his biographer and friend Ernest Jones managed to convince him to leave, and Jones arranged the complicated diplomatic details of Freud's emigration from Austria to England. However, the Nazis extracted their pound of flesh. They confiscated Freud's bank account and demanded a fugitive tax, without which they threatened to confiscate his library and art collection. During these trying times Freud worked an hour a day on his *Moses and Monotheism,* which tormented him like a "ghost not laid."

During his short stay in London Freud continued to practice psychoanalysis, kept up his correspondence, worked consistently on *Moses and Monotheism,* and received visiting dignitaries. His callers included the writer H. G. Wells, the anthropologist Bronislaw Malinowski, the painter Salvador Dali, and the Zionist leader Chaim Weizmann. Three secretaries of the Royal Society asked him to sign its Charter Book, which contained the signatures of Newton and Darwin. Although Freud was in agony from a jaw cancer that eventually claimed his life, he received these accolades with the grace of a nobleman and maintained his sense of humor to the end. Upon hearing a radio announcement to the effect that this war was to be the last war, a friend asked Freud if he believed that. Freud replied, "Anyhow it is my last war."

Freud's last will and testament was *Moses and Monotheism.* In this quasi-mystical, novelistic essay of self-discovery, Freud develops his general theory of monotheism, which focuses on Moses as the father figure and lawgiver of the Judeo-Christian tradition. Saul of Tarsus, the renegade rabbi who is commonly known as St. Paul, was to organize Christianity in early-second-century Rome on the foundations of original sin and salvation through sacrificial death. Saul's revelation was that human suffering is the effect of having murdered God the father, and his mission as the Apostle Paul was to preach that the sacrificial victim was indeed the long-awaited Messiah in the person of Jesus Christ, the Son of God. Freud argued that Christianity, which emerged from ancient Judaism, became a "Son religion" as a result of having displaced the slain primal father. In *Moses and*

Monotheism Freud not only amplified and extended the insights of *Totem and Taboo* and *The Future of an Illusion;* he was also reacting covertly to the oncoming pogrom. He concludes his book about Moses with the wry observation: "Only a part of the Jewish people accepted the new doctrine. Those who refused to do so are still called Jews."

Beyond the personal meaning that this rather speculative work had for Freud, *Moses and Monotheism* is highly suggestive theoretically. Its methodology rests on the projection of the psychoanalytic procedure onto the world historical plane. The history of a people may be read as if it were the history of an individual, with the intention of unearthing the cultural secrets or "repressed content" of the collectivity, whether the latter be a cult, a nation, a religion, or a civilization. Research along this line might illuminate the phenomenon of leadership in accordance with Freud's emphasis on leaders as embodiments of the collective superego. Such an approach would allow freer reign for what Mills called "the sociological imagination" to come to grips with what is going on in today's world at the fine point where biography intersects with society and history.

CRITICISM AND ADVANCES

Freud's theories gave rise to a flurry of psychological experiments in the 1930s and 1940s. Most of these were dubious tests of his hypotheses; for example, attempts were made to test repression by seeing if people find it harder to remember unpleasant things than pleasant ones, even though the mechanism of repression was postulated only for strong instinctual drives and their derivatives. A combination of behaviorist orthodoxy and middle-class America's reluctance to deal with any of the strong emotional drives that Freud was discussing has meant that academic psychology has done little to follow up his leads. Clinical practice, on the other hand, has heeded Freud's recommendations to pay attention to emotions and behaviors of which we are not ordinarily conscious (for example, childhood experiences, sex, and aggression). That clinical psychologists and psychiatrists are ambivalent about the veracity of Freudian theories and the effectiveness of his therapeutic methods should not obscure the fact that Freud's most basic discoveries have been vindicated, so much so that they have almost passed into the realm of common knowledge.

One criticism that may be leveled against Freud is that he reified his concepts. Notwithstanding his analytic disclaimers, he treated such mental ephemera as ego, id, superego, consciousness, and unconsciousness as if they were real objects; and Freudian terminology has come to be used by many professionals and laypeople in the same way. There is a measure of truth in the assertion that concepts, once entrenched in the literature, develop a life of their own; however, this linguistic phylogenesis must not blur the distinction between the real and the nominal. It should be underlined that Freud's conceptualizations are analytic tools rather than actual entities.

In addition, it may be said of Freud that he was culturally bound in his thought. His Eros/Thanatos duality is subject to this critique, in the sense that Freud's attitude toward death reflects a pessimistic period of Western thought. In conjunction with his contemporaries Freud regarded aging and death as the irresistible antithesis of life. This viewpoint contrasts with such recent Western European psychological paradigms of inner growth as Erikson's "ages of man" and Maslow's "hierarchy of needs," and contradicts Eastern doctrines of spiritual rebirth, through which aspirants attain enlightenment and come to see the world through the eyes of one newly born. Neither age nor sex is a barrier to this experience, as long as life is understood as a process of interior growth and personal development rather than as a slow decline into the grave.

The most valid criticism of Freud is that he observed repressed, middle-class, Victorian men and women and generalized from them to all humankind. Twentieth-century anthropological research by Bronislaw Malinowski, Margaret Mead, and others has shown that neither the latency period nor the Oedipus complex is universal. The type of adult sexual repression that Freud found in the social milieu of his day is by no means characteristic of all cultures. In addition to traditional societies on the Asian, African, and South American continents, contemporary lower- and middle-class subcultures in Europe and North America have mores different from Freud's formulations.

However, all of this does not invalidate Freud's work. It means, rather, that appropriate theoretical modifications must be made. Such innovations have been attempted by a group of "left-wing" Freudians, including Erik Erikson, Karen Horney, Erich Fromm, Geza Roheim, Herbert Marcuse, and Fritz Perls, who opened up a broad path for social and historical factors to enter this ongoing colloquy on human nature.

If Freud's work is understood as describing a particular historical period, it is a valuable complement to that of Weber. The Protestant-ethic personality—hard-working, uptight, repressed, puritanical—is exactly what Freud was depicting. Thus, the dictum, "Neurosis is the price we pay for civilization" is the clinical insight corresponding to Weber's pessimism about the effects of rationalization and bureaucratization on the quality of modern life.

Freud also complements Durkheim. Durkheim was of two minds about modern society. At first he argued that "organic solidarity" was a sufficient condition for social order, even though the contractual network first had to emerge from the emotionally binding "mechanical solidarity" of traditional societies. Later, after the Dreyfus affair and the tremendous conflict of turn-of-the-century France, Durkheim reconsidered and concluded that a purely formal, rules-and-regulations type of society created widespread anomie. As a social remedy for the normless state of affairs he advocated a return to workers' guilds, in which emotional solidarity could be found. Freud bolsters the later phase of his French contemporary's theory by suggesting that if people's feelings are overly repressed, any strains in the social order are likely to cause a channeling of pent-up emotion into social movements that allow them an outlet.

WAS FREUD A SEXIST?

With the resurgence of feminism, Freud again became controversial. On the one hand, he has been accused of being sexist. Psychoanalysis justifies traditional male and female roles in society, keeping women in the home while men pursue outside careers. On the other hand, some feminist theorists have tried to use and revise Freud precisely in order to explain the sexism that has dominated the social world.

On a certain level, it is true that Freud was an old-fashioned sexist. Despite the fact that most of his patients were women, he constantly wrote his theories from a male viewpoint. The Oedipus complex, the key to the psychic structure, is obviously a male problem: the little boy who must repress his desires for his mother and come to identify with his father. Freud never really explained how this worked in the case of females. His principal theory about women is one that has outraged feminists. Freud argued that a small girl, when she notices she lacks a penis, assumes that she has been castrated. This results in a lifelong sense of inferiority to men, and a more passive role in adult society. Should she exhibit aggressiveness or the desire to achieve in the masculine, public world, Freudians attribute this to her penis envy.

Nevertheless, despite these serious drawbacks, a number of feminist thinkers have attempted to revise Freud to help explain why we have had a male-dominated society. Their analyses are not designed to show the inevitable, but to see just what it is that needs to be changed. Juliet Mitchell, one of the first to argue that women are economically subjugated, went on to state that the patriarchal system of male domination is nevertheless older than capitalism, and constitutes an independent force behind sexism. To understand this, it is necessary to see how love, sexuality, and motherhood are internalized within the female psyche; and Freudian theory comes in handy for this purpose.

Among the most important of these feminist revisions of Freud is the theory of Nancy Chodorow. Her key question is, why do women do mothering in our society? Mothering, the process of taking care of a child, physically and especially emotionally, is not the same as sheer biological childbearing or the nursing of an infant at the breast. Once children are born, their own biological mother need not be the person who takes care of them. This has been true especially since bottle feeding was first practiced. In fact, however, women do most of the mothering, caring for toddlers, and even older children. Some feminists even argue that women are mothering their whole lives: They mother their husbands at home, just as on the job as secretaries, nurses, or waitresses they are expected to perform mother-like roles for male bosses and customers.

Mothering, then, is a social role, not a biological one. It is not instinctual, Chodorow points out; studies show that both men and women react similarly to infants' cries and smiles, and among animals even males will often care for an infant of their species if left alone with one. Similarly, women who are separated from their infants for medical reasons shortly after childbirth do not develop as much affection for them. The mothering role is learned. But how?

Chodorow draws on a version of Freudian themes for the answer. Both the infant boy and girl are cared for by a mother. In the original state of the child's psyche, there is no reality-oriented ego, but only a pleasurable merging with the other. It is this infant experience, according to Freud, that is the prototype of later sexuality; long afterwards, the child and then the grown adult seeks unconsciously to recapture this feeling by sexual contact (or some symbolic displacement of it). This transfer is inevitable; no one can remain an infant in mother's arms indefinitely. There are social pressures, too, in the form of incest taboos, which force the child to give up any sexual designs on the mother, and seek sex partners outside the family.

For a boy, this process results in the classic Oedipus complex. The jealous father has a special role in depriving the son of his mother. The little boy, fearing his punitive father, not only gives up his sexual desires for his mother, but internalizes his father in the form of a superego, a kind of fantasy father that he identifies with and carries around inside his head. For a little girl, though, the break is not so severe. She is given more permission to be close and affectionate with her mother, even in a physical way. True, she too has to pull away, and fathers normally carry on a degree of flirtatiousness with their daughters that is basic to encouraging them into a heterosexual role. But there is not the traumatic pressure as in the case of the boy. Moreover, the girl does not come to identify with her father, or internalize him as her superego. Instead she acquires a distinctively feminine superego, and indeed a whole feminine psychic apparatus or personality.

This feminine personality is characterized by an underseparation between herself and other people. Whereas the boy develops a sharp separation between himself and the world, due to the forceful and abrupt giving up of his mother in the Oedipal complex, the girl does not experience this sharp division. Men turn out to be distant, oriented toward the world of objects, domineering, and achievement-driven. Women prefer intimacy and warmth in personal relationships, and define themselves more in relation to a group of others.

And this, Chodorow concludes, is exactly what makes up the maternal personality. A mother is simply a typical female, finding her personality needs in being close to other people and submerging herself in the group— in this case, the group made up of her own family, and especially her children. Because of her continuing lack of psychic separation from her own mother, she has a need to continue this kind of close and nurturant relation with others. Mothering reproduces itself across the generations.

Chodorow concludes that if women are to break out of this sex-typed situation and take their places successfully in the larger society, this cycle of role reproduction must be broken. One way it can be broken is if men take a larger part in caring for children, especially emotionally. Then children will grow up with less radical separation between male and female worlds; psychologically, boys brought up in this way should have less of the depersonalizing split between self and others, while girls will identify more with fathers and acquire greater psychic entrée into the hitherto male-dominated worlds of work, politics, and achievement.

Chodorow's theory is not without its flaws. For one thing, sexist domination of society is not simply a matter of women willingly complying with nurturant feminine household roles. There are also the economic processes of which the Marxist feminists have written, and the sheer struggle for sexual domination from which men benefit. Moreover, Chodorow's women are too idealized: warm, loving, selfless creatures who have no demands of their own. In fact, plenty of women have been tough, aggressive, suspicious, or selfish, and have fought for position both inside the family and outside it. Chodorow fails to see enough conflict in society, either in the outer world where sexual discrimination is practiced, or in the family itself. Women have been quite capable of fighting with their husbands over family power when they have had the resources to do so. And mothering itself is not so idyllic as Chodorow makes it; women get angry at their children, sometimes even abusing them, and fight with their children over control more than they would like to admit.

What has to be borne in mind is that Freud's perspective is one of conflict, too. The tendencies that Chodorow describes probably do exist, but they coincide with other tendencies—assertive and selfish ones—what Freud called the id. A mother can simultaneously love her children and fight with them, just as she can both nurture her husband and hate his patriarchal controls. It is this kind of inner conflict and ambivalence, in fact, that makes divorces so bitter, and makes the struggle for women's rights one of the most emotionally difficult of battles.

Freudian theory thus continues to play an important part in our thinking today. Clearly the last word is not in on a theory of sexism in male-female relations. In addition to Chodorow and other feminist theorists who emphasize the mother role as the archetypal female activity, a theory of gender stratification has been developed from Freud's emphasis on sexual drives as a primary human desire. In this perspective, developed by Randall Collins on the basis of earlier theories of Kingsley Davis and Claude Lévi-Strauss, men have sought to control women as erotic property. In earlier tribal societies, women were exchanged among groups to make political alliances. In modern society, men and women bargain directly in a sexual marketplace, in which men have up until now held most of the economic bargaining cards. In this perspective, it is not surprising that as women acquire greater economic resources of their own, they can afford to bargain with men less for men's earning power and more for their own sexual attractiveness; hence the time of the feminist movement also turned out to be a time of erotic liberalization.

Freud, in fact, may have been closer to this than we realize. Freud's own theories were paternalistically sexist, but his data were not. Bearing in mind that the first great wave of women's liberation in Europe began in the German-speaking countries around the turn of the twentieth century, one can put into perspective Freud's patients, mostly neurotic women from this very era, suffering from the family stresses of a newly emerging situation in which women were beginning to assert some independent rights. Freud may have misinterpreted what was going on, claiming to see in these conflicts an eternal psychic pattern when it may only have been an historically temporary one, as women struggled over sexual repression as a strategy within a male-dominated society. But the genius of a theorist may be to point at the crucial processes, more than to arrive immediately at the correct answer.

CHAPTER NINE

The Discovery of the Invisible World: Simmel, Cooley, and Mead

SIMMEL

About the same time that Emile Durkheim was giving sociology a distinctive scientific identity in France, a similar attempt was being made in Germany. The German equivalent of Durkheim was Georg Simmel (1858–1918), whose career is strikingly similar to Durkheim's—and also strikingly different. For Durkheim was successful, and Simmel was not. Like Durkheim, Simmel formulated a view of society as a level of analysis independent of observable individuals, with laws of its own that required a separate science to investigate them. Simmel pointed out more clearly than anyone that since only individuals are physically real, the subject matter of sociology must be an invisible world of symbols and forms of interaction. He thus avoided some of the possible mystification inherent in Durkheim's "collective conscience." But Durkheim went on to become one of the most prominent thinkers in France, while Simmel spent twenty-nine long years waiting to be called to a professorship in Germany. All his life Simmel was an outsider, and his work shows both the strengths and weaknesses peculiar to that position.

Simmel came from a wealthy and cultured Jewish family, and indeed his work is full of echoes of music, art, and drawing-room conversation. After studying philosophy, he became a *privatdozent* (private lecturer) at the University of Berlin in 1885. Not until 1914—just four years before his death—was he to gain the long-sought promotion to full professor. Forces conspired to keep him out. He was a Jew in a time of growing anti-Semitism, a liberal in Imperial Germany, the proponent of a discipline, sociology, that was associated with the un-German politics of Comte and Spencer. Simmel retreated more and more into the world of art and sociability, his sociology becoming a collection of insights—a theory of society, as it were, as if seen by a passerby, catching a few features as they struck the eye but never penetrating to the heart of the edifice. Like the subject of one of his most famous essays, Simmel was the stranger who sees things that other humans, wrapped in their familiar routines, cannot see, a man privy to secrets given him because he has no one to tell them to.

The formal background of Simmel's sociology was the tradition of German philosophy—Kant, Hegel, Dilthey, Wundt—which showed how humans see the world through a veil of their own perceptual forms and how these forms were passed on through human history in language, artistic ideals, myths, and legal systems. Accordingly, Simmel argues that society is an *invisible world* with laws of its own. These laws are found in the flow of culture—language, technology, social institutions, art—which molds each new generation along the lines of the past, and in forms or patterns of interaction among humans that have effects on what they may individually do. But humans are also living individuals. The culture that molds them and the interactions that constrain them are what make them human, but they are also something external and alien. The drama of humankind is, then, a struggle between the individual and the society—a drama that is fundamentally a tragedy, for the two forces must always exist together in every living person.

Simmel's sensitivity to these two simultaneous levels of existence resulted in a striking insight, one that has been followed up only recently: The social institutions that make up the relatively permanent heritage of a society—the state, the family, the economy, the class structure—are only an extended version of the everyday interactions of men and women meeting on the street, in stores and offices, or at a party. Thus, by studying the formal structure of the more fleeting encounters, we reach the essence of our invisible society.

"The interactions we have in mind when we talk about `society' are crystallized as definable, consistent structures such as the state and the family, the guild and the church, social classes and organizations based on common interests," wrote Simmel.

> But in addition to these, there exists an immeasurable number of less conspicuous forms of relationship and kinds of interaction. Taken singly, they may appear negligible. But since in actuality they are inserted into the comprehensive and, as it were, official social formations, they alone produce society as we know it. . . . Without the interspersed effects of countless minor syntheses, society would break up into a multitude of discontinuous systems. Sociation continuously emerges and ceases and emerges again. Even where its eternal flux and pulsation are not sufficiently strong to form organizations proper, they link individuals together. That people look at one another and are jealous of one another; that they exchange letters or dine together; that irrespective of all tangible interests they strike one another as pleasant or unpleasant; that gratitude for altruistic acts makes for inseparable union; that one asks another man after a certain street, and that people dress and adorn themselves for one another—the whole gamut of relations that play from one person to another and that may be momentary or permanent, conscious or unconscious, ephemeral or of grave consequence (and from which these illustrations are quite casually chosen), all these

incessantly tie men together. Here are the interactions among the atoms of society. They account for all the toughness and elasticity, all the color and consistency of social life, that is so striking and yet so mysterious.[1]

In one of his essays, Simmel speaks of men whose profession is to sit at home in full dinner dress, ready for a call from superstitious hostesses who find that they have a dinner party of thirteen about to sit down at table. Simmel was himself something of a "fourteenth man at dinner." Always the outsider, even in his chosen sphere of fleeting encounters, Simmel could not divest himself of his sociologist's detachment. Even more so than his later incarnation Erving Goffman (whom we shall meet in Chapter 13), Simmel was simultaneously within and without; neither completely participant nor completely observer; and his writings are a texture of insights that never quite make a solid system.

Simmel was the first to remove sociability from the realm of the taken-for-granted and to analyze it as part of the social structure. Sociability, he pointed out, is a little world within the world, with laws all of its own. Here one did not allow practical and serious matters to intrude. The doings of the outer world might provide the starting place as subject matter for conversation, but the conversation was to rule the subjects and not vice versa. In the hands of skilled conversationalists, politics, business, art, gossip, the weather, all become the vehicle for talk that is carried on for the sake of talking, as raw material to be shaped by the formal requirements of these artists of fleeting symbols. Sociability is thus a world of make-believe, making the world of "outer" reality into a fantasyland that exists solely for the pleasure of the players.

In the same vein, Simmel offers a perceptive analysis of the game of flirtation (which suggests that he must have been experienced at it—as do his knowledgeable remarks on love affairs and secrets). In its most refined form flirtation takes the raw material of sex and weaves from it a fabric of delight and fantasy, a symbolic world which turns the simplicity of physical passion into the subtle universe of love. By such sketches Simmel takes us into the heart of the salon society of Europe in one of its most dazzling eras.

But Simmel never really pushes through to a sociological theory of the causes and effects of sociability or pursues the ramifications of his view of humankind's symbolic performances into a general model of society. He does not draw the implication, just recently being developed, that individuals create their worldviews out of just such encounters—not only in polite upper-bourgeois drawing rooms, but in all classes of society—and that it is just such shared fantasy worlds that bind some individuals together and set them off against others. Simmel's payoff is aesthetic rather than sociological. He concludes his discussion of sociability with the observation that polite conversation has the same sort of function as a majestic view of the

[1]Georg Simmel, *The Sociology of Georg Simmel,* Kurt H. Wolff, ed. Published in 1950 by The Free Press Division of the Macmillan Company. Reprinted by permission.

ocean: Both give pleasure because they transmute the turmoil of life into a pleasing spectacle, viewed from a distance. The tragedy of conflict and failure, of individual versus society, exists in sociability as in serious life, but as material for play, and hence no longer dangerous and uncontrolled. The conversationalist emerges victorious in his world of symbols.

Simmel's sociology ranged much wider than drawing rooms, to include the serious realms of power, money, and historical change. As always, this material yields insights to Simmel's eye as he abstracts out the formal properties of diverse situations. His analyses of the effects of group size are classic, demonstrating that a group too large for all its members to converse together will have a different structure than a smaller one.

The point is drawn even more sharply when he compares two-person groups with three-person groups. The dyad's fundamental reality is its perishability, for it will dissolve whenever one person decides to leave; this gives each partner a particular hold on the other. The triad, however, has a basic independence of its members, for it will still exist if one person leaves. The individual thus becomes less significant to the group. Moreover, new configurations open up here, as it becomes possible for two to form a coalition against the third, or one to play the other two off against each other. In short, the whole realm of organized society and its power relations opens up through shifts in numbers and in the resulting geometry of social relationships. Simmel thus develops the meaning of Thoreau's remark, "I have three chairs in my house: one for solitude, two for company, three for society."

Simmel had other insights, some of them brilliant, on the structure of group conflicts, on the social relationships created by secrets, on the way in which the variety of groups in modern society gives each individual a distinctive set of social ties and hence produces modern individualism. But Simmel never really carried these ideas far enough to produce a comprehensive sociological theory. Unlike Durkheim, he does not try to test causal propositions against empirical evidence, but only to display a philosophy of the forms that flicker across the human landscape. At bottom, Simmel, the lonely outsider, hated society. He wrote that people in groups are ruled by the lowest common denominator and that the higher forms of intellect and morality are always individual products. This personal disposition contradicted Simmel's own insights on the ways in which the individual is a product of society, and it kept him from pressing on to the breakthroughs that came to Durkheim when he realized that people's moralities and ideas have their origins in groups and their rituals.

But if Simmel, the outsider of the German intellectual world, could not produce a genuine sociology from the leads it offered, there were others who would. The American universities had been reformed in the 1870s and 1880s along German lines, and American intellectuals were shaking off the stupor of the era of petty religious colleges. American sociologists, full of the same German philosophy that sustained Simmel and impressed by the empirical approaches of the new experimental psychology, were to succeed where Simmel failed. In Cooley and Mead, the relationship between the invisible world of social symbols and the mind of the individual was to become a theory of considerable power.

THE LIFE AND WORK OF COOLEY

Charles Horton Cooley (1864–1929) was born in Ann Arbor, Michigan, the fourth of six children. His father was a migrant from western New York, who had a distinguished career as a justice on Michigan's Supreme Court. Charles was an introspective, imaginative, and ambitious boy who read profusely. He prepared himself for college at age sixteen; however, ill health forced him to take seven years to graduate from the University of Michigan. Before taking his doctorate in economics in 1894, Cooley studied mechanical engineering, worked for the Interstate Commerce Commission, and traveled abroad. For his doctoral dissertation he presented a theory of transportation relating a socioeconomic solution of the railway question to the study of territorial demography. This work remains a benchmark in "human ecology," a field that was to be fruitfully researched and developed by Roderick McKenzie, Robert Park, and Ernest Burgess in Chicago a generation hence.

Cooley's early inspiration came from Emerson, Goethe, and Darwin. From Herbert Spencer, whom he criticized subsequently for his subjectivity and lack of "culture," Cooley received his first broad outline of evolutionary knowledge. Franklin Giddings of Columbia University encouraged his aspirations to teach sociology as a university subject at Michigan. Cooley was a member of an academic clique that admired John Dewey, whose personality and lectures on political economy in 1893 and 1894 made a deep impression on Cooley's thought. Dewey criticized and went beyond Spencer by maintaining that society was an organism in a more profound way than the latter had perceived. Dewey's analysis of language as the "sensorium" of society corroborated Cooley's burgeoning interpretation of written language as the social medium of transmission par excellence.

While preparing his thesis, Cooley became intrigued by the "psychic mechanism"; he was especially concerned with the transmission and modes of recording language through space and time. He studied these processes in their historical and contemporary forms until he developed a conception of communication that was consistent with his organic view of society. In his lectures and studies he continually related his findings to such major aspects of the social process as conflict, survival, and adaptation. Cooley transcended the Darwinian climate of opinion by becoming a social psychologist. He came to the realization that he could never actually *see* the social life of humankind unless he understood the processes of mind with which society was indissolubly linked. He observed the mental-social development of his children as a method of organizing and expanding his theoretical insights. After beginning to teach, he read Walter Bagehot, William

James, Gabriel Tarde, and Mark Baldwin and readied himself for his first book, in 1902, *Human Nature and the Social Order*. Cooley preferred a life of contemplation and continued to teach at his midwestern alma mater all his life. He turned down a professorship at Columbia, although he did consent reluctantly to serve as president of the American Sociological Society in 1918.

COOLEY'S SYSTEM

Cooley's social thought encompasses several interrelated dimensions: (1) His approach was organic; (2) his viewpoint was evolutionary; (3) his outlook was moral and progressive; and (4) his ideal was democratic.

His organicism rested upon the theoretical assumption of the reciprocity of the individual and society. In his first book he systematically debunks the alleged antithesis of the individual versus society on the grounds that the latter is a psychical whole of which the individual is a particular expression. As the separate individual is a myth, so is society an illusion when conceived of apart from individual members. For Cooley "society" and "individuals" are collective and distributive aspects of the same thing rather than empirically separable phenomena. Thus, society becomes a living whole, or organism, composed of differentiated members, each of which has a special function. A university, for example, is composed of administrators, faculty, and students, with each status group having particular roles to perform within the organizational structure. This approach was a predecessor of the emerging functionalist system.

Cooley's evolutionary viewpoint suffuses his system; yet it differs from the social evolutionism of Spencer and the leading nineteenth-century anthropologists in its emphasis on individual rather than collective aspects of development. Cooley is more concerned with the evolution of the individual's social being (how the growing organism acquires a sense of the "I") than with grand historical sequences or stages of cultural evolution. His view encourages the student of human nature to believe in life as a creative process of which the human will is an integral ingredient. Far from being a passive element of society, each individual does his or her unique share in the work of the common whole. Cooley perceived each individual as a "fresh organization of life," which flows from the hereditary and social past. He envisioned each life history as containing a stream and a road; he discerned the stream as heredity, which comes through the germ plasm. He apprehended the road as "communication or social transmission," including language, interaction, and education. The road, which contemporary sociologists might call "culture," is a later development than the stream.

Cooley's moral outlook is expressed in his equation of rationality with the judgment of right. By rationality Cooley meant more than the product of formal reasoning; he pointed to the more profound rationality of conscience as an outcome of the social life of a person, including one's interactions with others and imaginary conversations with oneself. By locating society in the mind, Cooley, in his ethical treatise "The Social Aspect of Conscience," was able to explain the moral nature of confession as the opening of oneself to another, higher, more ideal person from whose vantage point one is able to obtain an outside view of oneself. Cooley's morality was thus rational, social, and progressive. While he did not feel, like some ethnocentric evolutionists, that twentieth-century culture was the apex of civilization, he did believe in the necessity for humankind to have a high and vivid image of personality that was morally edifying. One's reach, so to speak, should exceed one's grasp. He discerned three practically universal ideas of right: loyalty to the group, kindness to group members, and adherence to the customs of the tribe. Whereas his contemporary, Max Weber, understood the rationalization of the world in terms of continual disenchantment (for example, the recent demystification of the moon), Cooley stressed the possibilities for personal growth in a right (that is, rational) society efficiently organized according to democratic principles.

His conception of democracy embodied a philosophy of mind-enlarging consciousness. Cooley found the earliest forms of democratic unity in Western civilization among the pre-Roman Teutonic tribes, especially in the social units of the family, clan, and village group. Without indirect communications media such as the telegraph, telephone, radio, and television, people had to come together in face-to-face contact to experience the rising tide of social excitement that led to higher levels of consciousness. The people of old held feasts, games, and public assemblies and ceremonies as occasions for group exaltation and as opportunities for the expression of public opinion. Modern-day Americans celebrate the astronauts' space flights through the mass medium of television; the Romans fed Christians to the lions in stone stadiums; and the ancients chanted, sang, and danced festively around the campfire. Rock concerts and jazz, gospel, and country festivals are contemporary examples of a return to primitive modes of togetherness, with the added thrill of amplified sound made possible by recent technological and cultural developments. Cooley stated that although "democracy as a spirit is spontaneous," it could only have a large-scale spiritual effect with the liberation of the creative faculties of the members composing the body politic. He saw in the present epoch the potentiality for a "higher and freer consciousness" and understood democracy as the general phase of that enlarged consciousness.

Cooley comprehended institutions as definite and established products of the public mind which were the outcomes of the organization and crystallization of thought around the forms of customs, symbols, beliefs, and lasting sentiments. He perceived such institutions as language, the family, industry, education, religion, and law as continually responsive to the needs of human nature. He saw them as "apperceptive systems" of the public mind, which were inseparable from, and unreal without relation to, one another. Here again one can notice glimmerings of functionalism; Cooley, however, did not make the mistake of reifying the social system and locating needs in it rather than in the people who created it. Since *sociality* is mental, the institution is an individual habit of mind that is largely unconscious because of its commonality. The individual is not merely a passive effect of the social order; he or she is an effective cause as well.

The Looking-Glass Self and the Primary Group

In *Human Nature and the Social Order* Cooley presents his theory of the social self. Drawing upon Wilhelm Wundt and especially upon William James, he discusses the meaning of the "I" as observed in daily thought and speech. This "I" is the empirical self that can be verified by observation; it is neither an a priori Cartesian assumption nor a metaphysical entity. Cooley observed that this primal idea referred least often to the body and most often to either the "my feeling" or to the "looking-glass self." He regarded the self as a feeling state that is more or less consistent with ideas as they arise in our experience. The former "my" attitude refers to the individual's sense of appropriation toward various objects and people. He gives the example of gloating as a reflective self-feeling state in which the person who has either accomplished or acquired something that is pleasing thinks "mine, mine, mine" with a warm sensation. Cooley extends James's definition of psychology as the study of states of consciousness by establishing the sociality of selfhood as it relates to the thought of others. The social self emerges as an idea taken from the communicative life that the mind treasures as its own.

It was from this line of reasoning that the concept of the looking-glass self was born. In order to grasp this germinal idea, one should bear in mind Cooley's dictum: "The imaginations people have of one another are the solid facts of society." The dimensions of the looking-glass self are threefold: First, we imagine our appearance or image in the eyes of the other; second, we imagine some judgment of that appearance; and finally, we experience some sort of self-feeling such as pride or mortification. In other words, "I feel about me the way I think you think of me." For example, a person would be ashamed to appear ignorant in the presence of a learned man, or glad to be recognized by a celebrity. This phenomenon pervades our everyday existence in the social arena at even subtler levels than shame or joy. All the little looks and gestures that happen in daily encounters with others constitute the very fabric of society. This aspect of Cooley's sociology has been developed in the social thought of Erving Goffman, a man whom we shall meet in a later chapter.

In Cooley's primary theory of social psychology, that we are the imaginations that we have of one another, and that society is the organic whole of which all imagining individuals are parts, he asserted that these imaginations are the solid facts of society. In the relation of self to society, individuals project images of their selves, which, as James said, are basically of the modes of self-denial or self-affirmation. From the latter group come the stars in the institution of entertainment (or "show business"). The star system represents a stratification of social selves—from the "superstars" to the less famous—in relation to the nonstars—viewers, audience, fans, or public.

The old adage that stars are born and not made may be true; however, the promotion of the social self of a star is the secondary function of an effective agent with the right business connections and contacts in the industry as well as the charisma of the performer. The decline of the hero in our times has given rise in mass society to the phenomenon of the celebrity, a manufactured personality with or without talent. The celebrity's image is sold to the collectivity through advertising in the media (especially television, movies, radio, newspapers, and magazines).

The Hollywood-derived star image is an economic commodity competing with other marketable image-commodities of packaged personalities. Perceptive commentators on America have observed that we, and many of the other high-tech countries, are living in the era of the cult of the personality. Movies are to the twentieth century what oil paintings were to the nineteenth, and such legends as Al Jolson, Maurice Chevalier, Jimmy Durante, Bette Davis, John Wayne, Jack Benny, Judy Garland, Fred Astaire, Bing Crosby, Charlie Chaplin, Noel Coward, Marlene Dietrich, Bob Hope, Danny Kaye, Frank Sinatra, and Marilyn Monroe took time and space to magnify themselves in our imaginations.

As the movies are replaced by television as the primary entertainment medium, the marketplace of the star system shifts from the public place of the theater to the private locale of the home. Since advertising remains a constant factor of American society, the star system maintains itself in a modified form. Still, the mind, in which the stars themselves exist, remains the locus of society in the Cooleyan framework. Hollywood has been the dream factory and the center of Romantic America. As the scene switches more to television, "TV Guide" has become the log of that civilization. And now we are entering a new era in the evolution of communications, as well as a transition from one electronic source-dyad of the definition of "reality"—the movies and radio—to another—television and the computer.

In *Social Organization* (1909) Cooley introduced the concept of the primary group. Such an association is characterized by intimacy, face-to-face interaction, emotional warmth, and cooperation. These groups are the seedbeds of society in the sense that they are fundamental in forming the social nature of the individual and his or her primary ideals, including love, freedom, and justice. The outcome of a primary relationship involves a "we" feeling that makes for close identification of the self with the life of the group. Sociologically universal examples of this mode of association are the children's play group, the family, the neighborhood, and the council of elders. The basic experience of the primary group is the feeling of social unity with other members. In contemporary times primary groups have been emerging in the form of urban and rural communes, as people begin to band together with varying degrees of success for survival purposes and to reexperience a lost or shattered home life. For Cooley the self-governing, democratic village commune was the highest social form. He quotes

Tocqueville: "It is man who makes monarchies and establishes republics, but the commune seems to come directly from the hand of God."

In contrast to the primary group the secondary group is impersonal, contractual, formal, and rational. Relationships are cool rather than warm. Professional associations, corporate bureaucracies, and nation-states are classic examples of this group type. But primary and secondary groups should not be taken as mutually exclusive categories. For example, primary groups may emerge within the secondary bureaucracies in the forms of boards of directors, academic cliques, circles of confidants, and like-minded associations.

CRITICISM OF COOLEY

Cooley's methodology was one of "sympathetic introspection." By this he meant the process of the social scientist putting himself or herself in touch with various sorts of persons, attempting to imagine how the world appears to them, and then recollecting and describing as closely as possible their particular feeling states. By this method Cooley essayed to understand the inner lives of rich and poor, criminals and children, conservatives and radicals, idiots and idealists. No phase of human nature was alien to him, so deep and wide were his sympathies. He took his own nature as a reflecting prism of the whole, and by examining his responses to others' presentations of self, he sought to pierce the invisible veil of society.

Since Cooley's methodology was analogous to Max Weber's *verstehen* and Pitirim Sorokin's "logico-meaningful" method, it may be criticized on similar grounds. A major canon of scientific method is that its statements must be intersubjectively testable; otherwise, reliability of results becomes impossible. Indeed, one of the scientific dilemmas of Western sociology has been the immense difficulty of agreeing upon uniform methods and procedures. Since Cooley depended primarily on his personal powers of observation and drew his insights by an imaginative reconstruction of society from his peculiar vantage point, there would be no way for objective social scientists to test his conclusions empirically. Mead himself took Cooley to task for locating society in the mind instead of in the social world out of which psychical experiences arise. However, Cooley was breaking new ground by locating the self in consciousness rather than in behavior and therefore felt free to unload his mind of positivist baggage. Methodological precision concerned him far less than breadth of comprehension.

Cooley was a sanguine practitioner, whose small-town sociology is suffused with the mores and attitudes of midwestern, white, Anglo-Saxon, Protestant liberalism. Cooley spent most of his life with his family and in the academic cloister at Ann Arbor, preferring not to venture into the flow of surrounding society. The prime advantages of this sheltered existence were the opportunities to meditate calmly and deeply on the quality of social life and to consolidate an expanding sociology department at the

University of Michigan. The main disadvantage was Cooley's failure to come into direct or frequent contact with people of diverse modes of life. He understood the problems of social organization in terms of personal degeneracy; his analysis, while penetrating, was more speculative than empirical. His uplifting armchair sociology rings with a kind of idealization of the real, which disdained the painstaking task of data gathering.

Unlike Freud, Cooley was relatively out of touch with the world of unconscious wishes and motives. Cooley accepted Goethe's notion of the individual as a unified whole and rejected both biological and psychological determinism. The underlying theme of Cooley's theory of self was the metaphor of growth. His faith was in the individual's untapped potentialities, or what Dewey called "the infinite perfectability of man." Cooleyan sociology was a rationalistic blend of the provincial and the universal. The former attitude was a reflection of an isolationist America that had yet to be swept onto the international scene by a world war, while the latter pointed to the essentially Christian foundations of American civilization and the subsequent emergence of the national drive to "make the world safe for democracy."

THE LIFE AND WORK OF MEAD

George Herbert Mead (1863–1931) was born in South Hadley, Massachusetts, the son of a pastor. He studied at Harvard under the tutorship of Josiah Royce and William James. He traveled widely and took courses at overseas universities, mainly in Germany. In 1893 he was awarded a recently founded chair in philosophy at the University of Chicago, where John Dewey became a colleague and personal friend. Mead taught there until his death in 1931. He exercised a tremendous influence on several generations of students, principally through his oral teaching; his publications during his life consisted of scattered articles, notes, and critical studies in various philosophical, psychological, sociological, and pedagogical journals.

All those who knew Mead personally were unanimous in remembering him as a rare, high, and disinterested spirit. He was a professor who knew how to charm as well as interest his students. He had a manner well suited to the exposition of ideas; he reasoned in a spiral by returning to what he had already said and then integrating it at a higher level of understanding. He made a new point with each line of reasoning, weaving previous threads into a larger and more comprehensive fabric of thought. Colleagues and students admitted, moreover, that conversation was his medium; writing was a poor second best. Despite the pressure of the academic world to "publish or perish," Mead became chairman of the University of Chicago's philosophy department without having published a single book. Four volumes of lecture notes gathered by pupils and friends were issued posthumously under the titles of *The Philosophy of the Present* (1932), *Mind, Self, and*

Society (1934), *Movements of Thought in the Nineteenth Century* (1936), and *The Philosophy of the Act* (1938). Like Georg Simmel, he was a philosopher turned social scientist, and in order to get a clearer portrait of Mead's social psychology within the history of sociological theory it helps to consider his philosophical perspective.

MEAD'S SYSTEM

Mead's social thought is relational, evolutionary, and pragmatic. Upon reading Mead one is struck with a sense of what Alfred North Whitehead called "the interrelatedness of things." As a philosopher of science Mead understood the mechanical and atomistic bias of the nineteenth century as an outcome of past systems of ideas. The chemists and physicists of the preceding century were mainly preoccupied with the notion of matter as composed of static, solid, self-sufficient particles. Their focus was on the structure rather than on the activities of the atom. With the recent emergence of relativistic theories in the natural sciences, atoms were perceived in terms of "eigen states" or "patterns of stability." This shift in emphasis, which provided a wider theoretical frame of reference for explaining physical events, was paralleled in Mead's social psychology by the dissolution of the implicitly atomistic image of humankind of much nineteenth-century sociology.

The sociologies of Comte, Marx, Spencer, and even Durkheim apprehended the relationship between society and the individual primarily in a deterministic manner. The locus for action resided almost wholly in the social or economic system such that "the invisible hand of society" totally controlled human behavior. The human individual was portrayed as a kind of self-contained molecule within the larger social organism. Mead's relationism consisted of his theoretical joining of self and society in the ongoing social process such that the individual was neither isolated from his or her fellows nor wholly determined by any abstract system.

Mead's theoretical achievement was arrived at inductively by observation of what happens in the daily lives of human beings. For Mead the society in which we interact with one another in sundry groups constitutes an empirical reality. It is a product of evolution and is divisible into many modes of social reality, which are dependent upon variable definitions of the situation. He distinguished between Aristotelian and Darwinian ideas of evolution; according to the former doctrine, evolution is the development of the existing plant or animal species (which is the Latin word for the Greek term "form") without reference to the environment. In contrast, the theory presented in Darwin's *Origin of Species* is not concerned with the development of a particular species as such; rather, it is interested in showing how various forms evolve and survive in response to environmental pressures. Those forms survive that can best adapt themselves to changing life conditions. Behind this post-Aristotelian conception is the idea of a life process that takes on various forms (or species), which arise and decline through space and time. The human form is a relatively recent evolutionary development.

It was the German romantic idealists, culminating with Hegel, who formulated a philosophy relevant to the human life form in terms of the reflexive experience of ourselves as actors in the social world. According to this tradition the self is not a static unity that exists *in vacuo;* it is a dynamic, historical process that involves a subject-object relationship and arises as a result of interaction with other selves. The more we become aware of ourselves in the continuing social process, the more we increase our "species consciousness." In other words, we become more able to understand our human form as a consequence of life and social processes.

As a pragmatist philosopher Mead is heir to James and Dewey. Mead viewed modern research science, with its mathematical and experimental methods, as both a cultural outgrowth of the European Renaissance and Enlightenment and an emergent evolutionary tool whereby humans might intelligently control their social institutions. He was in agreement with Dewey that scientific method applied to the problems of society was the key to the door of progress. Mead interpreted pragmatist doctrine as having three phases and two primary sources. The former included the following assumptions: (1) that a hypothesis is "true" if it works when tested, (2) that the process of knowing lies within human conduct, and (3) that knowledge is a process of acquiring the necessary "scientific apparatus" (including ideas, concepts, units of analysis, theoretical models, paradigms, equations, and so forth) to carry out the desirable task of social reconstruction in a democratic state. He understood the sources of pragmatism to be (1) behavioristic psychology, which enables the social scientist to apprehend intelligence in terms of human activity, and (2) the process of research or scientific method, which is self-revising and tests an hypothesis by how it works.

Mead recognized the French Revolution as the pivot of modern history; it built the principle of revolution into social institutions by incorporating the people's right to change or amend the constitution upon which the state is founded. The fundamental scientific problem that emerged in Mead's mind, then, was how we become selves in a rapidly changing and seemingly chaotic world. How to preserve order and at the same time accommodate change was Mead's perennial question.

The Social Self

That the human being has a self is the major supposition of Mead's theoretical framework. It is no mystical conjuration but an empirical exercise to observe that human beings make indications to themselves in the course of everyday life. Mead defined these "self-indications" as anything of which one is conscious, such as a ringing telephone, a friend's remark, the lyrics of a song, a thought, the recognition of a familiar figure, and so forth. The importance of discerning the existence of these self-indications is twofold: (1) An object (physical, abstract, or social) may be extricated from its setting and acted upon; and (2) the fact of human self-indication enables the individual's action to be constructed rather than simply released.

Mead distinguished between the *stimulus* and the *object.* The former does not have an intrinsic character that acts upon individuals. In contrast, the meaning of the object is conferred upon it by the individual. Human beings *react* to a stimulus (for instance, an unexpected pin prick), but they *act toward* an object (for example, the determination not to flinch at an injection). Individuals are not surrounded by a world of preexisting objects that coerce them; rather, they build up their environment of objects according to their ongoing activities. From a myriad of prosaic everyday acts, such as getting dressed or preparing food, to major life decisions, such as choice of vocation or mate, the individual is making self-notations of objects, assigning them meaning, assessing their utility in reaching various goals, and then deciding what to do on the basis of such judgments. Mead understood this interpretive or self-conversational process as acting on a symbolic basis.

Mead made fuller sense of Dewey's notion of language as the sensorium of society by delving into the symbolic processes of human communication. He distinguished between gesture and symbol, deriving his concept of the former from Wundt's *Völkerpsychologie* and from Darwin's psychological classic *The Expression of the Emotions in Man and Animals.* By the term "gesture" Mead meant a social act that operates as a stimulus for the response of another form engaged in the same act. He presents as an example of a "conversation of gestures" the dogfight, in which the forms interact with one another on a nonsymbolic basis by growling, baring the teeth, and nipping the flanks. In such a situation each dog does not stop to ascertain the meaning of the other's aggressive behavior. One dog's response of growling to the other's baring of teeth is not made on the basis of what that gesture stands for. The first dog does not respond to the *meaning* of the second dog's gesture, because it does not indicate to itself the hostile intentions of that gesture. The adjustive behavior (that is, the ensuing fight) is called forth by the character of the stimulation, without any intermediary process of interpretation of meaning.

Human beings respond not to the gesture but to its meaning; thus, human language or communication is symbolically interactive. Take, for example, the baseball situation of "at bat." The pitcher peers down from the mound to receive the signal from the catcher as to what type of pitch to throw, while the batter checks with the third-base coach for hitting instructions relayed from the manager in the dugout. The catcher may indicate a curve ball by extending, say, two fingers, and the third-base coach may order a bunt by touching his ear and tipping his cap. Thus, before the delivery of the pitch, the situation has been structured according to prearranged signal systems, which have a common meaning (that is, evoke similar responses) for the actors involved. That the pitcher has the option of calling for another pitch and that the batter might be guessing that a curve will be thrown mean that the players are not merely reacting like dogs to gestures; they are interpreting symbolically the meaning of the signs, thereby organizing their activity to act intelligently toward the situation confronting them. When the gesture evokes the same attitude in the receiving as well as the sending form, it is a significant symbol. When the bodily or vocal gesture (speech) reaches that stage, it has become what we call "language."

What enables human beings to interact meaningfully (that is, symbolically) with one another in the ongoing social process is the primary mechanism of role taking. As human beings become objects to themselves and learn to act toward themselves in various ways, they also learn to assume the roles of others in constructing their behavior. They learn to cast themselves imaginatively into the other person's frame of reference and to assume an attitude toward themselves that reflects this sympathetic understanding. For example, a parole-board officer attempts to ascertain the prisoner's fitness for parole on the basis of his moral and sympathetic judgment of the prisoner's current attitude toward the law. The self is reflexive in the sense that it coils back upon itself in the communicative process, and it is social in the sense that it is built up continually in the course of daily encounters with other human beings. The social self is a product of a series of defining situations which arise in the life of the individual. In addition, the social self is an emergent process within society, which Mead construes as the fitting together of individual lines of action in human groups via role taking.

The social self is neither a static intellectual monad like Descartes' cerebral "I" nor a defense structure such as Freud's executive "ego"; rather, it is a dynamic and changing transaction between the individual and others. Mead described the contents of the social self in terms of "I" and "me" aspects. The conception of the self as binary rather than unitary was mentioned by James and developed by Cooley, but it found its fullest expression in Mead. Mead understood that the social act itself is phasic in that the human being delays his or her action toward other forms. In preparing the act, the individual can consider the possible responses of the other in lieu of reacting wholly on impulse. Furthermore, the self that organizes its behavior within the social act in relation to other forms is composed of conditioned and spontaneous phases. Mead identifies the former as the "me" and the latter as the "I."

The "me" represents the organized set of group attitudes that the member assumes. It is the conventional, habitual, and routinized aspect of self that is always there. The "me" determines our self-consciousness insofar as we are able to take the role of others within the larger community of selves. Each member of a choir, for example, knows the score he or she is supposed to sing, and the resulting harmony of sound is a product of cooperation among the sopranos, tenors, and basses. The "I" stands for the response of the individual to the organized attitudes of others. It is aware of the social "me" in the sense that the "I" of one moment is present in the "me" of the next. In other words, the "now" or what Mead called "the present" is the sphere of the "I," while the "me" consists of the organization of past attitudes. Mead's "I" accounts for such phenomena as novelty, spontaneity, artistic creativity, and social change in relation to social situations, which function as occasions for the emergence of a creative self. The "I" as construed by Mead is the sociological analogue to Werner Heisenberg's indeterminacy principle in physics. Mead's formulation cracks the ideological edifice of determinism by allowing for the element of chance or free will in human affairs.

Mead developed an original theory of social change from the "I" concept. He understood institutions as social habits that are necessary for the maintenance and preservation of social order. Social control rests ultimately on the exercise of self-control, whereby the individual feels inwardly obliged to respect the rights of others within the community. This relationship of the individual to society becomes highlighted when persons of great mind and moral character emerge and make the wider society a different one. A genius's behavior is as socially conditioned as that of the ordinary person, with the exception that the genius's response to the organized attitude of the group is unique and original. Einstein, for example, lived a relatively simple life; however, his response to physics' universe of discourse was such that the consequences of his theoretical synthesis changed society at large. The lives of such world teachers as Jesus, Buddha, and Socrates are symbolic in the sense that their personal relationships represented an emergent order that was implicit in the institutions of their respective communities. They were deviant with respect to particular public moralities, but conformist in giving complete expression to such central principles of the larger community as rationality, neighborliness, truthfulness, and brotherly love. They were manifestations, so to speak, of higher beings, who, as religious personages and as charismatic leaders endowed by their publics with spiritual authority, approached the social realm from the standpoint of the spiritual plane and were enabled thereby to effect major social change.

The Generalized Other

Mead's second major contribution to sociological theory was the concept of the "generalized other." In the growth and development of the self the generalized other represents the stage at which the individual is finally able to relate to himself or herself according to the attitude of the whole community. Prior stages in the genesis of this truly social self are the preplay, play, and game stages. In the earliest phase of self-genesis the child's baby talk is a reflection of its inability to make an object of itself through which it can approach itself. Mead objected to Tarde's theory of direct imitation because it failed to explain the manner in which individuals learn to make objects of themselves, a process that is inherent in the evolution of human selfhood.

During the play stage of socialization, children assume roles segmentally and arbitrarily. They play in a quasi-theatrical way at being mother, father, doctor, television star, or astronaut. During this interval children have a rich fantasy life and begin to take on roles in a rudimentary manner by assuming the vague personalities that populate their minds as a result of the McLuhanesque environment in which they dwell—a mass communications environment, which has become increasingly electrified since Mead's day. The successive radio and television generations of American youth have derived their symbolic worlds and their role models increasingly from the entertainment media, including comic books, movies, and record albums, rather than from literature or personal contact. The mind begins to develop during this formative stage as the child stimulates its imagination by assuming inwardly the attitudes of its heroes.

In the game stage, the child no longer assumes the attitude of particular individuals toward itself; it ceases taking discrete roles. The child who plays in a game must be ready to take the attitude of everyone else involved in that game and needs to understand how the different social roles are interrelated. The child is confronted by the ongoing activity of others, which is organized and has procedural rules. To grasp the group in terms of its activity is essential. The child learns the rules of the game not by rote acquisition, but in anticipating how others are going to act in the game situation and then adjusting its behavior toward their lines of action and building up its own. According to the framework of symbolic interactionism, learning includes role playing in a situation where the social self arises in the ongoing group process.

The final stage of self-development, according to the Meadian schema, is the generalized other. This concept parallels Durkheim's idea of the collective conscience and Freud's formulation of the cultural superego. What is significant about this phase is that the individual has transcended rule-following behavior by becoming conscious of his or her realization of the rules. This ability of making an object of one's consciousness, of one's own process of self-indication, enables the human being to take an abstract role, which stands for a series of concrete roles. For example, the president of an organization assumes an abstract role insofar as she is aware of the particular roles that constitute the status network of the hierarchy. Other instances of such complex roles would be those of the peace negotiator, political ambassador, labor arbitrator, football coach, United Nations representative, and presidential "troubleshooter." In each case the individual must be aware of invisible, informal webs of personal relationships in addition to the organizational loyalties of the involved social actors.

Mead identified the generalized other with the organized community or social group that gives the individual his or her sense of self-unity. The generalized other entails the extension of role taking into continuously expanding social circles, from the Cooleyan primary groups to such secondary associations as the workers' union, the university, the corporation, the political party, and the nation-state. The whole community, from the small group to the giant bureaucracy, can express an attitude only because it is represented in each individual's mind as the attitude of the generalized other. As the size of Spaceship Earth shrinks with technological progress in transportation and communication, a global consciousness begins to emerge in minds around the world. To Mead and those who follow him in his train of thought, the League of Nations and the United Nations appear as attempts to institutionalize a planetary generalized other in order to resolve national conflicts of interests by mediation and mutual understanding rather than by war.

The generalized other is an idea of high explanatory power which has had considerable influence in the formulation of empirical social research. Herbert Hyman's derivative concept of the "reference group" has become one of the central analytic tools in social psychology. Robert K. Merton and Alice S. Rossi interpreted it in terms of a "social frame of reference" while analyzing the causes of varying degrees of dissatisfaction among World War II troops. Muzafer Sherif employed related concepts in experimental studies of individual conformity to group judgments. Further implications of the concept of the generalized other remain to be explored by future generations of social psychologists.

CRITICISMS AND ASSESSMENTS OF MEAD

A major defect of Mead's sociology is its failure to account for the phenomena of power and stratification. Since he was more concerned with developing a social psychology in which the whole (society) is prior to the part (individual) and with describing the complex process by which the biologic individual acquires a self in the social process, Mead tended to ignore the ways in which humans dominate and manipulate one another in political, economic, and status hierarchies. His approach to society was discursive rather than rigorously structural, and his schema neglected to analyze social class and mobility. Although his philosophy was relatively apolitical, it did reflect an underlying liberal ideology of self-improvement through personal change. A radical element of Mead's thought that has not been fully appreciated is his theory of the social consequences of personal change.

Another problem with Mead's theory is the difficulty of operationalizing his concepts for research purposes. Such notions as the "I" and the "me" and the "generalized other" are too vague to quantify in an era when hard research is measured by elaborate indices, matrices, and tests of statistical significance. Since Mead's universe of discourse lends itself neither to the data-accounting approach to sociology nor to a calculus of theoretical propositions, his social psychology is sometimes regarded as useless for social research.

But the argument may also be reversed. Mead's relational perspective contains a covert critique of positivistic sociology. This critique has been most succinctly stated by Herbert Blumer, one of Mead's former pupils at the University of Chicago. According to Blumer the fundamental deficiency in contemporary sociology is that it operates with unrealistic images of human beings. Humankind is not merely a medium through which beliefs, values, norms, and roles work themselves out in behavior; the human being is an acting agent who takes these matters into account in constructing his or her behavior vis-à-vis the situations in which he or she acts. To be faithful to the character of human group life, it is necessary to recognize human beings as acting organisms organizing their own activity, rather than as neutral entities pushed into action by forces allegedly working through them.

For Blumer the trend in contemporary sociology is to remove sociologists from intimate familiarity with the life and experience of people in society. To the extent that this occurs, they become naïve about the world they propose to study and accept abstract theoretical constructions or answers to a few short survey questions as a sufficient contact with empirical reality. The Medians thus turn the tables on their positivistic detractors. As we shall see in Chapter 13, developments in social phenomenology have opened up the possibility of closing the gap between the two perspectives, of bringing about a close analysis of subjective experience as the foundation for more arm's-length research methods.

Finally, Mead may be criticized for being naïve in his equation of process with progress. He stressed consciousness and rationality, while paying little attention to the unconscious and irrationality. Indeed, for Mead the Freudian unconscious was a chimera, since whatever people fail to indicate to themselves are things of which they are unaware. Mead's optimism wears a bit thin in view of the violent holocaust that unfolded after his demise. However, one must remember that Mead was at bottom an ethical philosopher, who, like Durkheim toward the end of his career, was struggling to enunciate what he called a "method of morality." In essays collected under the title *Fragments on Ethics* Mead portrayed humans as rational beings, because they are social beings. By analyzing the philosophies of Kant and the utilitarians he arrived at a pragmatic position according to which the only rule ethics can present is that an individual should deal rationally with all the values that are found in a particular problem. Mead's analogue of the Golden Rule was to "act toward other people as you want them to act toward you under the same conditions." His method of morality would take into account the combined and interrelated interests of the individual and society.

PART III

The Vicissitudes of Twentieth-Century Sophistication

CHAPTER FOURTEEN
Contemporary Sociological Theory in France, Germany, and the United States

CHAPTER FIFTEEN
The Impact of Women in Sociology in the Late Twentieth Century

CHAPTER TEN

The Discovery of the Ordinary World: Thomas, Park, and the Chicago School; W.E.B. Du Bois and African-American Sociology

The year 1918 marked the beginning of a new era in American sociology. It saw not only the end of World War I, the coming of women's suffrage, and the decisive dominance of a new urban America, but also the publication of *The Polish Peasant in Europe and America* by William I. Thomas and Florian Znaniecki. This five-volume work, running to 2,244 pages, was a monument in more ways than one, for it represented the first major American effort to win attention by bringing together general sociological theory with large-scale empirical research. The age of systematic sociological research had just begun.

For its first few decades, such research had a very well marked home. It was the University of Chicago, from whose medieval stone walls and picturesque courtyards the sociologists of the "Chicago school" sallied forth to investigate the surrounding urban slum. The university enjoyed an intellectual position during the first half of the twentieth century rivaled only by Harvard; Enrico Fermi's cracking of the atom and Robert Hutchins' famous educational reforms were only some of its better-known accomplishments.

Founded in 1892 on John D. Rockefeller's millions, Chicago sought preeminence from the very beginning. Its first faculty consisted of many of the top thinkers in America, pirated away from rival institutions by Chicago's dynamic president, William Rainey Harper. The first department of sociology in the world was set up there at its outset, under the chairmanship of Albion W. Small, who had come directly from the presidency of Colby College in Maine.

THOMAS'S LIFE AND WORKS

William I. Thomas (1863–1947) was one of the first graduate students in the sociology department. He was already in his thirties, having previously taken a Ph.D. in English, held a professorship at Oberlin College, and studied philology and ethnology in Germany. Within a year after appearing at Chicago, he had a position on the faculty. Although he was the son of a rural southern preacher, Thomas became very much the sophisticated urbanite and *bon vivant.* Known as a snappy dresser and a lady charmer, Thomas eventually talked a wealthy Chicago heiress into putting up $50,000 for the study of race relations. This was quite a sum for its day (1908) and indeed constituted the first big research grant in the history of American social research.

With this money Thomas embarked on a study of Polish immigrants in Chicago. He originally intended to study other ethnic and racial groups as well, but his sense of empirical thoroughness led him to limit his focus. The Poles, as the biggest immigrant minority in Chicago at the time, posed an important enough question in themselves, especially since the Chicago newspapers were currently full of alarm about "Polish crime": the unpredictable outburst of violence from otherwise stolid and acquiescent people. Thomas, who had fully immersed himself in the social thought of his day (see Chapter 5), was already critical of simple evolutionist or racist theories of behavior. He expected that neither automatic modernization nor hereditarily determined failure would be the fate of these transplanted Polish peasants, and his research was designed to find out exactly what was happening.

Thomas drew for his approach on the latest developments in social psychology, especially the dynamic outlook of James and Mead. Social life must be seen from the inside, as people actually experience it, Thomas felt. Social structures operate on individuals only as the individuals interpret them and feel them bearing down against their own attitudes and motivations. He later formulated a key element of the symbolic interactionist approach in the statement that has since become known as the "Thomas Theorem": "If men define situations as real, they are real in their consequences."

In accordance with this methodology Thomas learned Polish, read the local immigrant press, and observed daily life in the Polish ghetto. His most famous methodological innovation was the use of letters that Polish immigrants had written to relatives at home. Thomas hit on this method fortuitously. One day, walking through the ghetto, he jumped back quickly to avoid a bundle of garbage thrown out of a window. In the pile of garbage he spied a pack of letters. Since he could read Polish, he looked through them and found a vivid account of immigrant life "from the inside." Subsequently, Thomas advertised in the Polish press for other collections of letters and used these as a major part of his documentary materials.

In 1913, while on a trip to Poland, Thomas met Florian Znaniecki (pronounced Znan-yet-ski), a young Polish philosopher, and they discussed Thomas's work. The next year the Germans invaded Poland and Znaniecki escaped to America. Completely unanticipated and uninvited, he showed up penniless at Thomas's house in Chicago. Thomas took him in and made him a collaborator in his research, especially in filling in the background on the peasants in Poland.

The completed work, which began appearing in 1918, had an immediate impact, at least within sociology. It established the superiority of large-scale systematic research over speculative and superficial approaches, and it at last brought theoretical issues down to where they belong—in confrontation with the real world. *The Polish Peasant* concluded, among other things, that crime was the result of the lack of mediating institutions to integrate the individual into the larger society. Accordingly, a strong Polish-language press, Polish parishes of the Catholic Church, and other immigrant cultural institutions were far from being alien and dangerous to the fabric of American society. On the contrary, Thomas and Znaniecki argued, it was just such institutions that integrated the Polish community around itself and hence provided the prerequisites for its eventual integration into the rest of society. Thomas and Znaniecki thus avoided the naïve positions—condemning the immigrants or demanding their immediate Americanization—and gave a more sophisticated analysis based on careful observation of the facts. Their work can be faulted, especially for its neglect of politics, but in general their view holds true and bears considerable relevance to the experience of other minority groups, including the black minority of today.

But, at the very moment of his triumph, Thomas's career had a sudden shock. Early in 1918 he was arrested by the F.B.I. in a hotel room with a Mrs. Granger, the wife of an army officer on duty in France. The charges—violating the Mann Act and registering in a hotel under a false name—were thrown out of court, but there was a great public scandal. The arrest appears to have been politically motivated, since Thomas's wife was currently prominent in Henry Ford's peace movement, then anathema to the Woodrow Wilson administration. The University of Chicago, under an onslaught of unfavorable publicity from the Chicago *Tribune* and similar quarters, abruptly dismissed Thomas. There was scarcely a protest from the faculty; for all his eminence, Thomas had enemies.

Thomas spent the rest of his career traveling and writing under grants from the Carnegie Corporation, the Social Science Research Council, and various wealthy heiresses. Except in the flashiness of his life style, Thomas might well be called the first sociologist of the modern era of research grantsmanship. Znaniecki went on to become a theorist of some note. Ironically, with its founding spirit in exile, the Chicago school emerged in the 1920s as a full-blown movement in sociology. Its new leader was, appropriately enough, a protégé of Thomas, Robert E. Park (1864–1944).

PARK AND THE CHICAGO SCHOOL

Park, too, had had a colorful nonacademic career. He also had come from a religious, rural family. He studied philosophy with John Dewey at the University of Michigan and with William James at Harvard, and in between he spent twelve years as a newspaper reporter, based from New York and Detroit to Denver, Minneapolis, and Chicago. Like most other intellectually oriented Americans, he put in his sojourn in Germany, where he encountered Simmel and earned a Ph.D. from Heidelberg in 1904. Park then became secretary of the Congo Reform Association and wrote a famous exposé of the barbaric conditions prevailing in the colonial regime of the Belgian Congo.

The racial situation in America attracted him next, and Park became a ghost writer and adviser to the black leader Booker T. Washington. Indeed, it has been urged that Park was the "power behind the throne" in Washington's movement. In any case it seems fair to say that the two men shared the same gradual, assimilationist, up-by-your-own-bootstraps philosophy of change. It was at Washington's Tuskegee Institute in Alabama that William Thomas discovered Park in 1914 and brought him to Chicago. After 1918, with Thomas gone from the scene, Park took over the leadership of the Chicago school. The ex-newspaperman gave the group just the impetus that was needed. The growing city was the big story of the day, Park exhorted, and he sent his students out to find "the big sociological news" in the everyday world around them. Before the 1920s were over, the Chicago school had produced a series of studies such as Nels Anderson's *The Hobo* (1923), Frederick M. Thrasher's *The Delinquent Gang* (1927), Louis Wirth's *The Ghetto* (1928), and Harvey W. Zorbaugh's *The Gold Coast and the Slum* (1929).

Park himself, with his colleagues Ernest W. Burgess and Roderick D. McKenzie, produced an overall picture of the city, with a perspective derived from animal ecology. Although their model may have been unduly shaped by Chicago's position on the shores of Lake Michigan, it gave an elegant picture of the city as a set of concentric rings: a downtown core where the very rich and the very poor lived nearby (if in drastically different conditions), surrounded by neighborhoods beginning with slums and becoming progressively better as one reached the suburbs. As the city grew and new immigrants arrived, the best-off inhabitants moved to the outskirts. Their previous places became filled by the more prosperous members of the next inner ring, who in turn vacated spaces for the ring inside them, and so on until we reach the center, where the newest immigrant groups found the poorest places from which to begin.

This model of ecological succession was elaborated theoretically in several ways. In the 1930s researchers began to map rates of suicide, mental illness, crime, and other forms of deviance onto such ecological diagrams and found they were concentrated in certain areas of the city. These were called "disorganized" areas and were believed to generate deviance. Another variation was Park's famous "race-relations cycle," which bears a metaphorical as well as a substantive relation to his ecological model. All groups, claimed Park, struggle for domination of available resources, both economic and territorial. After initial contact between alien groups, there is conflict. This stage is followed by the stage of accommodation, in which the boundaries between groups become clearly marked and respected on both sides (that is, the stage of segregation). Finally, there is assimilation, as the subordinate group adopts the ways of the dominant group and eventually disappears into it.

These theoretical models were fruitful in stimulating considerable research, but in the end they were not substantiated. The ecological picture of deviance suffers, we have discovered, from numerous flaws: It overlooks the fact that people can move into an area after becoming deviant, rather than becoming deviant because they are there; it ignores biases against reporting crime and other deviance by inhabitants of the more respectable areas; and it is guilty of the "ecological fallacy" in statistical inference (of which Durkheim was also frequently guilty) of supposing that the *average* characteristics of the people in an area can be taken as reliable evidence of how particular *individuals* are being affected. (For example, we cannot conclude anything if the area with the lowest average education has the highest suicide rate, for it may be the highly educated persons in that area who are committing suicide.) Similarly, Park's model of the race-relations cycle turns out to be purely speculative as far as the crucial stage— assimilation—is concerned. The experience of such groups as black Americans has shown us that assimilation may occur in language and politics without occurring in the economy or in personal relations. Nor is there an inevitable trend from conflict to accommodation; indeed, events can run in the opposite direction (as in the 1960s), and the theory does not tell us when or why this may happen.

In general, the principal shortcoming of the Chicago school turned out to be the thinness of its theorizing, and this in the end was to be its downfall. It has since lapsed into a preoccupation with statistical methods and descriptions, in the virtual absence of explanatory theory. Park's ecological model was merely an approach to describing the city and lacked any real substantive or predictive power. The naïve optimism of his theory of race relations is obvious today. Missing from Park's theory—and missing as far back as Thomas's *The Polish Peasant*—were clear ideas of stratification, of power, and of politics. An approach to these things, however, was developing outside the granite walls of the Chicago school.

In fact, the empirical tradition had already been launched. W. E. B. Du Bois, in 1899, had already carried out a massive research project called *The Philadelphia Negro*. But American sociology at the turn of the century, like the rest of the society, was segregated, and Du Bois remained scarcely known. Even among black leaders, Du Bois was regarded as a dangerous radical; his only recognition came from Max Weber, far away in Germany.

W.E.B. DU BOIS AND
AFRICAN-AMERICAN SOCIOLOGY

From Great Barrington to Harvard and Berlin

William Edward Burghardt Du Bois was born in Great Barrington, Massachusetts, in 1868, three years after the end of the Civil War and five years after the Emancipation Proclamation. His ancestry was a mixture of mostly African, some Dutch, and a strain of French. His grandfather, Tom Burghardt, fought in the American Revolutionary War, and his service freed him and his family from slavery before the Bill of Rights of 1780, which declared all slaves in Massachusetts free. Du Bois' boyhood was typical of today's single-parent households, and he credited his mother with being a strong and nurturing influence during his youth after his roaming father drifted away from his family.

The folkways and mores of polite New England society permeated the climate of opinion in Du Bois' small hometown in the valley of the Berkshires, and the precocious scholar did not feel the insult of prejudice until he realized gradually that some of the respectable Great Barringtonians considered his brown skin unfortunate. Du Bois became the local correspondent of the New York *Globe* at age fifteen, and used his position to better his race by giving short lectures and instructing fellow blacks on how to form their own political organizations. His growing racial awareness was evidenced by his senior oration on the life of Wendell Phillips, the antislavery writer.

Du Bois won a scholarship to Fisk University in Nashville, Tennessee. Although the Fisk faculty was white with one exception, Du Bois felt free from the shadow of the veil that divided the races to a much greater extent in the end-of-the-century South than at his northern home. He discovered the fabric of rural black southern culture, teaching summers at a country school in a log cabin with dirt floors built before the Civil War. While serving as the chief editor of the *Fisk Herald* and sharpening his comprehension of the race problem he prepared himself to fight the "color bar" in a peaceful but forthright manner.

Du Bois entered Harvard as a junior in 1888 and came under the intellectual influence of the idealist philosopher George Santayana, and especially of America's pragmatist psychologist William James. He took his Ph.D. degree from Harvard in 1895 with the dissertation *The Suppression of the African Slave Trade to the United States of America, 1638–1870*. Vernon Loggins, literary commentator and author of *The Negro Author* (1931), called that work "by far the greatest intellectual achievement which had by 1900 come from any American Negro." Du Bois praised the North for its efforts on behalf of education, yet scolded the region for not providing the Afro-Americans it had schooled with economic opportunities. He argued in a Marxist vein that the southern white oligarchy exploited its workers and that political participation would enable them to protect their economic interests.

Du Bois went on to the University of Berlin for postgraduate study in sociology, history, and economics under such figures as Heinrich von Treitschke and Max Weber. He assimilated from this experience the scientific methodologies of social research, including by extrapolation Weber's method of *verstehen*. Du Bois maintained a correspondence with the great German sociologist, and Du Bois' novels and sociological writings reveal an empathic understanding of people's subjective understandings. Weber requested that Du Bois write an article on "The Negro Question in the U.S." for the *Archiv für Sozialwissenschaft und Sozialpolitik*, which Weber edited.

The Founding of Afro-American Sociology

Du Bois experienced culture shock in returning to a racist American society and found no openings for teachers at the black colleges of Fisk, Howard, and Hampton. He did land a job at Wilberforce College in Ohio, teaching Latin and Greek. However, the political and church hierarchies at the college, which was administered by the African Methodist Episcopal Church, put a damper on his social scientific plans for Afro-American freedom. The school was in dire financial straits, and he barely received a sympathetic ear.

The University of Pennsylvania hired Du Bois, the first black to receive a Ph.D. from Harvard, as an assistant instructor in 1896 to conduct a research project in Philadelphia's Seventh Ward slums. Du Bois took advantage of this opportunity to study the life of the blacks as a social system. He moved into a neighborhood apartment with his new bride and applied the social research methods of participant observation, multivariate and statistical analysis, and demographic mapping for the black population. Du Bois believed that sociological method, including *verstehen*, would go a long way toward solving the race problem, and he interviewed five thousand respondents with various questionnaires. The resulting book, *The Philadelphia Negro*, is the first major empirical work in American sociology. Although he was critical of certain black social patterns, such as crime and prostitution, Du Bois eschewed the current genetic approach to social theory and blamed the social problems of the Afro-American community on the environment and the moral depradation of slavery, not innate racial inferiority. Franz Boas, anthropologist and colleague of Du Bois, says, "An unbiased estimate of the anthropological evidence so far brought forward does not permit us to countenance the belief in a racial inferiority which would unfit an individual of the Negro race to take his part in modern civilization."

In 1897, W. E. B. Du Bois took charge of the work in sociology at the University of Atlanta. He laid out a ten-year-cycle study (1896–1905) of institutional aspects of black society, including mortality, business, education, art, environment, religion, and crime. When World War I broke out in 1914 Du Bois planned a one-hundred-year study program of Afro-Americans, factoring in demography; biology; socialization according to family, group, and class; the cultural patterns of morals and manners; and law and government. The impact of the Atlanta Studies on Afro-American sociology (1897–1910) was phenomenal; it published 2,172 pages of sophisticated analysis on a variety of issues.

While Durkheim and Weber were laying the foundations for sociology in the industrial democracies of the West, Du Bois focused his energies on the foundation of an Afro-American sociology during the first four decades of the 1900s. At the first Pan-African Congress, organized by the Trinidadian English barrister H. Sylvester Williams and held in London in 1900, Du Bois declared, in his address "To the Nations of the World":

> The problem of the twentieth century is the problem of the color line, the question as to how far the differences of race—which show themselves chiefly in the color of the skin and the texture of the hair—will hereafter be made the basis of denying to over half the world the right of sharing to their utmost ability the opportunities and privileges of modern civilization. (*ABC of Color*, p. 20; *Souls of Black Folk*, p. 54)

Theoretical Influences

Weber and Marx had a greater influence on the development of Du Bois' thought and politics than the fin-de-siècle Social Darwinist climate of opinion. Du Bois understood the laissez-faire evolutionist Spencer's implied "survival of the fittest" viewpoint, but the pragmatic mode of instruction and philosophy he learned from James was more useful for his purposes. Weber's emphasis on the politics of stratification, in addition to the need for systematic, sustained, and exhaustive socioeconomic historical research, characterizes Du Bois' work. The Marxist undercurrent of his writing comes out increasingly in his considerations of the African slave trade. The slave traders who debased humanity by their economically profitable but ethically immoral machinations were equivalent to the racist white European colonial bourgeoisie who were exploiting the underclass of workers or the black proletariat, which Du Bois believed destined to overthrow the bonds of caste and discrimination.

The Social Evolution of Afro-American Leadership

Du Bois recognized Frederick Douglass (1817–1895) as the first national black leader. Douglass was the chief abolitionist, a lecturer and writer who escaped from slavery in 1838, bought his freedom, and then founded and edited the *North Star*, an abolitionist paper, between 1847 and 1860. He worked with the Underground Railroad, served as a consultant to President Abraham Lincoln, and met with John Brown, a fellow abolitionist of Puritan stock, austere life style, and Christian values. Du Bois writes in his preface to his biography *John Brown* (1909), "John Brown worked not simply for Black Men—he worked with them; and he was a companion of their daily life, knew their faults and virtues, and felt, as few white Americans have felt, the bitter tragedy of their lot."

For black America, 1895 was a watershed year, with the passing away of Douglass and the emergence of a new leader, Booker T. Washington. His "Atlanta Compromise" speech of 1895 favored a program of industrial and trade school education, and political conciliation of the South, until Afro-Americans could attain first-class citizenship by becoming an effective labor force. Washington was a great orator and charismatic leader who emerged as the spokesman of America's ten million blacks. Du Bois had both praise and criticism for the new leader in his essay "Of Mr. Booker T. Washington and Others" in *The Souls of Black Folk* (1903). Du Bois said

> It startled the nation to hear a Negro advocating such a programme after many decades of bitter complaint; it startled and won the applause of the South, it interested and won the admiration of the North; and after a confused murmur of protest, it silenced if it did not convert the Negroes themselves.

Washington founded Alabama's Tuskegee Institute with the financial help of northern industrialists, and especially Andrew Carnegie, who contributed six hundred thousand dollars. Tuskegee taught young black students such trades as carpentry, tailoring, printing, dressmaking, mattress making, plumbing, laundering, and domestic service. This was hardly a militant threat to the racial class structure. In the conservative atmosphere of the time, Tuskegee emerged as one of America's most famous training schools, and its president became the most sought-after Afro-American in the United States. The Tuskegeean's peak years were 1899–1905. He received honorary degrees from Dartmouth and Harvard and became an adviser to Presidents Theodore Roosevelt and William H. Taft. Tuskegee gained notoriety as the "White House" for black affairs.

Du Bois came into conflict with Washington because Du Bois believed strongly in the value of a college education, the vote, and self-assertion for political and civil rights. Although both were dedicated black nationalists, Du Bois believed that the higher education of a "Talented Tenth" could acquire the knowledge of modern culture to guide the progress of Afro-Americans to a higher civilization. Du Bois' concept of the "Talented Tenth" was developed in an essay in *The New Negro* (1903) and held that a trained minority was necessary to provide the service and leadership for mass advance.

Du Bois' interests went beyond empirical social science into politics; Herbert Aptheker called him a "prophet agitator" and Elliot Rudwick called his biography of Du Bois *W. E. B. Du Bois: Voice of the Black Protest Movement*. Du Bois launched the Niagra Movement in 1905, and served as its general secretary. He gave credit for its founding to F. L. McGhee, who suggested it, C. C. Bentley, who planned the organizational method, and W. M. Trotter, who firmed up the platform. Du Bois drafted the principles of membership and the plan of attack. The group consisted of members of the "Talented Tenth," who were committed to implementation of such constitutional rights as the First Amendment freedom of speech and criticism, free and unsubsidized press, the vote, abolition of caste distinctions based on race and color, recognition of human brotherhood as a practical creed for the present age, highest-quality training without monopoly of class or race, dignity of labor, and a "unified effort to realize these ideals under wise and courageous leadership" (Foner, 1890–1919, I, p. 146).

Du Bois urged the necessity of complaint against rather than compliance to social injustice. That position was the nexus of conflict with BTW, as Booker T. Washington was known. Du Bois, the Atlanta sage, urged his adherents to take radical action against the curtailment of Afro-American political rights. His program included urging blacks to vote intelligently and effectively, pushing civil rights, organizing business cooperation and increasing interest in college education, opening new avenues of employment and holding the old, distributing information on laws of health, pushing the study of black history, aligning white labor unions and blacks into mutual understanding, increasing the circulation of honest, unsubsidized periodicals and newspapers, and having all civilized agencies attack crime. Du Bois said, "In fact to do all in our power by word or deed to increase the efficiency of our race, the enjoyment of its manhood, rights and the performance of its just duties" (Foner, 1890–1919, I, p. 148).

Du Bois had the soul of a poet combined with the intellect of a scientist. In *The Voice of the Negro* (1905) he wrote:

God give us men! A time like this demands

Strong minds, great hearts, true faith, and ready hands;

Men whom lust of office does not kill;

Men whom the spoils of office cannot buy;

Men who possess opinions and a will;

Men who have honor, men who will not lie;

Men who can stand before a demagogue,

And damn his treacherous flatterers without winking.

Tall men, sun-crowned, who live above the fog

In public duty and private thinking.

For when the rabble, with their thumb-worn creeds,

Their large professions and their little deeds,

Mingling selfish strife—lo, Freedom weeps,

Wrong rules the land, and waiting Justice sleeps. (Foner, 1890–1919, I, p. 149)

The Niagra Movement ran for five years as the first Afro-American national organization that made aggressive and unconditional demands for the same civil rights enjoyed by all Americans. Washington continued his attempts to destroy the movement. Nevertheless, at its final meeting, the Niagra Movement took some credit for "increasing spiritual unrest, sterner impatience with cowardice and deeper determination to be men at any cost" (Foner, 1890–1919, I, p. 116). The Niagra Movement, which had filled the de facto leadership gap of the Afro-American Council, was the predecessor of the National Association for the Advancement of Colored People. Under Du Bois' leadership the Niagra Movement laid track for younger men and women to follow.

The twenty-year reign of Booker T. Washington ended in 1915 with his death. The next strong leader to emerge on the scene of black society was Marcus Garvey. World War I had motivated a rural to urban migration, and Garvey set up headquarters for his Universal Negro Improvement Association (UNIA) in Harlem, New York, with branches in several American cities and foreign countries. Garvey, a Jamaican, was a professional printer; he was also an even more intensely charismatic leader than Washington. Garvey had a genius for showmanship and a dynamic personality that he used to establish the first mass movement among black Americans. His dream was for black industry and commerce and the ultimate freedom of Africa. Although Du Bois agreed with the UNIA's goals of the instillation of black racial pride and community organization, he criticized Garvey's lack of business acumen and his attitude that the United States was the real estate of the white race and that the black should not fight for social equality within American society.

The NAACP and *The Crisis*

Du Bois was one of the founders of the interracial National Association for the Advancement of Colored People (NAACP) in 1909 and he was appointed by the board as director of publications and research and editor of its propaganda organ, *The Crisis*. His editorship from 1909 to 1934 gave Du Bois the opportunity to exercise his sociological imagination for an educated black public and present black role models for the Afro-American community of the times. Although Du Bois was in conflict with O. V. Villard, NAACP treasurer, and criticized by others for his personal aloofness and intellectual elitism, he persisted in his aim of cultural pluralism. Du Bois was considered radical for his emphasis on ongoing black nationalism and on a broader basis for his desire for a multiracial society. At the Universal Races Congress in London in 1910, Du Bois advocated an overarching transracial "human brotherhood." *The Crisis* and its controversial editor reached their high point during World War I, when there was an accompanying flood of democratic propaganda for the equal rights doctrine prior to the advent of Garvey. Gunnar Myrdal observed, "Under the influence both of the criticism from the Du Bois group and of much changed conditions, he came increasingly to move toward an ideology which incorporated and expressed the Negro protest in cautious but no uncertain terms" (Myrdal, *An American Dilemma*, New York: Harpers, 1944, p. 743).

Du Bois' Empirical and Theoretical Work

Du Bois emphasized the preeminence of the environmental approach over the genetic doctrine in his empirical work *The Philadelphia Negro* (1899) and later writings. Despite the prevailing tendency to stress nature over nurture in the scientific air at the turn of the nineteenth century, Du Bois disallowed any inherent or inherited racial superiority of white over black. In his chapter on "The Environment of the Negro" Du Bois described a stratification system for blacks of four grades: the well-to do, laborers, the poor, and criminals. This model adds a moral dimension to the earlier economic analysis of class in his chapter on "The Negro Family." Du Bois' stratification research foreshadowed the later research in American sociology of E. Franklin Frazier, W. Lloyd Warner, and C. Wright Mills. The empirical research methodology of *The Philadelphia Negro* includes a variety of representations, including maps of the Seventh Ward and the city, tables, graphs, demographic curves, and statistical data stimulated by the work of Charles Booth and Francis Galton in England. The work, based on detailed questionnaires for the five thousand recipients, was carried out by Du Bois singlehandedly.

Du Bois' classic work *The Souls of Black Folk* (1903) is an extraordinary collection of essays composed in a poetic prose that emphasizes the predictive power of sociology regarding the racial conflicts that continue to plague our species and urges the autonomy of the black community. Du Bois defined the main problem of the twentieth century as the problem of the color line. Yet he went further, injecting a note of evolutionary optimism into his historical explanation of sociological variables:

> It is, then, the strife of all honorable men of the twentieth century to see that in the future competition of races the survival of the fittest shall mean the triumph of the good, the beautiful, and the true; that we may be able to preserve for future civilization all that is really fine and noble and strong, and not continue to put a premium on greed and impudence and cruelty. (*Souls of Black Folk*, p. 188)

Du Bois' Role as Elder Statesman

In his later career, Du Bois became a global traveler, advocating Pan-Africanism and world peace. He stressed the context of slavery, disenfranchisement, Jim Crow legislation, and antiblack racial prejudice and discrimination as negative conditioning factors against the emergence of a rationally conscious mode of high self-esteem for Afro-Americans. Du Bois set the stage both for the integrationist "dream" of Dr. Martin Luther King and the politics of black pride of Malcolm X and others. Such organizations as the Congress of Racial Equality (CORE), Student Non-Violent Coordinating Committee (SNCC), Urban League, NAACP, and Black Panther party of the 1960s–1990s were all influenced in some manner by Du Bois' political activism and social thought.

Du Bois used his tenure as chairman of Atlanta University's sociology department, 1934–1944, to promote social studies for black colleges and graduate schools with requests for financial support from individuals, foundations, and governments. The Atlanta University Conference of 1943 was the first meeting of black land grant colleges to coordinate a program of cooperative social studies. Du Bois chaired the conference committee, which brought the support of Howard Odum, Edward Reuter, E. Franklin Frazier, Charles Johnson, Donald Young, and other eminent American sociologists. The idea of an Encyclopedia of the Negro was projected in 1909 by Du Bois, but backers did not come up with the funding until 1931. Robert E. Park of the University of Chicago and W. E. B. Du Bois were the first editorial board collaborators. Guy B. Johnson of the University of North Carolina succeeded Park in the late 1930s.

Du Bois pressed for the civil rights of blacks through the Thirteenth to Fifteenth amendments to the Constitution and for the human rights of blacks by founding the Pan-African Movement, which held five congresses from 1900 to 1945, stressing Africa for the Africans instead of for the colonial profit of European nations.

Du Bois, who was referred to as the "Old Man" by blacks in the 1960s, became a symbolic leader of his race by going to Africa when he was in his nineties. President Kwame Nkrumah of Ghana appointed him to direct a secretariat for an Encyclopedia Africana in Accra, the capital of Ghana. Du Bois coordinated these efforts, which were sponsored by the Ghana Academy of Sciences. The "Old Man," who had visited Nikita Khrushchev and Mao Tse-tung, lost faith in the United States and became a citizen of Ghana. The proud and prolific Atlanta sage, who founded Afro-American sociology, criticized his ex-country for having betrayed the American Revolution's concept of justice. When Martin Luther King lead the March for Jobs in Washington, D.C., in 1963 Du Bois led a parallel demonstration in Accra. Du Bois died on August 27, 1963, at the age of ninety-five, his prophetic black soul home in the land of his roots.

THE INVESTIGATION OF SOCIAL CLASS

Du Bois remained on the periphery of American sociology. More attention went to black sociologists in the 1930s and 1940s, especially those who were trained at the center of the sociological Establishment, at Chicago, and who were sponsored by Chicago networks. Thus E. Franklin Frazier, who took his degree at Chicago under the influence of Robert Park and Ernest W. Burgess, became the most famous black sociologist and eventually president of the American Sociological Association. His dissertation on *The Negro Family in Chicago*, published in 1932, launched a controversy within sociology over the question of lower-class black family structure as an obstacle to black social advancement. In the 1940s black sociologists from Chicago, St. Clair Drake and Horace Cayton, produced *Black Metropolis*, a famous study of class stratification within the black community.

By this time mainstream empirical research had shifted its focus. American sociologists had discovered the centrality of social class. Not just inequality between races, but a dimension of economic stratification within them, was becoming the center of attention. The first to bring attention to the themes of social stratification in American sociology was, strangely enough, a young theologian from Princeton Theological Seminary. This was Robert Lynd, who, with his wife Helen Merrill Lynd, was preparing to set out on missionary work in Africa when he received a grant from a religious foundation to study religious behavior in the United States. The Lynds chose Muncie, Indiana, a prospering industrial town in the Midwest. Their approach, influenced by anthropological studies of primitive tribes, was to take up residence, to participate and observe as widely as possible, and to interview local informants. The Lynds soon concluded that the gap between white-collar (middle-class) and manual (lower-class) workers was by far the most crucial element in determining people's life styles, and they proceeded to produce the first study of a community's stratification. After eighty years Marx's fundamental sociological ideas began to receive some systematic empirical verification. The studies of Muncie, reported under the title of *Middletown* (1929), with a follow-up study during the Depression (*Middletown in Transition*, 1937), were immediately recognized. Robert Lynd became a professor of sociology at Columbia in 1931 and thus helped found a second major center of empirical research. Lynd became something of a spokesman for a liberal-left position in sociology; his son, the historian Staughton Lynd, became a prominent antiwar leader in the 1960s.

At about the same time that Lynd was working in Muncie, the anthropologist W. Lloyd Warner was finishing a study of Australian aboriginal tribes (published under the title *A Black Civilization*) and deciding to apply his techniques to a study of the natives of the modern United States. He chose the staid old town of Newburyport, Massachusetts, which was to appear in the research reports from 1941 onward as "Yankee City." New England struck back in defense with a satirical novel about an anthropologist who comes to study a seacoast town, *Point of No Return* by John P. Marquand. In the end, however, Warner had the upper hand in this exchange. His research has been criticized in various ways, most notably for its overemphasis on a supposedly rigid status ranking of the populace, but Warner's analysis of the religious and patriotic rituals of the Newburyporters (in *The Living and the Dead*, 1959) is a brilliant application of Durkheim's perspective to a modern society. Only a person with the detachment of an experienced anthropologist could have carried it off.

Warner went on to study a midwestern town, national business leaders, and large-scale organizational trends in America, with increasing emphasis on surveys and statistics. This methodology has become increasingly popular throughout sociology. The percentage of articles reporting statistics in the major sociological journals increased from 10 percent during the period from 1915 to 1924 to 60 percent during the period from 1955 to 1964. This trend represents the self-conscious effort of sociologists to become "scientific." The effects of this change have been both good and bad for the discipline. In his presidential address before the American Sociological Society in 1929, the Chicago sociologist William F. Ogburn announced sociology's scientific coming-of-age and its exclusion of mere social do-gooders. This was also a personal confession for Ogburn, who had begun his career as a Socialist and had gradually shifted to an emphasis on detached quantitative research on population and technological trends.

Questionnaire surveys became the order of the day. George Gallup began his preelection polling in the 1936 presidential election, and in 1940 a Columbia research team began the first serious effort to study the determinants of people's votes. In the 1940s and 1950s survey research became the dominant mode of research and was applied to everything from political attitudes to religious beliefs, school achievement, social mobility, and sexual behavior. Great improvements were made in the collection of reliable data and in methods of analysis. By 1960 every major university had its buzzing computer center, surrounded by hosts of researchers, programmers, interviewers, coders, and statisticians. Research had become a large-scale enterprise, and sociologists had to become adept at securing grants from foundations or government agencies to foot the bills.

On the positive side sociology began to acquire a basis of hard knowledge. The old racial theories of behavior were among the first victims of this collection of facts, as sociologists documented the influence of social conditions on social success and social deviance. By the 1930s it was demonstrated that the range of intelligence is about the same among blacks as among whites. The biasing effect of social conditions on the IQ scores of people in deprived environments was also documented.

The effect on theory was a negative one—the destruction of the biological-evolutionist model. The collection of data tended to corroborate some theories—especially the general sociological positions of Marx and Weber on the importance of stratification in social behavior, although this theoretical connection had long gone unnoticed by American sociologists. Quite without premeditation, researchers found that social class was the best predictor of behavior of all sorts, from political preferences to religious beliefs, marriage and child-rearing patterns, media participation, life styles, and types of deviance. It is not the only determinant though; and the effects of other dimensions of stratification (Weber's cultural status distinctions, education, and religion) on all of these behaviors were also demonstrated.

American sociology was not exactly rushing forward in elaborating these theories, however. Indeed, a pronounced tendency toward foot dragging was apparent as far as theory construction was concerned. The methods for collecting data gradually became more sophisticated as sociologists learned how to achieve a reliable sample of the population, how to ask questions that did not bias the respondent, and how to apply the proper statistical test to show when results were not due merely to chance. The best of the survey researchers evolved a method known as multivariate analysis, which takes account of the fact that behavior usually has multiple causes and shows how to control each cause in relation to the others so that the effect of each might be assessed. But in general this approach tended to concentrate more and more on its own technical problems and to forget about using its data to build general explanatory theory. Not only did technique tend to become an end in itself, but the survey researchers began to make a fetish out of numbers, to the point where they came to regard "empirical" as meaning quantitative data only. Where taken as an absolute requirement, this has restricted research to a few tightly structured loopholes on the world, missing most of the action and struggle during which things actually happen.

The same sort of limitation can be found in the research in experimental social psychology that has grown up since the 1940s. The founding figure in this movement was the German gestalt psychologist Kurt Lewin, in exile in America since the 1930s, like so many of his colleagues. This research has made impressive demonstrations on such topics as how groups influence individual conformity in perceptions and beliefs and how groups solve problems. But although there have been long strings of cumulative experiments on particular topics, such research has been as yet little related to any of the major theories in sociology. Experimental social psychology is on the borderline of sociology and psychology and more often than not has proceeded from purely psychological (individual) perspectives, with a corresponding behaviorist-inspired emphasis on methodological purity to the exclusion of all else. Experimental study of small groups has nevertheless accumulated a fair amount of knowledge that yields some potentially important contributions to sociological theory.

THE SOCIOLOGY OF ORGANIZATIONS

The missing link seems likely to come through yet another modern area of research, one that occupies a strategic position in sociology, the field of organizations. Organizational research got its real start in the 1930s with a pair of contributions emanating from Harvard Business School. In 1927 the industrial psychologist Elton Mayo began carrying out a long series of experiments on worker productivity at the Hawthorne Works of the Western Electric Company in Chicago. The researchers began with a conventional industrial-engineering approach, treating workers as part of the machinery to be manipulated by an efficiency expert; their initial experiments varied the lighting in the factory to observe its effects on production.

But whether they turned the lights up or down, production seemed to increase. Mayo's associates hit on the idea that the workers were responding to being studied: Instead of treating them like cogs in a machine, someone was interested in them personally, and the workers appreciated the attention. To test this so-called "Hawthorne effect," the Mayo team set up further experiments in the factory, in which they paid attention to the personal reactions of the workers. These results were not interpreted entirely accurately, and the Mayo group tended to overstate their new philosophy: that management must concentrate on "human relations" (and implicitly ignore the economics of workers' pay, which is actually quite important). Nevertheless, the Hawthorne studies took organizations out of the hands of the purely technologically oriented engineers and "management scientists" and placed the emphasis squarely on the dynamics of the "informal group" of workers.

This work was complemented by the publication in 1938 of a book entitled *The Functions of the Executive,* by Chester I. Barnard. Barnard, then lecturing at Harvard Business School, was the former president of the New Jersey Bell Telephone Company. (Incidentally, Western Electric is the manufacturer of telephone equipment for the Bell system. It appears that this is a very research-oriented company. The Bell Telephone laboratories in New Jersey continue to be the leading nonacademic and nongovernment research center in the social sciences in America.) Barnard argued from his own experience that the lines of authority in an organization chart are a myth. The president of a company is like a politician, not a puppeteer, declared Barnard; his subordinates are the ones who run the organization, and his job is merely to create the right climate in which they will get the job done. Barnard's shrewd observations on organization politics at the top and middle ranks fitted nicely with the Hawthorne studies that showed that the workers enforced an informal norm over each other, so that no one individual would work too hard to show up the others in the eyes of management. Organizations were suddenly transformed into living things; they were no longer abstract charts or inert machines.

Since the 1930s a great deal of research has been generated on organizations. Much of the best of it came from Chicago, where Park's student Everett Hughes guided an enormous number of studies of various occupations "from the inside," ranging from undertakers, janitors, and policemen to physicians, lawyers, and scientists. By the 1960s the field of organizational research had accumulated data on a wide range of topics and had arrived at a fair degree of understanding of the ways people struggle to gain or to evade control in organizations, of the way an organization's goals and outputs are affected, and of the determinants of different sorts of organizational structure. Although far from completed, a genuine explanatory theory has evolved in the field of organizations. This theory is the product not only of sociologists but of researchers in business administration and political science, as well as in economics, psychology, and history.

Perhaps more than any other area of research, the field of organizations ties together and develops the great sociological theories, especially the stream proceeding from Weber on through Michels and Mannheim (see Chapter 12). By no means have all the researchers in this field been aware of this connection. For sociological research as a whole, the contributions of empirical research to theory building have remained more potential than actual.

This is not the full story, however. It is impossible for research to proceed for very long without some guiding questions being asked. American sociology got its start from the evolutionary and social-problem orientations of the nineteenth century. The wave of research since the 1920s has destroyed most of the old beliefs, but American research sociology as a whole acquired no new theory to replace what it had rejected. As a result, the old social-problem sorts of questions continued to guide research for a long time after they lost their original significance.

For example, sociology was agitated for decades by the question of whether social mobility had declined in America, of whether the society was becoming more rigid, or "closed," since the supposedly wide-open frontier era. By the late 1950s, after thirty years of speculation, argument, and research, it was possible to give a definitive answer to the question: The amount of social mobility in America had changed very little, at least during the twentieth century. (It was not so very great in the first place.) In the process of answering this question, sociologists had overcome a large number of technical difficulties entailed in accurately measuring and comparing mobility rates. But there has been little effort to ask the general theoretical question: What determines the amount of social mobility in a society? The latter sort of question requires a larger perspective, and recent decades have seen a revival of comparative and historical studies and an accompanying theoretical orientation that should eventually correct this deficiency. But this illustration shows just how much our highly technical research depends on old, perhaps forgotten, debates over social issues. The old river bed goes on even though the water has dried up.

Remarkably, all this has gone on after the time of the great intellectual revolution described in Part II of this volume. What happened in the twentieth century was that sociology split into a "high tradition" and a "low tradition." The latter has dominated America, where characteristically the most engrossing issues have come to be methodological debates, even though it should be apparent that the advance of sociological knowledge depends on melding the data generated by various methods around the construction of an integrated explanatory theory. This split should not be exaggerated, however. The intellectual revolution of Durkheim, Weber, Freud, and Mead has sent out its shock waves rather slowly, but the twentieth century has seen its gradual penetration into the far-flung territories of sociology. The following chapters take up the various streams of its progress.

CHAPTER ELEVEN

The Construction of the Social System: Pareto and Parsons

"Who now reads Spencer? It is difficult for us to realize how great a stir he made in the world. . . . He was the intimate confidant of a strange and rather unsatisfactory God, whom he called the principle of Evolution. His God has betrayed him. We have evolved beyond Spencer." Professor Brinton's verdict may be paraphrased as that of the coroner," Dead by suicide or at the hands of person or persons unknown." We must agree with the verdict. Spencer is dead. But who killed him and how? This is the problem.[1]

Talcott Parsons (1902–1979) entered the sociological arena in 1937 as a detective investigating the demise of the culminating system of liberal rationalism. Spencer died with the optimism of the nineteenth century. He was the last of the great system builders, explaining everything—why people act, why institutions exist, why history moves in certain directions. Talcott Parsons has been the only man of the twentieth century to attempt the same with any success while living up to the new standards of sophistication. His detective work was aimed at finding out why systems no longer seemed possible; he aimed not to gloat on the fact but to overcome the new obstacles.

Parsons was the first man to see clearly the breakdown of nineteenth-century rationalism and the great breakthroughs of Durkheim, Weber, and Freud. His system is an effort to synthesize these breakthroughs. He was only partly successful. His position is unmistakably more derivative of Durkheim than of Weber, and he overlooks the achievements of Mead and his tradition entirely.

Parsons also marks the schism in American sociology between the high tradition and the low tradition. Many sociologists have stuck with the concerns and issues of the nineteenth-century reformers—individual mobility, deviance, social disorganization and its cures—merely casting them in

[1]Talcott Parsons, *The Structure of Social Action,* Vol. 1, p. 3. Published in 1968 by The Free Press Division of The Macmillan Company (original edition 1937). Reprinted by permission.

more behavioristic terminology and going ahead with empirical studies only loosely related to any explanatory theory. Parsons represented an era in which general theory was largely divorced from detailed research, a split that has been slow in healing. Parsons himself was limited by the Anglo-American tradition whose grand theories he tried to revive, especially by a rather behavioristic interpretation of Freud, a patriotic naïveté about politics, and a propensity to elaborate too many abstractions. But more of this later.

First we must turn to a man very different in temperament from the optimistic Parsons—Vilfredo Pareto (1848–1923), probably the most cynical social thinker of modern times. Pareto, more than anyone else, represented the attack on the liberal rationalist tradition, and from him Parsons derived his sophistication about how to build a system in an era when no truly modern mind thought it still possible.

PARETO'S LIFE AND WORKS

Pareto's life coincides with the events that soured liberal positivist hopes in Europe to the point that they scarcely survived into the twentieth century. Born in Paris of an Italian father and a French mother, he grew up in Italy during the heroic years of Garibaldi. He studied science and engineering and began his career almost simultaneously with the rise of the newly united Italian constitutional monarchy in 1871. Like many another young man he was an ardent, idealistic democrat. He worked for a railroad company and then as a superintendent of iron mines in the booming industrial north. At age thirty-four, Pareto received an inheritance that enabled him to retire and devote himself to research and writing. His field was economics, the classical science of British liberalism. In this field one plots the results of individuals' acting as rational decision makers, following their independent interests in the network of contractual exchanges that creates a nation's wealth and measures out the common good with an invisible hand. Pareto soon distinguished himself as one of the great rigorists who introduced sophisticated mathematical methods into economics. His position in the discipline is still marked by the concept of "Pareto optimum," which bears his name. His efforts brought him a chair of economics at the University of Lausanne in 1892, when he was forty-four.

But Italian democracy was not going well. The old enemies had not given up; the nobles still kept the peasants in poverty and near-serfdom in the south; the priests still reconciled the faithful to their lot and warned against the godlessness of reformers. And new enemies arose: labor unionists, Socialist agitators fighting against the sixteen-hour day, the thirteen-hour day, and the eleven-hour day in the factories of Turin and Milan. Anarchists appeared from the teeming slums, proclaiming property to be theft and parliamentary democracy to be a sham. In 1900 an anarchist's bomb took the life of the constitutional monarch King Humbert. Parliaments went through one deadlock after another; politicians did what they could for friends and supporters by getting them paid government jobs. Grinding poverty was the lot not only of the workers but also of the underpaid lower-middle class, epitomized by the hardships of a young Socialist schoolteacher named Benito Mussolini.

Nearing the age of fifty, disillusioned, Pareto retired to his villa above Lake Lausanne to think. He became a mysterious figure; the world began to call him "the hermit of Celigny." Shortly after the turn of the twentieth century he emerged with a book, but not on economics. The science of rational behavior had betrayed him. What he needed now was sociology. His first sociological book was an attack on socialism, which Pareto declared a new form of religious superstition. In the guise of reason it created utopian worlds without struggle, which the Socialist and anarchist leaders used to inflame their followers against the upholders of democracy and of the nation. There was another long silence from Celigny as Europe plunged onward into World War I. In 1915, now an old man of sixty-seven, Pareto published his great work: the five-volume *General Treatise on Sociology*, to become famous under the English title, *The Mind and Society*.

PARETO'S SYSTEM

Pareto's system may be summarized as follows:

1. Societies have great stability. Whenever something happens to upset the old order—revolution, war, crime, natural catastrophe—there is a reaction, a conservative movement to restore order. After Robespierre came Thermidor and Napoleon; after 1848 came Napoleon II; after an assassination the nation recoils to the party of law and order. Most change is only apparent; new governments— republican, monarchist, Bonapartist, Socialist—only change the ruling ideology, while underneath things go on in much the same way. In the formal terms of the economist, society is a system in equilibrium. A change in one direction is compensated for by a change in the opposite direction. To the liberal faith in evolution and progress, Pareto answered with bitter wisdom: *"Plus ça change, plus c'est la même chose."*
2. The economist sees people as rational decision makers, choosing among alternatives, seeking the correct path to maximize gain and avoid loss. By that criterion we must recognize that most action is not logical. The reasons people give for what they do cannot stand up under examination. They act first, then justify what they have done. The judge hands down his decision to fit the power interest of his associates, then cloaks it in high-sounding legal terminology. Moreover, people are easily taken in by false reasoning. All that one needs to make them accept slavery is to give it the name of freedom. Many actions cannot even be assessed by the standards of rationality; like the kneeling of the peasants before the priest, they are rituals. Except for scientists, stockbrokers, and a few others, most individuals are nonlogical most of the time. Thus economics must be superseded as the main science of human behavior.
3. If one examines the reasons people give for their actions, one finds certain constant themes reappearing throughout history. These Pareto termed "residues," which may be interpreted as basic human motives. The main two residues are

called the instinct of combinations (inventiveness or creativity) and the instinct of group persistence, or persistence of aggregates (conservative or security needs). There are also changing elements in human beliefs, which Pareto termed "derivatives," consisting of such ideologies as Christianity, democracy, and socialism.

4. The basic forces in society, according to Pareto's hypothesis, are "sentiments." Sentiments can never be directly observed, since they are biological forces or instincts, presumably shifting with the genetic currents of the human race. One can only infer the sentiments from their manifestations, the residues and derivatives. Such inference is a risky business, but it is unavoidable if one is to capture the overall picture. Science solves complex problems by the method of successive approximations: Hypothesize a model of the forces at work; test it against the evidence; readjust the model where it fits badly; test it out on more evidence; and so on. This is presumably why Pareto needed five volumes to write his system. Moreover, his biological hypotheses were in the current scientific vogue of naturalistic explanations. Individual success and failure, crime, and mental illness were all attributed to racial or family heredity. Spencer's evolutionism had moved increasingly into a literal biological determinism.

5. Not everyone has the same mixture of sentiments. In most people the strongest sentiments are the conservative and social ones. This is what one would expect from an evolutionary point of view; if strong group-preserving instincts were not predominant, it is unlikely that societies would survive. This fact accounts for the stability of societies.

6. Some people, however, are cleverer, stronger, and more individualistic than others. In society, as in nature, there is a continual struggle for dominance. In this struggle the guileful people win out, both by using force and by appealing to the sentiments of the dull, conservative ones. There is thus always an elite, and revolutions change only the leaders. But there is a certain pattern to the changes in dominance. The guileful people, whom Pareto calls the foxes, rise to the top. If too many of them become concentrated at the top, however, the whole tone of society takes on too much originality, too much rationality, too much clever thinking, too many new ideas. Since the social order is built primarily on conservative instincts and feelings for security, the foxes eventually undermine their own position. Society is thrown increasingly into chaos—wars, revolutions, parliamentary strife—and a reaction sets in. The lions, the strong individuals who appeal to the conservative instincts of the masses, take over. Eventually the foxes begin to rise to the top again, using their guile against the stupidity of the lions, and the cycle begins again. In politics, as elsewhere in Pareto's system, the principle of dynamic equilibrium holds.

CRITICISMS OF PARETO

Pareto's theory is easy to criticize. It does not account for many of the observable changes in society. There may always be an elite, but why is it sometimes large and sometimes small, sometimes organized in a feudal system, sometimes in a patrimonial empire, sometimes in a mass party democracy? We may always fall short of equality, but what determines variations in the degree of concentration of wealth? Pareto's research methodology is sloppy, consisting mainly of analyzing and classifying what various classical authors (Plutarch, Cicero, Thucydides, and others) and miscellaneous newspaper clippings have said about the reasons people act the way they do. The biological explanation commits the fallacy of *obscurum per obscurius*—explaining something that is only dimly known by something completely hidden. The procedure results in explanations that cannot be tested. If Pareto were asked why the people of Sparta were more easily regimented by their leaders than were the Athenians, he would reply that the Spartans had more of the sentiment of group persistences. It should be said in fairness that Pareto's method might have paid off if indeed his hypothetical sentiments had some attributes that might make them independently verifiable, like the genes in genetic theory later discovered in the cell. This they lacked, and Durkheim's logic tells us why such attributes of *individuals* would never be an adequate explanation of *society* in any case.

But to end with this critique is to miss Pareto's significance and perhaps to fault him for something he was not trying to do. At the very general level on which he worked, Pareto is mostly right. People do have sentiments, not just practical interests. Economic humankind and liberal rationalism are false leads. Deviations from rational social exchange are not due merely to a lack of information about full market conditions, and more education and better communications will not basically change things. Individuals often act in the service of nonempirical, purely symbolic ends, to which the standards of rational behavior cannot be applied at all. Furthermore, it is the rationalists who have the unworkable image of society; society is held together by nonrational sentiments, not by a deliberate social contract. On the last point Pareto's theory converges with Durkheim's argument for the necessity of precontractual solidarity.

Parsons was to make much of these elements in Pareto's thought, plus his logical sophistication about the procedure of successive approximations and his concept of society as an abstract system of interacting parts in dynamic equilibrium. (The last concept is itself justified as something postulated under the method of successive approximations.) The more cynical side Parsons left out, ignoring Pareto's emphasis on force, deceit, and struggle in politics and substituting for Pareto's conservative pessimism a new evolutionary model of progress within the social system. But here Pareto was more perceptive than Parsons. Most politics most of the time certainly fits his general description. Observers who cannot (and do not want to) see through political ideologies are simply acting with that concern for social belonging that Pareto saw as such a widespread motive. In 1922, seven years after Pareto's treatise appeared, Mussolini came to power in Rome. Fascism, an innovation inconceivable to the nineteenth-century liberal mind, proved in fact what Durkheim, Weber, Freud, and Pareto had already proved in theory: that the naïve positivistic theory of humankind was inadequate to reality.

PARSONS' LIFE AND WORKS

It is a long jump from Fascist Italy and the morose Pareto to the sedate halls of Harvard University in the 1930s. But there is some slight continuity in our theme, for here Talcott Parsons was carrying out one of the great coups of academic politics. A young economics instructor, he had studied with the great anthropologist Bronislaw Malinowski at the London School of Economics and had learned the functionalist theories of Durkheim before they appeared in English. He went on to do his doctorate at Heidelberg on Weber's economic history and translated *The Protestant Ethic and the Spirit of Capitalism* for American publication. Arriving back at Harvard, he soon joined the sociology department, newly founded in 1930.

As the citadel of American scholarship, Harvard had waited thirty years to see if this new discipline would prove respectable. When the issue seemed finally decided in its favor, the usual search was made for the most eminent person in the field to head the new department. This person was judged to be Pitirim Sorokin. Sorokin was a Russian, formerly secretary to Alexander Kerensky (the head of the Provisional Government of 1917), once sentenced to death by the Bolsheviks, and later exiled. Like most Russian intellectuals he was full of grand ideas, none of which had emerged from the nineteenth century. He had published a notable book on social mobility, which marshaled all the statistical evidence of the day to embellish the theory that people owed their class positions largely to their hereditary ability. Then came his great work, the four-volume *Social and Cultural Dynamics,* a cyclical theory of world history, elaborately documented from the *Encyclopaedia Britannica,* which concerned itself mainly with a perceived trend from spiritualism to materialism and back again. Like most cyclical theories, it rested mostly on the single case of the fall of the Roman Empire, and showed scanty acquaintance with non-Western history.

Within a few years Parsons had displaced Sorokin as the dominant sociologist at Harvard. Through a strategic alliance with functionalist anthropologists and clinical psychologists, and with good support from far reaches of the Harvard faculty (Parsons was always a master of ecumenical movements), Parsons eventually had the sociology department replaced with a new, interdisciplinary Department of Social Relations, with himself as chairman. Sorokin found himself in exile for a second time, this time to his research institute for the study of altruistic behavior. But the coup was more than a purely local affair. Parsons brought the new European sociological theory into America at a famous university where many of the major theorists of the following decades were to receive their training. The dominance of the Chicago school was broken at about the same time, symbolized by the displacement of the Chicago-based *American Journal of Sociology* by the new, more theoretically oriented *American Sociological Review* as the official journal of the American Sociological Society.

The times were propitious for a general change in the orientation of sociology; it was not merely a matter of Parsons' intellectual and political brilliance alone. The old evolutionist and social-disorganization theories had degenerated into a form of biological racism that offended the awakening social conscience of the depression era. Pareto's lions and foxes and Durkheim's anomie provided some explanation for the Fascist movements of Europe and their smaller American reflections in Huey Long and Father Coughlin. At the same time the newly imported sociology offered some answer to the increasing popularity of Marxism among intellectuals; Weber in particular offered a rival theory in the very heart of economic sociology. What Parsons so successfully offered was a revived liberal sociology at a time when liberalism seemed to be breaking down on both sides.

Parsons' theory has changed somewhat from his first great attempt to synthesize Pareto, Durkheim, and Weber in *The Structure of Social Action*, whose opening words head this chapter. In the 1940s he grew increasingly interested in Freud and less interested in Weber. This period culminated in Parsons' major systematic work, *The Social System* (1951). At the same time, Parsons was engineering an interdisciplinary movement to establish a common ground for all the social sciences (possibly even all the sciences), a project expressed in *Toward a General Theory of Action* (1951). In the 1950s it became clear that Parsons had overstepped himself in his emulation of Spencer's encyclopedic system (recall that Spencer's *Synthetic Philosophy* ran all the way from cosmology to ethics): that his efforts to comprehend everything drove him to elaborating extremely abstract categorizations that did not constitute a workable explanatory theory. By the 1960s Parsons had apparently lowered his sights again. He began to revive the Weberian historical sociology with which he had started out and to offer new theories on political movements. Parsons' intellectual highway was by now clearly marked, but it continued to turn up new surprises until his death in 1980.

PARSONS' THEORY OF SOCIETY

Parsons' writings are usually quite complex, abstract, and difficult to read. C. Wright Mills, a bitter opponent of Parsons' abstract theorizing, charged that if Parsons' works were translated into plain English, no one would be impressed. He then proceeded to translate four paragraphs of Parsons' prose into one succinctly worded paragraph of his own. Nevertheless, there is a comprehensive theory to be derived from Parsons' writings, a theory of great sophistication and sometimes of considerable power.

Society as a System

Social causality is very complex, since all institutions (politics, economics, family, culture, and so forth) influence each other. There are chains of causes, vicious and benevolent circles; history is a seamless web. The nineteenth-century thinkers were naïve enough to think that one factor could be isolated as basic: either heredity, environment, or economics. Parsons knew that this is impossible. But the very interconnection suggests a solution: Society is a system of interrelated parts. The model is analogous to an economic system, in which many individuals acting independently neverthe-less contribute to a few predictable results (for example, prices go up or down) under the direction of an invisible hand that no one controls. The task of sociology is to search for the laws guiding the invisible hand in all of society. Parsons' major work is thus entitled *The Social System*.

Functionalism

Like Durkheim, Parsons believed that the causes of social structures must be found in their relations with other structures, not in smaller units such as individuals. The various parts of a society (polity, economy, education, religion, and so on) all serve functions for the other institutions, and they exchange these contributions for mutual support. For example, the schools train citizens and workers and in return are supported by state and industry; the church upholds family morality, and families are the bulwark of church membership—and so on. The basic idea goes back beyond economics to the old biological analogy (which Adam Smith had updated to begin modern economics) in which society is one large body, with the king as the head, the soldiers as the arms, the priests and counselors as the eyes and ears, and so on.

Parsons attempted to classify the basic functions that must be carried out in any society if it is to survive. With these tools it becomes possible to analyze all societies in the same way, even though they may not have the same institutions. What we call politics, for example, Parsons called the "goal attainment" function, by which the group makes decisions for collective action. War is the most obvious example of such community action; regulating the monetary system would be another. (This may seem a rather limited view of politics, but we will discuss that criticism later.) But not all societies have anything that could be called a state; a primitive tribe, for example, may be organized only as a large kinship network. Using Parsons' concepts, we look for the *function* of collective action instead of for something that looks like a modern state, and we find that function is one of the things that the kinship system does, in addition to what we ordinarily think of families as doing.

Parsons was fond of cross-classifying various distinctions to arrive at a related set of concepts, and his set of basic functions (there are four of them; almost everything in Parsons comes in sets of four) can be presented in that way. Everything can be classified as either a means or an end and also as either internal or external. Cross-classifying these factors we get the table shown.

	Means	Ends
External	A (adaptive)	G (goal attainment)
Internal	L (latent pattern maintenance)	I (integrative)

We begin to see (and this is the simplest of Parsons' classifications) why he has such a reputation for being abstruse. At any rate, the initials A-G-I-L (or L-I-G-A) can be used as a convenient mnemonic device. Any social organization must fulfill all these four functions: maintaining basic cultural patterns (education and family socialization do this for the larger society), integrating its members into harmonious participation (religion and the legal system do this), attaining community goals (performed by the polity), and adapting to the environment (performed by the economy). The need to fulfill these functions is one of the main limitations on any social organization and, therefore, one of its prime determinants.

The functional method can also be used to explain particular institutions. For example, William J. Goode, in his paper "The Theoretical Importance of Love," gives a functional analysis of romantic love in American society. Goode begins by noting that societies vary a great deal in their attitudes toward romantic attachments: Some, like modern America, view it as a good thing (in fact, a required norm, since people are not supposed to admit to marrying for any other reason). Others, like traditional China, view love as a foolish infatuation that interferes with the serious business of negotiating links between families through marriages of their children. Other societies, such as Japan, view love as neither particularly desirable nor particularly undesirable. Goode goes on to note that these differences in love norms are related to differences in the kind of kinship system: The extended kinship system in China, linked with a patriarchal household economy and a patrimonial form of polity, contrasts with the segmented nuclear family in the United States, which carries out virtually no functions other than child rearing and recreation. Thus, love is frowned upon in China because it is dysfunctional for the system, and it is virtually required in the United States because there are no other bonds except emotion to hold the family unit together and thus get the children reared.

This functional explanation is not the whole story, of course; to say that something is needed does not tell us why it comes to exist. There is also a historical side to it—the creation of the romantic ideal by the medieval troubadours and the perpetuation of the ideal in the Christian church and in the marriage ceremony—and also a social-psychological side, as individuals arrange their own feelings toward each other. But Goode's functional analysis puts the question into the larger structural context, even if it does not answer all the whys and hows.

Social Integration

The organic analogy suggests an equilibrium model, and many of the facts seem to fit: As Pareto noticed, societies recover after wars and disasters, people are aroused to punish deviants, and so on. How can we explain this? The old social-contract ideas of the nineteenth-century theorists, who thought that individuals rationally decide to uphold the rules because it is in their self-interest, were demolished by Durkheim's critique. Other theories—those of Sorokin, Spengler, and even Marx—never confronted the question at all, but assumed that societies were somehow held together. Parsons, in the forefront of mid-twentieth-century thought, could not evade the issue, which he called "the Hobbesian problem of order." This referred to Thomas Hobbes' seventeenth-century proof that the natural (that is, logical) state of self-interested humankind is not social harmony but "war of all against all."

Parsons' solution was to accept Durkheim's collective conscience, the nonrational feeling of solidarity that all ongoing societies have. Parsons renamed this the "value system," following the anthropologists who had come to talk about the cultural values that a society passes down through the generations. But how explain the coercive power that the value system (or collective conscience) has over individuals? Parsons threw out Durkheim's crowd psychology and substituted Freud. The collective conscience can be found in the individual conscience, that is, in the superego. Thus Freud's view of socialization—the child identifying with the punishing parent and internalizing the parent's commands—becomes the basis for society's influence over the individual. With this stroke Parsons draws the link between the psychological level and the social level, and the core of his system is complete. At last the age-old question of social order is resolved on a sound basis.

It follows from this that societies are different because they bring up children to hold different basic values. Parsons classifies these values into what he calls "pattern variables," or basic choices people are called upon to make when they encounter other people. For example, one can judge other people in terms of either what they do (achievement) or what they are (ascription). American society places a great emphasis on achievement, whereas medieval society was more concerned about whether a person was born an aristocrat, a peasant, a Christian, or a Jew. Another basic choice is between treating people according to abstract and general rules like the law (universalism) and treating them according to personal relationships like friendship (particularism). Societies can thus be described according to their combinations of basic values. In this regard, Parsons believed that the United States can be summed up as achievement-oriented and universalistic; Imperial China was achievement-oriented but particularistic; Germany is ascriptive and universalistic; and Latin America is ascriptive and particularistic. In the tabular form:

	Achievement	Ascription
Universalism	United States	Germany
Particularism	China	Latin America

Social Change

The social system changes by either "differentiation" or "de-differentiation." This means that the division of labor can increase, with structures becoming more specialized in their functions, or decrease, with structures taking on more functions. The idea is a familiar one in economics: The self-supporting family farm is part of a system with little division of labor, whereas the modern economy of specialized food producers, clothing manufacturers, railroads, and so forth, has a high division of labor. Extending the idea to the entire social structure and bearing in mind the functions that are served by the family, the church, and so on, one can place societies on a continuum from undifferentiated to highly differentiated. At the low end of the spectrum are primitive tribes, in which the kinship system is the only social structure, filling all the various functions itself. At the other end are the complex set of specialized social organizations found in the modern United States.

In sociology we find this idea worked out with increasingly greater sophistication in Comte, Spencer, Durkheim, and Parsons. As the division of labor increases, societies increase their efficiency and their productivity, just as the mass-production factories produce more with less cost than the old handicraft industries. Following Durkheim, Parsons noted that the cultural system changes along with the social structure; as societies become more complex and differentiated, the culture becomes "upgraded"—more abstract, more generalized. This is Parsons' explanation of the trend (described in Chapter 7) from particularistic, local, nature gods in primitive religions to the universalistic world religions and, finally, to the modern, transreligious, ethical universe. But differentiation also creates problems; in particular, the more division of labor between the specialized parts, the more pressure there is for integrating the system. In economics this means that the industrial division of labor has to be integrated by a new monetary and credit system. In societal change, increasing differentiation creates problems that must be solved by political means—by state-supported education, welfare, old-age insurance, and so forth.

What causes societies to change, to move from one level of differentiation to another? Science, for one thing; economic growth, for another. New technological inventions, like the steam engine, the gasoline-powered automobile, and the radio, have changed the ways in which people produce and move goods, transport themselves, and communicate, and they have thus set off changes in human organizations with ramifications throughout the interconnected web of the social structure. Economic growth brings more and more of the world into one large division of labor, promoting greater specialization at all points and calling forth new agencies to coordinate things. Another cause of change is imperfect integration of the parts, due to prior change. Thus, as the Parsonian sociologist Neil Smelser has shown, the early industrial revolution in England put a great strain on the old family system; since workers in factories could no longer appropriately keep their children with them and have them help while they worked, the state eventually had to take over responsibility for the children by setting up schools and prohibiting child labor. The family was thus transformed into its functionally appropriate modern nuclear form.

These are all short-run changes, which come into play only once the processes of scientific discovery and economic change have begun. To explain the long-run changes Parsons draws on Weber's theory of history (presented in Chapter 7). The main difference is that Parsons omits political struggle, which was the main engine of change for Weber, and concentrates instead on changes in religious beliefs. Since Parsons sees societies as determined by their fundamental value systems, changes in values are the prime movers of social change, and charismatic leaders—the great prophets of antiquity, Saint Paul, Martin Luther, John Calvin—are the key figures who set forth new values. But the cultural tradition is in the long run more important than the individual leaders, since they can only develop the potentialities already inherent in the tradition.

PARSONS' RELIGIOUS SOCIOLOGY

Parsons' students can remember him lecturing on the sociology of religion to a roomful of Catholic nuns, Buddhist priests in their saffron robes, bearded rabbis, and Harvard undergraduates in Levis and tweed jackets, capturing the cultural history of the world into one long sequence: Parsons moved from the animistic religions of remote antiquity to the "instrumental activism" of the Hebrew prophets and their vengeful almighty God; on through early Christianity and the medieval struggles to separate church from state, and thence to Martin Luther's abolition of the monkhood, which upgraded the obligations of Christianity and made monks of us all; to Calvin's puritanical insistence that the world be as righteous as the kingdom of heaven, carried to the new world by the Calvinistic settlers of Massachusetts Bay who laid down the value system of the United States; the gradual secularization of that Protestant ethic into an achievement orientation that tolerated all religions and set loose the economic and social changes of the mightiest nation in the history of the earth; until at last one could see cultural history devolving down through the ages to the very man standing before us, this son of a Calvinist preacher and heir (his very name told us) to a long line of preachers, holding our rapt attention with the culminating system in which cultural history at last comes to full self-understanding. Spencer was dwarfed by the performance. It called to mind the visionary giants of the past: Hegel, Dante, and Thomas Aquinas.

Indeed, Talcott Parsons' sociological system is an adaptation of the traditional Christian worldview to the sophisticated requirements of modern secular thought. Unlike most contemporary social scientists, Parsons believed in free will—a voluntaristic conception of humankind in society, as he put it in *The Structure of Social Action*. To this extent he breaks with the hard-nosed positivistic attempt to bring humankind under the deterministic canons of physical science. At the same time he holds that social order and predictable behavior are not only real but necessary, just as Christian theology maintains both that humankind is free and that God is nevertheless all-determining.

Parsons solves the religious paradox in sociological terms: Individuals are free to choose, but they always choose in the presence of other individuals who are also free. They can act together in harmony because they develop values that tell them what things are worth pursuing and norms that set the rules under which they pursue those ends. People do not have to live up to the values and norms of their society, but they find it best for themselves, as well as for others, if they do.

The norms that develop always must have some rewards built into them, so that people reward each other for doing what they must do. Like the utilitarians on back to Adam Smith, Parsons sees the world as held together by an invisible hand, a system in which people exchange things with each other. The exchanges are sometimes economic—pay for work, money for goods—but Parsons adds a Freudian dimension to make the exchange a moral matter as well as a material one. People trade not only goods but human contact and emotion—approval and disapproval, feelings of belonging, a sense of social solidarity. Thus, individuals who live up to the norms reap the rewards of feeling that they belong and are respected; those who do not conform punish themselves by isolating themselves from human society. Parsons incorporates the old moral lesson into his sociology: One can find happiness in being good, while evil is its own punishment—to be cut off from God (or society).

The functional imperatives of society thus take the place of the Christian God. People do not have to live up to them, but if they do not, retribution swiftly follows as their world crumbles around them. Durkheim, the ultrapositivist, had debunked religion in the name of science by showing that God is but a symbolic representation of the moral order of society. Parsons, the American secularized theologian, turned up the other face of the argument with his claim that society is fundamentally a spiritual order. All humans basically acknowledge the claims of social order, no matter how much they rebel against its claims on them personally; individuals may steal, cheat, lie, and fight, but no one would want a world in which everyone did so, for then society would not exist. God in the end is stronger than the devil, and the devil himself knows it. Even force and violence ultimately contribute to this order. Like Dostoevsky's Grand Inquisitor, Parsons sees that power is necessary to enforce the claims of society on the individual. The wielders of power—the kings and the generals and the politicians—may personally profit a great deal, but without them society would crumble into a chaos that no one would want. Thus humans are selected to do God's will, whether they know it or not.

Parsons incorporates not only the traditional Christian moral vision, but its optimistic nineteenth-century adaptation, liberal evolutionism. Society is not only becoming more productive and more powerful as it develops, it is also becoming more just. As the value system has shifted from ascription to achievement, from particularism to universalism, human beings are becoming more humanitarian. Torture, public executions, cruelty to the insane, the burning of witches—all these have gradually disappeared in the more modern societies. The sense of universal brotherhood has spread—from a society in which one trusted only one's relatives to the rise of feelings of national identification and now (optimistically) beyond nations to all humankind. Politics, too, has become increasingly participatory and just. In a list of evolutionary stages through which societies must pass if they are to become increasingly differentiated (and thereby more modern and more powerful), Parsons rather ethnocentrically includes democracy as a necessity for all truly modern systems. Whether or not some individuals want to allow democracy, it is the price they must pay if they want progress. In politics as elsewhere, Parsons' God manifests itself increasingly throughout history.

PARSONS' CONTRIBUTIONS

Parsons' liberal optimism betrays its weaknesses most clearly in his treatment of politics. Fascism, Parsons felt, was a transitional phenomenon caused by the struggle of a rationalized economy and a tradition-breaking scientific culture against an old world of family, community, and politics that had not yet adjusted. Parsons never took seriously Durkheim's fears that an extremely rationalized society would destroy social solidarity, or Weber's warnings that modern bureaucratic organizations eliminate responsible social leadership and condemn us to a world of bureaucratic drift. Like the early British liberals, Parsons held far too gentlemanly a view of politics, closing his eyes to the realities of power struggles where the interests of the various factions by no means coincide with the interest of the collective system. By concentrating entirely on the functional aspects of society, Parsons was powerless to explain the vast realm of phenomena that are not functional. Like his predecessors, Parsons had his gaze too much on the heights to fully understand what went on in the mundane world below.

The major fault in Parsons' method is overabstraction. When Durkheim identified the collective conscience, he was talking about something that real groups of people feel when they come together, not about a big invisible balloon in the sky neatly covering the boundaries of the United States or China or some other country and labeled "value system." In the same way, Parsons reified the very general idea of a social system and identified it with whole states, not noticing how many different, relatively nonconnected groups there are within every state, oblivious of or in conflict with each other. His error was in jumping from some aspects of reality that fit the metaphor to the assumption that they all do. Societies sometimes draw themselves together after a war, but quite as often they break up into new societies; the fundamental assumption of dynamic equilibrium is a variable to be explained, not a universal process to be taken for granted. The path forward from Durkheim's insight is not to make it more abstract, but to examine particular groups of people as they create the various kinds of collective conscience found at a tea party or a diplomatic reception, or in the corridors of a mental institution. Erving Goffman, as we shall see in Chapter 13, is the man who took up this latter task.

Parsons' major contributions to sociology have been to uphold the high theoretical tradition and to ask the fundamental questions in an era when few social scientists were even aware that they were there to ask. He carried out part of the crucial integration of the great insights of Durkheim and Freud and showed some of the places where Weber fits into the emerging grand pattern. If functionalist explanations fall far short of incorporating the realities of human conflict and explaining the links between the functions an institution serves and the fact of its existence, they nevertheless sometimes cast a spotlight on the manifold interconnections of the social structure. Finally, not the least of Parsons' contributions is one for the twenty-first century: He has preserved our knowledge of free will and human consciousness as facts until the time that our theories become adequate to explain those mysteries.

CHAPTER TWELVE

Hitler's Shadow: Michels, Mannheim, and Mills

The decade of the 1930s posed the biggest shock to popular worldviews since the French Revolution of the 1790s. The unimaginable happened: Fascism came to power in Germany. An authoritarian, antimodern, antiscientific, antirational, and antidemocratic movement, it negated all the ideals human beings had thought were in the ascendant for almost 200 years. Moreover, fascism was not simply a conspiracy of a few backward aristocrats, but a popular mass movement with literally millions of enthusiastic followers, and it sprang up in one of the most advanced industrial nations in the world.

The 1917 revolution in Russia that brought the Communists to power for the first time had already made a dent in the complacency of Western liberal beliefs, but not so great as the Fascist success. After all, at least one sector of Western thought had been predicting such a revolution for quite a while, and in any event it could be brushed off as a modernizing effort in a backward country. One way or another the Russian Revolution could be assimilated to existing modes of thought—but fascism! Until it happened, no one would even have thought it possible. And having happened, it required explanation, something that has dominated our attention ever since. The inferences drawn have not all been sound, but we have been thinking in Hitler's shadow for forty years.

Fascism did not appear out of nowhere, of course. Currents of anti-Semitism and antirationalism had been welling up since the latter part of the nineteenth century. In 1922 Benito Mussolini, a former Socialist leader, took power in Italy after marching on Rome with his black-shirted followers, promising an end to economic and political disorder. And in 1923 Adolf Hitler began his slow climb to prominence in an abortive *Putsch* organized in the beer halls of Munich. Fascism built up strength slowly and in full public view before Hitler was named chancellor in 1933. People of reason had plenty of time to listen to it and react to it, but for the most part they found it so incompatible with their assumptions that they dismissed its importance.

The Marxists, especially after the onset of the worldwide economic depression of 1929, made an effort to explain fascism as the death agony of capitalism. But why *this* death agony, so unlike what Marx seemed to predict? Moreover, the issue seemed not so much an economic one—Hitler was successful enough in restoring economic prosperity once he took power in Germany—as something more deeply rooted in people's social nature that made them respond irrationally to crises, whether economic or otherwise. Marxism had shared the rationalistic assumptions of the nineteenth century, but these seemed no longer to apply.

Marxism was breaking down in other ways as well. The Russian experiment in Soviet utopia was going badly. The power struggle between Stalin and Trotsky had turned into a reign of terror by the 1930s, and the world was treated to the spectacle of old revolutionary leaders being tried and executed on charges of treason and finally of the exiled Trotsky lying dead in his villa in Mexico with an assassin's pickax through his brain. Stalin's dictatorship wiped out most of the optimism of the left; Hitler's brought the rest of the world to its feet in shock. Science and industry were moving onward toward the innovations of television, the jet plane, and the atom bomb, but the old hopefulness was gone. The world suddenly lost its meaning, and modern individuals found themselves wandering amid their material creations like characters in the novels of Franz Kafka.

World War I already had begun to foreshadow this disillusionment with human rationality. It was a war that everyone, after the first spasms of patriotic enthusiasm, agreed was senseless—begun over a trivial issue in diplomacy, unstoppable once the mammoth machinery of warfare was set in motion, dragging on in the trenches of the Western Front at the cost of millions of lives, and ending by having settled nothing. It was during and after World War I that the characteristic disillusionment of modern literature became the universal outlook of thinking individuals, spread by the Dadaists, T. S. Eliot, Ernest Hemingway, and the rest of the "lost generation."

Disillusionment had been particularly acute on the left, for the Socialists had explicitly hoped to be able to prevent such wars. Wars are fought for the benefit of the ruling classes, they asserted, but it is the workers who die in the ranks; hence it would be absurd for the workers of one country to kill their class brothers and sisters for the benefit of their bosses. The Socialist movement, grown to considerable strength among the workers of Germany and France, was counted on to maintain peace. But when war was declared in 1914, after the assassination of the Austrian Archduke Ferdinand in Sarajevo, the Socialists for the most part fell in line with the prevailing mood of chauvinism. The Social Democrats in Germany, the strongest working-class party on the Continent, threw their support squarely behind the kaiser by voting to provide the emergency war funds for the army.

MICHELS' IRON LAW OF OLIGARCHY

At least one man was not surprised by this unprincipled turnabout. He was Robert Michels (1876–1936), a young historian who had been unable to get a job in the German university system, despite the recommendation of Max Weber, because he was a member of the Social Democrats. Michels had participated extensively in party activities and had come to the conclusion that the Socialists did not live up to their own ideals. Although the party advocated democracy, it was not internally democratic itself. The revolutionary Marxism of the speeches at conventions and on the floor of the Reichstag was just a way of whipping up support among the workers, while the party leaders built a bureaucratic trade union and party machine to provide sinecures for themselves.

Michels' analysis appeared in 1911 in a book called *Political Parties*. The phenomenon of party oligarchy was quite general, stated Michels; if internal democracy could not be found in an organization that was avowedly democratic, it would certainly not exist in parties which did not claim to be democratic. This principle was called the Iron Law of Oligarchy, and it constitutes one of the great generalizations about the functioning of mass-membership organizations, as subsequent research has borne out.

The Iron Law of Oligarchy works as follows: First of all, there is always a rather small number of persons in the organization who actually make decisions, even if the authority is formally vested in the body of the membership at large. The reason for this is purely functional and will be obvious to anyone who has attended a public meeting or even a large committee session. If everyone tries to have a say (as happens especially in the first blush of enthusiasm when a new, democratically controlled organization is created), then in fact nothing gets done. The discussion goes on at great length without even covering all the necessary issues, until finally most people leave or keep quiet and let a few persons present their plans. Before long, the group has delegated to a few of its members the authority to prepare plans and to carry them out, while most members confine themselves to formally selecting and approving plans presented to them.

Second, says Michels, the leaders who have this delegated authority tend to take on more power than the members who selected them. Once in power (whether this is an elected office or a purely informal leadership role), they tend to remain there for a long time and become relatively impervious to influences from below. New leaders enter their ranks primarily by being selected or co-opted from above by the old leaders, rather than by rising on their own from below. The reason for this is partly functional and partly because of the way resources of power are distributed in an organization.

The leaders are a much smaller group than the rank and file, but they have the advantage of being better organized. The members as a whole come together (if at all) only at occasional meetings or elections, but the leaders are in constant contact with each other. The leaders tend to form a united, behind-the-scenes, informal group, for it is much easier for them to make plans, carry out programs, and iron out disagreements in private personal negotiations than under the parliamentary rules of open meetings. But since the leaders operate in close contact with each other, out of the sight of the general membership, they tend to develop their own ways of looking at things. They are "insiders" who have a sophisticated view of how things are done, how bargains are struck, how strategies are formed. They know the ropes, and new leaders must become initiated into their world; hence they are selected from above, rather than projected from below.

Third, the leaders gradually develop values that are at odds with those of the members. Michels here applies the principle of Marx and Weber that men's outlooks are determined by their social positions. The social positions of party leaders are fundamentally different from the positions of mere party members, since their experiences of participating in the organization are different. For the ordinary member, the organization is something he or she belongs to and participates in from time to time, but it is not usually the center of his or her life. Members expect their union to fight for their interests and their values, but that is about all.

The leader's position is different. For that person, the organization is usually a full-time job, or at least a major part of his or her life. Especially if the organization is big and powerful enough to have paid officials, these officers receive money, power, and prestige from their positions, and often a chance to belong to a higher realm of other elites. The union leader gets to associate with corporation officials; the Socialist deputy sits in the legislature with other persons of power. It is not surprising, says Michels, that the values of such leaders become subtly corrupted. The leader becomes less concerned with the interests of the rank and file or the ideology of the party and more concerned with staying in office. Leaders become conservative, in the sense that they want only to preserve their organization and not jeopardize it on risky ventures, even if the organization's ideals call for it.

But doesn't this corruption of the leaders bring them into conflict with their followers? It sometimes does, says Michels, but the leadership has the upper hand in such struggles. Unless the membership is extremely upset about something—and maybe not even then—they are unlikely to mobilize their numbers to displace the leadership. For power in the organization goes to those who control its administrative resources, and these are in the hands of the leaders. They are better organized than the membership. They are better informed, for they are in constant contact with the latest developments both inside and outside the organization, and they can use this knowledge, which is usually kept secret among themselves, to attack their opponents as ill-informed and unrealistic. They control the communications within the organization: distributing its newsletter, calling its meetings, setting its agendas, making its official reports. They have full time to devote to organization business and organization politics, whereas their opponents are usually part-time amateurs; the leaders also have the finances, the staff assistance, the contacts, and the know-how.

And finally, they have the legitimacy of being the existing leadership who can claim to represent the organization, whereas their opponents can be called "factions" and "splitters" who represent only themselves and who aid the organization's enemies by creating internal dissension. The united leadership, then, can wield power out of all proportion to its numbers because it controls the material and ideological resources of the organization. Michels provides a sort of mini-Marxism of class conflict and the weapons that enable one class to prevail, only his setting is a single organization rather than the whole society. But Michels had no hopes that history would ever reverse this distribution of power resources. As long as we have large-scale organizations, these consequences are inevitable. "Who says organization," stated Michels, "says oligarchy."

Michels' analysis was remarkably perceptive. Subsequent research has revealed that the dispersion of power away from the membership and into the hands of the leaders who control the administrative apparatus occurs in all sorts of formally democratic membership organizations—in political parties all over the world, trade unions, clubs, legislatures, charities, PTAs, and professional associations ranging from the American Medical Association to the American Sociological Association. The Iron Law of Oligarchy is not, of course, an outright declaration that members never have any control of their organizations. Theories that state such absolutes are usually wrong, for reality is more complex and variable than that. Properly understood, Michels' theory tells how the different positions in an organization shape the interests of their holders and give them certain organizational weapons that they can use in the struggle with others for control of the organization. It does not state that the leaders are always completely corrupted or that they always have their way.

The history of political parties in America illustrates the point nicely. The Republican and Democratic parties in America, especially the latter, have always been strongly influenced by party bosses and professional politicians, from the spoils system of Andrew Jackson through the recent presidential campaigns. The techniques of organizational control that Michels describes are well illustrated in almost any political campaign. Nevertheless, some reforms have occurred from time to time; some politicians occasionally arise who make more than a token appeal to popular demands; and long-entrenched party bosses are sometimes displaced. Michels' theory, then, is not a matter of absolutes, but of variations, of which he described the most typical outcome. Subsequent research has shown us that the threat of organizational oligarchy, although always present, varies with the type and setting of the organization. The most oligarchic associations are those that have a very numerous and dispersed membership and large-scale centralized administrative machinery for the leaders to control. The less oligarchic organizations are those that depend on frequent participation by their members and that compete with other associations for their members' support. Michels' position on the chances of real democracy is pessimistic, but we have since seen that there are at least some possibilities of overcoming oligarchy.

Michels' theory has been fruitfully applied in yet another direction. The American sociologist Philip Selznick has shown that the same sort of processes can be found in government agencies in his classic analysis of the New Deal's TVA (Tennessee Valley Authority) project to help the poor farmers of Appalachia. Such bureaucracies are not like political parties, of course, since they do not claim to be controlled by their membership, but rather by the elected officials who head the government. But there are similar processes in both. The bureaucracy's members come to take on distinctive interests and outlooks from running the organization, which begin to cut them adrift from the official purposes of the legislators who originally created it. Like party officials, the bureaucrats become more interested in having the organization survive and prosper than in meeting any particular ideals. The TVA, for example, soon gave in to powerful conservative interests of the wealthier southern farmers and neglected the poorer farmers and the public as a whole. The liberal rhetoric of the organization's ideals continued, says Selznick, but only as a protective cover, analogous to the radical speeches of Michels' German party leaders.

The overall picture is of a world of organizations that control their own members, rather than vice versa. Bureaucracies and political parties alike operate according to the principle of self-protection and self-aggrandizement, regardless of what happens to the interests of the larger society or to the organization's own enunciated goals. Such ideals float over the surface, but serve only to cloud our eyes to the organizational realities below. We think the social world is rational and purposeful, but the appearance is deceptive, and things are not really under any individual's control.

His pessimism confirmed by the Social Democrats' support of World War I, Michels finally took a university position in Italy. The German academic system would not accept him in any case. When Mussolini's Fascist movement arose, Michels gave it his support. For Michels, its open disavowal of democracy was at least a sign of honesty, and he was convinced that if democracy was impossible, the only answer lay in strong leaders.

MANNHEIM'S THEORY OF SOCIAL RELATIVISM

Michels thus disappeared from the intellectual scene, but the questions he raised did not. Their implications were drawn out most thoroughly by another German, Karl Mannheim (1893–1947). Trained in sociology and philosophy, Mannheim became a professor of sociology at Frankfurt University in the late 1920s. Nearby was the first research institute for sociology to exist in Germany. Its funds came from a millionaire manufacturer, the father of one of the university students. It is doubtful that he knew quite what he was endowing, for the Frankfurt Institute became a crucible for the ideas of Weber, Freud, and a new revival of Marx. Around it gathered a remarkable collection of men, known as the "Frankfurt school," most of whom were to make their marks on social research in America after the Nazis forced them out of Germany. They included Theodore Adorno, the guiding spirit of the research for *The Authoritarian Personality;* the prominent neo-Freudian Erich Fromm; the leading sociologist of literature Leo Lowenthal; Karl Wittfogel, who reformulated Marxist analysis of Eastern societies in *Oriental Despotism;* the Marxist philosopher Max Horkheimer; and Herbert Marcuse, the chief neo-Marxist prophet of the mid-twentieth century. In this atmosphere appeared Mannheim, the most conservative figure on the scene and the most eminent.

Mannheim first stated his position in 1929 in *Ideology and Utopia.* His stance was essentially that of a liberal trying to find a place for his values in the modern world. These were the beliefs that reason and democracy were the best defenses of human welfare, freedom, and culture. But these values were threatened, and Mannheim squarely faced the threat: Nothing was truly believable anymore. No values were certain; no truths were sure.

What had happened was that human beings had penetrated beneath their old assumptions—first, of religious dogmatism, then, of secular humanism—to recognize the social relativism of ideas. Mannheim did not invent this relativism himself. Its most popular expositor in the 1920s was the German philosopher Max Scheler, but it went back through Nietzsche, Marx, and Hegel and ultimately had its roots in the Enlightenment effort to bring all assumptions under the test of scientific reasoning. To paraphrase Mannheim, we have come to see that there is no such thing as "truth" or "value" all by itself, but that these are always *somebody's* ideas. Moreover, the individuals who think these ideas do not confront the universe in the abstract; rather, they occupy particular positions that shape their outlooks. We can trace these influences on human beings' ideas more easily, says Mannheim, if we realize that most individuals do not originate any ideas at all, but just repeat what they have heard from others. The basic ideas of any social period come from a few elite groups of thinkers. If we look at the social positions that these intellectuals occupy, we can see the determinants of their thought.

For example, the only intellectuals of the European Middle Ages were priests and monks. They were organized in the Catholic Church, which claimed universal spiritual domination throughout Europe. Accordingly, their ideas took the form of a universal system of theology and philosophy, which claimed to reduce the entire world to order and which was dogmatically asserted to be true. This ideal was found, for example, in the *Summa Theologica* of Thomas Aquinas. This age of absolute faith began to break down when the Church began to lose its monopoly over the livelihoods of intellectuals. This came about first from the various reformations and schisms in the Church, then from the industrial revolution, which created a new, literate, middle-class audience. Intellectuals could now make a living by selling books and articles on an open market. This in turn meant that there was a competition of ideas, leading eventually to the recognition that there were innumerable points of view on the world. The free market of ideas created the philosophy of relativism.

But then is nothing true? What about the methods of natural science, which slowly build up a body of knowledge, verified by experiment and refined by generations of critical reasoning that holds good irrespective of time and place? Mannheim paid little attention to scientific knowledge, it is true, but this was because he considered it irrelevant to his main concerns. He was interested in thought about society and especially about politics, and it is for such thought that social relativism is especially crucial.

Political beliefs always combine our analysis of what exists in the world with our values of right and wrong. Concepts like "democracy" and "freedom" have this twofold nature; they state not merely how things work, which is the aim of natural science, but how they *ought* to work. The question of what the right political system is, then, is not amenable to the methods of natural science—at least not in any simple fashion. But this was what the liberal tradition of the Enlightenment had proposed to do—to find the right way to conduct human affairs through the use of reason, rather than by relying on dogma or force. As we shall see, Mannheim did not want to give up this hope of the eighteenth-century thinkers, but his reason told him that the issue of relativism must be faced before it would be possible to say if anything of this hope could be salvaged.

Political thought, says Mannheim, falls into five main camps: bureaucratic conservatism, traditional (historical) conservatism, bourgeois liberalism, socialism, and fascism.

Bureaucratic Conservatism. The position taken by administrators. Its principal tenet might be formulated as "Don't rock the boat." It declares that there are no issues other than technical questions of how to get things done and does not want to take the trouble of asking what should be done and why. It simply wants to continue as usual with existing operations. Bureaucrats, says Mannheim, try to reduce all questions of politics to questions of administration. This attitude is found among administrators and technical experts everywhere; it deals with questions of value by denying that they exist, although of course it contains the implicit value of keeping the bureaucratic machine running, and as such constitutes the ideology of the bureaucrats.

Traditional Conservatism. The viewpoint of privileged aristocrats, wealthy landowners, and established clergy. It declares, contrary to the bureaucratic ideology, that history cannot be controlled by plans or decisions. Such conservatives are fond of naturalistic metaphors: Society develops over the centuries like a spreading tree or a flowing river, and nothing anyone can do will have much effect on the natural course of events. Needless to say, this argument for respecting tradition is made by those who are most favored by what the past has wrought up to now; it is those who are sitting in the highest branches of the tree who extol its supposedly harmonious growth.

Bourgeois Liberalism. This philosophy declares that human beings do have the power to reason, to plan, to decide their fate. It points out the flaw in the conservative argument: that not everyone benefits equally from the traditional opinions on what is good for all; accordingly, the best form of government is that in which all the people, or their representatives, assemble to decide their common policy. Truth is not found merely in dogma and tradition, but is something that individuals may arrive at by rational discourse.

Socialist Thought.   This goes one step further and points out that human beings not only have intellectual disagreements but also have real conflicts of interest. Government, even democratic government, is not just a debating society in which people decide on the best interests of all; it upholds the laws and property of an economic system that favors certain individuals and enchains others. In short, Socialist thought exposes liberalism as an ideology averting people's eyes from their material situation, at the same time that material advantages determine who will be able to take part in the government debate. Truth, then, can be revealed only by the revolutionary class, the workers, who can strip away the bourgeois ideology because they have nothing to gain from it.

Fascism.   Finally, Fascism emerges after the lessons of socialism begin to sink in. Liberal democracy is unmasked as ideology, but socialism soon undergoes the same fate. There is nothing transcendental or compelling about the values of socialism, it is soon discovered. They represent only the interests of one more class or one more set of politicians, and all their talk about history being on their side is revealed to be a purely ideological claim. Fascism, says Mannheim, emerges from this sort of total relativism. Its reasoning is: If you can't be right, you can at least be on the winning side. Cynicism about the possibility of attaining political truth leads to opportunism and the worship of power for its own sake. Fascism is the ideology of the unsuccessful, the marginal politicians and intellectuals. It finds its followers among those who, for whatever reasons, want to return to dogmatic certainties; in a time of chaos, there are many who would sacrifice everything for guaranteed law and order.

If each of these positions is determined by the social interests of its respective social groups—bureaucrats, aristocrats, middle-class entrepreneurs, workers, and opportunistic ideologues—which position is right? How can we decide among them? Mannheim gives two answers. First, he points out, these philosophies were largely formulated by intellectuals, who then peddled their ideas to the classes most favorable to them. The intellectuals themselves were a motley group, recruited from many classes of society. This shows that the position of the intellectual is a distinctive one, detached from any social class and hence potentially attachable to any. Marx, for example, came from a bourgeois family but attached himself to the camp of the workers. The "free-floating intelligentsia," then, is in a position to transcend any particular class interests. If they can attach themselves to any class, they can also attach themselves to none and devote themselves to synthesizing the insights gained by each of the above ideologies. Out of their particular positions, the intellectuals should be able to formulate a general one.

But what can this position be? Mannheim's second answer derives from a historical view of values. No values are absolute, he says. What is believed in one age will not be believed in another, and each group has its own interests and outlook on life. Any group that tries to impose its values on others by declaring them universally valid is committing both an intellectual error and an exercise of coercion. The dilemma arises because we are always making choices of action, and hence we cannot do without values, be they explicit or implicit. But at least it is possible, says Mannheim, to be aware of this and to avoid beliefs that are inappropriate to the times. For example, the traditional conservative ideology which spoke of the world as a God-ordained order, in which nobles controlled and protected their serfs like fathers their children (and God his world), had some relevance to a medieval society. It becomes an ideology only when the modern landowner tries to keep down the wages of his farm workers by using the same arguments, even though he now operates in a market economy in which his main concern is profit.

Mannheim's criterion, then, is that ideas should be in harmony with historical development. We cannot have absolute truths and absolute rights and wrongs, but we can at least demand that ideas be realizable in action in the world as it currently exists. Mannheim makes a partial exception for those political ideas he calls "utopias," which he sees as preparing the way for a new stage of society. Thus, the Rousseauist ideals of freedom were a utopia of the eighteenth century, but they foreshadowed the bourgeois society of the nineteenth century and hence could be seen as serving some function in the light of history.

If we look back at Mannheim's list of the five main political ideologies, we see that with one exception, they form a historical sequence. The exception is bureaucratic conservatism. Ever since bureaucracies began to develop in the seventeenth century, they had taken an anti-ideological, antipolitical stance: Times change, and reasons for action change too, but bureaucracies go on and on. The other four ideologies fall into a historical progression: First, traditional conservatism reigned in the premodern society of aristocrats and priests. This was challenged by the bourgeois liberalism of the rising businessperson, which accordingly became most salient during the formative years of the industrial revolution. Advancing industrialism created the working class and its characteristic ideology of socialism. And, finally, modern society went into a period of crisis, caused by the failure of the previous ideologies to correctly express the nature of the modern world. The result was fascism.

But fascism was not the end of history, at least from Mannheim's standpoint. It was rather the ideology of chaos and frustration, and it simply embraced the crisis rather than pointing to a way to resolve it. What was still lacking was a politics appropriate for modern society, and this Mannheim himself proposed to provide. This was the aim of his next book, *Man and Society in an Age of Reconstruction* (1935).

MANNHEIM'S POLITICS FOR MODERN SOCIETY

Mannheim begins with an idea that has become familiar in modern liberalism: We have come to the end of laissez-faire in economics. Economic freedom for businesspeople was important during the nineteenth century as they struggled to free the market from traditional restrictions and thus to build up modern industrial society. But now that the free-market system has won out, and industrialism is an operating system, it must be controlled to keep it from destroying us. A planned economy, directed by the government through monetary and fiscal controls, has become necessary to avoid catastrophic depressions, inflation, unemployment, and other ills.

Similarly, says Mannheim, we have had a laissez-faire philosophy in social and political matters. This has been the characteristic ideology of the bourgeois period, when the model of the individual businessperson and his or her private property influenced people to think of themselves as independent and self-sustaining individuals, fashioning their own fates and requiring nothing of society except the freedom to go their own ways. But when the interactions of human beings in modern society produce seemingly irreconcilable conflicts (for example, class conflict, whether in unionized or revolutionary form), the individualistic philosophy provides no way out. We are left in chaos until people begin to turn to fascism, which promises to impose order by sheer force. But fascism does not solve the underlying problem; it only buries it under totalitarian repression. Just as a sort of Keynesian strategy must be applied in the economic sphere, Mannheim declares that we can have the benefits of modern society only by the creation of planning in the social sphere.

The social and political ills of modern society, as distinct from its economic problems, Mannheim finds to be caused by two major trends: the principles of fundamental democratization and of increasing interdependence.

There has been a seemingly irreversible trend to include more and more of the populace in political life. Alexis de Tocqueville noticed this in the 1830s, and by Mannheim's time it was becoming taken for granted, just as today we automatically assume it will happen in the new nations of the Third World. But, says Mannheim, fundamental democratization in the sense of political participation does *not* automatically lead to increased freedom and an improved political life for everyone. This impression was given by the first stages of democratization in the early nineteenth century, when the industrial revolution brought the well-educated and business-trained middle class into politics. As they won the vote and the right to hold office, they brought with them their characteristic rationalism. This gave a sense of improvement over the old traditionalism, an optimistic feeling that public affairs were now to be settled with intelligence and humaneness.

The later period of industrialization, however, mobilized the rest of the populace, and their entry into politics began to reverse the earlier effects. As urbanization, transportation, and the mass media made the lower classes (the small businessmen, workers, and farmers) a political force, they too won the franchise. But the effect was to lower the level of political debate to demagoguery: appeals to the emotions rather than to reason, to those who want quick, simplistic solutions rather than intelligent understanding of problems. Whereas the earlier phase of democracy enhanced the sense of freedom and rationality, the later phase of mass politics opened the way to potential dictatorship.

At the same time, the different sectors of modern society have become increasingly interdependent. We now have a national economy rather than a set of local economies, an increasingly powerful national government, nationwide transport, and nationally centralized mass media, all of which bring people functionally together in very large numbers. One result of all this is that crises and conflicts in one part of society can no longer remain isolated, but quickly affect the rest of the system. By becoming more interdependent, we have become more vulnerable. Human beings are affected by financial affairs, political decisions, or cultural fads in far-off places; they become haunted by things they can neither see nor control.

As things become more interdependent, the bases of power in society become more concentrated. The economy becomes dominated by a few far-flung corporations and by agencies of the central government that regulate money, credit, and trade. As society comes to depend on the smooth functioning of a complex and gigantic system of exchanges, the organizations that can regulate this activity become necessarily more important and more powerful. Our lives are thus affected by the decisions made in large bureaucracies, and those bureaucracies in turn are controlled by their technical experts and managers, who alone understand the complexities of the system. Thus, at the same time that the mass of humankind achieves the formal trappings of democracy, the situation puts real power in the hands of only a few.

The same shift in power occurs in the military sphere with the rise of modern weapons. In earlier times, says Mannheim, sheer numbers had some weight; one individual was worth one gun. But this equality of force disappears with modern tanks, airplanes, and bombs, which make one centrally controlled military organization more powerful than large numbers of individually armed people. In short, power necessarily becomes more concentrated in modern society, thus increasing the chances of dictatorship.

One might think from this argument that, at any rate, the centralized organizations arising in response to the increasing interdependence of the parts of society would provide the coordination necessary to prevent catastrophes. But no, says Mannheim, we can have large-scale organizations, with all their dangers to individual freedom, without gaining intelligent direction of social policy. This, in fact, constitutes the crucial problem of modern society, for which mass democracy and institutional interdependence provide only the background. Bureaucratic organizations provide rational control, says Mannheim, but there are two kinds of rationality.

On the one hand, there is *substantial rationality,* "an act of thought that reveals intelligent insight into the interrelations of events in a given situation." The model of substantial rationality is a person thinking realistically, calculating so that his or her actions reach their intended goals. On the other hand, there is *functional rationality,* "the fact that a series of actions is organized in such a way that it leads to a previously defined goal, every element in this series of actions receiving a functional position and role." Here Mannheim is talking about an industrial or administrative organization rather than a single person. The crucial difference is that whereas the individual's rationality involves his or her understanding of all his or her actions, the organization's rationality consists in reducing most of its members to cogs in a machine. Substantial rationality, then, is found only in the person at the head of the organization, whereas subordinates are made functionally rational by disciplining them to carry out orders, not to reflect on them.

These two kinds of rationality, then, are not the same thing. Indeed, substantial rationality can undermine functional rationality, as when the organization's members or outsiders foul up its operations by standing back and criticizing or offering competing plans as to how things should be done. The conflict of these two principles is shown in World War I, says Mannheim, in the dispute between the German army and German diplomats and political leaders. The latter soon saw that Germany could not win the war because it was isolated against the rest of the world, and hence the only (substantially) rational course was to negotiate for peace. The army, however, was organized as a highly efficient bureaucracy, and its members were trained to think only in terms of how to carry out war operations. They exhibited what Mannheim calls bureaucratic conservatism, the outlook that denies all policy questions in favor of "getting the job done." In the conflict between the two forms of rationality, the functional rationality of the military carried the day. Germany did not attempt to negotiate and eventually was crushed militarily. The same pattern, of course, has been seen many times over, most recently in the American military's attempt to treat the nuclear arms race as a purely technical question, quite apart from its moral or policy implications.

Mannheim's theory comes down to this basic issue. Modern industrial society will necessarily consist of powerful, centralized bureaucracies, run by their elites. The only question is: Will it be an intelligent and humanistic elite or a shortsighted and irrational elite? Mannheim views advanced industrial society through the lenses of Weber's and Michels' theories, which see supposedly rational organizations blindly drifting, following the imperatives of their internal functioning regardless of their consequences for the larger society. Business corporations, government bureaucracies, political parties, the military, the police, all follow their own patterns of self-aggrandizement, regardless of the disasters they may lead us into. Thus, we come into the modern era of enormously concentrated social power, controlled by blind and irresponsible elites who cloak their irrationality with the outdated ideologies of liberalism. The result, says Mannheim, is bound to be crisis—economic depression, senseless war, domestic disillusionment, and panic. Here two other possibilities open up: Either the Fascists will gain control, with their irrational glorification of order at any price—and this will, in the end, lead to enormous oppression and destruction—or, and this was Mannheim's hope, the organizations of modern society will be gotten back under control by a new elite, trained in social science, who will provide a planned society.

Mannheim gives no clear idea of what such a plan would be, but presumably it would take into account the interdependence of all the parts of society, the consequences of organizations that their own members could not see, and the ways in which individuals' emotions are channeled into aggression or sublimation. But if no plan yet exists, we must get to work on it, for these are the only choices: bumbling along in our network of powerful but unguided organizations and risking fascism whenever a crisis arises, or instituting planning.

But what happens to freedom in a planned society? This was a key question for Mannheim, since freedom was the main value he set out to defend against the forces of modern society. His answer invokes the perspective of historical relativism. It is useless to talk about freedom in the abstract, says Mannheim. Each age has its own conception of freedom, based on its particular problems and possibilities.

Earliest human societies are in the "stage of chance discovery." Their methods of dealing with the world consist of traditions, accidentally adopted and maintained because they work. This notion is like William Graham Sumner's concept of folkways. On this level of society, freedom means spontaneous physical action—the freedom to go where one pleases, to do what one wants when one wants to do it. The limitations on this freedom come primarily from the environment—wild animals, the weather, diseases, lack of food—which may keep human beings from being able to do everything they want.

More advanced civilization has reached the "stage of invention." People have learned to reflect on their world, to develop tools, crafts, machines, businesses, factories, organizations. The new techniques and organizations free us from the hardships of nature, but in return we must give up much of our physical spontaneity. The self-discipline of work with tools and in cooperation with others gives us much control over the physical environment, but it forces us to change our concept of freedom: It is no longer physical freedom of movement that is important, but the freedom to make one's own fortune by using tools and building one's business. It is the freedom of the inventor and the entrepreneur.

But if the stage of social inventions gives us control over the physical environment, it puts us at the mercy of the social environment. What good is formal freedom to choose one's own work, says Mannheim, to a worker who is at the mercy of the shifting trends of the labor market? Accordingly, we find ourselves at the dawn of the "stage of planning," in which we give up the free activity of each entrepreneur and inventor to go his or her own way regardless of the consequences for others in return for a new sort of freedom: the freedom to control our social world instead of being controlled by it. Democracy can be preserved in planning by incorporating the safeguards and procedures of democracy into the plan itself. At least, such was Mannheim's hope. He had to be optimistic about planning, for he felt there was no other acceptable choice.

What can we say about Mannheim's ideas in the light of the half-century since they were written? The Nazi regime, predictably enough, turned an enormous bureaucratic efficiency to the service of such irrational goals as destroying "the Jewish menace" and conquering the world, and eventually it perished from the response to its ill-calculated policies. Most modern societies have instituted economic controls, be they Socialist or Keynesian, which apparently serve to prevent the kind of economic crisis that brought the Nazis to power in the first place. But there remain other crises besides economic ones, especially those involving internal social conflicts and foreign wars, as well as societywide issues of the quality of life. In regard to these matters things remain much as they were in Mannheim's day.

MODERN APPLICATIONS OF MANNHEIM'S THEORIES

C. Wright Mills (1916–1962), the controversial, motorcycle-riding sociologist from Columbia University, made the most serious application of Mannheim's perspective in his analysis of power in America. Mills was a big, burly Texan, so full of energy that he even wrote standing up; he went through three marriages and wrote six major books before dying of a heart attack at the age of forty-six. His key work, *The Power Elite* (1956), gathered together the evidence to show that power has become highly centralized in all sectors of American society.

The American economy, according to Mills, is dominated by a few hundred giant corporations, whose top executives and owners make up a national upper class. In politics the national government far outweighs state and local governments as the locus of crucial decisions, and within the government the executive branch initiates policies that the elected representatives in Congress have only the power to rubber-stamp. Mills felt that the military had become a third major power center, going its own way in carrying out a worldwide policy of war preparation and finding its own allies, especially in its suppliers in the corporate economy. Mills documented the "military-industrial complex" before that notion became popular.

Mills' picture of America was widely challenged, especially his relegation of pluralistic competition to the secondary levels of local patronage politics and his conclusion that high government officials, military officers, and the corporate rich form a united power elite ruling America in their own interests. Much of this criticism was based on value judgments that saw nothing wrong with a state of affairs that Mills found reprehensible.

Most of his critics were supporters of the cold-war policies of the 1950s that Mills felt were based only on the self-interest of a coalition of businesspeople guarding their privileges and the military inflating their own importance and that threatened the world with nuclear catastrophe. Opinion has shifted more toward Mills since the 1960s. The Vietnam War provided a concrete example of how the momentum of a military bureaucracy is scarcely controlled by the rest of American society. We have discovered that the moral shock of the Eichmann trial, with its defense of concentration-camp slaughter as "just following orders," is not merely a historical relic of Mannheim's day, for Americans faced the same issue when functional rationality was applied to the extermination of Vietnamese peasants.

If we understand what Mills was saying in the light of Mannheim's larger picture of modern society, many of the disputes centering around just what Mills meant by power fade into triviality. Mills was documenting Mannheim's theories of interdependence and centralization in American society and the resulting transfer of power from local politics and political parties to a set of bureaucratic elites. In this perspective it is of little importance just how united those elites are or how consciously they try to manipulate our society (although even on this point, recent research has documented the disproportionate influence of a socially coherent upper class on national politics). Indeed, of the three alternatives Mannheim provides for modern society—the bumbling planlessness of organizations' functional rationality, the irrationality of a Fascist dictatorship, or planning by an intelligent and humanistic elite—Mills clearly put America in the first category. He was not, as some of his critics charged, hankering romantically for the bygone days of agrarian democracy. He accepted the concentration of organizational power in America as historically inevitable and only wanted it put under the control of persons who were aware of its dangers and responsible to the people at large.

In this perspective it appears that we are still more or less in the situation that Germany was in prior to the 1930s—bumbling through the nuclear arms race on the momentum of military organizations; drifting through our race conflict on the momentum of entrenched business interests, political parties, and government bureaucracies; allowing the police to exploit superstitions about psychedelic drugs and the youth culture for their own self-aggrandizement. Our situation remains what Mills called "organized irresponsibility"—and in the background, should current compromises fail too badly, are the incipient Fascist demagogues, with their slogans of nationalism and law and order. Only the existence of a controlled economy keeps at least the catalyst of a major depression from being a continuous danger.

What about Mannheim's solution—planning? Mannheim was rather vague about exactly what to do, and since Mannheim few thinkers of independent stature have addressed the question. It is true that a group of social scientists, jealous of the success of economists in achieving a policy voice through the Council of Economic Advisers, have been clamoring for a

Council of Social Science Advisers to offer policies on the overall state of society. Although the general theme is within the compass of Mannheim's hopes, these individuals have little of Mannheim's substantive insights into modern society or indeed of the knowledge accumulated by the major thinkers of the last century. Their proposals consist of little more than the old social-problems philosophy that has guided American sociology, without striking success, since its inception (see Chapter 4): Keep a survey team trained on ghetto "hot spots," and pour in a few more welfare dollars when the riot temperature is rising. This philosophy sounds much more like a well-known political strategy for domestic counterinsurgency than anything based on sociological knowledge. The mentality of the would-be planners at this point resembles that of the bureaucrat, who, as Mannheim said, reduces all policy questions to questions of technique and administration and blindly accepts and maintains the implicit values of the status quo.

Indeed, Mannheim correctly pointed out that the greatest dangers to modern society come not from rebellious individuals at the bottom of the social structure, but from the irresponsible momentum of military, business, and government bureaucracies. If we are to have any sort of successful planning to preserve our freedoms, it must be directed first of all at controlling the military, the police, the corporations, the mass media, the self-inflating educational system, rather than being controlled by their blind self-aggrandizement. It is here that the advances of sociology can have their most important application. Only if all of us—politicians, bureaucrats, and ordinary citizens alike—become aware of the intrinsic dynamics of our organizations will we ever stand a chance of getting them under our control and giving the world, at last, a semblance of substantial rationality.

CHAPTER THIRTEEN

Erving Goffman and the Theater of Social Encounters

Sociology today bears a surface resemblance to many of the dominant ideals of modern America: It is hard-nosed, quantitative, scientific, and practical-minded. Like technical experts behind, say, the atom bomb or a cost-accounting system, sociologists seem immersed in their statistics and their computer programs, oblivious to the human realities behind numbers and abstractions. Yet it would be a mistake to take the obvious, publicly visible side of sociology for the whole of the discipline, just as it would be wrong to conclude from the overwhelming impact of modern technology that we have become a nation of robots. The robots are here, to be sure, but the human element keeps reappearing alongside them. In American society there has been a youthful generation pushing for a cultural revolution in political ideals and in personal behavior; and in sociology, there has been the movement of radical empiricists whose most representative figure is the enigmatic Erving Goffman.

Goffman's sociology might well be called the sociology of the forgotten. Embarrassment, uneasiness, self-consciousness, awkward situations, faux pas, scandals, mental illness—these are his subjects. His colleagues and students have begun to map out the whole underside of society: drug users, delinquents, con men, suicides, flying-saucer cultists, prisoners, topless dancers, and policemen on patrol. But the new sociology is more than a peek into the hidden and the bizarre. It follows one of the great strategies of the sociological method, first laid down by Emile Durkheim: Since society is ordered by norms that are usually unnoticed because they are taken for granted, the sociologist should concentrate on cases where the norms are broken in order to see clearly what they are and what forces act to uphold them. It is this strategy of revelation through disruption that Goffman has adopted: to look at the places where smooth-functioning public order breaks down, in order to see what normally holds it together. The method has produced insights that have begun to restructure sociological theory from top to bottom; we have come to see how social reality itself is constructed out of tacit understandings among people meeting face to face.

Even death itself has a meaning only from the way it is enacted in the omnipresent human theater.

THE LABELING THEORY

The first elements of the new approach to become popular in sociology appeared in a new theory concerning deviance. The sociologist of juvenile delinquency David Matza illustrates this theory and how it differs from its predecessors with a set of arguments. How does one become a delinquent? One theory pointed to a stressful environment: Sally's parents fought bitterly and finally were divorced; her mother took a job and was rarely at home; Sally underwent a great deal of stress, became pregnant, and in due time became an unwed mother and thereby a delinquent. A second theory was that there are delinquent subcultures, so that a person need not be individually disturbed to become deviant but may merely belong to a group in which deviance is "normal." The argument thus read: Sally's family lived in a lower-class neighborhood; Sally began to hang around with a "tough" gang, and as a result she became an unwed mother and a delinquent.

The new theory, known as the labeling theory, argues that a majority of persons in supposedly delinquent areas do not become delinquent, that persons in "nice" neighborhoods may be just as likely to commit infractions but are less likely to be arrested or officially punished for them, and that it is the process of getting caught that transforms trivial offenses into the beginnings of a full-scale delinquent role. In terms of the labeling theory: Sally was in a parked car with her boyfriend one evening. After a few embraces she struggled free and insisted that it was time to go home. The boy was about to start the car when a police car rolled up, and a searchlight caught Sally buttoning her blouse. This was followed, through the rest of the night and the following days, by brusque commands, a ride in the squad car, fingerprinting, a personal search, a medical examination, calls to parents, charges of curfew violations and statutory rape, and lectures by police sergeants, juvenile court officials, probation officers, school administrators, and the family. As a result, Sally went out at the next opportunity and got pregnant.

Goffman gave much impetus to labeling theory with his analysis of the inner workings of a mental hospital, reported in his book *Asylums*. Mental hospitals are supposed to cure mentally ill persons. Goffman decided to look at the matter from the inside and got himself into a large, state-run institution for a year—not as a patient (he felt the role would confine him too much to just one section of the hospital), but as the next best thing, recreation assistant, with his true identity known only to the hospital superintendent. Once inside, attracting attention neither as a patient nor as an authority-wielding attendant, he blended in so closely with his surroundings that his comings and goings were hardly discernible. "I could have sworn there were only fourteen in this room a minute ago," a puzzled attendant would say. Through his brilliantly enacted plan Goffman collected the evidence for a radically unconventional insight: that mental illness is a social role just like any other and that the mental hospital is a place where people learn how to be properly mentally ill.

The theoretical underpinnings of Goffman's analysis hinge on his model of the self. The self is a social product, asserts Goffman, taking up G. H. Mead's insights. A person is not an isolated thing, but an image carved out of the whole life space of his or her interactions with others. A being alone is an animal; only in the society of others does a person acquire essential humanness. Each person's self is a reflection of the responses of others, and each person gives others parts of himself in return. Society is like holding hands in a circle, says Goffman, in which each one gets back on the right hand what he or she gives with the left.

Ordinarily, one derives one's feeling of self from acting with a variety of people in many contexts. But a mental hospital greatly simplifies the conditions of life: In place of a network of different relationships, one finds oneself in a world of only two social categories: patients, all of whom are considered basically flawed and incompetent, and staff, all of whom have freedoms patients are denied and the authority to control patients in major and minor ways. The hospital is large; bureaucratic exigencies require that large numbers of patients be fed, clothed, rested, exercised, watched, and— because of their lapses from ordinary social behavior—sometimes forced to bathe, be dressed, restrained from violence and destruction, and generally treated as persons whose selves carry no dignity or autonomy.

Moreover, the hospital, as a place to keep patients away from normal society, is necessarily a "total institution"—the patient spends every hour of the day within the same walls, subject to the same monolithic controls, and facing the abiding scrutiny of a regular staff that keeps permanent records of patients' behavior. The social sources that reflect his or her self, then, are not only degrading but monolithic; they offer the patient no escape into privacy or to alternative audiences who know nothing of his or her shortcomings. Much of the bizarre behavior of inmates, including such acts as slobbering, cursing, defecating in their clothes, fighting, and withdrawing from any contact, can be seen as desperate devices out of an impoverished repertoire of actions to give some autonomy to the self. The formal organization of a mental hospital, then, by its very nature, creates many of the symptoms that it is designed to cure.

The foregoing does not do justice to the many subtle and complex ways in which being mentally ill has been analyzed, by Goffman and others, as a social role rather than as inexplicable, random, and exotic behavior.[1] The general form of analysis has been applied to many areas: to showing how

---

[1] Current research on the biochemical bases of some mental illness only adds to the complexity of the analysis, rather than eliminating social factors. Whatever the physiological process involved, all humans live in a social world, and even a person with a malfunctioning body shapes a self in relation to the social world around him or her. Later in this chapter we will discuss Goffman's suggestion of just what it means *socially* to define someone as mentally ill.

social service agencies, subject to organizational exigencies, make "blind men" out of people who have trouble seeing, by teaching them permissible, recognized roles for blind men to follow; to showing how in ghetto schools the self-fulfilling prophecy makes children into failures by treating them as potential failures; and most notably, to showing how prisons, officially operating to rehabilitate prisoners, instead operate to socialize the novice lawbreaker into a subterranean inmate culture that furnishes him or her with a new self as a full-fledged criminal. This perspective lends itself to a cynical appreciation of institutional ironies and considerable skepticism about well-intentioned efforts to rescue deviants and unfortunates back into the dominant society that defined them as deviant in the first place.

But the labeling theory and its correlatives are only a small part of the revolution in worldviews that Goffman and his colleagues are bringing about in sociology. The marks of this larger perspective can be gleaned from the above. First, this revolution entails a radical empiricism that is not satisfied with statistical accounts or abstract theorizing about either individuals or society, but that looks in detail at exactly what happens in the situations its subjects are living through. Second, it demands that all acts and social statuses be viewed as the products of social interaction among persons; thus deviance is not to be explained merely in terms of the "deviant," but in terms of the workings of the groups that label him or her as such. Finally, it is based on a radically new view of social reality: not as something "out there" that is always fixed and need only be described and taken account of, but as something that individuals *construct* as they go along out of an infinite set of possibilities that may be realized in contradictory ways at different times and places. This plural, *enacted* view of social reality is the essence of the revolutionary breakthrough, and Goffman's conception of life as theater provides us with a key for building our understanding of it into a new sociology.

GOFFMAN'S THEATRICAL MODEL OF SOCIAL LIFE

Shared staging problems; concern for the way things appear; warranted and unwarranted feelings of shame; ambivalence about oneself and one's audience: these are some of the dramaturgical elements of the human situation.[2]

Since we all participate on teams we must all carry within ourselves something of the sweet guilt of conspirators. And since each team is engaged in maintaining the stability of some definitions of the situation, concealing or playing down certain facts in order to do this, we can expect the performer to live out his conspiratorial career in some furtiveness.[3]

---

[2]Erving Goffman, *The Presentation of Self in Everyday Life* (New York: Doubleday Anchor Books, 1959), p. 237.

[3] Ibid., p. 105.

When do people become uneasy? The answer provides Goffman with a key that opens up the everyday social encounters comprising virtually the whole of experienced society. Embarrassment, Goffman notes, occurs when one's claims to present a certain self are contradicted by the situation: when a purportedly well-to-do person asks an acquaintance for a loan, when a date is refused, when status unequals avoid each other's eyes in an elevator. Uneasiness also occurs when persons show themselves to be less than fully and spontaneously involved in a conversation: by self-consciousness, which communicates to others that one is more concerned with how one is presenting oneself than with the conversation itself; by "interaction-consciousness" brought about by an overmanipulative hostess or by uneasy pauses in the conversation; by "other-consciousness" caused by persons whose obvious affectation or insincerity draws attention to themselves and away from the flow of talk; and by preoccupation with things outside of the conversation. Conversation creates a little capsule of reality of its own, and those who violate its standards are the villains of ordinary social life. Correspondingly, there are heroes of sociability, as the famous tale of Sir Francis Drake's refusal to be distracted from his backgammon game by the approaching Spanish Armada well illustrates.

In general, then, social interaction is a kind of performance with its own guiding rules. Persons are expected to maintain a consistent social face and to help others in maintaining theirs. Living up to the latter rule is called tact. The rules of politeness serve these functions. Thus, conversationalists avoid threatening topics and contestable claims about themselves or overlook such gambits on the part of others and thus avoid insulting them; there is an effort to stay out of uncontrollable disagreement, to avoid lulls and unresponsiveness, which would suggest a lack of interest in the other's conversation, and to end the conversation in a way that seems natural and does not communicate that one has gotten tired of the other's talk.

Goffman works up such observations into a full-fledged theatrical model of social behavior. Behavior has an expressive element as well as a practical element; it is designed to communicate a definition of reality as much as to carry out tasks. Social performances are often put on by teams, such as the husband-and-wife combination entertaining guests in their home, the car salesman convincing a customer, the factory workers putting on a show of diligent effort for the superintendent's inspection. Accordingly, it is possible to view the social world as divided up into frontstage and backstage regions; in the former, a group project is the optimal definition of the group's situation; in the latter, the performers can let down their standards and relax under the cover of a carefully guarded privacy. As Goffman notes, social bonds are strongest between individuals who share common backstages, since they must trust each other to guard the secrets of their common strategy of presenting themselves to outsiders.

Why is life like a theater? Goffman suggests two main reasons. First, being able to control the reality that other people see is a prime weapon, available to almost everyone in some degree, for raising one's status, power, or freedom. Thus, aristocrats and upper-class people use their wealth and leisure to put on shows of grandeur and dignity that give them deference; middle-class people put on a show of respectability to set them above the working classes; managers try to enhance their authority by putting on an impressive demeanor before their subordinates; and workers protect their autonomy from the bosses by restricting their encounters to carefully guarded frontstages.

There is a second reason life must be like a theater: Performances are *necessary* if there is to be a clear, consistent, and recognizable social reality. Situations do not simply define themselves: They must be constructed by symbolic communication; and hence social life must be expressive, whatever else it may be. Goffman thus advances the viewpoint of Durkheim as well as Mead. Durkheim's concept of the collective conscience was a way of pointing out the existence of a shared consciousness as the essence of society. Goffman brings this notion down from the heights of abstraction, so that we no longer find ourselves trying to imagine a big balloon of consciousness hanging over France or England or the United States and making up the collective conscience of those societies; rather, we think in terms of millions of little social realities that come into existence whenever people are together.

Situations have a power of their own, transcending the individuals who make them up, just as Durkheim noted that the individual contributes to the collective conscience but is often powerless against its overwhelming force. The power of symbolic realities is found everywhere, from the deafening silence of a church communion or a public ceremony, which keeps individual observers from opening their mouths and gives novice speakers stage fright, to the tacit rules dividing the acceptable from the impermissible in polite conversation. By analyzing situations as processes of social theater, Goffman shows how collective consciences are created and have their powerful effects.

Our worlds, Goffman is saying, are full of abstract notions about what is real, both for ordinary members of society and even more so for sociologists. What we know firsthand is always something in the present time, in some particular place and situation; what we believe to be real is something inferred from this situation. We meet someone and infer from what he does and says his character (trustworthy or insincere, amusing or dull) and his status (an important personage or an ordinary guy). Thus, we are always presenting a self to other people, and we control our acts for their effects in expressing what we would like others to think we are like when we are not with them: We take care not to get to a party too early lest it seem that our lives are otherwise empty; we entertain guests in the cleaned-up frontstage of a living room and guard the bedroom backstage.

We not only construct characters and statuses for others to see as the permanent realities floating above any immediate here-and-now; we also construct the large organizations that we think of as the permanent, supraindividual structures of society. As we may recognize with some shock, organizations are invisible. No one has ever seen an organization. What we do see are buildings, which *belong to* an organization, and organizational charts, which are symbolic representations in geometric form of the formal rules relating to the members of the organization. As we can see from a little mental experimentation, an organization could still exist if its buildings were taken away; it could also exist without any of its present members, since it is made up of invisible positions that can be filled by new people when the old ones leave. Our world, then, is populated by entities (General Motors, the Pentagon, the University of California, the city of San Francisco) that exist only in people's minds; we are misled into thinking of them as physical things because the people who enact these symbolic entities are usually found in specific physical places. As long as some people believe in them, organizations are real in their effects, and people who do not accept their rules are punished as criminals, madmen, or revolutionaries. But to keep these organizations in existence, they must continually be enacted; when someone succeeds in changing the script of the play, the form of the organization changes, and we say that a power play has occurred.

Society, in a very important sense, is a theater, and its performances—symbolic social ceremonies—are crucial in maintaining it. Durkheim, sixty years earlier, had argued as a general theory that society is held together by ceremony and ritual; Goffman shows society-sustaining rituals at every point in daily encounters. As Goffman puts it:

> In so far as the expressive bias of performances comes to be accepted as reality, then that which is accepted at the moment as reality will have some of the characteristics of a celebration. To stay in one's room away from the place where the party is given, or away from where the practitioner attends his client, is to stay away from where reality is being performed. The world, in truth, is a wedding.[4]

This is a radical way of looking at reality. Social reality is what people say it is, and Goffman is suggesting that instead of trying to focus on some independent things that people seem to be talking about, we should watch them as they are talking about it. The ultimate reality is a puzzle, sometimes a myth, and the "realest" thing we can catch hold of is the behavior of the people constructing reality. A movement of radical empiricists calling themselves ethnomethodologists[5] has taken up just this problem: how people go about constructing in their own minds and conversations a view of the social world around them. This movement, led by UCLA sociologist Harold Garfinkel, builds on the insights of the German social philosopher Alfred Schutz (who in turn was influenced by Max Weber's concept of *verstehen*) and on modern logical and linguistic philosophy. It also carries out the more radical implications of Goffman's style of sociology.

---

[4]Ibid., pp. 35–36.

[5]"Ethnomethodology" means the ethnography (anthropologically detached description) of people's methodologies for dealing with everyday reality.

THE ETHNOMETHODOLOGISTS

The ethnomethodologists go beyond Goffman in their minute analysis of how people construct an everyday reality. Their main finding has been that people act as if reality were solid, given, and unambiguous, but the social world they communicate about is actually fluid, highly subject to interpretation, and not easily discoverable.

In Garfinkel's terms, social communication contains a large quotient of "indexical expressions"—terms that cannot be defined but can only be tacitly understood in the concrete situation by the particular people involved. Words like "this," "now," or "you" are simple examples of indexical expressions; whole systems of ideas can be more complex cases when they contain (as they usually do) concepts and connections that people understand well enough as long as they are in the swing of reading or talking about them, but about which, when pressed for a precise account, they must eventually say, "You know what I mean!"

Garfinkel uses the method of revelation through disruption to highlight these facets of people's "practical reasoning." His long-suffering students perform exercises in which they get into a conversation and then ask for full clarification of meanings:

SUBJECT: Hi, Ray. How is your girlfriend feeling?
EXPERIMENTER: What do you mean, "How is she feeling?" Do you mean physical or mental?
(S)   I mean how is she feeling? What's the matter with you? [He looked peeved.]
(E)   Nothing. Just explain a little clearer what you mean.
(S)   Skip it. How are your Med school applications coming?
(E)   What do you mean, "How are they?"
(S)   You know what I mean.
(E)   I really don't.
(S)   What's the matter with you? Are you sick?[6]

The point is not simply to show that people communicate mostly tacitly, taking for granted that their conversational partners know what they are talking about. These experiments also show that people eventually become angry when pressed to explain their statements and that the source of their exasperation comes from a growing recognition that this line of questioning is, *in principle*, endless. There are indexical expressions contained in virtually everything one says, and the effort to make such expressions objective, to reduce a statement to one in which "You know what I mean" is *not* ultimately necessary, is impossible.

People act as if the world has this objective character, and they expect others to act in the same way, even though this is not a true description of reality. Garfinkel's findings are that people can carry on social relationships

---

[6]Harold Garfinkel, *Studies in Ethnomethodology* (Englewood Cliffs, N.J.: Prentice-Hall, 1967), pp. 42–43. © 1967, Prentice-Hall, Inc.

while carrying around a patchwork-like, invisible, and ambiguous social order in their heads precisely because they act as if there were something solid there all the time. People do not usually ask each other to clarify their statements, even when they are patently ambiguous; they give each other the benefit of the doubt and assume that there is a solid meaning that will be forthcoming in due time.

The social world, then, is really quite a flimsy thing, but since people do not generally realize this, it can take on a considerable amount of solidity. People confronting a representative of an organization do not usually ask for the precise basis of his or her authority or whether there are rules that require what is being demanded of them. Instead, they assume that what is ordinarily done is proper and necessary, and they accept roles as docile customer, client, or employee that are not necessarily enforceable upon them. Garfinkel illustrated this by having his students go into a department store and offer a small fraction of the marked price for some items. The students found themselves approaching the task with considerable apprehension, because there is an implicit understanding in most American stores that things must be bought for their marked price. But they discovered that once they actually began to bargain—to offer, for example, twenty-five cents for a ninety-eight-cent item—it was like breaking through an invisible barrier. With sufficient assurance they gained command of the situation, and the salespeople became flustered and ill at ease. Often they felt that there was at least some chance of having their offers accepted. Obviously, the rule that the price you see is the price you pay has force only because everyone expects it to be followed; most of its force comes from the fact that it is never challenged.

The ethnomethodological viewpoint is potentially revolutionary in its implications. Social structures exist only because people believe that they exist, and those beliefs can be successfully challenged by people with sufficient power or self-assurance to override attempted sanctions. The whole fabric of daily interpersonal ceremony, deference, politeness, and authority exists because it is taken for granted, but it is usually backed up by nothing more than potential social disapproval for its violators by those who believe in its solidity. Persons who see social structure as social myth can puncture the bubble; their equanimity in refusing to accept a conventional definition of the situation gives them the psychological advantage, for the power of the upholders of these conventions rests on their self-assurance that their reality is objective rather than a matter of definition. The hippies led a cultural revolution against constraining formal definitions of situations precisely by their capacity to "blow people's minds" with a well-enacted expression of a counterdefinition of everyday realities.

Of course, not all enacted invisible social structures are so easily challengeable. A business organization is a network of rules and roles that exists only because people agree that it exists, but short of a general siege of amnesia, the people who run it are not likely suddenly to deny its existence. After all, there are material and psychological advantages to playing this symbolic game—those who do, make a living, gain some status and authority, and so on. The state, a police force, an army—all these exist only because their members (or at least a sufficient number of them) agree to act as if their rules and positions were real things; but if they can act as such, they can coerce others into believing, too.

But even with the advantages of power, comfort, and wealth that human organizational play-acting brings, such organizations are not as stable as they appear on the surface. The formal organizational chart rarely corresponds to the actual arrangements of power and cooperation; generals are often at the mercy of master sergeants, bosses may exercise less influence than their secretaries, and little-known politicians and bureaucrats can dictate to presidents. Reality is negotiable, even in organizations in which a total denial of the ultimate validity of the organization would be impossible, and how people negotiate it determines what will actually happen within it. Moreover, even an organization that can back up its claims to reality with coercive violence is sometimes subject to a crippling wave of disbelief. Revolutions occur when everyone comes to doubt the power of the state, much in the same way that a bank is destroyed when there is a run on its funds.[7] From the merest encounter of strangers avoiding each other's eyes on the street, to the mightiest empire, human social order is ultimately a symbolic reality that exists only as long as it is generally believed in, and it changes as people struggle to shift those beliefs to their own advantage.

GOFFMAN'S CONCEPT OF FUNCTIONAL NECESSITY

Goffman's position is more conservative than this. He is neither a revolutionary nor a hippie. Rather, he stands squarely in the Durkheimian functionalist tradition, a more empirically oriented Talcott Parsons. Life is full of nonpractical ceremonies, but Goffman sees ceremonies as functionally necessary to maintain social order. He explores the underside of life, but he is not really sympathetic to the underdog. *Asylums* does not condemn hospital personnel for destroying the selves of mental patients, but explains their behavior in terms of the exigencies of a necessarily bureaucratic total institution. In the same vein Goffman's analysis of the rules of politeness and social ceremony is carried out without irony. In his view individuals who do not live up to the rules of polite interaction are justly punished by embarrassment, self-consciousness, or ostracism, for such rules are functionally necessary for social reality to be kept alive. Indeed, Goffman defines mental illness as the incapacity or unwillingness to perform well and to obey the rules of social encounters. Social justice is harsh; if one does not live up to

---

[7]Some organizations, of course, are much flimsier than this. Most voluntary associations, such as new political parties, social clubs, softball leagues, and stamp collectors associations, go through a period of initial enthusiasm about the organization's objective reality. Then most of them find themselves sliding back down into nonexistence through an acceleration of doubt about the organization's survival, as its believers desert the invisible sinking ship of its reality.

such rules, one is punished by one's fellows; and since one's self is derived from others, one may well be stuck with a permanently spoiled identity as a faulty social interactant or a mental patient. But all this is necessary to uphold society, to preserve symbolic reality for those who can participate in it.

Like most functionalists, Goffman is too ready to see things as necessary simply because they exist. His descriptions of traditional middle-class politeness are becoming outdated. Although he argues that such formalities are necessary to protect the boundaries of the self and to maintain a clear definition of reality, the increasing informality and frankness of interpersonal manners in the most modern sectors of American life illustrates how flexible people can be. They are tougher than Goffman supposes, capable of more honesty, and willing, at times, to put up with an ambiguous, and freer, reality. In the end Goffman is not willing to follow through on his own radical realism to the point where he could see how individuals struggle to impose their own definitions of reality on others, and the potentially liberating effect when people begin to realize just how this operates. To be sure, the ethnomethodologists also, for the most part, fail to carry through the social implications of their thought. They confine themselves to analyzing in great detail the rules that seem to govern people's everyday behavior—in effect, turning the speculative philosophical field of epistemology into an empirical research enterprise.

THE IMPERIALISM OF PHILOSOPHY

A great driving force in the development of all this recent microsociology has, in fact, come from philosophy. There has been a philosophical revolution since the beginning of the twentieth century, and its waves have spread slowly to neighboring disciplines. The initial influence for change comes from even further afield—from a controversy that exercised mathematicians at the turn of the century. This was the conflict between the "formalists," who believed they could construct a complete system of basic axioms and definitions, from which they could rigorously deduce any possible mathematics; and the "intuitionists," who argued that mathematics could not be made into a closed system but that its advancement depended upon working out proofs for each new problem as it came along. In the early years of the twentieth century, the formalists made their most ambitious move. The British philosophers Bertrand Russell and Alfred North Whitehead tried to show that an axiomatic system of pure logic could be constructed to encompass the basic number system, and thus it would encompass the foundations of all mathematics. And Russell's student Ludwig Wittgenstein soon attempted to create a similar system for human language, thus formalizing the basis of the other side of culture.

But these formalist efforts failed. Russell and Whitehead found they had generated *paradoxes* within their system—contradictions in the basic logic itself. In 1931 the German mathematician Kurt Gödel proved that no set of axioms is ever complete, for it is always necessary to have *at least one* principle that stands outside the system; and if that principle is to be incorporated into a new, more comprehensive system, yet another principle must stand outside of that, and so on. At about the same time, Wittgenstein was abandoning his earlier effort at a closed philosophical system of language and coming to the conclusion that language is not just a finite universe of meanings that can be combined in different ways but a set of games that one might play—*actions* that one might do with words rather than merely a list of things at which one might point. Thus talking about things is only one language-game among many; asking, demanding attention, joking, impressing someone—all these actions are other language-games, just as real as the game of applying names to things that philosophers had taken as the only true discourse.

This victory of the intuitionists has been spilling over into sociology ever since about 1950. Garfinkel and the ethnomethodologists, with their concern for indexicalities and for infinite regresses of meanings, are translating Wittgenstein's and Gödel's discoveries into the language of sociology. Thus we come to see how social meanings are not so much given like concrete *things* we can point to, but are just contents of our social *actions*. And they are empirically visible in the language-games that make up most of our social realities.

In his recent work, Goffman, too, has captured the spirit of this philosophical revolution. With typical elegance, he sets out the main idea by expounding on the concept of "frames" and their contents. A situation is like what we see inside a picture frame while we observe it from the frame that surrounds it. Yet we can always step outside that frame and make it the content we are now observing, thereby putting a new frame around the content. Reality, then, is like boxes within boxes, *if we do not make certain social moves to focus it within a controllable frame.* Goffman shows that human actors are always concerned with keeping their frameworks in order; even when we are stepping in and out of frames, there is no escaping the dramaturgical impact of our framing behavior. In Goffman sociology and philosophy become merged, and on this spot the search for the stage machinery by which social reality is constructed comes into ever-sharper focus.

THE INFLUENCE OF MICROSOCIOLOGY

The potential effect of Goffman and the ethnomethodologists on the field of sociology is enormous. For the first time there opens up a real possibility of sociology's becoming a science—a precise and rigorous body of knowledge that explains why people act as they do in relation to each other and why the symbolic products that we call organizations, institutions, cultures, and societies take their particular patterns. This was not a real possibility as long as sociologists remained at arm's length from the observable reality they were trying to explain, dealing with it either through vague abstractions or through the static and secondhand accounts of what people do gleaned from survey questions about their attitudes. Human social behavior has finally become the central focus of attention, not in unrealistic laboratory situations but in the real-life encounters that make up the substance of society. Furthermore, Goffman's model of social performances provides us with a tool for fruitfully organizing this material, simultaneously pointing to the series of events that mold and express an individual personality, the actual dynamics of cooperation and authority that make up an organization, and the negotiation of bonds of sociability and intimacy that knit together social classes and endow them with a status and a group culture. The combination in Goffman of Durkheim and Mead foreshadows a new and powerful social psychology, in which Freud's paradoxes of the conscious and unconscious begin to yield to explanation. Goffman and the ethnomethodologists offer an approach to the empirical realities of organizations and classes that, applied through the heritage of Weber, can pinpoint the dynamics of the larger structures that link together face-to-face groups into a world society.

From this vantage point in time we are beginning to see a new vision of humankind, which was only dimly and partially perceived by the thinkers of the past. In the work of Freud, Darwin, and Spencer, of Durkheim, Weber, Mead, Goffman, and many others, we are reminded of human beings in the long perspective of biological evolution: distinctively gregarious and aggressive animals, linked to their fellows by elaborate emotional interactions, capable of symbolic communications that evoke unseen and unseeable realities, putting on collective symbol plays before the audience of their fellows and recapitulating them inside their own heads as symbolic thought, and thus filling our bare physical planet with that invisible world we call society. We struggle like animals for domination in a group that we need too much to wish to destroy; our weapons are not only teeth and nails and their mechanical extensions in human-made tools of violence, but rituals and communications that play on others' emotions and guide them by the images before their eyes and in their minds. Through these efforts groups are created and other people are excluded from them; organizations are formed and their control disputed; vast industries are produced; art and science and the rest of our symbolic culture arise, forming an invisible network that dominates even the dominators and comprises the spiraling complexity of human consciousness in the face of the inert chemical universe.

Our own realization of these processes is gradually taking shape into a sociology. And if the sociologies of the far past—of the times of Marx, Spencer, and Sumner—have helped to create the popular worldviews of our day, we may expect the popular awareness of the future to take on a new sophistication and a new tone from the sociological advances of today: a new sophistication and a new tone from the sociological advances of today: a new sophistication about the dilemmas and intricacies of a world in which human beings are free to conflict with each other, even as the chains of interdependence lock them in; and a new tone resulting from a new image of humankind. Thinkers of the past have seen human beings as creatures of their heredity or of their history of rewards and punishments, a thing of blind trial and error, or a cog in a larger structure or environment. All these models contain elements of truth, but the best sociology gives yet another image of the fundamental nature of human beings: creatures who *create* their own actions and their meanings and construct new realities where none existed before. Constrained as we are in what we can easily or are likely to create, nevertheless the social world is our own product. The solid world dissolves, opening up a universe of possibilities.

CHAPTER FOURTEEN

Contemporary Sociological Theory in France, Germany, and the United States

It is notoriously difficult to have detachment about one's own times. But we are already close to the end of the twentieth century. One era is passing away, another is in the making. No doubt some of the intellectual events that are happening right now are a significant part of our story of the discovery of society. But we will not really know what is significant until later, when such events can be considered retrospectively from the vantage point of many decades in the future. Only the twenty-first century will be able to judge the intellectual accomplishments of the late twentieth century.

It is in a tentative spirit, then, that we try here to bring the "discovery of society" up to date with some of the intellectual developments of our own times. We will provide a brief introduction to some of the representative theories of the sociological world: those of Michel Foucault and Pierre Bourdieu in France; Jurgen Habermas in Germany; and Randall Collins and Immanuel Wallerstein in the United States. One might argue with our selections; other theories could just as well be provided. Our only rationale is that we think these lines of thought are interesting. And for obvious reasons (considering that one of the theories we will deal with is that of one of the present authors), our selections have been those that were especially easy for us to produce.

MICHEL FOUCAULT: HISTORY AS DISCOURSE

Michel Foucault (1926–1984) has been in recent decades the most talked about of French intellectuals. Strictly speaking, he was a historian, not a sociologist. But he was crossing disciplinary boundaries from the very beginning, observing psychiatric practice in mental hospitals during the 1950s, and teaching classes in psychopathology at the Ecole Normale Supérieure in Paris. Combining these materials led him, naturally enough, to begin publishing on the history of madness and then broadening out into related topics. Thus we have a series ranging from *Madness and Civilization* (1961) to *The Birth of the Clinic* (1963) to *Discipline and Punish: The Birth of the Prison* (1975) to *The History of Sexuality* (1976). This is interesting enough material, all right, but how does it qualify Foucault as the leading intellectual in France, and a thinker that sociologists must take into account?

The answer is that Foucault was a man with a program. His most important book, *The Archeology of Knowledge* (1969), laid out an argument for a new way of conceiving history, and indeed any intellectual discipline. We can grasp how powerful his claim is when we realize that he means we must reconceptualize every intellectual discipline, not just the social sciences but the natural sciences as well, and not just the theoretical and scholarly ones but the applied, practical fields. What can all these have in common? They are all forms of *discourse.* Instead of reflecting or investigating the world, these disciplines construct the very nature of our world and determine the way we behave. They are ways of talking, and of not talking; as such they are intrinsically social, and they are sources of power in the deepest sense.

Concern with discourse did not originate with Foucault. It has been a theme of linguistics and literary studies, and more recently, of the philosophy of language; and the application of linguistic concepts (most notably by the anthropologist Claude Lévi-Strauss) to society and its products is the key to the movement known as French structuralism. But Foucault is not merely a structuralist, although he acknowledges some kinship to that movement. One might say Foucault took a fresh approach to the whole topic of discourse. Lévi-Strauss and the other structuralists examined societies and their products as systems, structured by signs in relationship to each other. Lévi- Strauss and others, for a while, seemed to be searching for the underlying code that governed the symbolic system of a society. Following some fundamental principles of linguistics, the structuralists expected these systems to be constructed out of *binary oppositions:* distinctions between pairs of categories. Later, the structuralist program came under attack, and "poststructuralists" and "deconstructionists" argued that the codes were not merely binary, or that no such code could be found, or that signs themselves are historical products which are endlessly subject to reinterpretation. Structuralism, which began as a search for some eternal, universal underlying properties of the human mind, eventually turned into a radical relativism in which nothing at all could validly be said. (The last is the position of the most famous of the "deconstructionists," Jacques Derrida.)

Foucault maintained his distance from these debates. Since he began as a historian rather than an anthropologist, literary critic, or philosopher, he was never tempted to imagine a closed system of signs; and he felt no need to break out from that system, either. His subject was always real human beings in the midst of the material conditions of their lives. His vivid description of the lepers in the Middle Ages, or the prison cells and factory buildings of the eighteenth and nineteenth centuries, exemplifies the kind of baseline from which Foucault worked, and which kept him immune from the idealist tendencies of the structuralist and poststructuralist intellectuals. Foucault always had his eye on power, control, struggle, and historical change. At the same time, he was concerned with the history of ideas. But this did not mean merely the history of intellectuals; it meant the history of ideas in practice, like the practice of the doctors, the prison reformers, the psychiatrists, and the factory managers whom Foucault studied. Foucault was thus able to offer a theory of how ideas interact with the social world, ordinary life at its most ordinary, even at its grubbiest level. There is a lot of shock value in Foucault's writings, but this is only the superficial part of what brought him attention. His fame comes from a deeper source—from his attempt at a theory of the connection between discourse, power, and history.

Discourse as a System of Constraints

What is discourse? At first glance, it is talking, communicating: It seems to use signs to designate things. This was the starting point of structuralist linguistics, the relationship between signifiers and that which they signify, together with the relations among the signs themselves. But Foucault argues that discourses are not merely groups of signs, but are practices which constitute the objects of which they are speaking. Discourse is more than signs pointing to things or oppositions among signs. Foucault sets as his task to analyze what is this "more than."

One way to look at this is to recognize a system of discourse as a system of *exclusion* or constraint. It is a set of boundaries as to what can be said and what cannot be said; and accordingly, if something cannot be said, it cannot even be thought about. Foucault suggests there are three great forms of exclusion: the division between madness and reason; prohibited words; and the will to truth. Let us look briefly at each of these.

Madness and Reason. Discourse is always supposed to be meaningful. No one listens to nonsense. But where is the dividing line drawn, and how? This is historically variable. Here we see a reason Foucault conceives his studies of madness and of psychiatry as uncovering a crucial form within civilization. At the beginning of the nineteenth century, the modern profession of psychiatry appeared. Foucault regards this as no minor development, but as a fundamentally new way of structuring the relationship between reason and unreason. It is a crucial fault line between historical epochs. He attempts to show this by examining the way in which the materials of the new psychiatry— the people who are its patients, the problems which are their diseases—were handled before and after the rise of the new discipline. The shift is not merely an intellectual one, as if the doctors' theories about mental disorders had changed from theories about fevers and affections of the brain to a new conception of "nervous diseases," and later, with Freud and his generation, to a purely psychological conception of causes and cures. For Foucault shows that the whole complex of practices surrounding the dividing line of madness and reason shifted its grounds during this time.

In the Middle Ages, madness was just another category of the untouchables, the outcasts of society. Just as lepers were segregated into their encampments of horror, the mad might be gathered together on a ship and put adrift in the sea. All this was connected with religious conceptions, with a notion of God's unfortunates, people who were accursed, but by the same token, had something of the holy about them. It was not a matter for the province of medicine, but a matter of the public organization of society. All the different classes of unfortunates were mixed together, and houses of confinement mingled the insane with the poor, the unemployed, with debtors, vagabonds, and prisoners. When we reach the watershed of the eighteenth and nineteenth centuries, the social connections are remolded in an entirely different direction. Modern psychiatry takes shape as a set of practices, designed no longer to exclude madness from society, but to contain and control it. Reformers like Tuke in England and Pinel in France cut the tethered madmen from their chains, and put them in specialized institutions under programs which were to inculcate them with reasonableness and self-restraint. It was a movement of humanitarianism and enlightenment; but at the same time, it placed a new stress on the inner control and reform of the individual.

Furthermore, the methods that were put into action were part of a complex which is found in many spheres. The mental hospital, the insane asylum, is an institution for surveillance, for control, for changing people's behavior; madness is to be dominated by reason. Parallel developments happen in other spheres. The poor and diseased had similarly been outcasts of medieval society; sometimes they were the objects of charity, and the focus of a religious message. They were a fact of life, part of the universe of sin, suffering, and atonement. But with the dawning of "modernity," the beggars too are brought under a program of social control, to be organized into workhouses and put to obligatory labor. Apparently further afield, but conceptually just around the corner, criminality undergoes a similar transformation. Where once criminals had been publicly tortured, mutilated, and executed, they too are put into the new institutions of discipline; ritual exclusion is replaced by specialized organizational control. And this shift is not merely at the margins of society; it affects even the central sphere of work, as laborers lose their independence and become herded into factories. Prisons, schools, army barracks, hospitals, factories, and reformatories all come to resemble each other.

This shift, taken as a whole, is a good example of what Foucault means by a "discoursive formation" or system of discourse. We find, at the modern end, a way of conceiving the world; in particular, we have a dividing line between reason and unreason, crystallized upon the technical discourse of the psychiatric profession. The way we think today, and hence the way we see the world, is based on this conception of reason and its boundaries. But the ideas of psychiatry did not simply come from observation of the world, nor are they a straightforward development from the earlier, less accurate theories of premodern medicine. They are part of a much wider shift in the organization of society, from one system of discourse to another. In the modern world, what is normal or abnormal is now judged by professionals with their specialized systems of control. This is the social transformation that constitutes the modern system of discourse.

Prohibited Words.   Another way in which a system of discourse shapes our world is by allowing what can be said, and excluding other things. There are many ways in which Foucault could illustrate this point. He chose sexuality, no doubt because it is such a striking example, in any society, of the difference between what is proper and improper. Foucault again draws on before-and-after portraits of the transformation of modern Europe. In the seventeenth century, there was considerable frankness in regard to sexual behavior; by modern standards, the codes regulating the coarse, the indecent, and the obscene were lax. Sexuality, one might say, was part of the public sphere, and its pleasures and power relations, physical attractions and repulsions were out in the open, subject to a conventional discourse. By the nineteenth century, there is an entirely different way of treating sex. Silence becomes the rule regarding most aspects of sex; conceptions of morality and virtue are elevated, and not only enjoin sexual monogamy but make any public attention to eroticism itself a scandalous violation.

Sexual behavior of course does not go away. The height of prudery in the Victorian era was also a time of massive prostitution, when proper bourgeois gentlemen frequently had mistresses, and society had a whole backstage of sexuality. Foucault stresses again that the issue is not behavior, but discourse. It is not just a matter of what people did, or what they thought about what they did; it is, rather, a field of conceptions and possible enunciations, of things that can be said and things that cannot be said. In other words, there is a new dividing line between the respectable and the unrespectable, enforced by the new system of sexual discourse. Sexual behavior can still go on, but it is shaped into its own sphere, where it must take account of this dividing line. It must hide itself away into privacy or even secretiveness. Hence the whole experience of sex takes on a new quality.

Foucault argues that Freud in the twentieth century, and the subsequent movement to open up sexuality as a new personal style of liberation, does not fundamentally transform the system of discourse and exclusion laid down in the previous century. Foucault charges that Freudian psychiatry only reinforces the mainstream conception of what is normal, and helps patients adjust to it. Whether Foucault is right about this may be open to question. That is, there may be a still newer, twentieth-century system of discourse which changes once again the field of possibilities in regard to sex. But it is probably too early to judge this very surely. And whatever the historical specifics turn out to be, any new system of discourse will no doubt turn out to have its own areas of exclusion, possibilities that it does not allow people to consciously consider.

The Will to Truth.   One of Foucault's most radical arguments is that the very conception of truth is itself one of the exclusionary systems of discourse. That discourse should be oriented toward truth is a characteristically modern idea. We live in this form of discourse, and hence we take it for granted. Again, Foucault shows the historical dividing line that brought us to where we are today. For example, the European penal laws of the seventeenth century and earlier were based on a notion of right; there were certain self-evident principles to be defended—obedience to God, the authority of the king, the dignities reserved for the nobility, and so on—and punishments were carried out to uphold these principles. The shift to modern penology is not merely a shift toward greater humanitarianism, a wave of sympathy which abolished the tortures and carnivallike public executions of the previous period. More fundamentally, Foucault argues, modern penology is a shift in how laws are justified. Henceforth, laws of all sorts are justified because they are based on "true discourse"; they are the products of rational discussion, leading to truthful conclusions. One might say that modern penal laws are supposed to be "scientific," but Foucault's point goes deeper than this: Modern science itself arises because of the ascendancy of this new form of discourse, discourse dominated by the "will to truth."

Foucault's use of this term "will to truth" echoes Nietzsche. As we have already seen in Chapter 4, Nietzsche proposed to turn modern scientific and critical consciousness back upon itself. Writing at the time when anthropologists were starting to explain the social institutions in remote tribes as the products of particular social causes, Nietzsche declared he would look at modern civilization in the same way. Our own institutions and moralities are no more eternal verities than those of any ancient or tribal society of the past; they are all the results of historical processes, and each is destined—so Nietzsche argued—to change into something else. One of the main traits of our modern civilization is the emphasis it places upon science, upon rationality, upon a faith in the power of the human mind to discover truth. But this attitude is more faith than actuality; it simply indicates a form of the human will to power in our times. It is a will to truth, that hides from itself by seeing only the truths that we have allegedly encountered.

Foucault is, at least partially, an heir to this Nietzschean way of looking at the modern world. Like Nietzsche, Foucault tries to uncover the ways in which we have socially constructed this emphasis on truth, and with it have excluded all the other ways that discourse can operate. What are these alternatives? One of them, Foucault points out, can be seen by looking at ancient Greek society, in the period just before the first philosophers (in the sixth and fifth centuries B.C.) created the modern ideal of the love of truth. (The word "philosophy" itself means "love of knowledge.") The earliest Greek society, as depicted in Homer, was enveloped in rituals: sacrifices to the gods, readings of omens to predict the future, attempts to ward off catastrophes. This was a form of discourse, Foucault argues, but it was a discourse concerned only with what it did, not what it said. Rituals were an attempt to react to the world, and to mold it. Rituals did not express a philosophy which saw the world as ruled by gods and invisible forces; its main thrust was not to describe the world at all, but to act on it. With Thales, Heraclitus, Socrates, and the other philosophers, the whole form of discourse changed. Discourse was now oriented toward truth, toward contemplation and description; discourse for the first time was judged by what it said, by what it pointed to beyond itself.

Foucault thus stresses that we should understand the basis of our own discourse, our own concern with truth. Truth is not an absolute but a historical product, the focus of a form of discourse that emerges only at particular times and places. The more basic form of discourse is practice, not consciousness. That we have elevated consciousness to the ideal form of discourse is just the particular, contemplative, and intellectual form of discursive practice in our own times.

Discourse and Power

Discourse is also a system of power. It implies who is authorized to speak, and who may not. Some persons must remain silent, at least in certain situations, or else their utterances are regarded as unworthy of attention. We see this in the example of the medicalization of madness. In medieval society the conception of madness was part of religious discourse and the practice of public segregation; the entire community was involved in recognizing and acting out the borderline between madness and normalcy. The watershed of the nineteenth century has given madness over into the hands of experts, whose opinions alone count on this subject. In a similar way, there is power underlying the system of discourse which constitutes sexuality. The sexual behavior which can be talked about openly has a different social status than sexual behavior which must remain behind the screen. The system of discourse produces repression at the level of feelings and thoughts; though a hidden and seemingly agentless system of control, it is a real power in society nonetheless.

The educational system itself, says Foucault, is primarily a system of power. The system of educational discourse focuses what we can say and think about; it constitutes what objects are real; what is public, what is private, what is under the province of technical specialists. The schools, in Foucault's eyes, are a set of rituals through which individuals pass; the end result is to divide persons into those who are authorized to speak of particular subjects and those who are ruled out from serious speaking by their lack of expertise. Modern society, unlike other societies, is dominated by the written word, by the form of discourse embodied in legal rules, bureaucratic reports, and professional technicalities. All this makes up the basic system of modern power.

Power, then, is Foucault's overarching theme. Most of his historical studies concern transformations in the system of power. Medieval society was rather coarse and brutal, a society in which everything took place under the pitiless eye of the public. Power was more nearly transparent, and everything was directed toward maintaining the boundaries by direct exclusion and repression: Lepers and madmen were herded to the outskirts of town, criminals and heretics were burned in the marketplace. Modernity, for Foucault, is a shift toward a different organization of power. Now there is a sharp split between public and private, and the border between them is controlled by specialists with their own professionalized discourse. The modern prison, the insane asylum, the factory, the bureaucratic welfare system, are all applications of the same structure; all institute discipline behind closed walls. Foucault would argue that the psychoanalyst's office is no more than an extension of this prevailing model. The means by which we attempt to escape from the confinements of modernity, Foucault suggests, are no more than continuations of the basic structure.

Foucault's analysis, of course, is not the last word on this subject. There are many ways in which the late twentieth century is different from the earlier "modern" times Foucault wrote about; and there may well be more historical shifts in the system of discourse than Foucault recognizes. There are probably more forms of power than he takes account of, and more ways in which people struggle against power. Foucault has popularized a way of seeing the entire world under the aspect of discourse; it remains to extend his model still further.

From the point of view of sociology, we might look at Foucault's fame in yet another way. In the narrower sense, Foucault might be regarded as a specialist in the historical sociology of deviance. But as Durkheim pointed out, deviance does not merely concern the margins of society. Deviance provides us with something like a natural experiment, showing us the conditions that hold society together by comparison with the occasions on which society falls apart. Foucault makes use of the history of deviance in exactly the same way. He is above all concerned with what it tells us about social control; he focuses on the abnormal for the light which it casts on the normal. The picture Foucault gives is that the normal is socially constructed, and historically changeable. This is a powerful continuation of one of the main insights of the sociological tradition.

PIERRE BOURDIEU:
SYMBOLIC VIOLENCE AND CULTURAL CAPITAL

The French intellectual milieu is rather different from the specialization which dominates in the English-speaking world. Leading French academics are also intellectuals in the broadest sense, who make their voices heard on philosophy and politics, literature and art, as well as in social science. We have already seen this in the case of Foucault. Similarly, the philosopher Jean-Paul Sartre wrote plays and novels, as well as an existentialist philosophy that included his own version of psychoanalysis; later in his career,

Sartre produced a quasi-Marxian philosophical system under the title of *Critique of Dialectical Reason* that can be regarded as a combination of philosophy and sociology. The anthropologist Claude Lévi-Strauss not only developed a theory of tribal kinship systems, but his works on primitive mythology were expanded into a system of analysis, structuralism, which exerted vast influence on philosophy and literary theory.

Within recent French sociology, the most important figure is perhaps Pierre Bourdieu. Bourdieu has not had the same degree of public fame as Foucault, Sartre, or Lévi-Strauss. But for sociology he is more immediately relevant. For one thing, unlike other French intellectuals who touch on the theory of society, Bourdieu is a professional sociologist, actively involved in research. For many years he has directed the Centre de Sociologie Européenne in Paris, the most important empirical research institute in France. Thus he has had the advantage, over the purely theoretical efforts of other French intellectuals, of being able to dig up new research information. It is worth noting, too, that although Bourdieu has reaped most of the fame for these research efforts, he has been assisted by many talented collaborators, such as Jean-Claude Passeron, Jean-Claude Chamboredon, Luc Boltanski, and others. His group has studied the cultural structure of modern life in the educational system of France, as well as other aspects of culture, high and low: museum going, amateur photography, home decor, the competitive field of the high-fashion designers, and the factional structure of intellectuals. From Bourdieu's research group, we learn more about the differences within a modern society than from any previous sociologist.

But Bourdieu is more than a describer of the worlds in which different social classes live. He is a theorist, who develops his own position by borrowing and synthesizing from Durkheim and Marx, as well as from the anthropologists Marcel Mauss and Lévi-Strauss. Moreover, Bourdieu adds a comparative dimension from his own experience, early in his career, when he did anthropological field work on the Kabyle tribe in the mountains of Algeria. Both in tribal societies and in industrial capitalist societies, Bourdieu proposes that culture is an arena of stratification and conflict. Culture is itself an "economy," which is simultaneously related to what we more conventionally call "the economy"—that is, the production and distribution of goods and services. Stratification in the cultural economy and in the material economy are reciprocally related, as cause and effect of each other. For Bourdieu, culture is a realm of power struggle, related to the struggle over the means of violence that characterizes the realm of politics.

Hence Bourdieu's central concept, *symbolic violence.* This is defined in *Reproduction: In Education, Society, and Culture,* which Bourdieu wrote with Jean-Claude Passeron, as "power which manages to impose meanings and to impose them as legitimate by concealing the power relations which are the basis of its force." Such power is very widespread. It makes up the content of formal schooling, but also of child rearing, of the styles people display in public, of religion, and of the communications media. Their legitimacy as cultural meanings by which people define the world and each other's place in it is based upon force. But this force is hidden, and necessarily so. The school teaches a culture authorized by the dominant class, but the school must claim to be neutral in all class conflicts, for only by appearing to be neutral can it add any power to the dominant side. One of Bourdieu's main contentions is that culture does have a relative autonomy, adding its own specific force to that of sheer physical and economic coercion. The culture of the school is an arbitrary selection from the universe of possibilities, but it must hide this arbitrariness; it cannot teach cultural relativism without undermining itself.

The theme comes out strongly in Bourdieu's most theoretical work, *Outline of a Theory of Practice,* where he draws heavily upon his Algerian tribal materials. Society, he claims, is held together by deception, or *misrecognition.* Here Bourdieu gives his own twist to the Durkheimian tradition. Durkheim had argued that society is held together by ritually created beliefs in its gods. In Bourdieu's sense, this involves a fundamental misrecognition, since society creates the gods, but must hide this fact from itself because only by believing in the gods as objective can the belief be effective. Marcel Mauss had extended Durkheim's ritual theory to the exchange of gifts which is the basis of the primitive economy. Giving, receiving, and reciprocating gifts is strongly hedged with social obligation, since it is an insult to refuse a gift, and a rejection of social ties if one does not repay one gift with a return gift. But the very idea of a gift is that it is felt to be voluntary rather than a mere payment for previous goods; hence one cannot carry out a gift exchange at all in the proper, and obligatory, spirit unless one denies there is any obligation involved in it.

This is the line Lévi-Strauss took up in his *Elementary Structures of Kinship,* to derive the various structures of tribal societies from the political and economic alliances produced by marriages—which Lévi-Strauss analyzes as gift exchanges of women between families. Bourdieu criticizes Lévi-Strauss for not placing enough emphasis on the ideological aspect of kinship rules; the official beliefs as to what constitutes a high-status marriage is itself imposed by the force of the dominant families, who are struggling for advantageous alliances. But Bourdieu also carries this model of misrecognized exchanges still further, by showing that not only marriages, but also tribal feuds and vendettas are a kind of gift economy. Among the Kabyle, insults and murders must be avenged, in order to keep up a family's honor. At the same time, a strong family must give insults and start fights, for it is only by having enemies that one can show honor. But one must carefully choose with whom one will fight. One dishonors oneself, for example, by challenging, or accepting a challenge from, an opponent who is too weak to fight properly. Carrying out fights with proper enemies, then, brings honor to both sides, and constitutes another hidden gift exchange. Bourdieu goes so far as to refer to it as an economy of "throats" cut by the murderer's knife, which are "lent" and "returned." It is an economy of honor, carried out under the guise of physical coercion. Here Bourdieu even manages to show symbolic violence misrecognized as real violence.

For Bourdieu, this case is not an extreme one. "Every exchange," he says, "contains a more or less dissimulated challenge, and the logic of challenge and riposte is but the limit toward which every act of communication tends."[1] This is Mauss's theme again, for every gift holds the prospect of dishonoring its recipient, if he or she cannot repay it with an equally prestigious return gift; it is upon this logic that the competitive gift-giving in the potlatch was played. And a theme of Lévi-Strauss as well: For the regularities of tribal marriage patterns breed not only alliances but also hatreds and wars when expected exchanges are not satisfactorily carried out. The borderlines from appeasement to alliance, and again from alliance to rivalry, are thin ones. It is this logic that Bourdieu has generalized.

The exchange of culture in this misrecognized form is the basis of the *reproduction* of the entire society. In modern society, schooling reproduces the distribution of *cultural capital* among social classes. The content of the dominant schooling is the culture that corresponds to the interests of the dominant classes. This constitutes cultural capital, the chief instrument of transforming power relations into legitimate authority. Each new generation passing through the school system thus reproduces the structure of legitimation: Those who are successful in the system acquire legitimate domination, while those who are unsuccessful acquire a sense of the legitimacy and inevitability of their own subordination.

This constitutes a double reproduction, in that both the structural relations among the classes are maintained, and particular families within each social class pass along their advantages, or disadvantages, from generation to generation. The principal means by which this transmission occurs Bourdieu calls the *habitus*. This means the internalization of an arbitrary cultural standard, at first in the family, later reinforced in the school. The habitus grows over time by feeding upon itself; consumption of a certain kind of culture, such as museum going, gradually develops into a need for more of the same. Hence children from culturally advantaged or disadvantaged homes not only start in the world with varying cultural dispositions and possessions, but increase their distances from one another as time goes along. Schooling, in this view, does not so much create symbolic capital as develop it into more refined forms; as in learning one's native language, one begins practically and customarily, later, consciously and systematically. Once finished with schooling, individuals carry a fund of culture which, if it is worth enough on the existing cultural market, gives them entrée to particular occupations and social circles. This movement of individuals through a system of cultural inculcation thus reconstitutes the structure of society.

In tribal societies, symbolic capital consists of honor, of kinship ties, and of myths such as those which define the dominant and subordinate places of men and women in the order of things. This culture hides stratification,

[1]Pierre Bourdieu, *Outline of a Theory of Practice* (Cambridge: Cambridge University Press, 1977), p. 14.

by defocusing it, and by creating the authorized categories through which group members must talk and think about the world. Culture reproduces the entire structure of society, including its material economy. Here again we find the logic of misrecognition and symbolic violence. The tribal economy seems to eschew strict economic calculations, and seems instead to work on an ethos of alternating penuriousness and extravagance. Kabyle families bankrupt themselves to put on a display of lavish spending at a wedding, or go to any lengths to hold on to traditional family lands. Yet all of these are moves in the economy of honor. Like the vendetta exchange of "cut throats," these extravagances and refusals of utilitarian considerations are means of gaining family honor and hence social power. For the family with much prestige will have a wide network of persons who are obligated to it by its extravagances; such a family can call upon many helpers when there are collective tasks to be done. Such a family will have many fighters when it engages in warfare, and many workers when there is agricultural work. Thus expenditures on the symbolic market bring their return in power and in renewed material wealth. The various realms flow into and reproduce one another.

This argument, Bourdieu believes, is quite general. Symbolic capital is always credit. In the tribal economy, it consists of obligations accumulated, which can be cashed in the form of a work force or fighters at the times when they are needed. Such symbolic capital circulates, like money, in a market. "Wealth, the ultimate basis of power, can exert power, and exert it durably, only in the form of symbolic capital."[2] Wealth can reproduce itself only if it is turned into forms that generate social obligation, and hence the alliances and deferences that make up social power. The same is true in a modern capitalist society, where the forms of cultural domination shift but the principle remains the same. In either case, the cultural market operates as symbolic violence: "the gentle, invisible form of violence, which is never recognized as such, and is not so much undergone as chosen, the violence of credit, confidence, obligation, personal loyalty, hospitality, gifts, gratitude, piety."[3] Such a circulation of cultural capital, in fact, is the most economical mode of domination.

Bourdieu's view of history consists of a typology of the two versions of society he has considered: rural Algeria and modern France. These correspond to two modes of domination. There is a domination which is constantly being made and remade in personal interactions; and a domination which is mediated by objective and impersonal media. The former consists of the ritual exchanges and vendettas of tribal society; the latter of the impersonal organizations which distribute titles, whether these consist of property deeds or academic degrees. The difference between the two types of society is "the degree of objectification of the accumulated social capital."[4] In the tribal society, power is continually negotiated by individu-

[2]Ibid., p. 195.
[3]Ibid., p. 192.
[4]Ibid., p. 184.

als on their own behalf. Hence such societies strike the modern observer as both more brutal and also more personal and humane than one's own. In the modern society, domination is based upon objective mechanisms—the competitive structures of the school system, the law courts, and the money economy—and hence its products appear divorced from people and take on "the opacity and permanence of things."[5]

The transition between the two types occurs when the culture is no longer the immediate possession of everyone who uses it, but becomes stored in writing. Then specialists begin to monopolize culture, and to develop it into esoteric forms of religion, art, and specialized knowledge. This primitive accumulation of cultural capital is Bourdieu's counterpart of the Marxian primitive accumulation; it marks the transition to class societies. A further stage in objectification of the system of domination occurs with the elaboration of the educational system. Whereas the personalized society of ritual exchanges is local and fragmented, the educational system unifies all cultural capitals into a single market. Formal educational degrees are to cultural exchange what money is to the material economy; both create a single standard of value, and guarantee free and universal circulation. Bourdieu goes so far as to say that an educational system producing certified degrees guarantees that one can always convert cultural capital back into money at an objectively fixed rate: that investment in culture always pays off economically at the same level.

Once a society organized in this way comes into being, Bourdieu sees only very limited possibilities for its transformation. Class society continuously and objectively reproduces itself. Political and economic upheavals cannot change its structure, precisely because of the relative autonomy of the cultural system. Neither the Marxists nor the Third World nationalists promise any relief, for these are movements formulated by intellectual rebels, who themselves have come to the top by virtue of their superior cultural capital. A Soviet type of society, dominated by the possessors of ideological capital, would constitute no formal change in the structure of domination. Nor can the school system itself be successfully destratified. Every movement in this direction has been a failure. Citing French data in the post–World War II period, Bourdieu shows that social classes have continued the same rank ordering of educational attainment, even though school attendance has expanded massively. Nor can reforms within the style and content of schooling change the situation. For the initiative in such reforms is always taken by highly cultivated intellectuals, themselves the products of the system that they are changing. The shift to the "free school" environment, to "soft" discipline and an emphasis on autonomy and creativity, remains nevertheless a mode of cultural inculcation and social selection, and one that most favors the children of avant-garde families. The newest, freest culture only adds another level of sophistication to an accumulation of cultural capital. There is no escape from the circle: The person who deliberates upon culture is already cultivated.

[5]Ibid., p. 184.

Not only formal education, but all spheres of culture are both stratified and stratifying. In Bourdieu's huge work, *Distinction*, he and his fellow researchers demonstrate that these relationships are found in all spheres of culture, from tastes in painting and music to the kinds of food one eats, the way one entertains friends, the furniture one buys, the sports one watches or participates in, the makeup one wears, the bodily contours one clothes or displays, as well as the politics and public issues one is concerned with or rejects. These are products of one's position within the structure of society, and they serve to reproduce that structure over time. For instance, the taste for art: Bourdieu shows that the upper-middle/upper-class elite divides rather sharply from the lower-middle/working-class nonelite over the kinds of art works it considers beautiful. The lower echelons insist upon a more substantive, content-oriented standard of beauty (a sunset, a picture of a first communion), while the elite rejects these as sentimental and prefers pictures which have a formal aesthetic, even if the content itself might be an everyday or even ugly object (a photograph of gnarled hands). The two aesthetics are hierarchizing, in that the "elite" overviews, transcends, and subsumes the lower classes' standards. The elite practices a one-upmanship that always stays one jump ahead of the "average" standard of appreciation. Not only can objects of ugliness be transformed into works of formal beauty; but when the lower-middle class becomes more educated into appreciating abstract art, the elite jumps ahead to prefer lower-class sentimental kitsch or "pop art," as an ironic distancing from what used to be the high-status art.

Tastes in art are only one illustration of the class struggle which goes on implicitly in every realm of culture. This form of struggle is particularly insidious because it appears to transcend the vulgar level of claims to economic domination and organized power. The upper-class aesthetic self-consciously distances itself from mere money, mere material things—as if there were not a tremendous material investment not only in the art objects themselves, but even in the years (or generations) of training necessary to appreciate art and to establish one's standards around them. Furthermore, the elites indulge in their standards dogmatically and without self-criticism, because these standards seem to deny mere mundane stratification. Social boundaries are maintained automatically because persons feel someone else would not be much fun to associate with, because they don't like the same kind of entertainment, and because conversation with them leads too easily to arguments over matters of taste. The same persons might be "liberal" or even radical in their avowed beliefs, and would never allow themselves to snub someone else on what they thought was a matter of social class. Aesthetics, and especially the aesthetics of everyday life and cultural consumption, are so powerful in reproducing the class structure precisely because they claim to stand outside it.

Bourdieu's system is completely closed. It is totally cynical, totally pessimistic. We are eternally doomed to stratification, and to misrecognition of our bonds. We cannot get outside our own skins; we can only change places inside an iron circle. In this respect, Bourdieu is probably too extreme. He places all his emphasis on the reproduction of the system of stratification, not enough on variations that have occurred between different times and places among human societies. A better-rounded picture would show more of the conflict which actually takes place in societies, and the organizational struggles by which groups do manage to reshape the stratification systems, at least to some degree.

The strength of Bourdieu's system is his effort to create a truly general economics. His analyses of cultural capitalism and symbolic violence might be called "a Marxism of the superstructure." More precisely, he claims that the distinction between the economic and noneconomic spheres must be abolished. Conventional economics is but "a particular case of a *general science of the economy of practices,* capable of treating all practices, including those purporting to be disinterested or gratuitous, and hence noneconomic, as economic practices directed towards the maximizing of material or symbolic profit."[6] So far, Bourdieu has provided us only with a sketch of this system. For Bourdieu's economics still lacks precisely what Marx attempted to provide, a dynamism for historical change, and a mechanism for internal struggle and revolution.

JURGEN HABERMAS AND THE SEARCH FOR REASON

It is the concern for transformation and revolution that strikes us most when we cross the Rhine into another intellectual scene. The most influential sociologist in Germany in recent years is Jurgen Habermas. Habermas is actually a philosopher by training, but he has argued that pure ideas themselves are empty without *praxis,* application to ameliorating our real social circumstances. As a result, he has pushed further than anyone else in turning all philosophical issues into questions for sociology, and in constructing a comprehensive theory about society and its direction of change. In all these respects, Habermas is the inheritor of the Frankfurt school, the group of neo-Marxists whom we have already mentioned in Chapter 2 (including Max Horkheimer, Theodor Adorno, and Herbert Marcuse). Habermas himself was trained by the Frankfurt school after World War II, and in the 1960s he was regarded as its leader in the younger generation. During the radical student movement of the late 1960s and early 1970s, Habermas called for a "critical sociology" which would examine the sources of alienation in the modern world, not only within the capitalist economy, but within every institution, including governments, bureaucratic agencies, and science itself. He advocated a "long march through institutions" to emancipate human capacities. But Habermas also criticized German student radicals over the issue of using violence to resist and change capitalist society, and eventually broke with the radical movement.

[6]Ibid., p. 183.

In the 1970s and 1980s, Habermas gradually moved away from Marxism, to build up his own general theory of society. This is expressed most comprehensively in his *Theory of Communicative Action*. Habermas takes on the heroic task of restoring the ideal of reason as the standard and goal by which every form of thought and action is to be guided. Although the entire twentieth century has been eroding such claims from the point of view of relativism, naturalism, subjectivism, or the fragmenting process of analytical sophistication, Habermas steps in to restore the Enlightenment ideal of all-penetrating reason. More than that: Habermas wants to defend the belief in progress, in a world-historical evolution toward the realization of reason in the world. It is not only the Enlightenment that Habermas wishes to revive, but a secularized version of Hegel.

As a sociological basis for this program, Habermas draws upon a particular version of Max Weber. Habermas interprets Weber as a cultural determinist. According to this view, Weber saw the driving force of world history as a long-term rationalization of worldviews in the West. From this flowed the type of personality dominated by the Protestant ethic, and the social institutions of modern capitalism, along with the rationalization of every other sphere of social life. Habermas claims he is following Weber, except to the extent that Weber was pessimistic about the rationalized society which had emerged in the twentieth century, the "iron cage" of bureaucratization and the heartless capitalist economy. Habermas intends to rescue the progress of reason, by claiming that it is the specifically capitalist version of rationalization that is to blame for differentiating the system's requisites from the lifeworld. In effect, capitalism has captured rationalization in a purposive-instrumental form; hence the task of social reconstruction is to free reason in all its dimensions from this narrower application. Habermas attempts to eliminate Weber's pessimism about the modern outcomes of this process, by reformulating his scheme in the context of twentieth-century philosophical Marxism. Habermas' end product is what he calls the critical theory of society.

Before describing Habermas' system, it is worth commenting on the way in which he claims to draw upon Weber. Weber is an extremely complex theorist; in one side of his argument he emphasized idealistic factors, while in other areas he stressed material conditions and conflict. Habermas places all the emphasis on the idealist side; and he makes Weber into much more of a linear evolutionist than he actually was. Although Weber often analyzed the effects of ideas on social action, he just as often revealed the social conditions under which particular kinds of ideas arose. Without an autonomous unfolding of culture, Habermas has much less grounds for his own theme of an immanent teleology toward reason in world history. Habermas shows very little interest in Weber's writings on material organization and interest groups. For Habermas, these provide only the "external factors" for the unfolding of the immanent logic of the rationalization of worldviews. But a different interpretation of Weber could say that these "external factors" are the driving mechanism in the whole development, and that the ideological sphere is derivative of them. In short, Habermas' view of world history is a good deal more like that of Talcott Parsons than what Weber actually said in many of his works. But let us now leave this point aside, and examine the system as Habermas constructs it.

The Theory of Communicative Competence

Habermas' basic strategy is to broaden the old conception of truth as objective knowledge, by placing it on a social foundation. In his earlier writings, Habermas discovered and discussed the work of George Herbert Mead (hitherto virtually unknown on the Continent) and his conception of thought as internalization of conversation. This places old epistemological problems in a new light. The problem of the isolated Cartesian ego attempting to deduce the existence of the external world dissolves once one realizes that thinking itself already implies the existence of other people, of an outside world from which thought is internalized. Cognition is social cognition. Habermas has never pressed the formal epistemological issue very hard, since he has always been more concerned with knowledge relevant to issues of social reform than with the precise extent to which one can establish the truth claims of any particular statement. It has been enough for him to guarantee *some* degree of objectivity in any statement, provided it is based on genuine social discourse. And since the social world has to a considerable degree a self-defining quality to it, Habermas can be content with the criterion of social agreement as sufficient grounds of objective truth. If a social movement can come to agreement, through open discussion, on its aims for reconstructing society "in the common public interest," then what further degree of objectivity might one want? At least so seems to run Habermas' line of reasoning.

Habermas embodies a vestige of the 1960s New Left, with its participatory democracy and its utopian ideals for social reconstruction. Add to this another popular movement, psychoanalysis, and particularly its most social form, the "encounter group," with its method of relentless honesty and self-revelation—and one has the background ingredients of Habermas' intellectual project. (The vogue of psychoanalysis in America, though, was in the 1930s and 1940s, while encounter groups have faded since the early 1970s. But in Europe of the 1980s, these remained relatively new movements of public interest, and they have inherited especially large hopes with the general decline in the popularity of Marxism.) Habermas, in other words, is something of a carryover from the activism of the 1960s. In many respects, this is probably a good thing, especially in our present era lacking in idealism and commitment. But it also gives Habermas certain liabilities from an intellectual point of view.

Habermas' main achievement is to broaden the concept of rationality. Traditional philosophy had confined this to propositional statements about the objective world or the logical connections of concepts. Habermas argues that ascertaining objective truths of this sort is only one kind of rationality.

Habermas believes there is a standard of rationality for other kinds of speech acts than constative assertions. Modern linguistic philosophers, following John Austin, have pointed out that many statements have "illocutionary" force: They do not merely *say* something (like "My house is gray."), but *do* something (like "I hereby declare you husband and wife."). According to Habermas, such "regulative" speech acts as excuses and apologies, and institutionally bound speech acts such as marrying and oath taking are interpreted as kinds of normatively regulated social action. They can be judged according to their degree of rightness in establishing interpersonal actions: That is, they are rational insofar as they conform to objectively recognized social norms. Hence such speech acts, too, are oriented toward reaching interpersonal understanding, and they can be criticized as to whether or not such understanding is reached, and whether the speech act was properly carried out according to accepted norms. Regulative speech acts thus have the same degree of objectivity as do constatives; the only difference is that in the latter case the referent is the natural world, in the former the social world.

A third type of speech acts—expressives—do not have this objective reference, since their function is to externalize an individual's subjective experience. As social actions, Habermas assimilates these to Erving Goffman's dramaturgical action, which he interprets as ways that one dramatizes to other persons the character of one's inner self. But even this subjectivity, and its aesthetic qualities in expression, are not exempt from the critical standards of rationality. For one's subjective world can be truthfully or falsely represented; hence there is a possibility of reaching complete social understanding, provided that the individual expresses him/herself honestly and effectively. To the extent that this does not happen, the procedure of open questioning—Do you really mean that? Was that what you meant to convey?—can ultimately bring the truth into the open. In this way, the whole world might be made transparent to social understanding, and rationally objective agreement established everywhere.

Of course Habermas is not so naïve as to provide nothing but an idealized picture of communication. Often, perhaps most of the time, communication falls short of these high standards. One way in which this happens is via a fourth category of social action, which Habermas labels "strategic action." This is self-interested action, oriented toward controlling or influencing others rather than coming to an understanding with them. Habermas includes Austin's category of "perlocutions" in this rubric, as speech acts oriented toward having a certain effect on the listener (confusing, embarrassing, flattering, and so forth). He also includes imperatives, as efforts to carry out one's own will rather than to arrive at a mutual agreement. Strategic action, of course, has a certain rationality, insofar as it can be judged according to standards of effectiveness in achieving its aims. But it is a rationality that Habermas does not approve of, since (1) it is carried out by selfish means, and hence does not have the mark of social agreement which is central in Habermas' conception; and (2) strategic speech action undermines the "rationality" of constative, regulative, and expressive speech actions, since its success depends precisely on deception rather than openness as to aims and means. Habermas admits that most everyday speech acts may contain an element of strategic action. But he believes that this is analytically secondary, and that such strategic elements can be removed.

How is this to be done? In the same way as any other imperfections in communicative action can be remedied: that is, by open, unimpeded discourse. The method is simply that questions can be asked until satisfaction is attained. For constatives, one questions whether the objective and logical conditions really hold; for regulatives, whether the norm is properly applied (and on a deeper level, whether the norm itself is to be accepted by the group); for expressives, whether there is sincerity and also aesthetic effectiveness. Openness to free speech is the key, an openness which must continue unimpeded until uncoerced agreement is reached.

Habermas thus provides an inspiring extension of the liberal tradition. Nevertheless, regrettably, one may question whether it is adequate either as social science, or as a realizable, or even a completely desirable, ideal in the world.

As Social Science. Habermas' effort to assimilate speech-act theory to categories of social action is laudable. But the version of social science that he uses is not a particularly sophisticated one. His scheme is rather like that of the structural-functional categories of Talcott Parsons. In particular, Habermas takes the very important type of speech acts—regulatives—and interprets them simply as normatively regulated action. To rest explanation upon "norms," as in the manner of the sociology of the 1950s, is superficial, since this practice typically confuses (a) the sociological observer's description of a pattern of behavior; (b) an imputation that the actor has an internalized standard of the rightness of that pattern; and (c) the theory that (b) explains or is the cause of (a). Normative theory in sociology, in other words, glibly jumped from description to explanation, without any empirical comparison of the conditions under which various patterns of action occur. It is largely for this reason that normative theorizing has faded away, and theories with more empirically explanatory leverage have taken its place.

On the level of social action, Habermas uses the work of Erving Goffman, from whom he derives the category of dramaturgical action. He draws heavily on Goffman's early book *The Presentation of Self in Everyday Life*, which Habermas interprets as being about how individuals express, or conceal, their subjective attitudes. In other words, Habermas picks up the popular, superficial impression of Goffman as how to be a con man in everyday life. Habermas then modifies this with his "rationality" theme, since if one can conceal something, nevertheless that implies a standard by which truthfulness can be established by *unconcealing* it. But this misses an important element in Goffman's analytical stance. First of all, Goffman is basically a Durkheimian, for whom the world is a moral order which happens to be constituted by rituals. Goffman's innovation is to show that such rituals take place throughout everyday life. So Goffman (and Durkheim) is giving us a theory of the causal conditions under which normative ideals are created socially. Ideals, including moral ones, are not a *deus ex machina* with which to explain social structure; they are, rather, products of social interaction. And they are variable products: Different kinds of ritual interactions, based on different situations of social class and power, produce different cultures, which establish the boundaries of particular (and often antagonistic) social groups. Goffmanian sociology is not just another subtype of speech act, with an aesthetic and subjectivistic core, but is a major tool for establishing the priority of sociological explanations over disembodied normative ones.

There is another respect in which Habermas misunderstands Goffman. Habermas thinks that Goffman is dealing with the expression or concealment of subjective states. But this is what Goffman explicitly denies. Much of Goffman's work is a crusade against the idea that there is a primordial subjectivity, which is then externalized by communication. As befits a Durkheimian viewpoint, Goffman argues that the self is actually a bundle of different things, really stances taken in various kinds of interactions. The self may be a "sacred object" to which we give ritual respect, but by the same token it is also a modern myth which actually fluctuates with the footings one takes in different levels of social interaction.

As Realizable Ideal.   Habermas' main concern, though, is not explanatory social theory but a practical guide to rational social reconstruction. This is a noble aim, and Habermas deserves to be honored for attempting it with such thoroughness against almost the entire weight of twentieth-century thought. But does his program promise success? Unfortunately, one might fear that it does not. His advice is that a situation of open discussion should be instituted, to go on until freely arrived at agreement is reached. The criterion of rationality is the existence of this discourse, the ability to put every speech action into debate, as a subject for questioning, against the standards of validity which Habermas has outlined. But we can still ask: Why and under what conditions would people actually engage in discussion of this sort? And if they did, would they arrive at the agreements he projects?

Habermas proposes that people *should* give up the use of imperatives, the engaging in strategic action, the pursuit of individual self-interest. Instead they should pursue the "common interest of all." But this seems to be a statement of exhortation and faith. There is nothing in sociological theory that suggests that people will generally, everywhere, and as a rule, give up on strategic action, or that they would be able to construe "the common interest" in a fashion which would be satisfactory to literally everyone in the world. Habermas does not even explore the social conditions under which some people will be moved, some of the time, to act toward such ideals.

The ideal of a lengthy, or even endless, discussion on all questions is not as practical as Habermas thinks. Robert Michels' Iron Law of Oligarchy, by which democratic-participatory organizations are taken over by a self-perpetuating elite, is partly due to the fact that discussions are tedious. The more people who try to speak, the longer it takes to get agreement on anything. Hence the sheer structural difficulty of arguing through to a general social consensus is implicitly a program for turning society over to a few specialized intellectuals, those who are most committed to lasting out these lengthy debates. Habermas actually may be formulating an ideology for such intellectuals, aggrandizing their own interests in taking the forefront by claiming that they are acting out an ethical imperative. Habermas' ideal is naïve from the point of view of contemporary sociology of science, concerned with exposing the social interests of intellectuals behind the objectified reality-constructing they perform.

One can ask, too, whether most questions are actually likely to lead to agreement. Habermas thinks this is unimportant, that it is enough to show the criterion under which agreement might be framed. But this is a hollow achievement, if particular issues cannot actually be resolved. Is it realistic to assume that any amount of argument between, say, proponents and opponents of abortion could finally change their minds? And this is aside from the problem of the sheer limitations of cognitive capabilities. Discussion, no matter how extensive, will not solve problems of social planning if there are complex contingencies on the macro level which lead to unpredictable outcomes. Here, even if agreement were reached, it does not follow that rationally effective action would follow from it.

As Desirable End. Habermas seems to envision the ideal society as an omnipresent encounter group, in which people everywhere will be questioning each other's every statement, and on every level. Constative, regulative, and expressive speech acts alike will be brought before the forum of group attention, and scrutinized until absolute truth, rectitude, and sincerity prevail. Perhaps this would be liberating, from the point of view of a certain ideal. But how would it be in real life? Leaving aside the fact that the discussion would be literally endless, taking up all of everyone's time and preventing anything else from being done, would we finally feel realized and made whole by this condition? I think, instead, that most people would revolt against this endless probing, this endless exposure. Although talk would ostensibly be going backward, digging toward its foundations, it would actually progress outward in time, building commentaries upon commentaries. It would produce a society of endless reflexivity. It would attempt to do what, in fact, Harold Garfinkel claims people in everyday life seek to avoid doing: falling into the pit of infinite regress of justifications and thereby making a cognitive chaos out of the taken-for-granted order of their lives.

On the whole, then, Habermas' effort to reconstruct society as a utopia of free and unconstrained communication appears to be a failure. But it is a heroic effort, and German sociology has again acquired world attention because such themes have even been raised. To be sure, other leading German sociologists, such as Niklas Luhman, have given a much more pessimistic vision of social constraints; and there are still other theoretical positions to be found. But the combination of philosophical depth and broad sociological concerns continues to be one of German sociology's most distinctive contributions. It is in German sociology that the utopian and emancipatory tradition is most likely to be found in the world today.

RANDALL COLLINS: CONFLICT THEORY AND INTERACTION RITUAL CHAINS

We come, finally, to North America. Here sociology operates in a specialized mode. There is less crossing over disciplinary boundaries, less political addresses to the public. American sociologists would no doubt like to have this wider impact, but intellectuals here simply do not play such a role as public figures as intellectuals do in Europe. But it is a mistake to believe that American sociology is merely an empirical enterprise, and that we import all our theoretical ideas from abroad. In previous chapters, we have already seen that the United States has its own tradition of constructing theories: for instance, Cooley, Mead, and the symbolic interactionists, and more recently Goffman and Garfinkel. America's most notable strength has been in microsociology, but it also has a tradition of building comprehensive theoretical syntheses, such as that of Talcott Parsons. As a contemporary sample, we include a section on one of the present authors' efforts at constructing a comprehensive sociological theory.

Randall Collins developed his theory during the 1970s and 1980s as a deliberate effort to cumulatively synthesize the sociological knowledge of the past century. His belief is that sociology has been gradually moving ahead, and can make still greater gains in the future. To be sure, sociology has always consisted of warring schools of thought, which prefer to emphasize their differences rather than their agreements, and tend to deny that anyone else has made much progress. But if we step back from the intellectual polemics, Collins believes, we can see a thread of developing knowledge from both theories and research. In its own way, sociology has been acquiring a core set of principles which make it into an explanatory science. The most important aspect of such a science, Collins holds, is not whether it states laws in mathematical form, backed up by statistical evidence. Often the nature of our laws is too complex to be stated in this way without losing their most important insights; and often the qualitative evidence—from historical comparisons, observational studies of organizations, participant observation, and interpretation of face-to-face interaction—has provided us with our most basic understanding of the way social processes work. This is not to rule out mathematical formulations and statistical research, but only to put them in proper focus, as contributors to a larger enterprise, rather than its central core.

In Collins' view, sociology can be a science in the sense that it produces explanations of why things happen in a particular way at a particular time. That is, we look for the conditions under which something happens, and the conditions under which it does not happen; and we pay attention to the conditions which produce variations all across the board. We look for the fundamental generative mechanisms in human interaction, from which all the features of different societies are derived. But societies are complex and historically changing; and within any one society, there are usually many different social groups. The generative principles we are looking for must be capable of producing a great deal of complexity, and many individual differences. The key is that there are multiple generative mechanisms—not a huge number, but at least a few. For instance, as we will shortly see, Collins believes that power processes and status processes are fundamental building blocks of stratification and organization. It is by combining and re-combining these elements in many crosscutting combinations that sociology is capable of explaining the diverse behavior of individuals and their relationships, which make up the social structure.

Collins takes his inspiration from theoretical principles of Weber and Durkheim, as they are backed up by more recent empirical research. From Weber, he takes the viewpoint that stratification and formal organizations are the two keys to all other areas of sociology. That is, virtually all groups can be seen as some aspect of stratification; and the institutions of human societies—political, economic, religious, educational, and so forth—are best analyzed according to the principles of organizational theory. If we can explain these two areas, we can derive most of the rest.

Stratification of Order-Givers and Order-Takers

Weber's theory of stratification is multidimensional, focusing on class, status, and power. *Class* refers to social divisions within the economic realm: the market relations of property and work. In Collins' view, this economic realm is not itself intrinsically organized; the very existence of classes depends upon the other two dimensions, status groups and power structures. *Status* always refers to groups, people who tend to associate together and to exclude outsiders. Status groups are one fundamental type of social network. These groups are a major influence of life styles and beliefs. As we shall see in Collins' micro theory, explaining status groups links Weber's theory with Durkheim's.

Power, for Weber, is a crucial category because it refers to the state and its politics. In Weber's macro theory, the state is a crucial organization because it is the ultimate location of coercive force as well as of legitimacy. The state undergirds the economic system; capitalism would not be possible without the legal system which upholds property and regulates financial transactions. Weber's theory of the state, moreover, is his theory of bureaucracy, and of related kinds of formal organization. In this way, the three-dimensional theory of stratification (class, status, power) links to organization theory, since power refers to positions within formal organizations. Weber himself was mainly concerned, in his macro theories, with the organizational structure of the military and the government. Collins broadens this theoretical emphasis. He treats power analytically. That is, power does not exist only in the realm of the state. There is a political aspect to every organization, including businesses, churches, schools, clubs—wherever there are formal structures divided into positions. In this sense, then, Collins proposes that the fundamental generative structure of economic class is really power. The way individuals make a living, their access to the material means of production, is most immediately structured by their power positions in organizations.

On the micro level, then, power and class collapse into a single dimension. Collins then proceeds to build a theory about this dimension of power-classes. People who are in positions of power are order-givers in everyday life. The process of giving orders, and of being responsible for their organizations, creates a particular worldview and set of motivations. Order-givers tend to be proud, self-assured, energetic, and formal; they identify themselves with their organization and its ideals. In effect, order-givers indoctrinate themselves with their own ideologies, becoming true believers in the ideas by which they justify giving orders. Collins uses Goffman's model of interaction rituals in everyday life to explain this pattern. Order-givers are "frontstage" personalities; they are constantly putting on performances, acting out the official side of their organization. This is intrinsic in the nature of power. For power has to be enacted, over and over again in face-to-face situations; the order-giver must convince others that he or she represents the organization, which will back up whatever he or she demands. But an organization is nothing more than a coalition of persons, and the order-giver is putting on a performance to convey the belief that his or her power coalition exists. The order-giver, then, must be always thinking of the organization, acting out its reality. The order-giver has an "official" outlook on the world, because he or she is always performing power rituals.

People who take orders have a different class culture. They are passive audiences of the power rituals carried out by their superiors. Consciously or unconsciously, they feel that these rituals are being used to push them around. Accordingly, order-takers tend to withdraw from official ideals. How much they withdraw depends on how coercively power is applied. In extreme power situations, order-takers become subservient, passive, and fatalistic, giving the dull compliance that was characteristic of slaves, serfs, and prisoners. Most of the working class today is not in such an extreme condition of powerlessness; accordingly, their class culture has shifted toward milder forms of alienation. Typically, there is cynicism about work and about bosses in general, and a tendency to identify with one's local group rather than with the organization and its official ideals. In our affluent modern societies, working-class culture consists in identifying *away from* formal organizations, placing most of one's emphasis upon one's leisure life.

In Goffmanian terms, the working-class culture of order-takers is a "backstage" culture, emphasizing one's private life and displaying cynicism about what goes on on the frontstage. The dominant class of order-givers, on the other hand, consists of "workaholics," people who identify strongly with their careers, and who let these structure most aspects of their lives. The foregoing description, of course, picks out only two abstract points of the continuum of class situations. Some persons are very high-ranking order-givers, in whom the most extreme versions of frontstage, official worldviews are dominant; others are middle-level order-givers, those who have power in some relationships, but have to take orders from others, while still other face-to-face relationships take place between equals. Collins uses the order-giver/order-taker model as a set of generative principles, from which the various intermediate positions can be derived as well as the extreme positions.

Collins' view of class conflict, then, is rather different from that of the orthodox Marxists. Power-classes exist wherever there are hierarchic formal organizations; they exist in Socialist societies as well as in capitalist ones, and in churches, schools, and many other realms as much as in businesses. Order-givers versus order-takers is a fundamental split, but one in which the two parties are usually quite unequal. For the order-givers are highly mobilized; they are already linked together in a network, and they are energized by their everyday interactions, while the order-takers tend to be localized, passive, and withdrawn. There is plenty of underlying strain between top and bottom in any organization, but this rarely comes out into overt conflict. Typically the order-taking class is fragmented, and its members withdraw psychologically from their formal organizations into their private lives.

Most conflict, Collins proposes, takes place at a different level: between different factions of order-givers themselves. It is mainly the higher classes who are engaged in conflict with each other. Conservatives and liberals are both led by members of the order-giving class; the main difference between them is in the kinds of organizations in which they work, and with which they identify. If holding power, after all, is the mechanism which makes persons identify with ideals, it is not surprising that the people who are most committed to fighting for their ideals are order-givers. The underlying splits are usually between organizations rather than between power-classes. Conservatives tend to come from the business world, whereas liberals are more likely to be employed in the nonprofit sector such as government agencies, education, and the media. Even radicals like the Marxists themselves can be best explained by the organizational positions held by certain types of intellectuals: typically in elite universities well insulated from outside pressures, or sometimes (as has been more common in Europe) as full-time officials of labor unions or journalists in the left-wing press. Left- and right-wing political activists try to mobilize the masses beneath them, to awaken the slumbering antagonism between order-giving and order-taking classes. But this happens only seldom, usually depending on an organizational crisis which shakes up the whole structure. Most of the time, politics is a maneuvering between rival groups of order-givers, who mask their own positions in their general statements of ideals and their claims to be representing the interests of lower groups.

The Horizontal Dimension of Status Rituals

There is a second dimension of social interaction which can crosscut the hierarchy of order-giving and order-taking. We can also ask: How tightly organized is the network of people who associate together? Here Collins draws on Durkheimian theory of social solidarity. Durkheim spoke of the "moral density" of interaction, which Collins prefers to call the "ritual density." Once again there are variables. How much of the time is an individual in the presence of other people? And are these always the same people, or are they different ones coming and going? If someone is constantly surrounded by people, and these people are always the same, the result is to subject the individual to very strong pressures for conformity. This group has a structure which Collins calls a "natural ritual." The process of interaction focuses people's attention on the same thing, and creates a strong sense of the boundary of the group. Symbols are generated which come to represent the group; and however arbitrary those symbols may be, the individual conforms strongly to them, and expects conformity from other people.

This is what Durkheim called "mechanical solidarity"; it is the situation of isolated small groups, of certain tribal societies, and of rural communities. But Collins uses this model analytically: That is, there is an aspect of this kind of structure within modern society as well. Some persons live in localized, relatively closed groups, little pockets of high social pressure on the individual, which are the main carriers of traditionalism and moralistic conformity. At the other end of the continuum, individuals may spend very little time with a group, and when they interact they do so with a great variety of different people. When individuals are in this situation—more time alone or in privacy, and interacting with cosmopolitan networks rather than an unchanging local group—they tend to think relativistically and abstractly.

This dimension, too, is an analytical one. Some persons are at the extremes of high or low ritual density, but there are also many gradations in between. And within the course of one's life, one may move in and out of different kinds of group situations. Small children, for example, are usually in a situation of high ritual density, always being in the presence of a small family group. Many of the characteristics of children's mentality and moral judgments follow from this structural situation, such as children's tendency to literal-mindedness and their expectations of complete conformity to the local customs with which they are familiar. Collins also proposes that adults can go through episodes of high ritual density; a couple in love, for instance, is creating a little private cult of extremely high ritual density, making each other into sacred objects.

We can see now how society can contain many different individuals, each one with a somewhat unique personality. There are only a few basic generative mechanisms, in Collins' view, but each person can have a slightly different combination of experiences on the dimensions of order-giving-and-taking and of ritual density. There are power experiences in different spheres of one's life: in all the different positions one has held at work, but also in the power structure of one's life at home, at school, and in other organizations. Not only do these experiences shape one's mentality as order-giver and order-taker, but these interactions will also have some degree of ritual density, which shapes one's tendency to identify with particular symbols and to expect conformity from other people. Every individual's "personality" is really the precipitate of all their social experiences as they have laid down their personal track through social networks.

Interaction Ritual Chains

Collins' later theory focuses on the dynamics by which individuals move through these dimensions of social experience. Collins proposes that each interaction is a kind of ritual, which can be analyzed as somewhere on a continuum of ritual intensity. Highly successful interaction rituals (IRs) are conversations in which the participants attain a strong focus of attention, create a common symbolic reality they believe in together for the moment. As the result of this, they come away with a recharged feeling of social solidarity. Collins calls this "emotional energy"; it is a generalized emotion of confidence and good feelings, a propensity to take the initiative, to act spontaneously in a certain direction. In what direction? Toward the persons and symbols which, in one's last set of encounters, have produced the most successful interaction rituals. For interactions also generate symbols: The things that one has talked about in a successful interaction become "sacred objects" in the Durkheimian sense, which symbolize membership in that little group. Each conversation in everyday life, banal as it may seem, nevertheless carries an unconscious freight of social meanings; gossip about friends can carry the significance of successful membership in some localized group of the recent past, just as certain buzzwords about politics, or technical terms used by a professional group, quickly signal who is a member of what larger network. Everyday interaction thus energizes certain symbols, by loading them with ritual significance as emblems of membership. Collins refers to this as "cultural capital" (a somewhat expanded version of what Bourdieu means by the same term).

In Collins' model, interaction proceeds according to a kind of social marketplace. Individuals gravitate toward those interactions in which they have received the most favorable amounts of emotional energy. But interactions are not always successful. Individuals who have better "market position" may not be very interested in spending much time, or much intimacy, in exchanging symbols with some other individual; those who are "rich" in cultural capital and network connections will tend to seek out their best deal, and that will be with persons who can provide a similar exchange of cultural capital, not with someone who is "poor" in cultural capital and net-

work connections. Furthermore, some interactions take place in formal organizations, in which one side is an order-giver, the other an order-taker.
These various interactions can either raise or lower one's emotional energy.
Collins hypothesizes that successfully giving orders raises one's emotional
energy, whereas taking orders reduces it. The result is that the order-giving
class also comprises the more dynamic individuals, who take initiative in
favor of their ideas (and thereby further their power); the order-taking class
tends to be more apathetic. This is one of the hidden dynamics of stratification: It is a stratification of emotional energy, as well as of more obvious
material goods.

Emotional energy can also be won or lost on the horizontal dimension of
status rituals. Being accepted into a group raises one's emotional energy, especially when the group is successful at generating a high level of emotional solidarity (which may be something as simple as laughing together at a
party). But being rejected by the group lowers one's emotional energy and
makes one depressed.

Collins thus visualizes society as made up of long intersecting chains of
interaction rituals. Each person comes into his or her next interaction with a
past history, coded in the form of certain symbolically charged ideas, and a
certain level of emotional energy. What will happen in the next interaction,
though, has to be negotiated; it cannot be predicted in advance even if we
knew all about the individual's cultural capital and emotional energy, because the interaction ritual is constructed by all its participants together.
How the cultural capitals and emotional energies match up in that situation
will determine how successfully the ritual goes, and who will be dominant
or subordinate, accepted or rejected, superficial or intimate. At the end of
the interaction ritual, each individual will come out of the situation with a
renewed level of his or her emotional energy, whether up or down or constant, and with a set of cultural symbols which have been charged with the
additional significance of group membership. Whether or not those particular individuals ever meet again, they have primed each other with the ingredients that will make up the next interaction.

The Micro–Macro Connection

Collins attempts to build up a systematic theory of the larger structures of
society, starting from these micro chains. His argument does not reduce society to the individual. As we have just seen, it is the interaction that loads
up the individual with motivations and ideas; personalities are precipitates
of the experience individuals have as they move through chains of interaction. The basic unit is not the person but the chain of situations. The macro
world consists of nothing but situational chains; "organizations," "states,"
"societies" are only words that people use, except insofar as there are real
chains of individuals acting them out. Collins thus attempts to derive the
principles of macro organizations as much as possible from the generative
mechanisms operating in situations. For example, his organizational theory

uses the principles of conflict and control deriving from the mechanism of order-giving-and-taking, together with the mechanism of solidarity through ritual group density.

But in doing so, Collins discovers the way in which the macro structure also exists in its own right. Organizations are nothing more than chains of social interactions, but the shape of these chains is itself a macro variable. The sheer number of persons and of interaction ritual chains, the way in which these chains are concentrated or spread out in space, and the amount of time over which chains form are macro variables. It is these that make up the macro structure, and they have a strong determining effect on what kinds of interaction rituals can take place within those chains. The individual personality is shaped by the local parts of the networks of interaction which make up the larger society. The upper power-classes, for instance, have their kinds of micro experience of giving orders because of the way they are located in the large-scale coalitions which link together organizational chains; the lower power-classes are equally fated by their peripheral locations, so to speak, at the loose ends of these chains. And other persons live in the middle realms of these networks, between the extremes. Ultimately, Collins proposes, sociology could provide a precise description of the factors operating on any given individual, setting their life chances as they construct their future ritual encounters. And on the macro level, we could translate the variables of political, organizational, and other ideological constructs into the real effects of micro generative mechanisms strung together in numerical patterns across time and space.

IMMANUEL WALLERSTEIN'S WORLD SYSTEM

Immanuel Wallerstein illustrates yet another side of current American sociology. In recent decades, there has been an upsurge of interest in historical sociology: that is, history as treated by sociologists themselves. Where most historians are specialized and avoid the theoretical implications of their own work, some sociologists have taken historical materials in order to make comparisons and construct explanatory models of the major features of society. Some notable works have been published in this vein, including Charles Tilly's resource mobilization theory of protest movements, based on his historical studies of revolutionary and nonrevolutionary movements in the history of France; Barrington Moore's analysis of the three routes to modernity—capitalist democracy, socialism, and fascism; and Theda Skocpol's comparative theory based on the great revolutions in France, Russia, and China. Perhaps the most ambitious of the historical sociologists is Immanuel Wallerstein. Working with a dedicated group of collaborators, and making use of a terrific range of historical sources, Wallerstein has developed a model of the entire world as a unit of social transformation.

In Wallerstein's model, individual societies do not control their own fates. To understand the development of any particular society, we must place it in the context of the world system. The capitalist world system which has come into being since the sixteenth century has relegated particular societies to positions of nondevelopment. To be more precise, the world is divided into a network between areas which are *core* and those which are *periphery*, together with those in the *semiperiphery* and in the *external area*.

For Wallerstein, the term "world" is not to be taken strictly literally. A *world system* does not mean the whole globe, but a world-in-itself, a set of societies that are linked together but are relatively autonomous from what lies outside the set. There are two main types of world systems: *world empires*, which are tied together by a dominating state which extracts economic tribute from the others; and *world economies*, which have a multiplicity of political units tied together by warfare and by economic exchange. There is also a third possible type, a socialist world government, which does not exist, although Wallerstein believes it may in the future. Wallerstein doubts there truly are Socialist economies in the twentieth century, but only Socialist-controlled states within the capitalist world economy.

The crucial distinction is between situations in which a conquest state dominates the economy by taking tribute (that is, a world empire), and those in which no state is strong enough to do so (a world economy). An imperial state, like ancient Rome or medieval China, limits the autonomous development of the economy. State officials are supreme and need make no concessions to low-status merchants; nor, in the absence of military competition among states, is there an incentive to rationalize the state apparatus and its economic policy. On this point Wallerstein follows Max Weber's ideas about the obstacles to early capitalist development. On the other hand, competition among states means that rulers must make concessions to mercantile and financial interests. The sheer pluralism of political power in the world system, then, is a crucial element in economic growth.

Within a world economy, some states are stronger than others, politically and economically. These are the core states. They are able militarily and economically to dominate the periphery, thus creating an international division of labor among different types of labor systems. Cheap labor on the periphery (in the form of plantations, slavery, or other cheap-labor systems) builds up wealth for the core. This structure is crucial for several reasons. It enables the core states to have a free and relatively well paid labor force, thus reducing the amount of costly class warfare internally, and provides a mass consumer market for economic products. Core states tend to become cumulatively richer: Their wealth enhances their military power, which in turn increases their wealth.

A core position also enables the state to escape the vicious cycle that tends to undermine state finances. States attempting to build up their military strength need officials to collect taxes, and money to pay their armies. But the state officials tend to eat up much of the wealth themselves. This was particularly so in medieval states, in which the nobility kept much of the revenue, and passed along the burden of taxes to the peasants below. If the peasants were squeezed too hard, though, they were likely to revolt, which in turn raised still further the cost of controlling them militarily. There is a vicious circle of expanding power and the economic costs of supporting that power. This is a reason states tend to rise and fall, sometimes getting ahead of others in power, and then losing out as the costs of their wars and their domestic struggles for control mount up.

Some powerful states, like Spain and France in the sixteenth century, got caught in ruinous wars against each other, and suffered internal economic crisis and social upheaval as a result. Hence they fell out of their core positions, and in the case of Spain, became part of the semiperiphery. The way out of this vicious circle, Wallerstein points out, was successful expansion into the periphery. Thus England, with lower military expenses and fewer foreign entanglements, emerged from the sixteenth century economically and politically stronger than its rivals, Spain and France. England went on to dominate the next phase of colonial expansion, into the Americas and Asia, reaping economic benefits from her colonies that enabled her to become dominant in Europe.

But just as Spain and France had their rise and fall, so eventually did England; and the United States, which rose to become the most powerful core state of the mid-twentieth century, also seems destined to lose world hegemony. There is a mechanism behind this which Wallerstein attempts to isolate. The capitalist world-system process is inherently cyclical. The cycles are analogous to the periodic crises of Marxian economics (described in Chapter 2), except that in Marx's theory their periodicity is about ten years; in Wallerstein, about one hundred to one hundred twenty-five years. In effect, Wallerstein has enlarged the Marxian model from the internal dynamic of particular societies to the entire world system. Like Marx, Wallerstein too expects the cycles to end with a Socialist revolution; but for Wallerstein, the only kind of revolution that can truly transform the capitalist system must be a world revolution.

Wallerstein's cyclical dynamics go as follows. Core societies have high-skill, high-wage economies of production; peripheral societies have low-skill, low-wage economies. Prosperity in the core societies depends upon their ability to exploit the low-wage periphery, and also upon the effective demand for the high-priced goods which their own labor force provides. An expansionary cycle (A phase) begins when the demand for high-wage goods (for example, manufactured products) is greater than the supply, and the demand for low-wage goods (for example, raw materials) is also greater than the supply. Hence the core societies expand their economic tentacles into new regions of the globe. This results in an increased flow of goods from the periphery, which in turn expands production of high-priced goods in the core. The whole world economy is in a boom phase.

The turning point comes when the supply of goods from the periphery exceeds demand (B phase). Foreign expansion slows down, because it is no longer profitable. This causes core production to stagnate. There is a downturn in the growth of the world economy. Eventually the cycle bottoms out.

During this time, capital becomes more centralized, preparing the way for a new expansion. The accumulation of capital is a recurrent process through each trough of the cycle. Also during the time of stagnation, unemployment and other economic miseries for the working class cause an upsurge of class struggle. The result is to force some redistribution of income. This increases demand for goods, setting the expansion cycle in motion once again.

Wallerstein and his colleagues propose that there is a double cycle (A1–B1–A2–B2). The first cycle of the pair has a milder downturn than the second; at the end of the pair of cycles, there is an especially great crash, in which low-wage production not only stagnates but also contracts, and high-wage production (which is always more elastic) takes a very sharp drop.

The political side of this cycle is not only that class conflict increases during the downturn phases, but also that rivalry between core states erupts into especially severe warfare at those times. It takes the entire double cycle, making up one hundred years or more, for political hegemony in the world system to shift, when the older hegemonic core state drops down and its place is taken by another. A new world power emerges during the A1 phase, comes to predominance through B1, reaches its height in A2, and declines in B2. The shift of hegemony from one core state to another is not accidental, but is tied to economic advantages. A state becomes hegemonic when its production, commerce, and finance exceed those of other states; hence, it can invest in the military force that enables it to dominate the international arena. But such hegemony always slips away. Ultimately hegemony depends upon a technological edge and upon relatively low internal costs of maintaining order. In order to keep class conflict within bounds, increasing concessions must be made to the workers. These concessions raise the costs of production. Since technology always diffuses away from its home country through imitation elsewhere in the world, another state with lower initial labor costs can seize the edge. Thus there is a continuous movement in and out of the core, and also in and out of the semiperiphery. As one can see, although Wallerstein is writing about the past, many elements in his model look like they are applicable to the current situation in which world economic domination by the United States is being challenged by Japan.

Wallerstein sets forth his theory in a massive four-volume work, *The Modern World-System*. To date, three of the volumes have appeared. Each volume comprises one major cycle of the world system. Volume I describes the initial takeoff of the capitalist world economy in Western Europe from 1450 to its final crash around 1640; politically, this was the period of the rise and fall of the Spanish empire. Volume II goes from the crisis of the 1600s to another turning point around 1750; during this time the Netherlands rose to become a hegemonic empire, challenged by the absolutist regime in France and by the rise of English power. Wallerstein's Volume III deals with the period from 1750 to 1917; this is the period of what we conventionally call the industrial revolution, but in world-system terms it is the period of the

British Empire and its rise to overwhelming economic and political power. That period comes to its crisis in the world wars of the early twentieth century. In Wallerstein's long-term perspective, World Wars I and II (1914–1918 and 1939–1945) are really the same world military crisis, punctuated by an uneasy truce. They mark the turning point which will take up Volume IV: the twentieth century, in which Britain declined and domination passed to the United States. This cycle, too, if Wallerstein's model is correct, will have its closing crisis, sometime in the twenty-first century.

Today's commentators are suggesting that the new successor to world hegemony is already on the horizon, in the shape of Japan. Wallerstein's fourth volume has not yet appeared, so we do not know the details of his prognosis. But Wallerstein does not expect that the cycles will go on forever. It is not necessarily the case that Japan will emerge as the core power of the capitalist world economy in the next century, because the theory also contemplates that the current cycle may be the last one.

For one thing, the evidence suggests that the cycles have been growing shorter, presumably because the mobility of capital around the world has accelerated. Even more important, there are trends that have inherent limits. These are the trends to include a greater percentage of the world area in the capitalist world economy, a greater percentage of personal incomes in the form of wages (rather than unpaid coerced or traditional labor), and a greater percentage of capital in the form of machinery and goods rather than land. Once the reserves of unexploited land, labor, and nonmechanized production have dried up, the core states will no longer be able to expand into the external area. No new colonies can be created, no new societies added onto the periphery for the core to exploit. The basic mechanism of capitalist growth in the world system will have disappeared. Class conflict at a high level of mobilization will become unavoidable throughout the world. The system will only be able to survive this final crisis by transforming itself into something entirely new. Wallerstein's bet is that this final resting place will be a socialist world government.

Wallerstein's projection of the future ending of capitalist cycles expresses the Marxian revolutionary theory in a new form. Marx's predictions of revolution within the leading capitalist societies failed because those societies drew their economic strength from their positions in the world system. The Communist states that existed during the twentieth century in Russia, China, and elsewhere came to power, not because of capitalist crisis in the economies of those countries, but because of the way former governments were destroyed in the wars engendered by the world system. It is for this reason that they are not truly socialist societies, as envisioned by Marx. Wallerstein thus reformulates the whole Marxian model, and proposes a logic by which Marx's predictions will come true in the end, but only on a much more massive scale.

A crucial question nevertheless arises. From the perspective of the 1990s, can we still say that a Marxian analysis has any relevance? Did not the anti-Communist revolutions of East Europe and Russia during

1989–1991 change the nature of the whole ball game? The answer, surprisingly, may still be no. Wallerstein has argued that the world system as a whole has been capitalist for a long time; the socialist states tried to opt out of the system, but they could not. Whenever they engaged in international trade they did it on capitalist terms. At best they could act as a kind of a business corporation organized along socialist lines internally; but externally they had to deal with world markets and finances the same as any other capitalist. Thus Wallerstein argues that one of the reasons the socialist states fell was because they became tied into the capitalist world system to such a degree that their own economies were squeezed by capitalist competition; and their heavy investment in military expenditures could only make the situation worse. To understand the downfall of the socialist bloc, one of the key theories that we need may be the dynamics of the capitalist world. And we will need it even more in order to understand the future of Russia and the other fragments of its former empire as they become increasingly capitalist.

The question remains whether this theory is true. Many elements of it are attractive, and may well be good approximations of how the world system affects the position of societies within it. In effect, Wallerstein tells us that the individual society is not a useful level of analysis, and that the causes of social change come from the outside in. This seems to be on the right track. But there are other aspects that are less convincing. How severe are the crises of the world economy? Are they severe enough to bring the whole system to an end? This is not to downplay the struggles and conflicts which take place within capitalism; but it is not yet theoretically convincing that these processes could not go on for centuries into the future, without coming to an end. Wallerstein projects that world socialism is the only transition point which can bring the cycles of world capitalism to an end. It is a good question, though, whether world socialism or any other stable resting point will ever exist, even hundreds of years from now.

To whatever degree we are convinced by Wallerstein's model, its intellectual ambitiousness and scope cannot be denied. It shows, once again, sociologists at their best, taking up the major challenges of explaining what goes on in our world. Whatever modifications eventually need to be made in Wallerstein's theory, it is a guidepost toward a wider understanding.

CHAPTER FIFTEEN

The Impact of Women in Sociology in the Late Twentieth Century

You may have noticed that most of the names dealt with in this book are men's. Some women have always been involved in the study of society, but until recently they have been submerged. Men have dominated the formative period of sociology, much as they have exercised domination elsewhere in society. This was also true in most other intellectual fields, including philosophy, history, and science; the main exception has been in literature, where women have had the most creative influence. It is with the women's revolution of the late twentieth century that male domination has been challenged and broken through; and it now appears that sociology at the turn of the twenty-first century is going to take a major part of its leadership from women.

As with everything else, we can use sociology to explain how this pattern has come about. We need to combine two lines of analysis: the sociology of gender stratification and the sociology of intellectual life. Gender stratification has varied in degree throughout different periods of world history and different types of societies. In tribal and kinship-based societies, before the rise of the state, the position of women was often fairly favorable. In some of these tribal structures the religious system and the symbols and myths centered on females. But the influence of women in the ideological sphere did not carry over into the intellectual specialties of philosophy and science, for the simple reason that these specialties did not exist, for either men or women. What knowledge existed was embedded in practical or religious activities; there were no separate communities of intellectuals to carry on specialized research and build up their own traditions of thought.

One of the ironies of history is that as the so-called civilizations arose, with their urban-based upper classes and their literate traditions, the intellectual traditions that emerged were largely monopolized by men. This male monopoly over the means of intellectual production was part of a larger pattern in which men controlled the structures of politics and economics as well. This is not to say there were no splits and conflicts among men; but the intellectual battles, as well as the political, religious, and economic ones, were largely carried out between one faction of men and another.

Women were not homogeneous either, but they were carried along in the class structure of male society. Thus upper-class women were largely confined to status-oriented activities around the household; women were sometimes idealized as members of the aristocracy, or prized as sexual objects and confined to harems; in either case their sphere was restricted and separated from men, who controlled the realm of production. Things were different with women of the working class; they did a great deal of work, but it was the dirty work relegated to servants, or the tasks of manual labor in such areas as textiles and farming. So neither the women of the upper nor of the lower classes had many opportunities to become intellectual leaders. Even the women who specialized in religion did not have the resources of men, who were priests and monks; women could become devotional mystics but not theologians.

The one intellectual arena in which women had advantages was literature. This was especially true in the times when literature was centered around upper-class courts and the salons of the aristocrats. Thus we find in ancient Greece the famous woman poet Sappho, prominent in the literary circle on the island of Lesbos. In medieval Japan, for a period the great writers were all women, including Lady Murasaki Shikibu, who wrote the epic Japanese novel *The Tale of Genji*. It is not surprising that the contents of the great novels centered on a combination of love affairs and the careers of upper-class families, because this arena of sexual intrigue and marriage politics dominated the lives of people in the upper-class households. This was a realm in which men and women both participated, and the early novelists tended to be women who specialized in their observations of what was going on around them.

One might even say that the earliest sociological research and analysis took form in these novels; where the men writers were busy idealizing the exploits of warriors and conquerors in their unrealistic epics, the women writers were taking a cool and realistic look at the backstage maneuverings that made up the real content of upper-class life. Thus in Europe some of the first sociologists appear in the guise of novelists; Jane Austen and Charlotte and Emily Brontë dissected the world of the marriage market and the status struggles of the middle and upper classes even before a more formal sociology emerged with Comte and Marx.

Let us consider now how ideas develop in intellectual disciplines. Creativity typically occurs in social networks. The individuals whose ideas become influential are usually connected to other thinkers who are already in the center of intellectual life. Using Bourdieu's term, one can say that cultural capital is passed along in these networks; in Collins' analysis, creativity is a kind of emotional energy that builds up in their interactions. We have seen many instances of this throughout *The Discovery of Society:* Comte comes from the main network of Paris intellectuals and he gets his start as secretary to Saint-Simon; Marx and Engels begin in the network of the revolutionary Young Hegelians in Germany who branch off from their master, Hegel. Durkheim was in a group which led the reform of the French universities around the beginning of the twentieth century; Weber grew up in the main German political and intellectual network at Berlin and later became the center of a network at Heidelberg.

If we apply this model of intellectual life to the position of women, we can see that one of the ways in which women got excluded from intellectual influence was that they usually were not allowed into these male networks. The most important intellectual capital was being passed along in places that typically were not open to women. Some women, however, were able to get into the networks; at first, this happened mainly through their family connections. For instance, the first woman to become truly famous in psychology was Anna Freud, Sigmund Freud's daughter.

This was true for the novelists, too. Mary Shelley, who wrote *Frankenstein*, was the daughter of the famous anarchist writer William Godwin and the early feminist Mary Wollstonecraft, and she married the famous poet Percy Shelley. Mary Ann Evans, who took the masculine pen name George Eliot, became a famous novelist in the 1860s after she began living with one of the members of the intellectual circle in London around Herbert Spencer and the evolutionists. Max Weber's wife, Marianne Weber, was a noted scholar in her own right; she was one of the leaders of the German feminist movement in the early twentieth century, and she wrote a comparative history of the legal rights of women which influenced her husband's comparative sociology.[1]

Family and personal connections, though, were usually not a strong enough basis for women to become the influential leaders of the intellectual world. These connections provided a foot in the door, but they needed to be expanded before women would start to have a distinctive impact in a field like sociology. One arena in which women independently moved into positions of leadership was radical political movements and their more moderate reformist counterparts. Rosa Luxemburg was the first woman to make a major contribution to Marxist theory. She developed the analysis of imperialism in the early twentieth century, arguing that capitalism could survive only as long as there was a noncapitalist market outside of it where it could find consumers for its surplus production. Capitalism thus rested on its overseas colonies and its spheres of influence in what we now call the Third World. According to Luxemburg, capitalism would collapse as soon as it had brought the whole world into one big capitalist market. When the

---

[1]Many of the distinguished women sociologists in the earlier generations of the twentieth century were related to men sociologists. Helen Lynd co-authored the pioneering community studies of "Middletown" with her husband Robert Lynd; the "Thomas principle" (if situations are defined as real, they are real in their consequences) was jointly published by W. I. Thomas and his wife Dorothy Swaine Thomas. Jessie Bernard, the pioneering sociologist in the study of male and female spheres, was married to Luther Bernard, an early president of the American Sociological Association; Helena Lopata, an important sociologist of the family, is the daughter of Florian Znaniecki, whom we met in Chapter 10.

monarchist government of the German Kaiser fell at the end of World War I, Luxemburg helped to lead a left-wing uprising that attempted to establish a socialist state. The revolt was crushed by conservative forces, however, and Luxemburg was killed in 1919 in Berlin.

At about the same time in the United States, Jane Addams was pursuing a more reformist version of Rosa Luxemburg's attempt at social revolution. Inspired by a visit to the program for workers' education that was developing in London in the late 1800s, she founded Hull House in Chicago, one of the pioneering institutions in social work. She was a leader in the crusade for humane treatment of new immigrants to America, for overcoming the conditions of slum housing in the cities, and for factory inspection to guard against dangerous work conditions. She fought for protection of children and for the rights of women, including the campaign for women's suffrage. For her pacifist activities, she was awarded the Nobel Peace Prize in 1931. Addams had connections with the early sociologists at the University of Chicago; and George Herbert Mead threw his political support to the activities of Hull House and the reform movements in Chicago.

We should note the difference, though, between the kinds of influence that the men at the university had and the influence that Addams had at Hull House. The male sociologists, although active in various social reform movements, had their greatest long-term influence in the style of research that was carried out and in the general theories they developed. Reform movements and practical activities, by their very nature, tend to be embedded in local conditions. The issues of slum housing in Chicago and of factory regulation at the turn of the century have been forgotten with the passage of time; other local issues have emerged and superseded these. The theoretical schemes tend to be more permanent, since they are more easily passed along to subsequent generations through the intellectual networks. George Herbert Mead's theories of the mind and the social self are better remembered than his participation in Chicago reforms.

Jane Addams had a powerful impact upon the social reforms of her day, and she left her legacy in building up the profession of social work. Still, the theorists and the researchers whose findings become part of our general picture of the patterns of social life have a long-term advantage, because their ideas become propagated through the intellectual networks and the educational system and are transplanted to many different contexts. Jane Addams and other women like her (along with men whose careers were centered on social work) did not become central figures in the development of sociology because of this difference in where they are located in the networks. The scholars who dominated the academic system of sociology had a wider sphere of influence because they controlled the more general and abstract ideas; and these scholars continued to be predominantly men.

Perhaps we can see now why the impact of women in the intellectual core of sociology waited until the last part of the twentieth century. By the 1960s, two major developments occurred simultaneously. One was that women began to become a considerable proportion of university students;

by the 1970s, there were more women than men students. Women were closing in on the core academic networks where the main traditions of ideas were being developed. And in the 1960s, there was a massive student movement on university campuses, connected to the civil rights movement to end the segregation of blacks from whites in the United States. Activists called this simply the Movement, since it comprised many different branches, including civil rights, opposition to nuclear arms and to the Vietnam War, and later the women's movement. As we have just seen, women had become influential leaders in radical and reform movements several generations before women had won more than a foothold in the academic world. By the 1960s and 1970s, everything was coming together: Women political and social reform activists now were riding a wave with the expanding presence of women in the universities themselves. It is not surprising that the major impact of women in sociology dates from this time.

Women from the student generation of the 1960s and 1970s have become a large proportion of the leaders of sociology at the end of the twentieth century. Where previously women had practiced sociology under a different guise—as in literature—or were lodged in practical activities, they are now at the core of the discipline. This period begins what one might call the Golden Age of women in sociology. The following sketches just a few of their contributions.

A REVOLUTIONARY THEORY OF REVOLUTIONS: THEDA SKOCPOL

The 1960s made American students aware of massive social conflict to a degree that did not exist for a long time before or since. One could no longer assume that the state was always the good guy, the democratic guarantor of law and order; some of us who lived through that period remember the police dogs that were unleashed on the crowd of civil rights marchers in Selma, Alabama, and other violent repression by the respectable agents of society. The authors of this book were in the concerned crowds that gathered when voting rights volunteers in the South returned to their college campuses after the summer of 1964, when several of their fellows had been murdered by deputy sheriffs in Mississippi. The atmosphere grew increasingly polarized; university officials often joined in the crackdown on the civil rights demonstrators, obstructing them from organizing on campuses to demonstrate against racial segregation in the surrounding communities.

Most students in this phase were committed to what was called "nonviolent direct action"; taking their inspiration from Mahatma Gandhi's movement to free India from the British in the 1940s, they put their bodies in the way of their opponents but offered no resistance when force was used against them. One of the authors remembers carrying a sociology book into a huge demonstration at the administration building in Berkeley, which we were occupying nonviolently to protest the suspension of several students who had led civil rights demonstrations. The sociology book was by Georges Sorel—it is described in Chapter 6 of this book—and the setting made for a wonderfully vivid lesson of how group solidarity arises from taking part in a conflict when one feels one is morally right. It was our experience of minirevolution; for a few tumultuous days the work of the university ground to a halt while everyone focused on the student revolt, and eventually the university gave in and granted new political rights for students on campus.

Events like this took place on many student campuses across the United States during those years. The tactic of nonviolence was not always maintained; and things heated up especially in the latter part of the 1960s as the struggle for civil rights boiled over into violent uprisings in many black communities. In the summer of 1967, fighting raged for several weeks in the streets of Detroit and Newark, and dozens of people were killed. Other issues came in, including the demonstrations against United States participation in the Vietnam War. Conflict escalated, and then began to decline. By the early 1970s, some measure of civil rights reform had been enacted, most of the official segregation was abolished, and both the black communities and the university campuses settled down.

For students who lived through that period, social movements, conflict, and revolution were not abstract ideas, but vivid realities; we believed we knew what they were about. Of course nothing like a real revolution ever beset the U.S. government during that period; there were minirevolutions in particular communities and on one campus or another. Nevertheless all this left a residue in the thinking of sociologists who grew up in that setting. Part of this was the recognition that revolutions could occur without necessarily falling into the classical Marxian scenario; a revolution did not have to be set off by an economic crisis, and it did not have to involve the uprising of an economic class. Theda Skocpol was the young sociologist who most thoroughly reaped the consequences of that insight.

Skocpol was a student at Michigan State University during this period. In her autobiographical sketch, she describes herself as coming from a small-town midwestern family to a huge university during the boom in student enrollments. There was something for everyone: Football, fraternities, and sororities for those who wanted a good time; serious study groups for others; and enough student political activists, too, to sweep one into the sense of the larger movements that were happening across America. Skocpol joined a civil rights education project in Mississippi, where she met her husband; she credits her marriage to an egalitarian male as one of the factors that encouraged her career at a time when women—especially married women—were not taken very seriously in the academic world. As we know, intellectual creativity usually involves linking into the network of important thinkers of the previous generation; and Skocpol did this with her next step, going on to graduate studies at Harvard and picking up the key advances of the time.

Just a few years before, the Harvard scholar Barrington Moore, Jr., had published his monumental comparative work on the trajectory of revolu-

tions in agrarian societies. Moore was concerned not so much with the causes of revolutions as with their outcomes; he asked why some revolutions
led to capitalist democracies, others to communism, and still others to
Fascist authoritarian regimes. Skocpol saw that the causes still had to be explained: Why do the major revolutions happen in the first place? The result
appeared in 1979 with her book *States and Social Revolutions.*

The focus was the three great revolutions which transformed the modern world: the French Revolution of 1789, the Russian Revolution of 1917,
and the Chinese Revolution of 1949. Skocpol reverses some long-standing
Marxian ideas. Revolutions are not caused, she asserts, by economic contradictions bursting through the bonds of existing political relations, and revolutionary agents are not rising social classes. New economic organizations
and new classes appear not before, but after a successful revolutionary
transformation. Thus the French Revolution cleared the way for large-scale
markets and for the bourgeois class to appear in the nineteenth century; the
Russian and Chinese revolutions created socialism at the same time that
they created a mass industrial working class. It used to be believed that the
socialist revolutions were anomalies, skipping stages in the natural sequence from feudal to capitalist to socialist economies. Not so, Skocpol argues; the revolution creates the economic structure that comes after it.

The main causes of revolutions are not economic at all, but political.
This is not to say that politics is just a free play of power, and that revolutionaries can do whatever they wish if only they have the will. The crucial
point is that politics too is grounded in a structure, the state; and the state
goes through its own crises. Borrowing a theme from Weber, Skocpol
points out that the state has interests of its own. These interests are above
all international: political chiefs are concerned about their international
prestige, and hence with the military power that enables them to get prestige. If the state faces outward, it must also look inward; the leaders of the
state must compete with the dominant classes inside their boundaries for
the economic surplus to put to use in paying their military bills. As a number of historical sociologists have shown since Skocpol wrote, the administrative apparatus of the state grew up initially as a device for supporting
armies and navies; eventually the state bureaucracy became so big that it
needed huge sums to support itself.

Skocpol broadens the way we think about class conflict. The members of
the state thus constitute a kind of social class. They represent a distinctive
way of making a living: by military and administrative appropriation. The
state, we now see, is not merely political; it is also an economic agent in its
own right.

If the state is military at its core, we have the starting point of a new theory of revolutions. Revolutions are not possible as long as the military apparatus of the state holds together. The most basic condition for revolution
is the breakup of the army and internal security forces which keep the state
in power. Previous theorists of revolution had concentrated on other factors
which miss the central point. One cannot simply point to the motivation of
the rebels; whether they are motivated by economic grievances, relative de-

privation, or cultural strain, they still can have little effect as long as the state maintains its military strength. What, then, causes military break-down? Here Skocpol turns to her comparison of the great revolutions.

France, Russia, and China all had the potential to be Great Powers on the world scene, but were overextended or poorly organized militarily. Their efforts to keep up with more powerful states brought about fiscal crises in the state budget; for some of these states, too, there were actual de-feats on the battlefield which disintegrated the armies. Moreover, one could see the revolutionary crisis coming long before the event, because the inter-national dynamic behind it had been going on for a long time. States at-tempt to keep up with their military rivals, and whatever their enemies do they must emulate. Thus the French in the 1700s felt it necessary to keep up with the naval power of the English; the Russian rulers around 1900 at-tempted to modernize to keep up with the European states; China's reforms responded to Japan and to the Western colonial powers. In attempting to keep up with outsiders, rulers introduce changes which in the long run tend to seal their own fates.

For revolutions to be truly major, the military breakdown above and outside must be combined with pressures from within and below. The older theories of revolution are not entirely wrong; the uprising of mass movements is part of the dynamic that makes a revolution especially sweeping in its effect. Skocpol notes that there are several different types of revolutions. In the first category are the so-called Great Revolutions, in which there is not only a political but also a social transformation, and in which these changes are accompanied by a class upheaval. In the French, Russian, and Chinese revolutions, these class uprisings took the form of peasant rebellions.

Another type of revolution, however, consists essentially of political revolutions. Examples of these include the English revolutions of the 1600s, which brought about the dominance of liberal parliamentary government, and the American Revolution of 1776–1783. There are also nation-building revolutions of the sort that have happened throughout the Third World in the middle of the twentieth century. In all these cases, the main dynamic is the breakdown of the military control of the old ruling apparatus. In other words, there is a breakdown at the top and a resulting revolution in politi-cal structures; but in the case of a merely political revolution this does not coincide with a massive uprising at the bottom that feeds into transforming the entire social structure.

Skocpol weaves together her historical comparisons to prove her point. France, Russia, and China had the conjuncture of external-plus-internal crises. On the other hand, England had a political revolution, triggered by a fiscal strain based on its foreign policy expenditures; but there was no social revolution, since the crisis from above was not accompanied by a peasant revolt from below. Similarly, the Meiji Restoration in Japan, which over-threw the rule of the Shogun in 1867 and set off the period of rapid modern-ization, was the result of a military crisis as outside powers intruded into

Japan; there was no massive internal upheaval, and the brief civil war was among different factions of the aristocracy.

In the "Great Revolutions" of France, China, and Russia, there were structural bases for internal revolt as well as for state breakdown. In all of these places, there were long-standing problems of the rural economy, and these were pushed to the point of revolt by the very efforts of the autocratic state to reform from above. Following up the themes of her teacher Barrington Moore, Skocpol points out that these governments unwittingly built up the ability of the peasants to revolt. The aristocrats were often removed from direct supervision of the day-to-day work on the farms, leaving the peasants alienated against a distant ruling class. And the government encouraged a collective organization of the peasants in each local area; this was done for administrative purposes of making it easier to collect taxes, but it had the effect of giving the peasants an organizational base which they could use in mounting a revolt. Once the central apparatus of the state broke down from external pressures, these internal conditions guaranteed that the social revolt would be very powerful indeed.

One of Skocpol's major contributions comes at the point where most theories of revolution ended. She asks: Why is revolutionary reconstruction possible after the initial breakdown? Most of the other theories never raise the question at all, since they apply only to the initial phase. Yet there is no intrinsic reason the state should reemerge, and in a more centralized and strengthened form at that. Why shouldn't the state just keep on fragmenting after the first round of revolution, until it ends up in small parts or is swallowed up by foreign conquerors? Why does the state come out of these Great Revolutions vastly strengthened?

The logic of Skocpol's argument is that the structural conditions behind the major social revolutions are ultimately in the military apparatus and in its international relations. The long-term cause of the military breakdown was that these states attempted unsuccessfully to expand their military capacity. In order to do this, prerevolutionary states tried to extract more surplus from their own population by tightening up their internal controls. These states became paralyzed in an effort to do this; for their own aristocracies resisted the efforts of the state bureaucrats to squeeze more taxes out of these economies. The effort of the state to become externally stronger led to internal conflicts, and this is what finally precipitated the process of revolution.

In the long run, the revolution enabled the state to do better what it had set out to do initially: to become more streamlined and more powerful. It just happens that the old rulers of the state were no longer around to see this outcome; neither were their main opponents, the aristocrats who tried to stand in their way. The leaders of the revolution, in every case, came from the class of minor officials, the class that was most involved in prerevolutionary administrative reform. They were not the Marxian class rising from the new economy; in France, they were not the rising bourgeoisie breaking through the ranks of the aristocracy; in Russia and China, they were not the workers rising up to challenge the bourgeoisie. They were instead the aspiring administrators, those who were acquiring new positions as the state bureaucracy expanded.

In the great revolutions, a two-edged crisis broke out around these cadres of the expanding state. Militarily things broke down at the top, leading to fiscal crisis and the disorganization of the army; socially the peasants were revolting from the bottom, often with destructive violence. Both of these crises were solved by the revolution. The military crisis eventually was overcome because these states had the potential resources to build a powerful apparatus of coercion; the old-line aristocrats who stood in the way of the expanding state were destroyed in the peasant revolt. The peasants, on the other hand, supplied the energy of the revolution but they were in the wrong place in the structure to reap its rewards. They could destroy but they could not take over. What did take over was the centralizing state, now in the hands of its young, junior officials. When the other pieces of the wreckage of the old regime were swept away, they were left on the center of the stage.

Skocpol's argument in 1979 made a powerful impact because it answered one of the big questions left over from the Marxist theory of revolution. Why didn't the Communist revolutions in Russia, in its Eastern European satellites, and in China lead to a withering away of state power? Why wasn't the result of the revolutions an increase in human freedom? Why instead did they give rise to highly centralized forms of authority, and to totalitarian dictatorship? Skocpol showed that the state is the central focus in leading up to a revolution; it is a battle all along over how powerful the state is going to be, and how many resources it is going to extract from the rest of society.

History of course moves along. There have been other revolutions besides the great social revolutions of France, Russia, and China. Many of these have fitted Skocpol's model of political revolutions which occur without much change in the social structure; and here too her model of external pressures and military/fiscal breakdown has done good service. By the late 1980s, it was apparent that the Russian state itself was breaking down; first it lost control over its East European satellites, and then by the early 1990s it was undergoing an anti-Communist revolution on its home ground. Is the advance in sociological theory which Skocpol represents capable of explaining these processes as well?

Some of the main elements of her theory play an important part. The Soviet state began to break down at the center before popular movements were allowed to mobilize against it from below. Military and fiscal strain weakened the center; factional battles broke out between rival groups of conservatives and reformers over how to improve the power of the state. As these struggles intensified, the Russian-dominated Soviet Union was no longer able to control its East European satellites; the breakdown at the center spread to the periphery. Skocpol's model of state breakdown through international military relations once more shows one of the keys to a revolution.

On the other hand, can we call this a great revolution, a social revolution as well as a political revolution? As of the early 1990s, there is clearly a path toward a social revolution as well, as reformers attempt to radically dismantle the Socialist economies and replace them with capitalism. This is a great surprise for a Marxian theory, but it is not so strange for Skocpol's model; after all, she indicates that the economic structures and classes tend to be formed as the result of revolutions, rather than beforehand as causes of them. Perhaps we will come to see history as more like a series of grand flip-flops, with the switching mechanism coming from the international arena of military strains and budget crises. When such a crisis coincides with internal conditions which organize a class revolt, the economy is switched: from capitalism to socialism, or the other way. Probably we have not seen the last of this sort of dynamic.

Here Skocpol's work brings us up to the frontier of our knowledge. She has not been alone in working on the theory of revolutions. We now understand much more about the various kinds of revolutions; we understand more about the economic role of the state inside a society, and about the geopolitical principles which affect the power of the state externally. The "minirevolutions" of the United States during the 1960s, which attuned a generation of sociologists to think in new ways about revolutions, have paid off with a broader theoretical understanding of the dynamics which change our world. Through work like that of Theda Skocpol, sociology's older traditions are revised and expanded; doubtless the generation of her successors will take them even farther.

BUILDING THE THEORY OF GENDER STRATIFICATION: RAE BLUMBERG, JANET CHAFETZ, AND JOAN HUBER

As a member of the 1960s generation, Theda Skocpol became attuned to the issue of revolution. Other women of that generation focused on the issue of the women's revolution. The feminist movement has a long history, going back to the activists of the 1800s who fought for women's rights. With the achieving of women's right to vote in the United States, England, and other countries around 1920, this so-called "first wave" of feminism died down. A small group of activists kept the issue alive, but the larger public was not listening. The 1950s was a period when the public ideology stressed the role of women as mothers and homemakers and denied that women should be working at careers outside the home. Ironically, this was a time when the white-collar work force was expanding to include a very large number of women: but in positions such as secretaries, taking orders from men.

Other features of the situation were undermining the ideology of separate male and female spheres. If women were expected to devote their lives to bringing up a family, the first order of business was to get married, and this meant finding a man. And since middle-class men were now all attending college, women had a good reason to go to college too. But once they were there, other possibilities for women arose besides the marriage market: learning about professional careers, becoming intellectuals or political activists. When the student movement took off in the 1960s, women were very much a part of it. Thus the "second wave" of the women's movement began in the late 1960s, as a branching off from "the Movement" for civil rights and peace.

The best-known feminist theorists of that period were especially likely to come from literature. This is not surprising, in the light of the fact that women first made their mark in the intellectual world as novelists and poets. Literary critics like Kate Millett and Germaine Greer wrote critiques of male domination and of the ideologies that uphold it. Marxist activism had been the other arena in which women intellectuals had gained a hold; so we find the use of Marxian theory by feminist writers like Juliet Mitchell and Shulamith Firestone. It was an expanded Marxian tradition, featuring not only class struggle but also sexual domination based on patriarchy and relations of reproduction. A number of feminist writers drew also on Freudian theory, purged of Freud's own male biases and modified to account for the roots of gender inequality. In Chapter 8 we reviewed Nancy Chodorow's theory of mothering, which attempts to explain gender inequality in terms of personality differences deeply rooted in early childhood.

The traditions of women intellectuals were strongest in literature and in psychoanalysis, and specifically sociological contributions to feminism were a little slower to receive attention. Nevertheless sociology was in an especially good position to explain the dynamics of gender change. The issues are essentially these. Cultural and psychological approaches to gender inequality are good at description and critique; one is able to show how deep and pervasive are the aspects of male and female differences and inequalities. The resulting picture, though, is a static one. If there are many subtle and deeply rooted processes reproducing the system of male domination, how is it possible to change them? Cultural and psychological models of gender domination must end up either as pessimistic or as putting their hopes on a sudden, almost miraculous, change in consciousness.

Marxian theories, on the other hand, have a dynamic of change; but they have a problem in applying this specifically to gender. For one thing, gender stratification existed before capitalism, and it continues to exist in the Socialist societies; accordingly, there is an additional process of gender stratification which exists over and above class domination. This is usually labeled "patriarchy." But to label something is not to explain it; and there is still the problem of showing how this "patriarchal" inequality rises and falls. If "patriarchy" is immutable, then we are back with the same problem as the cultural and psychological theories, unable to show a path toward a different future.

Sociology is in an excellent position to solve this problem. For sociology is the theory of the causes and effects of social patterns; and if most sociologists did not take a very good look at gender inequality before the 1960s, there was nothing to prevent the new generation from doing just that. In order to understand the causes of a social pattern, we need to examine the widest range of variation we can find, and to isolate the factors which make the difference. Max Weber, for instance, had done this in looking at state, religion, and economy across world history, trying to isolate the factors which gave rise to modern capitalism. Durkheim had done something similar with his comparison of mechanical and organic solidarity. In the mid-1960s, Gerhard Lenski had assembled the data on economic inequality across societies ranging from small hunting-and-gathering bands up through the great agrarian empires and the systems built upon industrial technology. When sociologists began looking for the general causes of gender inequality in the 1970s, they drew upon this comparative method.

A number of women sociologists were involved in this kind of comparative analysis, including Rae Lesser Blumberg, Janet Saltzman Chafetz, and Joan Huber. (Some men worked in this area too, but they have received enough attention, so we will leave them aside here.) The resulting theories play up different aspects of the situation, but there is an overall viewpoint which has been supported by different angles of approach to the evidence. So we can describe the building up of a general theory of gender stratification.

Among the most colorful of the comparative sociologists of gender is Rae Lesser Blumberg. She has pursued comparisons from many sorts of data. From the library and the computer files she makes use of the anthropological comparisons in the Human Relations Area Files, as well as the kinds of historical accounts that Lenski used to study economic inequality in medieval agrarian societies. Rae Blumberg is also a field researcher of world-ranging scope. Coming from the idealistic generation of activists of the 1960s and early 1970s, she joined the Peace Corps and was sent to South America. Revolutionary and anti-American movements abounded. On the other side, U.S. agencies were active in trying to head off Communist influence in the hemisphere, pushing both covert and overt programs. Rae Blumberg found herself in the middle of all this. The Peace Corps and the Agency for International Development (AID) worked directly with the poor, trying to foster economic development; and this brought American staff members into the arena where the movements of discontent thrived. At the same time, the Central Intelligence Agency (CIA) and the military attachés worked through the U.S. embassies, coordinating military aid to forces that were considered to be friendly to the United States, and attempting to undermine movements and even governments that were considered unfriendly.

Blumberg describes the situation in Bolivia in the early 1970s. The government, which had come to power in a previous coup, was considered too left-wing by the United States, which supported conservative generals attempting to overthrow it. On the other side were ultra-left guerrillas. Between the two, rumors of impending coups swept through the capital every few weeks. From time to time, one had to duck gunfire in the streets, or hope for luck in not being at the places where a bomb blew up. The circles of embassies and international organizations were full of deception and intrigue. Arms merchants and arms purchasers mingled under varied cover, ranging from the Middle East to militarized Asian bastians like Taiwan and Korea. Blumberg found that she was being followed by the representative of an American religious charity, apparently an agent who was suspicious of her knowledge of U.S. plans to bring down the leftist Bolivian government by economic manipulations. Pulling connections, she got herself out of Bolivia.

Over the years, both in her Peace Corps days and later, Blumberg has continued her firsthand comparative studies. To understand the position of women, she argues, one must see their position within the economic division of labor. And to understand why these positions differ, one must see a wide range of such arrangements. Blumberg has flown into the remote jungles of Venezuela, to study horticultural tribes where raiding and female infanticide were practiced. She has studied the Indian tribes of the Andes, some of which had old traditions of female crafts which constituted a crucial part of economic production. The harsh realities of politics and violent conflict were often present. Working in Guatemala in the 1980s, she came across whole villages that were burned out by government forces, destroying the population to put down resistance movements and keep a dictatorial government in power. In Venezuela, she wrestled with an attacker who broke into the university laboratory where she was working on her data.

Flying into Nigeria late at night, she found herself being "assisted" through customs by a couple of men who were very curious about the money and jewelry she was carrying; unable to shake them off outside the airport as she searched for a taxi, she finally approached a soldier with a submachine gun. Nigeria was split between three warring tribal groups; it was a gamble of two chances in three, she felt, that the soldier was of a different tribe than the men who were escorting her into the dark. The gamble paid off; she got free, with the soldier's aid, and drove off into the curfew of nighttime Lagos to follow up her latest research project. In her studies of women in the developing economies, Blumberg has found herself traveling inconspicuously in a crowded bus to avoid demonstrations, sometimes in government vehicles or even armored cars, sometimes with nervous drivers making their way through a road known for ambushes. The discovery of society, for Rae Blumberg, is both a dedication and an adventure.

Blumberg's approach to the theory of gender stratification can be illustrated by her examination of the Israeli kibbutz, and her answer to the puzzle: Why do these experiments in social equality, which minimize the organization of the family and bring children up communally, nevertheless end up with men dominating the important positions? The answer, Blumberg decided, is a two-step chain. Men and women are supposed to share the work of the kibbutz equally, but in fact men do the main work, such as driving the tractors in the fields; women tend to be in charge of the children's nursery and the laundry. And since the economic prosperity of the kibbutz depends on its agricultural output, men's work in this sphere gives them greater prestige and greater power in the community. The most important sector economically is the one that determines gender power.

So now for the second step in the chain: How did women become concentrated in the laundry and men in the fields? The answer is of general significance for the way societies have been organized at different times in history. Where work is compatible with the activities of women in bearing and caring for small children, that work tends to be done by women. Work which would take women away from the home, whether driving tractors in the fields or hunting for game in early tribal societies, tends to be monopolized by men.

Let us consider now the general theory to which Blumberg contributed, along with Chafetz, Huber, and others. First, let us consider the overall pattern of world history. Since the approach of this general theory is economic, we need to begin with the differences in the economic base. In *hunting-and-gathering societies*, gender inequality was usually fairly low. (Blumberg and Chafetz here are following the classification of social types developed by Lenski, which was mentioned above.) In *horticultural societies*, the picture is more mixed. These societies are supported by growing crops in small gardens. Typically there is a complicated kinship system, sometimes organized around women's lineages and/or women's place of residence, sometimes organized around male lineage and residence. In some of these societies women are fairly prominent in power and ideology; some are male-dominated; some are split into sharply separate spheres, which amounts to an open "war of the sexes." Here we may find adult men living in separate houses for warriors, maintaining taboos against the women, who live in their own huts with the children and see the men mainly for sexual contact.

Agrarian societies are the civilizations of ancient and medieval history that we mentioned at the beginning of this chapter. Here the economy has expanded to large-scale farming, using plows, animals, and sometimes massive irrigation systems. There is much more economic surplus than before, and this goes into building a class system dominated by the aristocracy. Women now depend upon the class position of the men in their families, and have little autonomous power. Upper-class women are often tightly controlled. Along with this went a cult of virginity; women were regarded primarily as sexual objects who were to be guarded at all costs. For men, there was the other side of a dual standard: Men's sexual exploits were often admired, just as women's were restricted. Women of the working class were the most exploited group in these societies; not only did they perform most of the menial work but they were also targets for the sexual *machismo* of upper-class men.

When we come to *industrial societies*, as they developed from the 1700s in Europe, we find that gender inequality drops somewhat from the extremes of agrarian societies. But change comes slowly and goes through two large phases. In the earlier phase of industrial societies, gender relations change in all social classes. Upper-class women are not so restricted; working-class women, on the other hand, begin to get some protections from exploitation at work and sexually. The ideal woman in this phase comes to be regarded as the middle-class housewife and mother; she is considered to be supreme in her own sphere, but it was also considered desirable to protect her by separation from the male sphere of work.

Finally there is the phase when a women's movement mobilizes against this separation of spheres. There is a trend toward integration and equality in the traditional male realms of work and politics and also of bringing men into the traditional female realms of housework and child rearing. In the late twentieth century, these trends obviously are still a long way from finished.

How can these differences across human history be explained? The general theory of gender stratification focuses on the intersection of several causes: (1) women's economic position; (2) women's reproductive position; and (3) male and female politics.

With regard to *economic position,* both Blumberg and Chafetz point out that the historical differences correlate with the kind of work that women do. In hunting-and-gathering systems, most of the food production comes from gathering rather than hunting; and since women do most of the gathering, this gives them a key economic base and gives them a fair degree of social power and prestige. In horticultural systems, women again contribute the most production, since it is typically women who do the gardening. But now we arrive at a complication. It is not simply who does the *work* that determines stratification, but who controls the *property.* In some horticultural tribes, for instance, there is a male supremacist complex; the women do the work but the men appropriate it because they are organized into military groups which dominate the macrostructure of society. This kind of economic analysis, we can see, is leading toward another kind of factor which determines the property system.

In agrarian societies, women's social position sinks to the lowest scale in world history. This is related to the fact that women now tend to have the lowest input into economic productivity. The center of the economy is in heavy agriculture, or in herding animals, or again sometimes in seafaring and in long-distance trade; all of these activities are monopolized by men, while women work as servants or perform the smaller tasks around the farm. And even where a woman works, men tend to control her property as their own. Here we have a strong negative on both dimensions: women's economic power and women's social status and power are both low.

Finally, industrial societies. Here we have evidence that as women get more income under their own control, their power position increases both inside the home and in the larger society. Sometimes this happens through inheritance, but most often through women's own careers; a woman's power now tends to depend upon how much she makes in comparison to her husband or to other men around her.

These comparisons lead us to two further questions: Why do women have the kinds of work they do in these different societies and why are women only *sometimes* able to control their own property, while at other times the fruits of their labor are taken over by males? The first question leads us to consider the reproductive sphere; the second to consider politics.

With regard to the *reproductive sphere*, Blumberg, Chafetz, and other theorists have pointed to the extent to which work is compatible with women's pregnancies, nursing, and child rearing. This leads to a further issue. Why is it that women sometimes are heavily concentrated in having babies and spend much of their lives caring for children? Yet in other times, women have far fewer children, or spread the child-care responsibility around so that some of the women at least are free to do other things. Joan Huber and other contributors have put together a theory to answer this point. When a society has a high death rate or a big demand for children for other reasons, women are especially valued as mothers. Women tend to be pregnant through much of their adult lives; when they are not pregnant they are breast-feeding small children. There is a vicious circle: Societies with a high death rate have poor health and medical conditions, making childbirths very dangerous, so many women die in childbirth. Add to this the fact that many children die before they grow up, and we see a vicious circle which feeds the death rate and keeps up the demand for still more childbirths. And since women are continuously bound up in the reproductive sphere, they have little opportunity to get the kinds of economic productivity which would give them a source of social power.

How can they escape this vicious cycle? Several conditions have sometimes intervened. When medical conditions improved or the environment was favorable, the death rate was lowered, taking some of the pressure off to have many children. In addition, through technologies of birth control, especially the invention of effective contraceptives in the early twentieth century, the birth rate could be dropped lower still. And finally the invention of the sanitary baby bottle around 1910 made it possible, at least in principle, for a mother not to be constantly in close proximity to her small children in order for them to be fed. As the result of all these factors, birth rates have generally fallen in the twentieth century, and so have the proportion of their lives that women spend in child rearing. At the same time, women's economic opportunities have gradually widened.

We still need to examine one more factor in explaining gender stratification. Both of the previous factors—economic position and the reproductive sphere—are sometimes overriden by a third factor. Women sometimes do much of the work but reap few of the rewards because men end up appropriating the property. And although women in the twentieth century are no longer forced by social conditions to spend their lives breeding children, it still took most of the century for a change in their career patterns to come about.

The third factor that intervenes is the political system, operating at the larger, macro level. Blumberg, Chafetz, and other gender theorists recognize how large-scale politics can keep women from gaining the economic positions they might otherwise have. In some colonial societies in Africa, for instance, European rulers bypassed the women's networks which were traditionally in control of local economic life and appointed male chiefs. In the early twentieth century, labor unions often pushed for laws which restricted women from certain types of factory work; this was supposed to protect women from heavy working conditions, but it also guaranteed jobs for men. How then do we account for male advantage in controlling politics? This part of the theory of gender is not as well developed in those theories that start from an economic or reproductive viewpoint. One line of theory, based on some ideas of Max Weber and developed by Randall Collins, points out that much depends on how the state is organized militarily.

Men have usually monopolized weapons and fighting; and when the state consisted primarily of bands of warriors or of aristocratic families living in armed castles, this military monopoly translated into a male control of the state. As long as men controlled the state, all the state ideologies were male oriented too; and whenever the state intervened in private life, it did so to back up the property and sexual advantages of males. According to this political theory of gender, the crucial turning point came when the modern bureaucratic state emerged. The state is separated from the aristocratic families which used to dominate its policies; the way is opened to reform movements and eventually to peaceful control by voting rather than by the wars and alliances of the aristocrats. This provided an opening for women to negate traditional male control at the macro level; it remained only potential, though, until women were actually mobilized to throw their weight into politics.

Now we encounter a crucial problem for all three of our lines of theory: economic, reproductive, and political. By the time industrial societies are fairly advanced, the conditions in all three of these theories have swung toward those favoring relative equality for women. Why, then, have the changes taken so long to come? The bureaucratic state under civilian control already existed in the 1800s; a low death rate, baby bottles, and birth control existed by around 1910; jobs in the industrial society moved predominantly toward the white-collar sector where women's labor was easily available. Why then was there a 60-year or so lag before women really got mobilized to break down the barriers of gender segregation?

Janet Chafetz suggests a theory for this lag. Male control of the macro-level structures of society translates into ideological beliefs of the appropriate way to behave in micro-level situations. When men control the higher occupational positions, women have few role models like themselves in these kinds of positions. Their self-images, rather, are of women they see most frequently: mothers, homemakers, secretaries, and nurses; or in the mass media, actresses who specialize in sex appeal. The ideological definitions of male and female activities thus reinforce the way jobs are actually divided up; it is another vicious circle. How can women break through this circle? Chafetz points out that if the circle can be reversed, so that there are many women in professional and managerial careers, it will provide a new definition of male and female and mobilize even more women to seek these kinds of careers. And since economic position flows into power position in the home, the whole social structure will move in an egalitarian direction.

What seems to break through this ideological stumbling block is primarily in the realm of politics. Political movements that bring women into the public eye stir up widespread feelings that go far beyond the people who take part in the movements. This is why feminist movements have been mobilized during the periods when women's career ambitions suddenly rise. It happened to a lesser degree around the turn of the twentieth century, when the feminist movement mobilized for suffrage. And it happened again in the 1970s and 1980s, with the second wave of the women's movement.

Politics consists of conflicts, and it is not surprising that the period of women's mobilization in the 1970s gave rise to tremendous controversy. One aspect was the appearance of backlash movements, the mobilization of conservative women as well as men against the new legal and social trends. Thus movements arose which stressed the preeminent value of women as mothers and homemakers and opposed women's careers outside the home.

Nevertheless, as Chafetz and her collaborators point out, these backlash movements are usually not as strong as the movement for gender change. The size of the backlash movement depends on the size of the movement it is mobilizing against, which means that the conditions that mobilize women into demanding better economic payoffs are already present. An antifeminist movement is always too late to bring the structure back to its old condition, because those changes in the structure in the first place (the changes we listed earlier in this theoretical account) were already shifting the balance of power. The political movement of women is like a spring which has been loaded by underlying structural changes; the ideological conditions we just outlined keep the spring down, but once a mobilization starts, it is like unleashing the spring.

All of these varieties of gender stratification theory are optimistic about the long run. The conditions which favor gender equality have been shifting for a century toward the women's side. The question is, how long will it take? Chafetz offers the most explicit projection. If favorable economic trends continue, she suggests, the demand for women's labor will continue to grow; this should be especially strong as the white-collar sector comes to dominate the occupational structure. When the current cohort of baby boomers retires around 2010–2020, the next cohort with its mobilized female labor force should be a gender-egalitarian one.

Chafetz also casts a wary eye on a pessimistic projection. When there have been economic downturns in the past, men usually pushed women back out of the labor force; short-term economic gains that women had won were subsequently lost. Under this scenario, the big danger is another economic catastrophe, like the Great Depression of the 1930s. If that happens— and the rickety financial structure of the world economy in the 1990s is none too reassuring on this score—women may again be pushed back out of the labor force, and male domination in all spheres will return.

Perhaps both of these scenarios omit some crucial pieces that we have not foreseen. Political factors have been the joker in the deck at various times in the past, and we should not expect economic and reproductive trends alone to totally determine the future either. We can expect the politics of gender to be involved in more battles: over new aspects of job legislation, child care, reproductive rights and restrictions, and family laws. Sociological understanding of the dynamics of gender stratification has been maturing; doubtless we will have more to learn about it in the future.

WOMEN AND THE FUTURE OF SOCIOLOGY

We could go on, if there were more space, to discuss the theories and discoveries of women in a wide range of sociology. Today, talking about the work of women sociologists is tantamount to talking about the field as a whole. In the macrosociology of the world system, for example, one would have to consider Janet Abu-Lughod, who shows us that the capitalist world system which arose in the sixteenth century out of a European core was not the first world system. Abu-Lughod takes us back to a previous world system in the thirteenth century, the "High Middle Ages," when Europe was just one end of an economic chain that stretched all the way to China, and in which India and above all the Islamic world were at the center. Instead of "the rise of the West," Abu-Lughod tells us, our real problem in explaining modern history is to account for "the fall of the East."

Women are prominent in microsociology as well. In any survey of the field one would have to deal with Karen Cook, a leader in exchange theory and social networks. In the sociology of science, Karin Knorr-Cetina formulated a radical "social constructionist" position to show how what is considered to be knowledge is created in the activities of scientists in the face-to-face action in their laboratories. In the sociology of organizations, a leading figure is Rosabeth Moss Kanter, with her insightful portrait of the way careers—of both men and women—are made in the internal politics of the big corporation. The methodological approaches pioneered by women range from hard to soft; Nancy Tuma is one of the creators of the statistical method of "event history analysis"; Arlie Hochschild developed an interpretive theory of emotions stressing the fluid and cognitive processes by which people define their feelings through "emotion work." Dorothy Smith developed her "standpoint theory," which argues that any group, men or women, majority or minority, produces a theory which expresses the standpoint of that particular group. Smith thus interprets feminist theory as a standpoint which opposes male viewpoints with a distinctive feminist viewpoint.

It has been argued that men's methods in sociology are hard and impersonal; that women's methods avoid mathematics, statistics, and objectivity, and instead concentrate on qualitative data and subjective understanding.

Men, it is said, go for abstractions and generalities; women go for the unique and particular. To be honest, the authors of this book can hardly endorse a position which calls for cutting sociology into two uncommunicating halves. On this issue, we are old-fashioned liberals: we believe in equality, participation, and cooperation. We do not wish to retire into a men's zone of sociology, while the women retire into their separate zone. As we have examined the discovery of society throughout this book, we have seen that many kinds of methods were used. Many standpoints were the bases from which sociological explorations have been launched; nevertheless they all come together into an ongoing body of knowledge that is called sociology.

The men who were first in the kinds of social settings in which sociology could be done analyzed society from both objective and subjective viewpoints. Marx had both economics and dialectics; Weber focused both on bureaucracy and on *verstehen*. Thinkers like Mead, Goffman, and Garfinkel showed the objective elements in the subjective and the subjective side of objective structures. Since the 1960s, when women began to fill the forefront of the discipline, women sociologists have done important work in virtually every kind of sociology. As women, they often bring distinctive standpoints from their social backgrounds and sensitivities. Yet another crucial part of their social surroundings as sociologists is that which they share with male sociologists: the intellectual networks in which creativity always operates and the passing along of cultural capital from the generations of the past.

Future historians of sociology will see our lifetimes as a period in which several new streams flow together into the older river. Sociology is a community, stretching over the generations, comprising now both men and women, engaged in the ongoing discovery of society.

Bibliographical Suggestions

There is no satisfactory overview of the whole development of sociology, but the scope of its history can be gathered from Howard Becker and Harry Elmer Barnes, *Social Thought from Lore to Science,* 3 vols. (New York: Dover, 1961), which tells about most of the main figures plus an extraordinary number of minor ones, ranging from ancient Greece to modern Afghanistan. At the other extreme there are books such as Raymond Aron, *Main Currents in Sociological Thought* (Garden City, N.Y.: Doubleday, 1968), and Robert Nisbet, *The Sociological Tradition* (New York: Basic Books, 1966), which treat just a few of the classical European thinkers. Much information on the lives and sociopolitical surroundings of the great sociologists is found in Lewis Coser, *Masters of Sociological Thought* (New York: Harcourt, Brace, 1971). We are also beginning to apply the sociology of science to sociology's history in a serious way. One of the best of such efforts is Nicholas Mullins, *Theories and Theory Groups in Contemporary American Sociology* (New York: Harper & Row, 1973). Recent developments are analyzed in Randall Collins, *Sociology Since Mid-Century* (New York: Academic Press, 1981). For neighboring disciplines, the reader could consult Joseph Schumpeter's masterful *History of Economic Analysis* (New York: Oxford University Press, 1954), and Marvin Harris, *The Rise of Anthropological Theory* (New York: Crowell, 1968).

Chapter One
The Prophets of Paris: Saint-Simon and Comte

The Enlightenment background of the early French sociologists is brought wonderfully alive by the Frenchman Paul Hazard in *European Thought in the Eighteenth Century* (New York: Meridian, 1963) and is given a thorough German treatment by Ernst Cassirer in *The Philosophy of the Enlightenment* (Boston: Beacon Press, 1955). The lives of Saint-Simon, Comte, Fourier, and others are found in Frank Manuel, *The Prophets of Paris* (Cambridge, Mass.: Harvard University Press, 1963). A good selection of Saint-Simon's work in paperback is Henri de Saint-Simon, *Social Organization and Other Writings,* Felix Markham (ed.) (New York: Harper Torchbooks, 1964), and of Comte's work, *Auguste Comte: Sire of Sociology,* George Simpson (ed.) (New York: Crowell, 1969). Comte's lengthy *System of Positive Philosophy* is heavy going.

Chapter Two
Sociology in the Underground: Karl Marx

Marx is still eminently readable, although this is least true of his masterpiece, *Capital* (New York: Kerr, 1906). A good selection of his and Engels' writings is in Lewis S. Feuer, *Marx and Engels: Basic Writings on Politics and*

Philosophy (Garden City, N.Y.: Doubleday, 1959). *The Eighteenth Brumaire of Louis Bonaparte* (New York: International, 1963) is a fine example of Marx as a historian of contemporary events. The theory of gender stratification is given in Friedrich Engels, *The Origin of the Family, Private Property, and the State* (New York: International Publishers, 1972). Marx's uncompleted system is sketched in his unpublished manuscript, *Grundrisse* (New York: Random House, 1973). Erich Fromm's *Marx's Concept of Man* (New York: Frederick Ungar, 1961) gives Marx's early humanist philosophy; Fromm's introduction is a useful guide to some rather difficult writing. Herbert Marcuse, *Reason and Revolution* (New York: Humanities Press, 1954), is the classic exposition of Hegel's system and its transformation into Marx's; Marcuse's *One-Dimensional Man* (Boston: Beacon Press, 1964) contains his revival of these themes, now popular with factions of the new left. The history of Marxism is most absorbingly told in Edmund Wilson, *To the Finland Station* (Garden City, N.Y.: Doubleday, 1953), beginning with Marx's eighteenth-century predecessors and continuing up to Lenin in 1917; Isaac Deutscher, *Trotsky,* 3 vols. (New York: Vintage, 1965), continues the story through the tragedy of Russia in the 1920s and 1930s. George Lichtheim, *Marxism* (New York: Praeger, 1965), gives a scholarly analysis of the Marxian system from the 1830s up to the present. The major modern biography of Marx is David McLennan, *Karl Marx, His Life and Thought* (London: Macmillan, 1973). Marx's economics is updated for current issues in Paul A. Baran and Paul A. Sweezy, *Monopoly Capital* (New York: Monthly Review Press, 1966), Andrew Gunder Frank, *Capitalism and Underdevelopment in Latin America* (New York: Monthly Review Press, 1967), Arghiri Emmanuel, *Unequal Exchange* (New York: Monthly Review Press, 1972), and James O'Connor, *The Fiscal Crisis of the State* (New York: St. Martin's Press, 1973). Other developments in Marxist thought include Jurgen Habermas, *Legitimation Crisis* (Boston: Beacon Press, 1975) and Louis Althusser, *For Marx* (New York: Pantheon, 1969). The continuing power of a sophisticated and nondogmatic Marxian sociology is illustrated by Barrington Moore, *Social Origins of Dictatorship and Democracy* (Boston: Beacon Press, 1966), Immanuel Wallerstein, *The Modern World System* (New York: Academic Press, Vol. 1, 1974; Vol. 2, 1980; Vol. 3, 1989), Samuel Bowles and Herbert Gintis, *Schooling in Capitalist America* (New York: Basic Books, 1975), Perry Anderson, *Lineages of the Absolutist State* (London: New Left Books, 1974), and Theda Skocpol, *States and Social Revolutions* (New York: Cambridge University Press, 1979). Marxian and feminist theories are compared in Natalie J. Sokolov, *Between Money and Love: The Dialectics of Women's Home and Market Work* (New York: Praeger, 1980).

Chapter Three
The Last Gentleman: Alexis de Tocqueville

Tocqueville's *Democracy in America,* 2 vols. (New York: Knopf, 1945), is read everywhere; his *Old Regime and the French Revolution* (Garden City, N.Y.: Anchor, 1955) is even more worthwhile—short, concise, delightful in idea and expression. Tocqueville tells much of his own life story in his *Recollections* (New York: Columbia University Press, 1949). Tocqueville's work, as well as that of Saint-Simon, Comte, Durkheim, Sorel, and many others in this book, can hardly be understood apart from the history of France; Alfred Cobban, *A History of Modern France* (London: Penguin, 1957), outlines the story extremely well. George Pierson, *Tocqueville and Beaumont in America* (New York: Oxford University Press, 1938), describes what Tocqueville saw and did not see on his visit to America. Tocqueville's ideas about mass society have been given modern currency by J. L. Talmon, *The Rise of Totalitarian Democracy* (Boston: Beacon Press, 1952), and Hannah Arendt, *The Origins of Totalitarianism* (New York: Harcourt, Brace & World, 1954).

Chapter Four
Nietzsche's Madness

Nietzsche's collected works are published in many editions. *The Portable Nietzsche*, edited by Walter Kaufmann (New York: Viking Press, 1954), is a good paperback reader, including all of *Thus Spake Zarathustra*, *The Twilight of the Idols*, and *The Antichrist*, as well as selections from other works. *The Birth of Tragedy* and *The Genealogy of Morals* are published together in a Doubleday paperback (Garden City, N.Y.: 1956). Important secondary sources on Nietzsche include Walter Kaufmann, *Nietzsche* (Princeton, N.J.: Princeton University Press, 1950), Erich Podach, *The Madness of Nietzsche* (London: Routledge, 1931), and numerous works in French and German. Rudolph Binion, *Frau Lou: Nietzsche's Wayward Disciple* (Princeton, N.J.: Princeton University Press, 1968), tells of the woman who was a friend of both Nietzsche and Freud. Perhaps the most revealing picture of Nietzsche is in Peter Fuss and Henry Shapiro (eds.), *Nietzsche: A Self-Portrait from His Letters* (Cambridge, Mass.: Harvard University Press, 1971).

Chapter Five
Do-Gooders, Evolutionists, and Racists

Of the Anglo-American tradition, the works most worth reading today are William Graham Sumner, *Folkways* (New York: Mentor, 1961), and Herbert Spencer, *Principles of Sociology* (New York: Appleton-Century-Crofts, 1884), Vol. 1. Spencer's work must be sampled selectively, as it is padded out to enormous length by all sorts of curious examples—but one must remember that he was being paid to serialize his work for a magazine monthly. The utilitarian tradition is described in Elie Halevy, *The Growth of Philosophical Radicalism* (Boston: Beacon Press, 1955). About all that anyone would ever want to know about early American sociology is found in L. L. and Jessie Bernard, *Origins of American Sociology* (New York: Russell & Russell, 1965), and Roscoe C. and Gisela J. Hinkle, *The Development of Modern Sociology* (New York: Random House, 1954). Herman and Julia Schwendinger, *Sociologists of the Chair* (New York: Basic Books, 1974), put this development in its political context. Richard Hofstadter's *The Age of Reform* (New York:

Vintage, 1955) and his *Anti-Intellectualism in American Life* (New York: Vintage, 1966) give the proper historical setting. The vogue of biological and racial explanations is hard to grasp from most modern histories, which leave this out because of their own bias as to what is important (and a good image) for the field. An exception is Pitirim Sorokin's *Contemporary Sociological Theories* (New York: Harper, 1928), which gives the full flavor of the pre-World War I intellectual milieu. The basic text for Edward O. Wilson is *Sociobiology: The Abridged Edition* (Cambridge, Mass.: Harvard University Press, 1980), which is divided into sections on Social Evolution, Social Mechanisms, and The Social Species. It emerged from the sourcebook in research, *Sociobiology: The New Synthesis* (Cambridge, Mass.: Harvard University Press, 1975). *On Human Nature* (Cambridge, Mass.: Harvard University Press, 1978) is a Pulitzer Prize winner which deals with the perspective on the challenge of human survival and the question of free will versus genetic determinism. A primary sourcebook of John C. Lilly is *Lilly on Dolphins: Humans of the Sea* (Garden City, N.Y.: Anchor Press, 1975), a revised edition of two earlier works: *Man and Dolphin* (New York: Doubleday & Company, Inc., 1961) and *The Mind of the Dolphin* (New York: Doubleday & Company, Inc., 1967). Lilly's personal, social, and intellectual growth is described in *The Scientist: A Novel Autobiography* (New York: Bantam Books, 1981).

Chapter Six
Dreyfus's Empire: Emile Durkheim and Georges Sorel

Durkheim's major works are *The Division of Labor in Society* (New York: Free Press, 1964), *Suicide* (New York: Free Press, 1966), *The Roles of the Sociological Method* (New York: Free Press, 1938), *Socialism* (New York: Collier, 1962), *Professional Ethics and Civic Morals* (New York: Free Press, 1958), and *The Elementary Forms of the Religious Life* (New York: Collier, 1961). They are all well worth reading. Miscellaneous papers on and by Durkheim are in Kurt H. Wolff (ed.), *Emile Durkheim: Essays on Sociology and Philosophy* (New York: Harper Torchbooks, 1965). Talcott Parsons, *The Structure of Social Action* (New York: McGraw-Hill, 1937), Vol. 1, and Edward A. Tiryakian, *Sociologism and Existentialism* (Englewood Cliffs, N.J.: Prentice-Hall, 1962), give critical assessments. Major works in the French Durkheimian tradition are Marcel Mauss, *The Gift* (New York: Norton, 1967), and the writings of Claude Lévi-Strauss, to which the best introduction is his *Structural Anthropology* (Garden City, N.Y.: Anchor, 1967). Important empirical developments of Durkheim's theories include Guy Swanson, *The Birth of the Gods* (Ann Arbor: University of Michigan Press, 1962); Kai Erikson, *Wayward Puritans* (New York: Wiley, 1966); Mary Douglas, *Natural Symbols* (London: Routledge and Kegan Paul, 1970); and the materials summarized in Randall Collins, *Conflict Sociology* (New York: Academic Press, 1975), chapters 2 through 4 and 7. The definitive intellectual biography of Durkheim is Steven Lukes, *Emile Durkheim, His Life and Work* (New York: Allen Lane,

1973). A brilliant sociology of science analysis of Durkheim's milieu is given in Terry N. Clark, *Prophets and Patrons: The French University and the Emergence of the Social Sciences* (Cambridge, Mass.: Harvard University Press, 1973). Georges Sorel, in addition to *Reflections on Violence* (New York: Collier, 1961), wrote *The Illusions of Progress* (Berkeley and Los Angeles: University of California Press, 1969). A good collection of his works is in John L. Stanley (ed.), *From Georges Sorel: Essays in Socialism and Philosophy* (New York: Oxford University Press, 1976). Sorel's intellectual biography is given in James H. Meisel, *The Genesis of Georges Sorel* (Ann Arbor, Mich.: Wahr Publishing, 1951). Sorel, Durkheim, and others of the fin de siècle generation in Europe are treated in H. Stuart Hughes, *Consciousness and Society* (New York: Vintage, 1961).

Chapter Seven
Max Weber: The Disenchantment of the World

Max Weber's works are voluminous and still of great value. His great (and uncompleted) lifework, the comparative studies of the world religions, is found in *The Protestant Ethic and the Spirit of Capitalism* (New York: Scribners, 1958), *The Religion of China* (New York: Free Press, 1951), *The Religion of India* (New York: Free Press, 1958), and *Ancient Judaism* (New York: Free Press, 1952). A short summary, based on his lectures, is in *General Economic History* (New York: Free Press, 1950). Weber's main generalizing efforts are found in *Economy and Society*, 3 vols. (New York: Bedminster Press, 1968); parts of this are in paperback as *The Theory of Social and Economic Organization* (New York: Free Press, 1964), *The Sociology of Religion* (Boston: Beacon Press, 1963), *The City* (New York: Free Press, 1968), *Max Weber on Law in Economy and Society* (Cambridge, Mass.: Harvard University Press, 1954), and *From Max Weber: Essays in Sociology* (New York: Oxford University Press, 1946). The last also contains Weber's famous lectures "Science as a Vocation" and "Politics as a Vocation." Other writings are collected in *The Methodology of the Social Sciences* (New York: Free Press, 1959). Finally, Weber's *Rational and Social Foundations of Music* (Carbondale: Southern Illinois Press, 1958) is a tour de force in the sociology of cultural history. The major commentary on Weber is Reinhard Bendix, *Max Weber: An Intellectual Portrait* (Garden City, N.Y.: Anchor, 1962); see also Talcott Parsons, *The Structure of Social Action* (New York: McGraw-Hill, 1937), Vol. 2; Randall Collins, "Weber's Last Theory of Capitalism: A Systematization," *American Sociological Review* 45 (1980); and Randall Collins, *Max Weber: A Skeleton Key* (Beverly Hills, Calif.: Sage, 1986). Some applications of Weber's analysis from very different points of view are found in Reinhard Bendix, *Kings or People* (Berkeley: University of California Press, 1978), Talcott Parsons, *Societies: Comparative and Evolutionary Perspectives* (Englewood Cliffs, N.J.: Prentice-Hall, 1966), Bryan S. Turner, *For Weber* (London: Routledge, 1981), and Randall Collins, *Weberian Sociological Theory* (New York: Cambridge University Press, 1986).

No truly satisfactory personal biography of Weber is yet available.

Marianne Weber, *Max Weber: A Biography* (New York: Wiley, 1975), provides his wife's viewpoint. Arthur Mitzman, *The Iron Cage* (New York: Knopf, 1970), gives a speculative psychoanalytic interpretation that sees Weber's life as a persistent failure. Martin Green, *The Von Richthofen Sisters* (New York: Basic Books, 1974), fills in information on the liberated milieu of Weber's later life, when he became connected via his mistress to such people as D. H. Lawrence and the radical Freudian fringe.

Chapter Eight
Sigmund Freud: Conquistador of the Irrational

An excellent anthology of Freud's classic essays is A. A. Brill, *The Basic Writings of Sigmund Freud* (New York: Modern Library, 1938), which includes selections from *Psychopathology of Everyday Life, The Interpretation of Dreams, Three Contributions to the Theory of Sex, Wit and Its Relation to the Unconscious, Totem and Taboo,* and *The History of the Psychoanalytic Movement.* The *Collected Papers*, 5 vols. (London: Hogarth Press, 1953–1956), contains substantial and wide-ranging material for the serious student, while John Rickman, *A General Selection from the Works of Sigmund Freud* (Garden City, N.Y.: Anchor, 1957), is a top-notch sampler for beginners. The classic biography is Ernest Jones, *The Life and Work of Sigmund Freud* (New York: Basic Books, 1961); however, Maryse Choisy, *Sigmund Freud: A New Appraisal* (New York: Philosophical Library, 1963), is the most intimate, in-depth psychological portrait of the founder. Freud's views on religion and culture are amplified in *The Future of an Illusion* (Garden City, N.Y.: Anchor, 1957) and *Civilization and Its Discontents* (New York: Norton, 1961).

Outstanding secondary sources include Erich Fromm, *Sigmund Freud's Mission* (New York: Harper & Row, 1959); Philip Reiff, *Freud: The Mind of the Moralist* (New York: Doubleday, 1961); Paul Roazen, *Freud: Political and Social Thought* (New York: Knopf, 1968); and David Bakan, *Sigmund Freud and the Jewish Mystical Tradition* (New York: Van Nostrand, 1958). In *Life Against Death* (Middletown, Conn.: Wesleyan University Press, 1959), Norman O. Brown applies psychoanalysis to history in an illuminating manner. Herbert Marcuse's *Eros and Civilization* (New York: Vintage, 1962) explores humankind's potentialities for regeneration in terms of freedom from repression. Hendrik M. Ruitenbeek (ed.), *Psychoanalysis and Social Science* (New York: Dutton, 1964), selects eleven key essays that probe the integration of the social sciences and psychoanalysis in America. Paul Robinson, *The Freudian Left* (New York: Harper & Row, 1969), sums up the contributions of Reich, Roheim, and Marcuse. Feminist treatments of Freud include Shulamith Firestone, *The Dialectic of Sex* (New York: Morrow, 1970), and Juliet Mitchell, *Psychoanalysis and Feminism* (New York: Pantheon, 1974). Nancy Chodorow's important revision of Freud is *The Reproduction of Mothering* (Berkeley: University of California Press, 1978).

Source material for Jung includes the following works: *Modern Man in Search of a Soul* (New York: Harcourt, Brace, & World, 1933) is a presentation of the contemporary crisis of humanity in psychohistorical, cultural, and transpersonal, or spiritual terms; *Memories, Dreams, Reflections* (New York: Vintage, 1961) is a fascinating scientific autobiography; *Man and His Symbols* (London: Aldus Books Limited, 1964) is a good beginner's textbook for students of Jung. Refer to his *Collected Works* (Princeton, N.J.: Princeton University Press, 1953–1967) for in-depth research. Excellent secondary sources with social orientation are by I. Progoff, *Jung's Psychology and Its Social Meaning* (New York: Evergreen Books, 1955); E. Neumann, *The Origins and History of Consciousness* (Princeton, N.J.: Princeton University Press, 1954); M. Serrano, *C. G. Jung and Hermann Hesse: A Record of Two Friendships* (London: Routledge, 1966); E. Whitmont, *The Symbolic Quest* (New York: Putnam, 1969); and R. Wilhelm and C. G. Jung, *The Secret of the Golden Flower* (London: Routledge, 1962).

Chapter Nine
The Discovery of the Invisible World: Simmel, Cooley, and Mead

Simmel's works are available in Kurt. H. Wolff (ed.), *The Sociology of Georg Simmel* (New York: Free Press, 1950), and *Conflict and the Web of Group-Affiliations* (New York: Free Press, 1955). Essays by and about Simmel are in Kurt H. Wolff (ed.), *Essays on Sociology, Philosophy, and Aesthetics by Georg Simmel et al.* (New York: Harper Torchbooks, 1965), and Lewis A. Coser, *Georg Simmel* (Englewood Cliffs, N.J.: Prentice-Hall, 1965). On Simmel, see Nicholas J. Spykman, *The Social Theory of Georg Simmel* (Chicago: University of Chicago Press, 1925), and Lewis A. Coser, *The Functions of Social Conflict* (New York: Free Press, 1956).

The major works of Charles H. Cooley are *Human Nature and the Social Order* (New York: Schocken, 1964), *Social Organization: A Study of the Larger Mind* (New York: Schocken, 1962), and *Social Process* (Carbondale: Southern Illinois Press, 1966). He lays down his optimistic, beginning-of-the-century sociology in this trilogy. Cooley displays his breadth and depth of interest in *Sociological Theory and Social Research* (New York: Kelley, 1969), which contains selected early papers. The best secondary source is Albert J. Reiss (ed.), *Cooley and Sociological Analysis* (Ann Arbor: University of Michigan Press, 1968), which is a collection of essays on Cooley's significance by contemporary theorists.

George H. Mead's primary contribution to social psychology is found in *Mind, Self, and Society*, Charles W. Morris (ed.) (Chicago: University of Chicago Press, 1934). *The Philosophy of the Act* (Chicago: University of Chicago Press, 1938) contains an analysis of the stages of the act, which is relevant to Mead's theory; *The Philosophy of the Present* (La Salle, Ill.: Open Court, 1959) includes important material on the self in relation to time; and *Movements of Thought in the Nineteenth Century* (Chicago: University of Chicago Press, 1936) presents a classic chapter on the problem of society, in addition to valuable work on the philosophic foundations of twentieth-century scientific sociology.

Worthwhile secondary sources are Jerome G. Manis and Bernard N. Meltzer, *Symbolic Interaction: A Reader in Social Psychology* (Boston: Allyn &

Bacon, 1967), and Herbert Blumer, *Symbolic Interactionism: Perspective and Method* (Englewood Cliffs, N.J.: Prentice-Hall, 1969). The latter is an exposition of symbolic interactionism by Mead's foremost sociological pupil. A different slant on contemporary schools is given in Sheldon Stryker, *Symbolic Interactionism: A Social Structural Version* (Menlo Park, Calif.: Cummings, 1980). John Dewey's *Human Nature and Conduct* (New York: Modern Library, 1957) is his treatise on social psychology, and William James, *Psychology: Briefer Course* (New York: Collier, 1962), contains valuable material for understanding the development of self theory. See also John J. McDermott (ed.), *The Writing of William James* (New York: Random House, 1967), and Paul E. Pfeutze's original work, *Self, Society, Existence: Human Nature and Dialogue in the Thought of George Herbert Mead and Martin Buber* (New York: Harper Torchbooks, 1961). The entire movement is reassessed by J. D. Lewis and R. Smith, *American Sociology and Pragmatism* (Chicago: University of Chicago Press, 1980). The best treatment of Mead as philosopher is David L. Miller, *George Herbert Mead: Self, Language and the World* (Austin: University of Texas Press, 1973).

Chapter Ten
The Discovery of the Ordinary World:
Thomas, Park, and the Chicago School

The history of the Chicago school is given in Robert E. L. Faris, *Chicago Sociology* (San Francisco: Chandler, 1967). The studies of Thomas and Znaniecki, Park, and their followers are described in John Madge, *The Rise of Scientific Sociology* (New York: Free Press, 1962). Representative writings may be sampled in Morris Janowitz (ed.), *W. I. Thomas on Social Organization and Social Personality* (Chicago: University of Chicago Press, 1967), Ralph H. Turner (ed.), *Robert E. Park on Social Control and Collective Behavior* (Chicago: University of Chicago Press, 1967), Otis Dudley Duncan (ed.), *William F. Ogburn on Culture and Social Change* (Chicago: University of Chicago Press, 1964), and Albert J. Reiss, Jr. (ed.), *Louis Wirth on Cities and Social Life* (Chicago: University of Chicago Press, 1966). Also of interest is the famous textbook by Robert E. Park and Ernest W. Burgess, *Introduction to the Science of Sociology* (Chicago: University of Chicago Press, 1921).

Primary source material on W. E. Burghardt Du Bois includes the following: *The Autobiography of W.E.B. Du Bois: A Soliloquy on Viewing My Life from the Last Decade of Its First Century* (New York: International Publishers, 1988) includes a comprehensive bibliography plus a calendar of his public life. *The Souls of Black Folk* (New York: Signet, 1982) is a collection of essays, originally published in 1903, *Against Racism: Unpublished Essays, Papers, Addresses, 1887–1961*, edited by Herbert Aptheker (Amherst: The University of Massachusetts Press, 1985), provides new material. Du Bois' oratory is collected in *W.E.B. Du Bois Speaks: Speeches and Addresses 1890–1919, 1920–1963* edited by Philip S. Foner (New York: Pathfinder, 1988). Du Bois writes of the richness of African civilization and culture in *The Negro* (New

York: Kraus-Thomson, 1988) with a new introduction by Herbert Aptheker. *John Brown* (New York: International Publishers, 1987) is the historical biography of the abolitionist martyr. Many of Du Bois' writings for *The Crisis* are included in *An ABC of Color* (New York: International Publishers, 1969). *The Philadelphia Negro: A Social Study* (New York: Schocken Books, 1967) is Du Bois' most enduring empirical work, originally published in 1899. *Black Reconstruction in America, 1860–1880* (Cleveland: Meridian, 1962) is his historical defense of Reconstruction governments with an economic interpretation of northern discrimination. *The Suppression of the African Slave Trade to the United States of America, 1638–1870* (New York: Dover Publications, Inc., 1970) is still a classic in the field. Key secondary sources include Elliot Rudwick, *W.E.B. Du Bois: Voice of the Black Protest Movement* (Chicago: University of Illinois Press, 1982); Rayford W. Logan (ed.), *W.E.B. Du Bois: A Profile* (New York: Hill and Wang, 1971); Arnold Rampersad, *The Art and Imagination of W.E.B. Du Bois* (New York: Schocken Books, 1990); and Leslie Alexander Lacy, *The Life of W.E.B. Du Bois: Cheer the Lonesome Traveler* (New York: Dial Press, 1970).

On E. Franklin Frazier see the chapter by G. Franklin Edwards in Robert K. Merton and Matilda White Riley, *Sociological Traditions from Generation to Generation* (Norwood, N.J.: Ablex, 1980).

Chapter Eleven
The Construction of the Social System: Pareto and Parsons

Pareto's *The Mind and Society*, 5 vols. (New York: Harcourt, Brace, 1935), is best approached through the selections in Joseph Lopreato (ed.), *Vilfredo Pareto* (New York: Crowell, 1955). The most notable recent interpretation of Pareto is Charles Powers and Robert Hanneman, "Pareto's Equilibrium Theory: A Formal Model and Simulation," in Randall Collins (ed.), *Sociological Theory 1983* (San Francisco: Jossey-Bass, 1983). Talcott Parsons' first major work, *The Structure of Social Action* (New York: McGraw-Hill, 1937), contains an important interpretation of Pareto as well as of Alfred Marshall, Durkheim, and Weber. Parsons' other works include *The Social System* (New York: Free Press, 1951), *Essays in Sociological Theory* (New York: Free Press, 1954), *Toward a General Theory of Action* (with Edward Shils) (Cambridge, Mass.: Harvard University Press, 1951), *Economy and Society* (with Neil J. Smelser) (New York: Free Press, 1956), *Societies: Comparative and Evolutionary Perspectives* (Englewood Cliffs, N.J.: Prentice-Hall, 1966), and the introductory essays in *Theories of Society* (edited with Edward Shils, Jesse R. Pitts, and Kaspar Naegele) (New York: Free Press, 1961). Commentaries are found in Max Black (ed.), *The Social Theories of Talcott Parsons* (Englewood Cliffs, N.J.: Prentice-Hall, 1961), and Alvin W. Gouldner, *The Coming Crisis in Western Sociology* (New York: Basic Books, 1970). Other varieties of functionalism are presented in Kingsley Davis, *Human Society* (New York: Macmillan, 1949), and Robert K. Merton, *Social Theory and Social Structure* (New York: Free Press, 1968), and are debated in the papers collected in N. J. Demerath III and Richard A. Peterson (eds.), *System, Change, and Conflict* (New York: Free Press, 1967). Representative works of modern functionalists include Neil J. Smelser, *Theory of Collective Behavior* (New York: Free Press, 1963); S. N. Eisenstadt, *The Political Systems of Empires* (New York: Free Press, 1963); and Robert N. Bellah, *Tokugawa Religion* (New York: Free Press, 1957). Parsons' evolutionism has been extended by recent German sociologists: Wolfgang Schlachter, *The Rise of Western Rationalism* (Berkeley: University of California Press, 1981); also Niklas Luhman, *Trust—Power* (London: Wiley, 1979). Parsons' works have been reappraised in the four-volume work of Jeffrey Alexander, *Theoretical Logic in Sociology* (Berkeley: University of California Press, 1981–1983).

Chapter Twelve
Hitler's Shadow: Michels, Mannheim, and Mills

Robert Michels' main work is *Political Parties* (New York: Collier, 1962); also available in English is his *Introductory Lectures on Political Sociology* (New York: Harper Torchbooks, 1966). Karl Mannheim's translated works include *Ideology and Utopia* (New York: Harcourt, Brace, 1936), *Man and Society in an Age of Reconstruction* (New York: Harcourt, Brace, 1940), *Diagnosis of Our Time* (London: Routledge & Kegan Paul, 1943), *Essays on the Sociology of Knowledge* (New York: Oxford University Press, 1952), and *Freedom, Power, and Democratic Planning* (New York: Oxford University Press, 1950). C. Wright Mills wrote *The New Men of Power* (New York: Harcourt, Brace, 1948), *The Puerto Rican Journey* (New York: Oxford University Press, 1950), *White Collar* (New York: Oxford University Press, 1951), *Character and Social Structure* (with Hans Gerth) (New York: Harcourt, Brace & World, 1953), *The Power Elite* (New York: Oxford University Press, 1956), *The Causes of World War Three* (New York: Simon and Schuster, 1958), and *The Sociological Imagination* (New York: Oxford University Press, 1959). His collected papers are edited by Irving Louis Horowitz under the title *Power, Politics, and People* (New York: Oxford University Press, 1963). A continuation of the spirit of both Mannheim and Mills is found in Alvin W. Gouldner, *The Dialectic of Ideology and Technology* (New York: Seabury Press, 1976).

Chapter Thirteen
Erving Goffman and the Theater of Social Encounters

Erving Goffman's main works are *The Presentation of Self in Everyday Life* (Garden City, N.Y.: Doubleday, 1959), *Asylums* (Garden City, N.Y.: Doubleday, 1961), *Encounters* (Indianapolis: Bobbs-Merrill, 1961), *Behavior in Public Places* (New York: Free Press, 1963), *Interaction Ritual* (Garden City, N.Y.: Doubleday, 1967), *Strategic Interaction* (Philadelphia: University of Pennsylvania Press, 1969), *Frame Analysis* (New York: Harper & Row, 1974), *Gender Advertisements* (Cambridge, Mass.: Harvard University Press, 1979), and *Forms of Talk* (Philadelphia: University of Pennsylvania Press, 1981). A collection of commentaries is found in Jason Ditton (ed.), *The View from Goffman* (London: Macmillan, 1979). Harold Garfinkel's work is presented in *Studies in Ethnomethodology* (Englewood Cliffs, N.J.: Prentice-Hall, 1967). Important background for American ethnomethodology is Alfred Schutz, *Collected Papers* (The Hague: Nijhoff, 1962–1966). Schutz's work has also been developed in Peter Berger and Thomas Luckmann, *The Social Construction of Reality* (Garden City, N.Y.: Doubleday, 1967). Also important are Ludwig Wittgenstein, *Philosophical Investigations* (New York: Macmillan, 1953), and John Austin, *How to Do Things with Words* (Cambridge, Mass.: Harvard University Press, 1962). Recent developments in ethnomethodology are introduced in Hugh Mehan and Houston Wood, *The Reality of Ethnomethodology* (New York: Wiley, 1975), and are given in advanced form in Aaron Cicourel, *Cognitive Sociology* (Baltimore, Md.: Penguin Books, 1973). The British version of ethnomethodology and Marxism is shown in Barry Sandywell, David Silverman, Maurice Roche, Paul Filmer, and Michael Phillipson, *Problems of Reflexivity and Dialectics in Sociological Inquiry* (London: Routledge & Kegan Paul, 1975). Efforts to tie this modern microsociology to traditional sociological concerns are in Karin Knorr-Cetina and Aaron Cicourel, *Advances in Social Theory and Methodology: Toward an Integration of Micro- and Macro-Sociologies* (Boston: Routledge and Kegan Paul, 1981). Anthony Giddens draws upon Goffman and the ethnomethodologists in *The Constitution of Society* (Oxford: Polity Press, 1984).

Chapter Fourteen
Sociology in the Late Twentieth Century

Primary source material of Michel Foucault includes the following: *Madness and Civilization: A History of Insanity in the Age of Reason* (New York: Random House, 1973; French original, 1961), a study of madness from 1500 to 1800 and the birth of the asylum. *The Birth of the Clinic: An Archaeology of Medical Perception* (New York: Random House, 1975; original, 1963) is a history of the emergence of clinical medicine. *The Order of Things: An Archaeology of the Human Sciences* (New York: Random House, 1970) is a detailed historicolinguistic analysis of the emergence of the human sciences and the recent concept of "man." *The Archaeology of Knowledge and the Discourse on Language* (New York: Random House, 1972; original, 1969) is his main methodological work on history and the discursive regularities. *I, Pierre Riviere, having slaughtered my mother, my sister, and my brother: A Case of Parricide in the 19th Century* (New York: Random House, 1975) is Foucault's editorial version of the intersections of medicine and law in the case of a madman and a glimpse into the birth of the psychiatrization of law. *Discipline and Punish: The Birth of the Prison* (New York: Random House, 1979; original, 1975) is a classic in criminology and portrays the development of the prison system from the late seventeenth to the middle nineteenth centuries. In *The History of Sexuality: Volume I: An Introduction* (New York: Random House, 1980; original, 1976), Foucault explores our compulsion to analyze and discuss sex since the seventeenth century. He writes the introduction to a fascinating case study, *Herculine Barbin: Being the Recently Discovered Memoirs of a Nineteenth Century French Hermaphrodite* (New York:

Random House, 1980). *The Use of Pleasure: The History of Sexuality: Volume Two* (New York: Random House, 1986) is a short treatise on ethics and erotics in ancient Greek society. Foucault's final work, *The Care of the Self: The History of Sexuality: Volume Three* (New York: Random House, 1986), represents the theoretical peak of his vocation as a social scientist as he explores sex, ethics, marriage, and a new erotics in the Golden Age of Rome. The best collection of original writings is Paul Rabinow's *Foucault Reader: An Introduction to Foucault's Thought, with Major New Unpublished Material* (New York: Random House, 1984). Another important work is *Language, Counter-Memory, Practice: Selected Essays and Interviews by Michel Foucault* (Ithaca, N.Y.: Cornell University, 1977), edited by Donald F. Bouchard. *Power/Knowledge: Selected Interviews and Other Writings, 1972–1977 by Michel Foucault* (New York: Random House, 1980) is Colin Gordon's key editorial guide. *This Is Not a Pipe: With Illustrations and Letters by Rene Magritte* (Berkeley: The Regents of the University of California, 1983) is Foucault's artistic tribute to the surrealist painter.

Recommended secondary source material includes the following: Alan Sheridan, *Michel Foucault: The Will to Truth* (London: Tavistock Publications, 1980), John Rajchman, *Michel Foucault: The Freedom of Philosophy* (New York: Columbia University Press, 1985), Edith Kurzweil, *The Age of Structuralism: Lévi-Strauss to Foucault* (New York: Columbia University Press, 1980), Barry Smart, *Michel Foucault* (New York: Barry Smart/Ellis Horwood Limited, 1985), presents Foucault as one of the new key sociologists. Hubert L. Dreyfus and Paul Rabinow, *Michel Foucault: Beyond Structuralism and Hermeneutics, With an Afterword by Michel Foucault* (Chicago: The University of Chicago Press, 1982), is a sophisticated version of Foucault's writings, theories, and methodology. Mark Cousins and Athar Hussain, *Michel Foucault* (New York: St. Martin's Press, 1984), places Foucault in the context of theoretical traditions in the social sciences and provides the most extensive references and bibliography to material about the author.

The major works of Pierre Bourdieu are *Reproduction: In Education, Society, and Culture,* written with Jean-Claude Passeron (Beverly Hills, Calif.: Sage, 1977; French original, 1970), *Outline of a Theory of Practice* (Cambridge, England: Cambridge University Press, 1977; French original, 1972), *Distinction. A Social Critique of the Judgment of Taste* (Cambridge, Mass.: Harvard University Press, 1984; French original, 1979).

Jurgen Habermas' principal works include *Legitimation Crisis* (Boston: Beacon Press, 1975), *Communication and the Evolution of Society* (Boston: Beacon Press, 1979), and *The Theory of Communicative Action* (Boston: Beacon Press, 1984).

Randall Collins' principal works are *Conflict Sociology: Toward an Explanatory Science* (New York: Academic Press, 1975), *The Credential Society: An Historical Sociology of Education and Stratification* (New York: Academic Press, 1979), *Sociology since Midcentury: Essays in Theory Cumulation* (New York: Academic Press, 1981), which includes his essay "On the Micro Foundations of Macro-sociology," *Weberian Sociological Theory* (New York:

Cambridge University Press, 1986), and *Theoretical Sociology* (San Diego: Harcourt, Brace, Jovanovich, 1988).

Some important works of recent historical sociology are listed above in the latter part of the bibliography for Chapter 2. Immanuel Wallerstein's volumes of *The Modern World-System* are cited there. To this can be added Charles Tilly's important works, *The Vendée, A Sociological Analysis of the Counterrevolution of 1793* (Cambridge, Mass.: Harvard University Press, 1964) and *From Mobilization to Revolution* (Reading, Mass.: Addison-Wesley, 1978), Craig Calhoun, *The Question of Class Struggle* (Chicago: University of Chicago Press, 1982), Orlando Patterson, *Slavery and Social Death* (Cambridge, Mass.: Harvard University Press, 1982), and Michael Mann, *The Sources of Social Power* (New York: Cambridge University Press, 1986).

Chapter 15
The Impact of Women in Sociology in the Late Twentieth Century

On the position of women in creative literature in earlier periods see Ivar Morris, *The World of the Shining Prince. Court Life in Ancient Japan* (New York: Oxford University Press, 1964); Sarah B. Pomeroy, *Goddesses, Whores, Wives, and Slaves: Women in Classical Antiquity* (New York: Schocken, 1975). On women in radical and reformist movements see Leszek Kolakowski, *Main Currents of Marxism*, Vol. 2, Chapter III: "Rosa Luxemburg and the Revolutionary Left" (New York: Oxford University Press, 1978); Mary Jo Deegan, *Jane Addams and the Men of the Chicago School, 1892–1918* (New Brunswick, N.J.: Transaction Books, 1988). For the upheavals that set off the most recent wave of the women's movement, see Todd Gitlin, *The Sixties: Years of Hope, Days of Rage* (New York: Basic Books, 1987).

The modern comparative analysis of revolutions begins with Barrington Moore, Jr., *Social Origins of Dictatorship and Democracy* (Boston: Beacon Press, 1966). Theda Skocpol's major work is *States and Social Revolutions* (New York: Cambridge University Press, 1979). She reflects on the social conditions of her career in "An `Uppity Generation' and the Revitalization of Macroscopic Sociology: Reflections at Midcareer by a Woman from the 1960s," in Matilda White Riley (ed.), *Sociological Lives* (Beverly Hills, Calif.: Sage, 1988). This volume also contains autobiographies by other distinguished women sociologists, including Rosabeth Moss Kanter and Alice S. Rossi. Other works by Skocpol include her edited volumes *Bringing the State Back In* (New York: Cambridge University Press, 1985), and *The Politics of Social Policy in the United States* (Princeton, N.J.: Princeton University Press, 1988).

The early round of feminist theorists from the late 1960s and early 1970s, with their predominantly Marxian and Freudian themes, includes Kate Millett, *Sexual Politics* (New York: Doubleday, 1970); Germaine Greer, *The Female Eunuch* (London: MacGibbon and Kee, 1970); Shulamith Firestone, *The Dialectic of Sex* (New York: William Morrow, 1970); and Juliet Mitchell, *Psychoanalysis and Feminism* (New York: Pantheon, 1974). The range of feminist sociology in the last two decades is described in Janet Saltzman

Chafetz, *Feminist Sociology: An Overview of Contemporary Theories* (Itasca, Ill.: Peacock, 1988).

Background for the comparative theory of social inequality comes from Gerhard E. Lenski, *Power and Privilege. A Theory of Stratification* (New York: McGraw-Hill, 1966). The sociological theory of gender stratification was developed by Rae Lesser Blumberg, *Stratification: Socioeconomic and Sexual Inequality* (Dubuque, Iowa: William C. Brown, 1978), and "A General Theory of Gender Stratification," in *Sociological Theory 1984*, ed. Randall Collins (San Francisco: Jossey-Bass, 1984); by Janet Saltzman Chafetz, *Sex and Advantage: A Comparative Macro-Structural Theory of Sexual Stratification* (Totowa, N.J.: Rowman and Allanheld, 1984), and *Gender Equity: An Integrated Theory of Stability and Change* (Newbury Park, Calif.: Sage, 1990); and by Joan Huber and Glenna Spitze, *Sex Stratification: Children, Housework, and Jobs* (New York: Academic Press, 1983). Chafetz's treatment of the dynamics of women's movements and antifeminist movements, written with A. Gary Dworkin, is *Female Revolt: Women's Movements in World and Historical Perspective* (Totowa, N.J.: Rowman and Allanheld, 1986), and "In the Face of Threat: Organized Antifeminism in Comparative Perspective," *Gender and Society* 1 (1987): 33–60. Randall Collins' comparative theory of sex and politics was first published as "A Conflict Theory of Sexual Stratification," *Social Problems* 19 (1971), 3–21, and later developed in "Courtly Politics and the Status of Women," in Collins, *Weberian Sociological Theory* (New York: Cambridge University Press, 1986).

Path-breaking work by women sociologists ranges from macro to micro. It includes Janet Abu-Lughod, *Before European Hegemony: The World System AD 1250–1350* (New York: Oxford University Press, 1989); Karen S. Cook, "Network Structures from an Exchange Perspective," in Peter V. Marsden and Nan Lin (eds.), *Social Structure and Network Analysis* (Beverly Hills, Calif.: Sage, 1982); and Rosabeth M. Kanter, *Men and Women of the Corporation* (New York: Basic Books, 1977). Arlie R. Hochschild's major theory of the construction of emotions through "emotion work" is presented in *The Managed Heart: The Commercialization of Human Feeling* (Berkeley: University of California Press, 1983). Sophisticated mathematical sociology is advanced by Nancy Brandon Tuma and Michael T. Hanna, *Social Dynamics: Models and Methods* (New York: Academic Press, 1984); and by Pamela E. Oliver and Gerald Marwell, "The Paradox of Group Size in Collective Action: A Theory of the Critical Mass," *American Sociological Review* 53 (1988): 1–8. Dorothy Smith's "standpoint theory" is presented in "A Sociology for Women," in J. A. Sherman and E. T. Beck, *The Prism of Sex: Essays in the Sociology of Knowledge* (Madison: University of Wisconsin Press, 1979).

Index